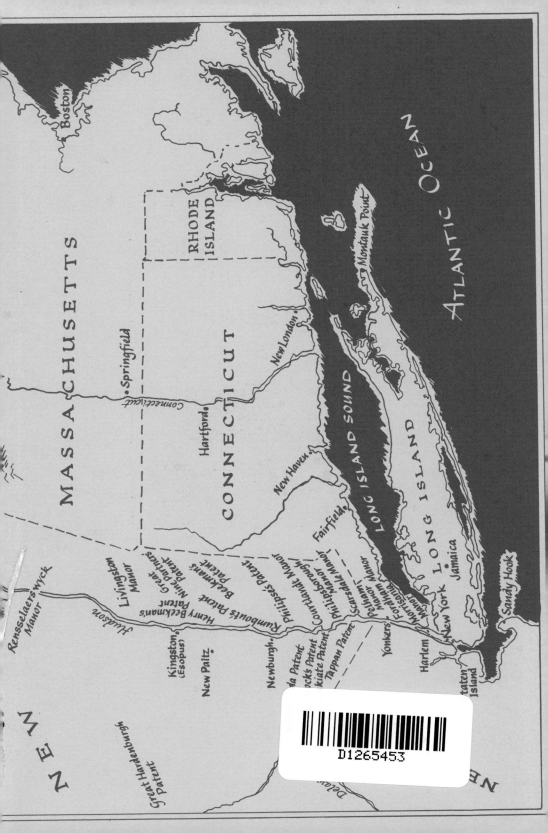

ROBERT LIVINGSTON
1654 - 1728
and the
POLITICS OF
COLONIAL NEW YORK

The Institute of Early American History and Culture is sponsored jointly by the College of William and Mary and Colonial Williamsburg, Incorporated. Publication of this book has been assisted by a grant from the Lilly Endowment, Inc.

This book is a winner of the Institute Manuscript Award and the Dixon Ryan Fox Fellowship of the New York State Historical Association.

ROBERT LIVINGSTON. From the original portrait owned by
the late H. H. Livingston. Reproduced by courtesy of his
son, Herman H. Livingston, Jr.

Robert Livingston
1654-1728
AND THE
POLITICS OF
COLONIAL NEW YORK

By

LAWRENCE H. LEDER

PUBLISHED FOR

*The Institute of Early American History and Culture
at Williamsburg, Virginia*

by The University of North Carolina Press   •   Chapel Hill

PREFACE

Hist. A3617 Pub. July 17, 1961

THIS VOLUME is a biographical approach to the politics of provincial New York, a case study of a wily Scotsman with his eye to the main chance who carved himself a niche out of the first British empire. An emigrant who arrived in New York with but two resources—a family background as the youngest son of a dissenting Scottish minister, and an ability to speak and write fluently in both Dutch and English—Robert Livingston utilized his native talents so effectively that he became one of the colony's wealthiest and most influential leaders.

Livingston's career illuminates some of the issues, personalities, and motivations of a formative epoch in the history of colonial and provincial America. His life encompassed a period described by Charles M. Andrews as one of "silent and peaceful revolution," an era more recently referred to by Clinton Rossiter as the "Seedtime of the Republic." Both appelations are justified, for these years witnessed the formulation of the basic ideals and methodology of American politics, the transmutation of the colonial Englishman into the American.

Yet, it is somewhat disconcerting to realize that this era has remained, as it were, a "Dark Age" in American history, especially insofar as politics are concerned. In the past half century, there has been but one major effort to synthesize the political growth of the provinces during those crucial years.[1]

One reason for this neglect may well be the attention devoted by scholars to that July day in 1776 when the representatives of the provinces in Congress assembled took their lives in their hands and renounced their allegiance to George III. This focus has led to a minute examination of the institutions and problems that were to loom large in the imperial crisis—governors, assemblies, Board of Trade, Privy Council, Indian relations, mercantile legislation, land speculation, and local sectional conflicts.

The emphasis on institutional development, however, may have been carried too far. Assuredly, it has an honored place in history, but can we understand the institutions of any period without first understanding the men who created and ran them? In order to comprehend the reasons and motivations behind the "silent and peaceful revolution," we must first learn something of the men responsible for them.

Robert Livingston is especially deserving of treatment because of the significance of his own career, the availability of material, and the importance of the family he founded, a clan whose record of public service parallels that of the Adams and Winthrops of New England. During his half-century of public service, Livingston rose from a minor town and county official in the frontier outpost of Albany to become Lord of Livingston Manor, financier for the New York government, secretary for Indian affairs, member of the governor's Council, and member and finally speaker of the New York Assembly. At the same time, he achieved prominence as one of the colony's leading merchants.

Livingston played a vital role in many of the leading events of his time. He led the group that fought against Jacob Leisler and eventually brought that misguided zealot to a rebel's death on the gallows. He helped to secure the recall of two royal governors, Benjamin Fletcher and Lord Cornbury, afterwards Earl of Clarendon. He promoted Captain William Kidd's disastrous privateering expedition. He participated in the settlement of the Palatines in New York from which only he really benefitted. He was an architect of the *modus operandi* whereby Governor Robert Hunter achieved an amicable

1. Herbert L. Osgood, *The American Colonies in the Eighteenth Century* (4 vols., N.Y., 1924).

settlement with the Assembly and won an enviable reputation among colonial administrators. Finally, he assisted in the formulation of Governor William Burnet's Indian trade policy which was designed to extend English influence into the Ohio Valley.

The exceptional scope of Robert Livingston's activities is indicative of New York's state of transition during the years 1674-1728. It was gradually changing from a Dutch West India Company outpost to a ducal proprietary and finally to a royal province. Indeed, it was the very rapidity of these changes which allowed Livingston to utilize his varied talents and accumulate personal power and wealth, although he had a deep and often fruitful concern for the welfare of the colony and the empire. He was one of that rare breed of colonial politicians who could often visualize the problems of their own locality from the broader imperial vantage point.

The basic problem facing the British empire during these five decades was its rivalry with France for domination of the North American continent. Of all the colonies, New York was most intimately associated with this problem, for the Hudson and Mohawk valleys became the arena of contention. Although the contest often took the form of an uneasy armed truce, it twice erupted into imperial wars during Livingston's lifetime. But I have not attempted to present an exhaustive history of the colony for the years 1674-1728. Instead, I have tried to examine some of the major developments as one individual participated in them, to assess Livingston's role in the politics of transition.

Since I have been most interested in evaluating the interaction between the individual and the political community, I have not explored certain phases of Livingston's life. There are also other reasons for this decision. For instance, there is a wealth of commercial material among his papers, but his account books have not survived, and there is no way of determining his annual income or his net worth at death. Also, very little attention has been devoted to the running of the Manor, for that was left to his capable wife, Alida. Descriptions of the duties of Livingston's many public offices have been purposely omitted; many of them were primarily clerical in nature rather than policy-making, and whatever influence Livingston may have acquired through them came not from their inherent powers and duties but from the knowledge that he gained and the contacts that he made with powerful figures in the colony and in England.

ACKNOWLEDGMENTS

T HE PROBLEMS of writing a biography are numerous, and without the assistance of many people in varying ways, the difficulties would be even more formidable. Several people have given liberally of their wisdom and knowledge, thereby keeping me from making many missteps: Professor Brooke Hindle of New York University, who directed the original dissertation; Mr. Charles E. Baker of The New-York Historical Society, who permitted me to utilize his extensive knowledge as an editor and as a scholar of early New York's life; and the members of the Awards Committee and the editorial staff of the Institute of Early American History and Culture, who have supplied me with many constructive criticisms.

Much of the initial work on this volume was made financially possible by a Penfield Fellowship from the Faculty and Council of New York University. The New York State Historical Association's award of a Dixon Ryan Fox Fellowship, and the receipt of the First Annual Manuscript Award of the Institute of Early American History and Culture not only provided the financial means to bring the book to press, but also the incentive to complete its revision.

This volume would not have been possible without the work of the staffs of many institutions in making their resources available to scholars. A special note must be made of the courtesy of Mr. Herman Kahn, director of the Franklin D. Roosevelt Library which is the depository for the Livingston-Redmond Manuscripts, and Mrs. William H. Osborn, owner of those papers, in allowing me to use them freely. Other institutions whose holdings have been consulted in the course of writing this book are: New York Public Library, The New-York Historical Society, Museum of the City of New York, New York State Library, Albany County Clerk's Office, Massachusetts Historical Society, American Antiquarian Society, Connecticut Valley Historical Museum, Library of Congress, Colonial Williamsburg, Incorporated, Institute of Early American History and Culture, William L. Clements Library, and the Henry E. Huntington Library and Art Gallery.

Certain individuals deserve personal notice for their friendship and help which often transcended their official responsibilities: Mr. Wilbur Leech, Mr. Alfred Baragwanath, Miss Juliette Tomlinson, Mr. Paul A. W. Wallace, and Dr. Louis C. Jones. To Professors Bayrd Still, Wesley Frank Craven, and Vincent P. Carosso, I am especially indebted. To Mr. Dunbar M. Hinrichs, for several interesting sessions on Captain Kidd, go my deep thanks.

Two highly personal obligations must also be acknowledged. To my late mother for her encouragement and her aid in typing much of the original dissertation, and to my wife, Bernice K. Leder, for her criticisms, typing aid, and forbearance, go my deepest appreciation.

Although many have aided me in preparing this biography, I alone accept full responsibility for the result.

L. H. L.

October 1960
Lexington, Massachusetts

Contents

PART THREE

Political Maturity, 1710-1728

Illustrations

PART ONE

Foundations of a Career
1603-1689

CHAPTER I

The Old World and the New

IN JUNE 1673, Robert Livingston, an ambitious young Scot of nineteen, stepped ashore at Charlestown, Massachusetts, to seek his fortune and find a new home. His choice of destination had probably been influenced by his father, the Reverend John Livingstone, who had twice sought to emigrate to the Puritan Commonwealth. Although the elder Livingstone had been unsuccessful both times, Massachusetts Bay had remained for him "the land where a great part of my heart is already." [1] Robert's decision was therefore a logical one, especially since his father's reputation had preceded him—the elder Livingstone was one of Calvin's leading disciples in the Scottish Reformed Church, a movement whose fame "reached even to America."

On both sides of Robert Livingston's family there was a heritage of service to God. His paternal grandfather, the Reverend William Livingstone, had ministered to flocks in Monybroch and Lanark. His maternal grandfather, Bartholomew Fleeming, although a merchant, was considered "a most religious man, and a great entertainer and encourager of all honest [i.e., Presbyterian] ministers and professors of his time." John Livingstone, son of the Reverend William Livingstone and father of Robert, continued the family tradition and was known

---

1. John Livingstone to John Winthrop, Jr., Jan. 5, 1634/5, *Winthrop Papers* (5 vols., Boston, 1929-47), III, 187-88. Robert dropped the final letter from his surname, but the Scottish members of the family retained the original spelling.

as the preacher "more honoured of God as the means of converting sinners to Christ than almost any minister of the Church of Scotland since the Reformation." [2]

Born in Monybroch in 1603, John Livingstone was taught to read and write at home and then sent to the Latin School at Stirling. As a student at the College of Glasgow, his first ambition was to become a doctor of medicine, but his father refused to sanction studies in France. At Glasgow, however, John came under the influence of Robert Blair, a leader of Scotland's Calvinism, and determined to become a healer of men's souls. He received his master of arts degree in 1621 and returned to his father at Lanark.

On January 2, 1625, John Livingstone delivered his first public sermon. This unlicensed preaching continued for two years until the Bishop of St. Andrews refused him ordination and forbade further clerical activity by him. For the next three years he served the Earl and Countess of Wigtown as chaplain at Cumbernauld, but in 1630 he went to Northern Ireland where his ordination was finally arranged by the Presbyterian sympathizer, Andrew Knox, Bishop of Raphoe. The ceremony was most unorthodox: Knox, an Episcopal official, presided, but the service was conducted by three Presbyterian ministers in their manner of "the laying on of hands." Knox then handed the neophyte the Book of Ordination and suggested that he strike out passages to which he scrupled. Livingstone found "that it had been so marked by some others before, that I needed not mark anything." Thus ordained in the forms of both the Episcopalian and Presbyterian ministries, although clearly in the spirit of the latter alone, John Livingstone took up his duties at Killinchy, where he was shortly suspended for nonconformity.

Though his suspension was soon lifted, the situation of the Presbyterian clergy remained intolerable because of the persecutions of Charles I. To a devout minister in 1634, there were but two choices: stand and be martyred, or seek out a place where true believers could congregate unhindered by bishops. Livingstone and a group of his fellows focused their hopes upon the Calvinist refuge founded just

2. Thomas Houston, ed., *A Brief Historical Relation of the Life of Mr. John Livingstone...Written By Himself....With a Historical Introduction and Notes* (Edinburgh, 1848), (intro.), 12, 25, 63; (notes), 280. (For this work, "intro.," "life," or "notes" will be cited.) James Aikman, *Annals of the Persecution in Scotland, from the Restoration to the Revolution* (Edinburgh, 1842), 90.

four years earlier on the shores of Massachusetts Bay. Illness and inclement weather disrupted the grand scheme, but it was not forgotten. Livingstone's interest remained in Massachusetts, and he spoke and corresponded with John Winthrop, Jr., and encouraged others to do likewise.[3]

During this interlude, Livingstone married. The Reverend Robert Blair, his old mentor, had wed Beatrice Fleeming, and he suggested that his sister-in-law would make a good wife for a minister. If Livingstone had any doubts, Janet Fleeming soon swept them away by her "judicious and spiritual" advice on the text for a sermon. She was devout in her faith, and she was strong-willed. John Livingstone foresaw that she would be an invaluable helpmate, and the two were married by his father on June 23, 1635. It was not a union born of love. As John Livingstone so quaintly phrased it, "albeit I was thus fully cleared, I may truly say it was above a month after before I got marriage-affection to her ... and I got it not until I obtained it by prayer. But thereafter I had a great difficulty to moderate it." [4]

In the following November, Livingstone was deposed from the ministry and excommunicated, a victim of the renewed persecution of Presbyterians by the Stuarts. Livingstone then led a group of Irish Presbyterians who, at the invitation of Governor Winthrop of Massachusetts Bay, decided to cross the Atlantic to find freedom "from the bondage of the prelates." But this attempt to reach the New World was halted by a hurricane.[5]

Back in Scotland, the Great Civil War neared. Livingstone spent much of his time in Stranraer on the Firth of Clyde, for there, near the Irish Sea, he was available to both Scots and Irish. Known to his compatriots as "a traffiquer with the English who wer affected to our reformation, bot with all to the discipline of New England," he served in many posts. His most important state missions, however, came in the next decade. In the summer of 1650, he reluctantly accepted appoint-

3. Houston, ed., *John Livingstone*, (life), 63-67, 71-72, 76-77, 81, 85-87; (intro.), 34; Livingstone to Winthrop, Jan. 5, 1634/5, *Winthrop Papers*, III, 187-88.

4. Houston, ed., John Livingstone, (life), 88-89; James Anderson, *The Ladies of the Covenant. Memoirs of Distinguished Scottish Female Characters, Embracing the Period of the Covenant and the Persecution* (Edinburgh, c. 1850), 79-88.

5. Houston, ed., *John Livingstone*, (life), 91-94. See also Thomas M'Crie, ed., *The Life of Mr. Robert Blair, Minister of St. Andrews, Containing His Autobiography, from 1593 to 1636* (Edinburgh, 1848), 104-7.

ment as a commissioner to treat with the exiled Charles II at Breda. The task was distasteful to him, for he disliked the idea of clergymen meddling "in public employments and State matters," and he feared his own insufficiency in diplomacy. The first qualm he expressed to the Commission of the Kirk; the second he suppressed. Actually, he was the wisest of the nine commissioners, for he envisioned their ultimate failure. Charles II's "bare subscribing and swearing some words," he believed, gave no assurance that "it was done from the heart." [6]

In April of 1654, the Reverend John Livingstone undertook his last state mission. He and two others were summoned to London by Lord Protector Cromwell, who had determined to do what no one else had been able to accomplish—settle the affairs of the Kirk of Scotland. Livingstone went, hoping to "procure some good to Scotland . . . But I found no great advantage, so I left the other two there, and came home." [7]

Home for the Reverend John Livingstone and his family was now the parish of Ancrum, Roxburghshire. There, on December 12, 1654, his wife gave birth to their fourteenth child, a son, whom they named Robert.[8] Little is known about Robert Livingston's childhood; much must be inferred and still more must be assumed. Until he reached the age of eight, Robert's childhood must have been very similar to that of any other minister's son in troubled Scotland. Since Ancrum was too small a village to offer formal schooling, he was probably taught within the family circle. His moral education seems to have been based wholly upon Scottish Calvinism, with all its attributes and deficiencies. The boy was enlisted in "the eternal war between God and Satan," for he exhibited in later life a quality which a friendly critic of Presbyterianism has called the Scot's greatest failing: he was "too intent upon his salvation . . . to see the men about him in comic relief. He was too serious minded to laugh at the incongruities of life." By example and precept he learned the doctrines of predestination and election,

6. Houston, ed., *John Livingstone*, (life), 103, 112-16; Robert Baillie to William Spang, Sept. 1640, *The Letters and Journals of Robert Baillie, A.M. Principal of the University of Glasgow* (3 vols., Edinburgh, 1841-42), I, 250.

7. John Nicoll, *A Diary of Public Transactions and Other Occurrences, Chiefly in Scotland, from January 1650 to June 1657* (Edinburgh, 1836), 127; Houston, ed., *John Livingstone*, (life), 137.

8. Edwin Brockholst Livingston, *The Livingstons of Livingston Manor* (N.Y., 1910), 52-54.

the duty to "work through and with God to bring about his kingdom on earth by doing away with evil and injustice." [9]

Shortly before Robert's eighth birthday, the Livingstone family was faced with a great crisis. After Charles II had been restored to the throne of England in 1660, the Reverend John Livingstone feared that "there would ensue an overturning of the whole work of reformation, and a trial to those who would adhere thereunto." And so it was. In 1662, the Scottish Parliament and Council decreed that all ministers were to keep May 29, the anniversary of the king's return, as a holy day. By November, word leaked out that charges had been preferred against recalcitrant ministers, one of whom was Livingstone. He went to Edinburgh, but kept himself close for several days awaiting word of the Council's intentions. Having no desire for martyrdom, Livingstone resolved to show himself only if those in power intended to impose banishment; if they demanded a blood sacrifice, he would remain hidden. On December 11, he publicly rejected the oath to Charles II. The Council thereupon prohibited his return to his family at Ancrum and ordered that he depart the king's dominions within two months. In April 1663, he boarded "old John Allan's ship" and, after an eight-day voyage, set foot in Rotterdam.

In December of the same year, Janet Livingstone followed her husband into exile, taking with her their two youngest children, Robert and Elizabeth. The five other surviving children were old enough to fend for themselves and remained in Scotland. Thus the family circle was broken, never to be mended. Elizabeth died in 1667, leaving Robert, for all practical purposes, an only child on whom his parents could lavish full attention.[10] It is hardly surprising that Robert had no strong ties with his brothers and sisters in later life.

To nine-year-old Robert, Holland in the 1660's must have been truly amazing.[11] Here was a lightness and freedom unknown to Scotland. The Netherlands had won their political and religious liberty

9. Wallace Notestein, *The Scot in History: A Study of the Interplay of Character and History* (N.Y., 1947), 155, 166.

10. Houston, ed., *John Livingstone*, (life), 139-42; Livingston, *Livingstons of Livingston Manor*, 50.

11. This and the following paragraph are based on: G. N. Clark, *The Seventeenth Century* (Oxford, 1947), *passim*; Notestein, *Scot in History*, *passim*; Petrus Johannes Blok, *History of the People of the Netherlands*, trans. by O. A. Bierstadt and R. Putnam (5 vols., N.Y., 1898-1912), IV, Chap. "Land and People about 1660"; Bertus Harry Wabeke, *Dutch Migration to North America, 1624-1860* (N.Y., 1944), Chap. I.

a century earlier, but Scotland was convulsed by civil and religious
upheavals; Leiden and the other Dutch universities sought the new
knowledge, while the Scottish universities were blinded by theological
controversies.

The boy had moved from a rural to an urban setting, from a country of relative poverty to a prosperous land in which wealth was more
equitably distributed than in almost any other European nation.
Standing at the crossroads of northern Europe, Holland was rich in
trade, and even the Dutch farmer was far more financially independent than the Scotsman who worked the rocky highland soil. The
Livingstones' new home, the port city of Rotterdam, was a commercial entrepôt without equal. At its piers docked ships which
brought it not only wealth, but a cosmopolitan spirit which accepted
the foreigner without undue hesitation. In Scotland, the Highlanders
and Lowlanders viewed each other with suspicion, uniting only to
view the Englishman with hostility.

Despite Rotterdam's attractiveness, the Reverend John Livingstone
made little effort to participate in its varied life; rather, he busied
himself in the theological disputes perpetuated by the Scottish colony
of exiles. He wrote his memoirs, edited an attack on Jacob Arminius'
abandonment of the doctrine of predestination, and prepared a Latin
version of the Scriptures. On occasion, the "worthy and warm Mr.
Livingstone" preached in the Scottish Reformed Church which had
been established by the exiles; to them, he remained "that burning and
shining light . . . , who used to preach as within the sight of Christ, and
the glory to be revealed." [12]

With such a formidable ecclesiastical background, Robert might
well have followed his father into the ministry. He did not. Possibly
his father's difficulties dissuaded him—as an adult he studiously avoided
religious controversy. Perhaps he found the heady atmosphere of a
seaport a powerful inducement toward the more worldly life. Young
Livingston's imagination must have been stirred by the exotic goods
in Rotterdam's shops and the foreign ships at its docks. In later life,
he claimed that he had been bred to trade.[13] Whatever the reason, the
ministry was not his calling.

12. William Steven, The History of the Scottish Church, Rotterdam (Edinburgh,
1833), 24, 33, 53, 370. See also Houston, ed., John Livingstone, (intro.), 55.
13. Robert Livingston to [William Burnet], Nov. 17, 1724, N.-Y. Hist. Soc., Collections, 67 (1937), 176.

Robert Livingston began to practice the mysteries of mercantile life in 1669, when only fifteen years of age, probably having been initiated into them by some Dutch merchant. During the year 1670, he kept an account book in Dutch; it begins with a statement of his assets and his liabilities, continues as a daybook for the year, and ends with a summation of the year's financial activities. How he obtained his initial capital is unknown; perhaps it was advanced by one of his brothers-in-law, Andrew Russell or James Miller, both merchants in Rotterdam.[14] Robert began the year with assets of 57,069 florins, including shipments of Bordeaux wine en route to Antwerp, pepper to Nantes, rye to Danzig, tobacco to Bordeaux, and herring to Hamburg. Among his liabilities, which totaled 18,891 florins, were the expenses of these voyages, several outstanding loans at 4 percent, and rent for space he occupied in the "House of the Whitewashed Hound," where he presumably conducted his business. When the year ended, he summed up his condition and found, "*Godt Danck*," that he had a net profit of 8,287 florins to add to his capital.[15]

Nothing further is known of Robert Livingston in Holland, except for a fragmentary letter in Dutch expressing his filial affections to his parents on New Year's Day 1670. Less than two years later, his father died. Despite the Anglo-Dutch War, Janet Livingstone returned to Edinburgh where her two eldest sons, both merchants, were residing.[16] In all probability, Robert accompanied his bereaved mother to their homeland.

Had he reviewed his first eighteen years, Robert Livingston would have found many creditable things in his background—a firm religious faith shorn of the excesses that still typified Scottish Presbyterianism, a good basic education, an excellent training in one of the most highly advanced business communities of the day, and a fluency in both Dutch and English. On the other hand, he probably had little money, and opportunities in Edinburgh were very limited for a poor

14. Russell married Janet, and Miller married Barbara Livingstone, both probably before 1669. Livingston, *Livingstons of Livingston Manor*, 52-53.

15. Robert Livingston's Account Book, 1670, Livingston-Redmond Mss., Franklin D. Roosevelt Lib., Hyde Park, N. Y. (trans. from Dutch for me by Mrs. Alida J. Kolk O'Loughlin; such translations will be noted by the term "Dutch"). The collection at the Roosevelt Library will be cited hereafter as Livingston-Redmond Mss.

16. Robert Livingston to John and Janet Livingstone, Jan. 1, 1671 (Rotterdam), (Dutch), *ibid.*; Livingston, *Livingstons of Livingston Manor*, 51n; Anderson, *Ladies of the Covenant*, 79.

youth. His brothers and sisters were strangers to him—indeed, his native Scotland must have seemed strange and oppressive after the freedom he had experienced in Rotterdam. With little to hold him in Edinburgh, and with war preventing his return to Rotterdam, Livingston turned to the New World. On April 28, 1673, he embarked for Massachusetts Bay.[17]

When he stepped ashore in the Puritan Commonwealth in June 1673, he faced the necessity of earning a livelihood. Though little is known of his first year in the New World, it seems logical that he would have associated himself with a Boston merchant until he became acclimated to his new surroundings. He had little capital, but his most important asset was his father's reputation. Livingston was in the one colony where his father's achievements as a leading disciple of John Calvin were known and respected. In September 1674, John Hull, one of the foremost Puritan merchants and treasurer of the Bay Colony, advanced Livingston £34 in "duffels, stokins, sattin &c" on the basis of the young man's parentage and prospects. Hull was a "cautious businessman, undertaking no rash speculations," but a son of the "Godly Livingstone" could not be classified as a "rash speculation."[18]

The conflict between merchant and cleric in Massachusetts had created an atmosphere that reminded Livingston too much of his native Scotland.[19] He probably solicited the loan from Hull with the idea of establishing himself in a place where business, political, and social success did not involve the Puritan ethic. The possibilities of New York were brought to Livingston's attention by news of the Treaty of Westminster between England and The Netherlands. In February 1673/4, the colony of New Netherland, now New York, was transferred for the second and last time to Charles II, who shortly re-granted it to his brother James, Duke of York. Word of this must have reached Livingston by September when he applied to Hull for

17. Livingston, "Anno 1673.... A Journal of our good intended voyage," Livingston-Redmond Mss.
18. Samuel Eliot Morison, *Builders of the Bay Colony* (Boston, 1930), 159-60, 170; Hull to Livingston, Jan. 30, 1678/9, Livingston-Redmond Mss.; Hull's private acct. book, 89, New Eng. Hist. & Gen. Soc.
19. Bernard Bailyn, *The New England Merchants in the Seventeenth Century* (Cambridge, 1955), 140.

the loan.[20] Perhaps Hull's willingness to grant it was spurred by the realization that the young Scotsman could now capitalize on another asset—his bilingual fluency.

In December 1674 or January 1674/5, Robert Livingston went to Albany, where he found the atmosphere much more akin to Rotterdam's. But he also discovered that the customary channels of trade had been disrupted by New York's restoration to the English. Massachusetts merchants had long been interested in the fur trade as a means of providing much-needed returns for the manufactured goods they purchased from England. However, the fur resources of the Bay Colony and its hinterland had been rapidly exhausted. By the 1650's those merchants had turned toward the Iroquois-controlled furs of the west. Prior to the transfer of New Netherland to England in 1664, the Englishmen of Massachusetts interfered with the Dutch domination of the Iroquois trade. But after the Duke of York became proprietor of New York, an international controversy sank to the level of a colonial boundary dispute.[21] However, Massachusetts had been on safer ground in an international dispute with the Dutch than in a local dispute with the Duke of York; James was heir presumptive to the throne, and Massachusetts was striving valiantly to avoid royal controls. Thus the New Englanders had to tread more cautiously after 1664 for fear of evoking retaliatory measures by the Crown.

But the temporary re-conquest of New York by the Dutch in July 1673 had given the Massachusetts merchants an opportunity to renew their contacts with the Dutch merchants of Albany. John Pynchon, a leader in the effort to secure the fur trade for the Bay Colony, took the initiative in opening a correspondence with at least one such merchant. Conversely, the restoration of English sovereignty over New York in 1674 made it impossible to continue the direct trade between Albany and Springfield. Now, the beaver skins were required to move southward through New York City where a duty of one shilling three pence apiece was paid into the Duke's coffers before they were shipped to Boston.[22] Since the Massachusetts merchants were forced to oper-

20. This news reached Massachusetts by June. Pynchon to Dreyer and Van Slichtenhorst, June 29, 1674, Livingston-Redmond Mss.

21. Arthur H. Buffinton, "New England and the Western Fur Trade, 1629-1675," Col. Soc. of Mass., *Publications*, 17 (1917), 177, 183.

22. Bartlett B. James and J. Franklin Jameson, eds., *Journal of Jasper Danckaerts, 1679-1680* (N.Y., 1913), 235*n*; Charles M. Andrews, *The Colonial Period of American*

ate through these channels established by the Duke and his agents, they found it necessary to have trustworthy factors in Albany to supervise their affairs. Pynchon sent Timothy Cooper of Springfield to Albany in the summer of 1675 under a seven-year partnership contract; [23] when Livingston arrived in Albany in the winter of 1674-75, he and Hull presumably had reached an understanding, though not as definitive a one as the Pynchon-Cooper contract.

Albany's ideal geographic position gave the city control of the Iroquois fur trade. The Mohawk River was an avenue to the furs of the Ohio Valley, the Hudson River a route to the markets of Europe, and Albany rested at their junction. This situation also had disadvantages. As the only gap in the Appalachian mountain range through which the French could penetrate, the Mohawk remained a crucial defense line for the English colonies until the French were ousted from the continent in 1763. But the French, more often than not, found this gateway closed by the Iroquois, the Confederacy of the Five Nations.

Throughout the seventeenth and eighteenth centuries, New Netherland and later New York enjoyed a doubly fruitful alliance with the Iroquois. The Five Nations provided military protection for the colony and brought furs to Albany from the western tribes for whom they acted as middlemen, and the English provided the Indians with manufactured goods at less expensive prices than the French. The fur trade was one of New York's major occupations, and it was completely dominated by Albany. [24]

In Albany the most influential citizens were the Dutch *handlaers*, or merchants, around whom the town's entire economic life revolved. To maintain cordial relations with the Iroquois sachems and retain the fur trade's profits, the merchants cultivated the friendship of the Indians at considerable expense and no little trouble. But trading was so

---

History (4 vols., New Haven, 1934-37), III, 95-96; Pynchon to Van Slichtenhorst, Dec. 12, 1673, Livingston-Redmond Mss.; Instructions to Gov. Andros, July 1, 1674, Edmund B. O'Callaghan, ed., *Documents Relative to the Colonial History of the State of New York* (11 vols., Albany, 1853-67), III, 217 (hereafter cited as O'Callaghan, ed., *N.Y. Col. Docs.*).

23. Contract between Pynchon and Cooper, Apr. 28, 1675, Pynchon Acct. Books (6 vols.), V (part 2), 476-77, Conn. Valley Hist. Museum, Springfield, Mass.

24. Ruth L. Higgins, *Expansion in New York with Especial Reference to the Eighteenth Century* (Columbus, 1931), 34-35; Peter Wraxall, *An Abridgment of the Indian Affairs...from the year 1678 to the year 1751*, ed., Charles H. McIlwain (Cambridge, Mass., 1915), xxxvi-xxxvii.

profitable that the *handlaers* exerted every effort to retain it as their monopoly. Intruders of any sort, whether the Patroon of Rensselaerswyck, the town of Schenectady, or newly arrived Englishmen, were unwelcome.[25]

Yet, if any outsider could allay the merchants' suspicions and win acceptance, it was Robert Livingston. Though a Scot, he had lived in Rotterdam for nine years, spoke the *handlaers'* language, knew their commercial methods, and understood their customs. He was also a very personable young man, a quality he relied on whenever all other means of achieving his objectives failed. As a result, he was an ideal factor for John Hull, who was eager to garner profits from the fur trade.

When Livingston surveyed Albany, he found a small, square town nestled on the side of a hill. It contained eighty or ninety houses, about five or six hundred people, and two churches—a Dutch Reformed and a Lutheran. Fort Orange lay near the riverbank and was set off by palisades filled with earth. "Clear, fresh, cool water" was piped into several fountains from a nearby spring. Albany itself was surrounded by palisades with gates at the ends of the streets. At either end of town were lodges where the Indians were received and entertained during the fur trading season.[26]

Upon his arrival, Livingston lodged with Gabriel Thomasz, but he quickly signified his intention of becoming a permanent resident, purchasing a town lot in March 1674/5.[27] This was a sign of stability, but he soon exhibited an argumentative quality that could be harmful to an aspiring merchant. On March 25, 1675, while visiting the Reverend Gideon Schaets, minister of the Dutch Reformed Church,

25. Arthur H. Buffinton, "The Policy of Albany and English Westward Expansion," *Miss. Valley Hist. Rev.*, 8 (1922), 330.

26. James and Jameson, eds., *Danckaerts' Journal*, 216-17; Evarts B. Greene and Virginia D. Harrington, *American Population Before the Federal Census of 1790* (N.Y., 1932), xxiii.

27. Deposition of Adriaen Van Ilpendam, Jan. 29, 1674/5, Arnold J. F. Van Laer, ed., *Early Records of the City and County of Albany and Colony of Rensselaerswyck* (3 vols., Albany, 1916-19), III, 329 (hereafter cited as Van Laer, ed., *Early Records*); Deed from Johannes Provoost [i.e., Jan Conell], Mar. 11, 1674/5, Jonathan Pearson, trans., *Early Records of the City and County of Albany, and Colony of Rensselaerswyck (1656-1675)*, (Albany, 1869), 108; Wheeler B. Melius and Frank H. Burnap, eds., *Index to the Public Records of the County of Albany, State of New York, 1630-1894: Grantees* (12 vols., Albany, 1908-11), VII, 4588.

Livingston quarreled with Hendrick Roseboom over some unspecified subject. Desirous of patching up the quarrel, Roseboom enlisted
the aid of Schaets and Adriaen Van Ilpendam as mediators. "With
much reasoning," they attempted to induce Livingston to settle the
matter, but he "would not consent thereto and gave for answer that
expenses had been incurred and that the matter must be decided before
the judges." Evidently, the mediators' persuasions proved more force-
ful, for there seems to have been no court adjudication.[28]

Livingston's immediate goal in the community was the establishment of a reputation as a responsible merchant. By mid-March 1675,
he reported some progress to his Boston creditor. Hull replied that he
was "glad to heare of your nearness to an Honnerable & gainfull im-
ployment," though he cautioned the young merchant "to serve God
& your generation & keep your selfe from the defilements of the place
and time." Hull also accepted Livingston's offer to formalize their
trade relationship, but added these stipulations: he would supply goods,
Livingston would bear the risk on all shipments, and the accounts
would have to be settled every six months in beaver. A cautious businessman, Hull was not inclined to take risks he could force others to
assume. At this stage in his career, Livingston could do little but accept Hull's terms.[29]

Livingston's ambitions encompassed more than commercial success
alone. In the colonies, a man might prosper by adhering solely to
trade, but even greater rewards could be won by participating in government as well. Public service in these years was closely intertwined
with private profit; holding public office was a means of both protecting commercial activities and gaining the positive benefits which accrued to government officials. There were many pitfalls, of course, in
blending these two; but John Hull's injunction, to "serve God & your
generation" and to avoid the "defilements of the place and time," was
the key to a successful career.

The Van Rensselaer family, majority owners of the Colony or
Manor of Rensselaerswyck, gave Livingston his first opportunity to

28. Depositions of Adriaen Van Ilpendam, Jan. 28, 29, 1674/5, Van Laer, ed., *Early
Records*, III, 329.
29. Livingston apparently agreed to this relationship because a year later he ordered goods from Hull. Hull to Livingston, Mar. 31, 1675, Mar. 13, 1675/6, John Hull's
Letterbook, 1670-1685, Amer. Antiq. Soc.

serve the public. The Manor, an enormous tract of land surrounding Albany and covering several modern counties, had been granted to a group of Dutch merchants by the Dutch West India Company. The Reverend Nicholas Van Rensselaer, who had arrived in New York at about the same time as Livingston, assumed the duties of the directorship after the death of his elder brother in October 1674. A minister of the Dutch Reformed Church, though ordained by the Anglican Bishop of Sarum, Nicholas Van Rensselaer's career in the New World was as unusual and stormy as it had been in the Old.[30] Nearly two months before he had made application for legal appointment as director, he had exercised that office's prerogatives by hiring Livingston as secretary of Rensselaerswyck on August 24, 1675. Although the annual salary of 200 guilders, or 40 schepels (i.e., 30 bushels) of wheat, may have been agreed upon then, the contract was not formalized for two years, and Livingston did not receive his salary arrears until August 24, 1677.[31]

Livingston's acceptance of that post opened still another office to him—secretary of Albany. The relatively small populations of Rensselaerswyck and Albany in the 1670's meant that neither could afford to pay an attractive salary to a clerk of its own, although together they could provide a recompense large enough for a competent secretary. Livingston took on the added duty in September 1675.[32] He received a third post when Governor Andros established a board of Indian commissioners in the fall of 1675. This agency's purpose was to bring some order into the conduct of the all-important Iroquois negotiations at the same time that they were brought under the authority, if not the control, of the governor and Council. Someone was needed

30. The first Kiliaen Van Rensselaer owned 60 percent of the original grant. His share, according to Dutch inheritance laws, was equally divided among his heirs. Nicholas' share was 14.8 percent of the Van Rensselaer portion, or 10.4 percent of the entire Manor. Samuel G. Nissenson, *The Patroon's Domain* (N.Y., 1937), 291, 387. See also Lawrence H. Leder, "The Unorthodox Domine: Nicholas Van Rensselaer," *N. Y. Hist.*, 35 (1954), 166-76.

31. Nicholas Van Rensselaer's petition, Oct. 15, 1675, N. Y. Col. Mss., XXIV, 158, N. Y. State Lib., Albany; Maria Van Rensselaer to Jan Van Wely and Jan Baptist Van Rensselaer, Nov. 1675, Arnold J. F. Van Laer, ed., *Correspondence of Maria Van Rensselaer, 1669-1689* (Albany, 1935), 13 (hereafter cited as Van Laer, ed., *Correspondence*); Contract, Aug. 2, 1677, Van Laer, ed., *Early Records*, III, 441.

32. On Sept. 8, 1675, Livingston was officially described as "Secretary of Albany, colony of Rensselaerswyck, etc." Pearson, ed., *Records of Albany*, 121. For a contrary interpretation, see Nissenson, *Patroon's Domain*, 273.

to maintain the board's records, and Livingston was the most readily available candidate.[33]

Through these three offices, Livingston laid the foundations for his future career. He became acquainted with the officialdom of New York and assisted them in the performance of their duties in Albany. He also aided various prominent New York City residents, serving as their attorney in civil lawsuits before the Albany courts.[34] And he gained an invaluable knowledge of the machinery of government on the local and intra-colonial levels, as well as an insight into the problems inherent in the conduct of Anglo-Iroquois relations.

Livingston's early life in Albany was not all business, either private or public. He was a young man of twenty-two, ambitious and eager for success, but also possessed of a convivial and engaging personality which won him many friends.[35] Some hint of the lighter side of Livingston's life is provided by a lawsuit. Jan Conell, with whom he had several business dealings, charged that Livingston borrowed a violin from Conell's wife and took it to James Penniman's house "to be merry." The instrument, Conell alleged, was returned "broken into three pieces." This charge Livingston apparently refuted, but it is noteworthy that Livingston's reputation encompassed making so merry with a violin that it failed to survive the ordeal.[36]

Early in 1677, Livingston found himself the subject of, though not a participant in, another lawsuit, one which carried embarrassing implications for his reputation. Sometime in January, at a gathering in Albany from which Livingston was absent, William Loveridge, Sr., made a chance remark about having sold wine to Livingston on credit. John Hammill embroidered the comment so as to sound as if Livingston could not have gotten the wine unless Loveridge had given him

33. Higgins, *Expansion in New York*, 33; John R. Brodhead, *History of the State of New York* (2 vols., N.Y., 1853-71), II, 287. Livingston declared in 1704 that he had "*acted* as secretary of the Indian affairs for twenty years before [receiving his first commission in 1696]...without fee or reward." Livingston's memorial to Sidney, Lord Godolphin, July 12, 1704 (draft), Livingston-Redmond Mss.

34. Matthias Nicolls to Livingston, June 25, 1678, Livingston-Redmond Mss.; Arnold J. F. Van Laer, ed., *Minutes of the Court of Albany, Rensselaerswyck, and Schenectady, 1668-1685* (3 vols., Albany, 1926-32), II, 67, 84, 93, 334, 340-41 (hereafter cited as Van Laer, ed., *Court Minutes*).

35. Richard Bingley to Livingston, Oct. 30, 1677, George Hall to Livingston, Feb. 24, 1677/8, Wentworth Greenhalgh to Livingston, Apr. 19, 1678, Livingston-Redmond Mss.

36. Van Laer, ed., *Court Minutes*, II, 175-76.

credit. To protect himself from any claim by Livingston, who was an important town official, Loveridge sued Hammill for defamation. The magistrates threw the case out of court, astutely observing that Hammill's statement had not defamed Loveridge, but "if it were true it would be Secretary Livingston, rather than the plaintiff, who would feel insulted." The very fact that Livingston made no effort to prosecute lends weight to the assumption that the statement was not far from the truth.[37]

One factor contributing to Livingston's financial difficulties early in 1677 was the lack of payment for his official duties. The salary for the secretaryship of Rensselaerswyck had been agreed upon but it had not yet been paid, and his reimbursement as secretary of Albany had not even been determined. Although the fees of the latter office produced some income, Livingston performed other tasks, such as that of tax collector, and presumably received no compensation. In March 1676/7, he appeared before the town magistrates and demanded 600 guilders a year salary, plus 5 percent of the town's revenues for keeping its books. Despite his contention that his predecessor had received this sum, the magistrates countered with the unacceptable offer of 400 guilders and 8 beaverskins a year. When Governor Andros visited Albany in April, he compromised the difference by ordering the magistrates to pay 600 guilders annually and 4 percent of the town's revenue.[38]

Even this salary and the arrears which Livingston received from Nicholas Van Rensselaer in August did not exorcise the specter of financial embarrassment. By October, various creditors began to press him and, for a time, it must have seemed as though Hammill's alleged defamation might be true after all.[39]

Livingston apparently considered an interesting solution to his financial predicament. It was not uncommon for young men newly arrived in the colony to marry well-to-do widows, and Livingston seems to have contemplated such a step.[40] A friend, known affectionately to

37. *Ibid.*, 189-90, 218-19.
38. *Ibid.*, 120-21, 160, 186, 225-26.
39. Gibb to Livingston, Oct. 12, 1677, Palmer to Livingston, Oct. 10, 1677, Bingley to Livingston, Oct. 30, 1677, Livingston-Redmond Mss.
40. Examples of this are Leisler, who married the widow of Pieter Cornelius Van der Veen in 1663 and gained a prosperous wine importing business, and Capt. Kidd, who married the twice-widowed Sarah Cox and gained a flour warehouse and real estate in New York City. Edwin R. Purple, *Genealogical Notes Relating to Lieut.-*

Livingston and his group as "the auld gossep," wrote that she was "vere sorey to hear that you are not mared yet for i think it is a great pety But I hope ere Long to come to Mrs. Benig weaden [wedding] and yours So go at her." A year later, another friend wrote that he was romantically inclined toward a "Mrs Susana." [41] At this time, however, Livingston's alternative to matrimony was a partnership with Timothy Cooper, who had come to Albany in 1675 as John Pynchon's agent. Their positions were clearly complementary: Cooper had great difficulty breaking into the *handlaers'* monopoly, while Livingston, with his Dutch background and ingratiating personality, had a good chance of success; Cooper had access to extensive credit and supplies through Pynchon, while Livingston's sources of supply must have been extremely limited. The mutual solution of their problems was simple enough—Cooper would obtain goods at wholesale, and Livingston would retail them to the Iroquois. By October of 1678, the two men were acting jointly in business transactions, an arrangement that must have been in effect for at least a year. Possibly, John Pynchon himself had suggested it during his visit to Albany in April 1677.[42]

The Cooper-Livingston arrangement was disrupted by the machinations of the *handlaers* soon after Governor Sir Edmund Andros' return from England. During the summer of 1678, the recently knighted governor was anxiously awaited; his arrival would signal a renewal of the colony's political, economic, and social life. Livingston planned to go to New York City for the occasion, and the magistrates of Albany selected two of their number to accompany their secretary to advise the governor of developments on the frontier during his absence.[43] The citizenry of Albany desired two things of the governor: a declaration of their exclusive rights in the fur trade, and official assurances which would keep the Indians living near Albany from being enticed away by the French in Canada. The second goal was achieved when

---

Gov. Jacob Leisler and his Family Connections in New York (N.Y., 1877), 6-7; John H. Innes, *New Amsterdam and Its People* (N.Y., 1902), 251.

41. Bingley to Livingston, Oct. 30, 1677, Shaw to Livingston, Oct. 8, 1678, Livingston-Redmond Mss. See also Greenhalgh to Livingston, Apr. 19, Aug. 6, 1678, *ibid*.

42. Cooper to Livingston, Oct. 2, 1678, *ibid.*; "Proposicons made ... At Albany the 24th of Aprill 1677," Lawrence H. Leder, ed., *The Livingston Indian Records, 1666-1723* (Harrisburg, Pa., 1956), 39.

43. Nicolls to Livingston, June 25, 1678, Livingston-Redmond Mss.; O'Callaghan, ed., *N. Y. Col. Docs.*, II, 741*n;* Van Laer, ed., *Court Minutes*, II, 348-49; "Calendar of Council Minutes," N. Y. State Lib., *Bulletin 58: History 6* (March, 1902), 31.

Sir Edmund issued an order on August 22 promising the Mohawks, Mahicans, and River Indians that their lands and way of life would be preserved. The first and, to the *handlaers*, most important point was won on the next day, but at great expense to themselves. The governor reserved the fur trade for resident merchants of Albany, but he also reserved the overseas trade for resident merchants of New York City. This placed the Albany traders at the mercy of their counterparts in New York City. Despite vigorous protests from the Albany authorities, Andros was adamant.[44]

Having won their fur trade monopoly, the Albany burghers intended to enforce it vigorously. (Indeed, elimination of outsiders became a perpetual theme in that town's history throughout the colonial period.) Timothy Cooper, agent of Pynchon and partner of Livingston, was an intruder marked for attack. Although he did not fall under the governor's ban, the *handlaers* soon found an excuse for getting rid of him. In February 1677/8, he wrote an indiscreet letter to Pynchon deprecating the attitude of the burghers towards two Massachusetts men who had gone to Albany seeking aid in retrieving their families from Indian captivity. The letter was intercepted by the Albany magistrates, who termed it "Schandilas" and turned it over to Sir Edmund. Hailed before the governor and Council in October 1678, Cooper presented a stout defense of the letter's meaning and intent, but he was ordered to leave Albany by the following spring.[45]

Even before Cooper's appearance before the governor, John Pynchon had sent his brother-in-law Elizur Holyoke to Albany to aid Cooper in settling his accounts. After the interception of Cooper's letter, his expulsion was only a matter of time. One of Cooper's largest debtors was Livingston, who was still in New York City when Holyoke reached Albany. Cooper wrote to his partner, urging him to "make what possible Speed you Can up so you may come to some composition with Mr. Holyoke." Fearful that Livingston might stay in New York City "to weary me out," Holyoke decided to attach the

44. N. Y. Council Minutes, Aug. 20-23, 1678, Berthold Fernow, ed., *Documents Relative to the History and Settlements of the Towns along the Hudson and Mohawk (with the exception of Albany), from 1630 to 1684* (Albany, 1881), 531-32; Edmund B. O'Callaghan, ed., *Calendar of Historical Manuscripts in the Office of the Secretary of State, Albany, N. Y.* (2 vols., Albany, 1866), II, 78; Nicolls to Livingston, May 11, 1679, Livingston-Redmond Mss.

45. Cooper to Governor and Council, c. Oct. 1678, N. Y. Council Minutes, Oct. 23, 1678, N. Y. Col. Mss., XXVIII, 28, 27a-d, 27c, N. Y. State Lib.

merchant's Albany property and then go to New York City to settle matters. Cooper dissuaded him from such rash action—nothing would more effectively destroy a young trader's reputation—and again urged Livingston "While all things are Privat as you tender your owne Credit hasten up." Holyoke reassured Livingston that "it is not [publicly] knowne what I come for as yett & my Designe Is so to Remaine untill I speake with you." [46]

Since official business before the Court of Assizes detained Livingston, Holyoke finally agreed to meet him in New York City where, through Governor Andros' mediation, the two reached an amicable settlement. Livingston paid a portion of the debt in goods, and he wrote to Pynchon promising that he "would be always Sending Something." In return, Holyoke agreed, "non need to know but what you Did Cleere that account with me when I was at york." [47]

But this did not end Livingston's financial difficulties. In 1679, he was dunned by John Hull for the loan made in September 1674—"consider what is just and Send me my moneys . . . that I may have Cause to say you have Some regard of your honnored fathers stepps." Evidently, that letter was ignored, for eleven months later Hull wrote again and implied something more drastic: "pray Sir do not any longer delay it nor occation me to take any severe Cours . . . that will not neither be for your profitt nor Creditt remember your Ancestors & ther good Example." In addition, Holyoke found it necessary to prod Livingston about his promise to John Pynchon.[48]

Plagued by creditors and, at the same time, desirous of starting a family—he was now twenty-four—Livingston sought a bride. He had been courting a "Mrs. Susana," and when he arrived in New York City in August 1678, he sent her a basket of pineapples and oranges, a rare and exotic gift in colonial New York. The offering went through the hands of a friend who reported to Livingston that "Mrs. Susana was pleased to say shee wold not have them if send from you." The lady was very distressed at "the report of your Extravagances at york & your putting in for other mens places." Such conduct, asserted Liv-

46. Henry M. Burt, *The First Century of the History of Springfield* (2 vols., Springfield, Mass., 1898-99), II, 29; Cooper to Livingston, Oct. 2, 1678, Holyoke to Livingston, Oct. 3, 1678, Livingston-Redmond Mss.

47. Shaw to Livingston, Oct. 8, 1678, Holyoke to Livingston, May 8, 1679, *ibid.*

48. Hull to Livingston, Jan. 30, 1678/9, Holyoke to Livingston, May 8, 1679, *ibid.*; Hull to Livingston, Dec. 31, 1679, Hull's Letterbook, 1670-1685, Amer. Antiq. Soc.

ingston's go-between, "is lyk to purchase you no reputation with her or any other." [49]

Aggressiveness may have cost Livingston his reputation with "Mrs. Susana," but the loss was not irreparable. His affections soon turned to Alida Schuyler Van Rensselaer, the attractive young widow of Nicholas Van Rensselaer. When Livingston began courting her, she was but twenty-two years old.[50]

Alida Schuyler Van Rensselaer and Robert Livingston were not strangers, for he had worked for her husband. Indeed, an apocryphal family story about their relationship reported that when Nicholas Van Rensselaer lay dying, he asked for a lawyer to make his will. Peter Schuyler, his brother-in-law, brought in Livingston, but Van Rensselaer ordered him out of the room. Alida, "in deep sorrow, asked why he had been so capricious—with a solemn voice he replied 'that man will be your husband.'" The dying man's prophecy, if he really made it, soon came true. After allowing a decent interval to elapse, Alida Schuyler Van Rensselaer and Robert Livingston were wed in the Albany Dutch Reformed Church on July 9, 1679.[51]

Alida could not bring her new husband great wealth, but her dowry was very important—an alliance with some of the most powerful families in New York. Her family was well established in Albany commerce and politics: her father, Philip Pieterse Schuyler, was one of the town's most substantial citizens, and her five brothers were young men with promising futures. One of her sisters, Gertruyd, had married Stephanus Van Cortlandt, a prominent merchant and politician in New York City; his sister, Maria Van Cortlandt, had married Jeremias Van Rensselaer, late director of Rensselaerswyck.[52] Through his marriage, Livingston gained social standing, an intangible but invaluable asset. This was a turning point in his life; without this asset, his future successes would have been impossible.

After the nuptial plans were announced, Livingston's changed status was reflected by the tone of the correspondence he received. Instead of dunning letters, he got solicitations for business and offers of assist-

49. Shaw to Livingston, Oct. 8, 1678, Livingston-Redmond Mss.
50. Nissenson, *Patroon's Domain*, 292; George W. Schuyler, *Colonial New York; Philip Schuyler and His Family* (2 vols., N.Y., 1885), I, 185.
51. Janet Livingston Montgomery to Gen. Gates, n.d., Misc. Montgomery Mss. (typed), N.-Y. Hist. Soc.; Livingston, *Livingstons of Livingston Manor*, 58.
52. Schuyler, *Colonial New York*, I, 185.

ance. The very news of the impending marriage was enough to induce James Graham, a fellow Scot, to offer "upon all occasions to serve you according to my capacity." Matthias Nicolls, secretary of New York, restated his desire for Livingston's aid in the execution of official duties in Albany, promising him that "you may depend on mine for you here" in New York City.[53]

From a relatively minor merchant and local official in a frontier outpost, Livingston was to rise quickly in landownership, government service, and commerce. Thomas De Lavall, in his estimate of the significance of this marriage, was more prophetic than he realized when he commented that Livingston had "now . . . come into the Ranke of honest men." [54]

53. Graham to Livingston, Apr. 7, 1679, Nicolls to Livingston, May 11, 1679, Livingston-Redmond Mss.
54. De Lavall to Livingston, Aug. 22, 1679, *ibid.*

CHAPTER II

Land and Status

O F THE MANY European heritages brought to America by the colonists, one of the most significant was the equation of land and status. In Europe, where the territory seemed too small to support the population, the hallmark of social status was landownership. The most acceptable means of acquiring land was by inheritance, but the *nouveau riche*, whether or not a cadet member of an ancient line, had to be content with its acquisition either by marriage or purchase. The obsession for land, instilled in men's minds for countless generations, was brought to the New World.

That New World conditions were totally different mattered little. The colonists, possessed of a deep-rooted land hunger, satiated themselves in a virtually uninhabited continent by staking out vast tracts of virgin forest. Despite the lack of population necessary to make the land productive, the early settlers envisioned the not too distant day when the wilderness would become prosperous farms.

Not everyone who migrated to the New World could appease his greed for land. Some of the prerequisites to a large landed estate were talent, capital, political and family connections, and ambition. Of all these, Robert Livingston's greatest assets were talent and ambition. He was possessed of a consuming drive for success and recognition which could only be symbolized by the ownership of his own large tract of land.

Soon after his arrival in New York, Livingston began cultivating important political connections. Matthias Nicolls, secretary of New York, had proffered his assistance whenever the young man should want it. By December 1678, he had won Governor Andros' gratitude by supplying information on Indian affairs. After his marriage, Livingston had the support of the Schuyler clan, a potent factor in New York politics, and of his new brother-in-law, Stephanus Van Cortlandt, who was elevated to the Governor's Council in 1680. Through them, his commercial prosperity was also assured, thereby providing him with the necessary capital.[1]

Having gained the basic prerequisites, Livingston moved towards the acquisition of a landed estate by pressing a tenuous claim to the Manor of Rensselaerswyck. A princely estate of some million acres, the Manor was one of the most desirable properties in the colony; Livingston's efforts to acquire it engendered a violent family feud and provided a most revealing study of his persistence, aggressiveness, and shrewdness.

Nicholas Van Rensselaer died intestate, and his widow, Alida, applied for letters of administration which were granted on November 30, 1678, and recorded in Albany a month later. Immediately after marrying Alida, Livingston took over his predecessor's estate, gaining control of two valuable farms, and paid Nicholas' local debts. He demanded an accounting of Nicholas' share of the Manor of Rensselaerswyck from Maria, widow of Jeremias Van Rensselaer, the former director. She could "not give it to him," however, because it was "not complete." Turning to her brother, Stephanus Van Cortlandt, the interim director, she asked to be "relieved of this trouble, for it is too much for me." She did not realize that this was just the beginning of Livingston's importunities. Seven months later, he was still treating her "so uncivilly and wants money." [2]

But Maria was not a key figure in the developing controversy. Those directly involved were Livingston and the Van Rensselaers in The Netherlands, particularly the head of that family, Richard. He entered the dispute in 1680, when Livingston demanded to see the will

1. Andros to Livingston, Dec. 4, 1678, Livingston-Redmond Mss.; "Cal. Council Minutes," N. Y. State Lib., *Bulletin 58*, 7.
2. Andros' order, Nov. 30, 1678, Van Laer, ed., *Court Minutes*, II, 379; N.-Y. Hist. Soc., *Collections*, 25 (1893), 68; Nissenson, *Patroon's Domain*, 293; Maria Van Rensselaer to Stephanus Van Cortlandt, Nov. 1679, John Darvall to Maria Van Rensselaer, June 17, 1680, Van Laer, ed., *Correspondence*, 30, 32.

of Jan Van Wely, maternal uncle of Nicholas, in order to learn what Alida Livingston had inherited from Van Wely through her first husband. Richard advised his sister-in-law Maria that Nicholas had died before his uncle. Therefore, Robert and Alida Livingston had no claim on Van Wely's estate.[3]

On November 6, 1680, Livingston obtained an audience with Governor Andros from whom he received certain assurances. The most important matter, Livingston wrote his wife, was the last will and testament of Nicholas' mother. The will of Nicholas' uncle, Jan Van Wely, would cause no trouble, nor would Philip Pieterse Schuyler's claim on Nicholas' estate. However, he continued, "you should get together all debts you have paid since his death, and when I come up I will obtain a certificate of the Court that I have paid the debts in this country, and obtain from the Governor my quietus. I do not worry about it, the debts abroad may take care of themselves. I am not afraid of them, I keep possession. The Governor said that I should come again on Monday, then we will discuss it further." The basic problem was this: Nicholas had not only died intestate, but insolvent as well. He owed his father's estate some 3,000 florins, along with other debts both in England and The Netherlands.[4]

Nicholas' estate was scattered over two continents. In New York, his assets, including his share in the Manor, slightly exceeded his liabilities; in Europe, his liabilities far exceeded his assets. Livingston's plans called for a divorce of the two estates and his retention of the New York one. By attempting to use the Atlantic as a legal barrier, he was engaging in a highly questionable tactic. Later, when this appeared to be failing, he attempted to divert the estate's creditors by hinting that Nicholas' inheritances from his mother and uncle were greater than the Van Rensselaers were willing to admit.[5]

After securing the governor's advice, Livingston returned to Albany. On December 7, 1680, he applied to the court for an evaluation of Nicholas' estate, and four men were appointed to "appraise all but his share in the Colony of Rensselaerswyck." The estate, valued at

3. Richard Van Rensselaer to Maria Van Rensselaer, July 12, 1680, Van Laer, ed., *Correspondence*, 35.

4. Robert Livingston to Alida Livingston, Nov. 6, 1680 (Dutch), Livingston-Redmond Mss.; Nissenson, *Patroon's Domain*, 294; Richard Van Rensselaer to Maria Van Rensselaer, May 4/14, 1682, Van Laer, ed., *Correspondence*, 63.

5. Stephanus Van Cortlandt to Maria Van Rensselaer, Dec. 1680, Richard Van Rensselaer to Livingston, May 4/14, 1682, Van Laer, ed., *Correspondence*, 43, 65.

3,440 florins, included a house and lot in Albany, "13 pictures with the King's Arms," and "about 200 books, quarto and octavo, the most of them in Strange Languages." Note was also taken of the debts Livingston claimed to have paid for Nicholas' estate. These totaled 5,851 florins, "for which I debit his share in the colony," Livingston declared, for 2,411 florins.

Carefully reviewing those debts, the appraisers "were not sufficiently satisfied." Their skepticism was aroused, and justifiably so, by the 1,908 florins Livingston claimed to have paid, "for various goods received," to Philip Pieterse Schuyler, lately Nicholas' father-in-law and now Livingston's. The vagueness of the obligation, the fact that it nearly equalled the deficit, and the kinship of creditor, debtor, and administrator, all combined to arouse suspicions. The elder Schuyler, however, was an honorable man, and his offer to "swear to the said account and . . . to make good account with those who might question the same" abated the appraisers' skepticism. On December 30, 1680, the court finally approved Livingston's administration of the estate.[6]

According to his plan, Livingston would seek from the governor a *quietus*, or release from all future claims; he could then regain his 2,411 florins by forcing a partition of Rensselaerswyck. But Sir Edmund was suddenly called home on January 7, 1680/1, to answer charges against his administration, leaving Commander-in-Chief Anthony Brockholls in charge. The governor's departure necessitated a complete revision of Livingston's plan, because Brockholls, a more timid creature than Sir Edmund, certainly would not involve himself in a scheme as potentially explosive as this one.[7]

Furthermore, Livingston found himself faced with another problem—a lawsuit. He was sued for thirty-eight florins that Nicholas Van Rensselaer had owed in Amsterdam. It is difficult to avoid seeing Richard Van Rensselaer's hand in this, for the sum was hardly worth the effort, but the principle was crucial to the Van Rensselaers. This was, in effect, a test case to determine the responsibility for Nicholas' European debts, a responsibility Livingston had rejected. When the case came to trial in Albany, Livingston sought a decision on the central issue; he declared that he was "nowise bound to pay the same, as the

6. Van Laer, ed., *Court Minutes*, III, 47-56.
7. "Cal. Council Minutes," N. Y. State Lib., *Bulletin 58*, 6; Brodhead, *History of New York*, II, 51.

estate was not accepted unconditionally, but administered under benefit of inventory, and the defendant had paid a considerable sum of money over and above the amount of the inventory." But the court was very hesitant even to consider such a momentous matter, and dismissed the case on a technicality that avoided the central issue.[8]

Actually, nothing could have been more fortunate for Livingston. An indication of what might have happened had the case been appealed to England was provided in an opinion of the attorney general of England a quarter of a century later. In a similar matter, he ruled that the "whole personal estate in England and the Plantations will be lyable to all the Intestate's Debts in both Places."[9] Substituting "The Netherlands" for "England," it is evident that Livingston's legal position was very weak.

By upsetting Livingston's plans for a quick end to the whole affair, Sir Edmund's departure for England set off a family feud of magnificent proportions. On the one hand, Livingston and the Schuylers were determined to break up the Manor. The former wanted Nicholas Van Rensselaer's share, while the latter wanted some of the Manor's farms. On the other hand, Maria Van Rensselaer and her in-laws in The Netherlands were equally determined to preserve the Manor as an entity. Maria hoped that her son might become director; the Van Rensselaers did not wish to arouse the long-dormant interests of the other owners by a partition. Vacillating between the combatants for several years was Stephanus Van Cortlandt, brother of Maria Van Rensselaer and brother-in-law of Livingston and the Schuylers. Although Van Cortlandt's own acquisitive instincts finally led him to advocate partition, his father, in March 1682, attempted to use him as a peacemaker. "Your brother," wrote Oloffe Stevense Van Cortlandt to Maria Van Rensselaer, "now goes up the river. I hope that together you may come to an agreement with the farmers, with Leuvensteyn, [and with] Captain Schuyler."[10]

It was a vain hope, however, for the key figures were unwilling to compromise. Richard wrote to Maria in May 1682 and advised her of the steps necessary to bring about Livingston's defeat, stressing his

8. Van Laer, ed., *Court Minutes*, III, 127.
9. Attorney General Northey's opinion, c. Mar. 1707, O'Callaghan, ed., *N. Y. Col. Docs.*, V, 2-3.
10. Nissenson, *Patroon's Domain*, 296-97; Oloffe Stevense Van Cortlandt to Maria Van Rensselaer, Mar. 1682, Van Laer, ed., *Correspondence*, 59.

liability for Nicholas' European debts. Specifically, he alleged that Nicholas owed his father's estate 3,324 florins. Insisting upon that payment, "besides the accrued interest," Richard pithily commented that Livingston, because he refused to accept that responsibility, was a "solicitor of fraudulent affairs." Furthermore, Richard charged, since Nicholas had gone to the New World as a penniless immigrant, his whole estate must have been mulcted out of the Manor, a property in which he had only a minority interest.[11]

None of this apparently distressed Livingston. Some eight months later, at Maria's request, he prepared a statement of his intentions. He reaffirmed his intention to retain whatever he could of Nicholas' and refused to render an accounting until the Van Rensselaers supplied an accounting of the proceeds of the estates of Nicholas' mother and uncle. To Maria's plaintive request for the use of the Patroon's farm and garden where her husband and children were buried, Livingston turned a deaf ear. He "rather expected to get something else in addition." [12]

When Maria realized that she could no longer cope with this persistent and ambitious Scot, she advised Richard that the Van Rensselaer family hire an attorney to bring Livingston to terms, suggesting Peter Delanoy, "an honest, Godfearing man." By the spring of 1683, however, Livingston must have realized how vulnerable he was to Nicholas' creditors. That, plus the pressure undoubtedly being exerted by Stephanus Van Cortlandt for an amicable settlement, may well have been the factor behind Livingston's more moderate demands. Now, he intimated, he would be satisfied with one farm and a nearby saw mill. Richard brushed this aside. The Van Rensselaers were working for a new patent and it would be impractical to consider any partition. "I wish," he disdainfully concluded, "that hereafter you would not trouble me any more with such and similar matters." [13]

On April 15, 1683, Richard followed Maria's suggestion by preparing a power of attorney for Peter Delanoy and outlining the three weak-

11. Richard Van Rensselaer to Maria Van Rensselaer, May 4/14, 1682, Richard Van Rensselaer to Livingston, May 4/14, 1682, Van Laer, ed., *Correspondence*, 63, 65-69.

12. Livingston's statement, c. Jan. 1682/3, Maria Van Rensselaer to Livingston, Jan. 1682/3, *ibid.*, 79-80, 86.

13. Maria Van Rensselaer to Richard Van Rensselaer, Jan. 1682/3, Stephanus Van Cortlandt to Maria Van Rensselaer, Feb. 1682/3, Richard Van Rensselaer to Livingston, Apr. 11/21, 1683, *ibid.*, 86, 91, 96-99.

nesses in Livingston's position. The Scot had ignored Nicholas' European debts. His wife had accepted Nicholas' estate under benefit of inventory and eliminated liability for debts discovered after court approval of the estate's administration, in spite of the fact that she had wed Nicholas under a communal property agreement and was, therefore, equally responsible for his European and New York debts. And, Livingston had seized the joint property of several partners because of the minority interest held by one of them.[14]

Richard advised Maria to warn Livingston that he would find it advantageous "to let everything go, for he might have a good deal of trouble with some creditors." She might also inform him that Nicholas' share in his mother's estate, according to the testament, was to be impounded until Nicholas had repaid his father's estate. Since Nicholas had no claim on his uncle's estate, this meant that Nicholas' creditors could only turn to Robert and Alida Livingston for satisfaction.[15]

If Richard believed that he could force Livingston to retract, he was mistaken. Being much too resourceful to admit defeat so readily, Livingston was cultivating various government officials in New York, and when the new governor, Thomas Dongan, arrived in August 1683, Livingston must have immediately sought his support. Since Peter Delanoy had already started planning his strategy along the lines suggested by Richard, Livingston undertook the offensive.[16]

Livingston's sights were set on the one obvious chink in the Van Rensselaer armor. Richard, as family head, could speak for the owners of 60 percent of the Manor. What of the other 40 percent? At Governor Dongan's suggestion, Livingston aroused the long-dormant interest of the other owners in their property. This was done openly, for Livingston obviously expected victory from the prospect of the campaign rather than from the ensuing battle.[17]

Maria was fully apprized of Livingston's activities and, as expected, she recounted all to Richard. It was at the instigation of the Schuylers, "that bitter family," that Livingston was now writing "to the par-

14. Richard Van Rensselaer to Delanoy, Apr. 2, 1683, *ibid.*, 99-100; Victor Hugo Paltsits, ed., *Inventory of the Rensselaerswyck Manuscripts* (N.Y., 1924), 35.

15. Richard Van Rensselaer to Maria Van Rensselaer, Apr. 12/22, 1683, Van Laer, ed., *Correspondence*, 101-2.

16. Catherine Darvall to Maria Van Rensselaer, July 9, 1683, Delanoy to [Richard Van Rensselaer], [Aug.] 1683, *ibid.*, 111-12, 117-18.

17. Livingston to Participants in Rensselaerswyck, Oct. 29, 1683 (draft), (Dutch), Livingston-Redmond Mss.

ticipants to get them to side with him and come to a division of the estate and thus to gain his object." He "will not let the matter rest, but insists on seeing it through, even if he should lose by it." To make matters worse, Stephanus Van Cortlandt had been fully converted to the Livingston-Schuyler cause. Maria was thoroughly disheartened: "It is here at present so sad, one does not know whether one deals with friend or foe. Yes, one dares not trust one's brother." Above all, she warned Richard, do not write to Stephanus Van Cortlandt, "for the house of Schuyler knows that immediately." [18]

On October 29, 1683, Governor Dongan and the Council received a request from Livingston for a partition of Rensselaerswyck. They recommended that it be transmitted to the various owners of the Manor before any official action was taken, and Livingston immediately sent an emissary with a circular letter to the Dutch owners. He also informed Richard that the dispute had been referred to the governor and Council and repaid him in his own coin by concluding: "I will not trouble you with any more *with such and similar* matters." [19]

Just as Livingston hoped, his offensive brought quick results. Nicolaes Van Beeck, spokesman for the Blommaert and Bessels heirs who owned a one-fifth share of the Manor, was very distressed that "the Rensselaers have for 50 years lived on [the income from the Colony] without giving the participants any revenue from it or rendering any account" despite an order from the Estates General of The Netherlands in 1650 to give such an accounting. The heirs forwarded a power of attorney to Cornelis Steenwyck to represent them in "the division [which] will necessarily have to take place." In a direct reply to Livingston, they stated that it was only "through usurpation" that the Van Rensselaers had taken to themselves both the control and the profits of the Manor. Agreeing in the desirability of a partition, they concluded with this ominous remark: "If Richard Van Rensselaer will not wish to agree to this, we will use such means as we feel will help us, and we hope that you will also, in this way, get what you want." [20]

18. Maria Van Rensselaer to Richard Van Rensselaer, Oct. 12, Oct. and Nov. 1683, Van Laer, ed., *Correspondence*, 125-26, 127-28, 135-36.

19. Livingston's petition, Oct. 29, 1683, O'Callaghan, ed., *Cal. Hist. Mss.*, II, 106; Livingston to Participants in Rensselaerswyck, Oct. 29, 1683 (draft), (Dutch), to Richard Van Rensselaer, Oct. 29, 1683 (Dutch), Livingston-Redmond Mss.

20. Nicolaes Van Beeck to Godfredius Dellius, May 29, 1684, Van Laer, ed., *Correspondence*, 151-52; Bessels, Van Beeck, Vroman, and Bessels to Livingston, May 29, 1684 (Amsterdam), (Dutch), Livingston-Redmond Mss.

Livingston must have received this communication with joy. Could the Van Rensselaers provide the other owners with an accounting of the past half-century's proceeds of the Manor? Could they explain the sale of farms, the proceeds of which had gone into the Van Rensselaer coffers alone? Such were the questions which would now be put to Richard. Even though his persistence in the matter of Nicholas' debts had made it impossible for Livingston to win, a victory was now equally impossible for Richard. The battle was stalemated.

Despite the inevitability of compromise, some skirmishing continued, probably because of the time lag in transatlantic communications. Richard did not oppose Livington's request for a partition because opposition would add impetus to the movement. Instead, he re-emphasized the responsibility of Alida Livingston for Nicholas' debts, and he urged that "a proper preference and ratio might be kept among the various creditors," once Nicholas' share in the Manor had been ascertained. The Van Rensselaers, of course, were the largest creditors. Little wonder, then, that Richard wrote that Livingston "knocks at the wrong door." Nevertheless, Richard was not as confident as he seemed, for he wrote to Maria and requested her to let him "know sometime whether the participants have written [to Livingston] in answer to his letter," and he urged Peter Delanoy "for the last time to prosecute the matter . . . diligently." [21]

But Richard's affairs were not going well in The Netherlands. He may have been reluctant to discuss his difficulties, but Maria was not. Word had already reached New York that he was not only in trouble with the Blommaert and Bessels heirs, but he was also involved in litigation with his nephew Kiliaen Van Rensselaer, the young Patroon. Maria, though sympathetic, was pessimistic: "From what I have heard I fear that you will get involved in even more serious litigation with the co-participants. Livingston will have his way," she concluded; "he has the governor on his side and the governor himself told me that he would not benefit the Rensselaers who are in Holland." The blame for this Maria placed equally upon Robert Livingston and "the house of Schuyler." [22]

The inevitable compromise was finally reached in 1685. On July 15

21. Richard Van Rensselaer to Dongan, Sept. 1/11, 1684, to Maria Van Rensselaer, Sept. 1/11, 1684, to Delanoy, Sept. 1/11, 1684, Van Laer, ed., *Correspondence*, 160-61, 156-59.

22. Maria Van Rensselaer to Richard Van Rensselaer, Nov. 12, 1684, *ibid.*, 168-69.

Governor Dongan issued an order which officially closed the quarrel, and four days later an agreement signed in the governor's presence settled the dispute. Livingston was completely absolved of responsibility for any of Nicholas' unpaid debts, payment for his occupation of portions of the Manor was waived, and 800 schepels of wheat were awarded to him. In return, Livingston agreed to restore to the Van Rensselaers all the Manor lands he had seized and to withdraw all objections to the issuance of a new patent to the young Patroon. The *quietus* so long desired by Livingston was finally signed by the governor on September 1, 1685.[23]

Although he had failed to appease his land hunger by a rape of Rensselaerswyck, Livingston continued his quest for land, for he had been too shrewd to place full reliance on that one effort, even though it had afforded him his greatest opportunity. He turned now to an authorization he had received in November 1680 from Governor Andros to purchase Indian lands "Lying upon Roeloff Johnson's [i.e., Jansen's] kill or Creeke upon the East side of hudsons River, near Cats kill." This permit, granted on the very day it had been requested, was revived by Livingston when he realized that he could not get what he wanted from Rensselaerswyck.[24]

In July 1683, Livingston had come to terms with two groups of Mahican Indians for the tract mentioned in Andros' authorization. Like most such transactions in colonial New York, these two deeds were noted for neither clarity nor precision. The boundaries were described by such terms as the "place the Indians called Saaskahampka" and the thicket "called Mahaakakock." For several hundred florins' worth of trade goods, Livingston obtained a parcel of land, but its extent was subject to conjecture and the largesse of the new governor.[25]

23. "Cal. Council Minutes," N. Y. State Lib., *Bulletin 58*, 43; Dongan's *quietus*, Sept. 1, 1685, Livingston-Redmond Mss. The agreement was probably the work of the Schuylers, who had lost their bid to buy lands in the Manor, and of Stephanus Van Cortlandt; Nissenson, *Patroon's Domain*, 302. For the concluding details, see Livingston to Peter Schuyler, May 2, 1687 (Dutch), Livingston-Redmond Mss.; O'Callaghan, ed., *Cal. Hist. Mss.*, II, 143; Paltsits, ed., *Rensselaerswyck Mss.*, 9, 36; Livingston to Kiliaen Van Rensselaer, Apr. 30, 1686 (Albany), Misc. Mss., no. 11346(4), N. Y. State Lib.

24. Livingston's petition, Nov. 12, 1680, Edmund B. O'Callaghan, ed., *The Documentary History of the State of New York* (4 vols., Albany, 1849-50), III, 611; Andros' order, Nov. 12, 1680, Fernow, ed., *Docs. of Hudson River Towns*, 546.

25. Copies may be found in "Deeds 1678-1687," 185-86, 187-89, Albany County Clerk's Office; Van Laer, ed., *Early Records*, II, 189-92; O'Callaghan, ed., *Doc. Hist. N. Y.*, III, 612-15. See Cadwallader Colden on Indian land titles in *ibid.*, I, 383.

Since it took him a little while to cultivate Governor Dongan, Livingston did nothing during the next year with the title he had purchased. In the meantime, he rounded out his landholdings in Albany. To the lot he had bought in March 1674/5, he added a house and lot from the estate of Nicholas Van Rensselaer, another house next door, and a pasture outside the north gate of Albany. When Livingston was sure of Dongan's friendship, he presented several petitions to the governor on November 4, 1684. It was Dongan's purpose to strengthen the aristocracy of New York and to bind its leading figures to himself and his master, the Duke of York. One means of accomplishing this was liberality in granting lands. Thus Livingston had no difficulty in securing the governor's assent to confirmatory patents for his lands in Albany and at Roeloff Jansen's Kill.[26]

On the same day, Dongan issued a third patent, one in which Livingston had no ostensible interest. It was given to four partners, who, in July 1683, had purchased land at Saratoga from the Mohawk Indians. Livingston's influence, however, must have been placed behind the patent's passage; when it was divided some five months later, the tract was split into seven lots with Livingston, David Schuyler, and Dirk Wessels being brought in as equal partners.[27]

Nevertheless, Livingston's holdings at Roeloff Jansen's Kill and his share of the Saratoga patent did not give him what he really wanted—lands that would rival those of the Van Rensselaers in extent and value. Therefore, on June 3, 1685, Livingston requested permission from Governor Dongan to buy some 200 or 300 acres of land from the Indian owners of Taconic, east of Roeloff Jansen's Kill. He explained that his previous patent included land which was "much Contrare to Expectation, very little being fitt to be Improved." Dongan assented to this petition with the stipulation that the confirmatory patent must be taken out prior to September 30, 1685. Livingston concluded the purchase on August 10. Once again, the bounds were vague—"a hill calld by the Indians Mananosick" and the "flatt or Plain over against Minnissichtanock where Two Trees are marked." The deed was pre-

26. Van Laer, ed., Early Records, II, 15-16, 16-17n, 200-1, 250-51; Andrews, Colonial Period, III, 121; Dongan's patents to Livingston, Nov. 4, 1684, Livingston-Redmond Mss.

27. Deeds from Mohawks to Van Dyck, Bleecker, Schuyler, and Wendel, July 26, 1683, Deed of David Schuyler to Livingston, Mar. 11, 1686/7, Van Laer, ed., Early Records, II, 195, 345-46; Articles of Agreement, Apr. 19, 1685, N. Y. Counties, Land Papers I, Bayard-Campbell-Pearsall Collection, N. Y. Pub. Lib.

Map of Livingston Manor, 1714

sented to the governor and Council, and the confirmatory patent was issued, not for 200 or 300 acres, but for 600.[28]

Livingston had now set the stage for a manor of his own. Almost a year to the day after Governor Dongan had presided at the compromise between Livingston and the Van Rensselaers, a patent was issued for the Lordship and Manor of Livingston. This development must be viewed in the context of the Livingston-Van Rensselaer compromise. The chronologies of the two events arouse suspicions that Livingston Manor was compensation for Livingston's relinquishment of his claims against Rensselaerswyck. Indeed, the terms of the 1686 patent for the Manor make such a conclusion almost inevitable. Dongan took two widely separated tracts—the Jansen's Kill patent for 2,000 acres on the Hudson and the Taconic grant of 600 acres on the Massachusetts border—and treated them as contiguous, converting them into a unified manor. The new patent granted no additional lands; it merely confirmed the earlier titles. Yet, when the Manor was finally surveyed years later, 2,600 acres had mysteriously become 160,000! This was one of the grossest land frauds ever perpetrated in an age noted for unethical dealings.[29]

Truly, Livingston had satiated his land hunger. At the age of thirty-two, a decade after his arrival in the colony, he had acquired a ducal estate. Though his lands were as yet uninhabited—even he did not choose to build on them for thirteen years—he doubtless envisioned the day when they would present a panorama of farms, meadows, and orchards. Nor did Robert Livingston stop here: the same political and family connections, fierce ambition, and lack of scruples which had won him the Manor of Livingston also brought him simultaneous success in commerce and politics during the 1680's.

28. Livingston's petition, June 3, 1685, Dongan's patent to Livingston, Aug. 27, 1685, O'Callaghan, ed., *Doc. Hist. N. Y.*, III, 617, 620-21; Indian deed, Aug. 10, 1685, Van Laer, ed., *Early Records*, II, 281-82.
29. Dongan's patent to Livingston, July 22, 1686, O'Callaghan, ed., *Doc. Hist. N. Y.*, III, 622-27. The Surveyor's map of 1714 is in *ibid.*, opposite page 690. There is a fragmentary Indian "Deed for remnant of Taghkonick, Quesichkook, and Woodland," Feb. 17, 1687/8, which conveys the intervening tract to Livingston. However, the deed was never recorded; *ibid.*, 628. When Gov. Hunter ordered a confirmatory patent in 1715, he outlined the Taconic and Jansen's Kill tracts and then referred to the "other land adjoyning which he [Livingston] did purchase of the Indians"; *ibid.*, 689. Absence of a clear title to the intervening land led to a serious, but unsuccessful, attack on the Manor in the 1850's. The defense in the ensuing trial did not attempt to prove title by Indian purchase. *Livingston Manor Case. Opinion of Mr. Justice Wright, in the Case of the People agt. Hermon Livingston. Supreme Court—Columbia County* (Hudson, N.Y., 1851), *passim*.

CHAPTER III

Commerce and Politics

As a result of his marriage to Alida Schuyler Van Rensselaer in 1679, Livingston gained opportunities to broaden his commercial transactions and make new contacts in both local and overseas markets. His increasing prominence as a merchant in the decade of the 1680's tended to involve him more and more deeply in public service, because the government relied heavily upon the credit of private individuals as a temporary solution to its recurrent problem of inadequate revenues and increasing expenditures. A rising merchant such as Livingston, dependent upon official favors in many of his activities, rallied to the government's assistance when it urgently needed money.

Historians have generally assumed that the one "feature in the growth of a privileged class in New York which Livingston's career does not adequately portray . . . is the mercantile interest." [1] However, if he was a successful politician—and there has never been any controversy on that score—it was primarily the result of his success as a merchant. Before he could rise from a local officeholder in Albany to a colonial politician of consequence, he had to make himself useful to the New York government, and he did so by lending it money.

As the year 1679 opened, there was little indication of these developments; Livingston's only large-scale transactions were with John

1. John A. Krout, "Behind the Coat of Arms: A Phase of Prestige in Colonial New York," *N. Y. Hist.*, 16 (1935), 51.

Pynchon of Boston. However, the pattern of his commerce was altered drastically by Sir Edmund Andros' ruling of 1678 that the overseas trade could be carried on only by New York City merchants. This forced the Albany merchants to relinquish their contacts outside the colony and to purchase their goods from New York City merchants. The latter were understandably anxious to capitalize on this monopoly, and one of them, James Graham, wrote to Livingston in April 1679 to solicit his business: "If you will give me any Incouradgement I will per every occasione send you Such goods as you advice proper for the place, and also if any Barbados goods be proper, viz., Rhum, Maleasses, Sugar . . . I haveing a great Quantity of that trade." He also added a flattering note, requesting Livingston's assistance in binding his brother as an apprentice to some Albany merchant, "hopeing he may better learn the dutch tongue with you than he Can here."

Graham's proposal was a sign of Livingston's growing reputation as a sound merchant, but he had already opened a correspondence in October 1678 with another New Yorker, his prospective brother-in-law, Stephanus Van Cortlandt. This arrangement continued for the next two and a half years. The amount involved was small, only 823 florins, but Livingston's remittances provide an interesting commentary on the relationship between his marriage in June 1679 and his financial status. He repaid 5 florins in December 1678 to Van Cortlandt, another 690 in August 1679, and the balance of 128 florins in April 1681.[2]

While Van Cortlandt provided a means by which Livingston could conform to Andros' decree, he also assisted him in evading it. Through the use of an obliging New York City merchant's name, Livingston could carry on an overseas trade. A small quantity of goods was shipped for his account by Van Cortlandt in January 1680/1 to an unnamed Barbados merchant; three years later, another small consignment was sent for him to an unnamed Amsterdam merchant.[3] By doing this, Van Cortlandt also introduced Livingston to new markets. Indeed, that was probably the more important service. Later, when New York City became the colony's exclusive port rather than New

2. Graham to Livingston, Apr. 7, 1679, Livingston's account with Van Cortlandt, Oct. 7, 1678-Apr. 26, 1681, Livingston-Redmond Mss.
3. Livingston's sales in Barbados, Jan. 11, 1680/1; Livingston's sales in the pink *New York*, 1684, *ibid.*

Yorkers the exclusive overseas traders, Livingston shipped goods abroad under his own name. By 1683, he sent flour to Arent Van Dyck and Robert Stanford in Barbados and, a few years later, he was trading to Amsterdam.[4]

Concurrently with his entry into overseas trade, Livingston's domestic commerce was altered to conform to Andros' 1678 order. He severed his ties with John Pynchon in October 1680, turning from Boston to New York City as a source of supply. Once again, Van Cortlandt came to his brother-in-law's aid, collecting money owed to Livingston by residents of that city. At the same time, Livingston began purchasing a wide assortment of goods from various merchants in the colony. The transactions involved large sums of money, indicating that his main reliance was now on local suppliers.[5]

As long as Andros' order remained effective (until 1683 or 1684), Livingston could not openly participate in the overseas trade. He could either trade with the Indians or become a general merchant in Albany. Apparently, he made the latter choice, because he imported a sizable quantity of rum and brandy from New York City and paid the excise duty which was only levied if the liquor was to be retailed in Albany. Further, he offered to purchase furs from his brother-in-

4. Livingston's acct. with Van Dyck & Stanford, 1683, Livingston's sales, 1687 (Amsterdam), *ibid.* The overseas trade monopoly of New York City had a vague history. It was closely enforced until July 1681; then, it was more honored in the breach than in the observance. In 1683, the city petitioned Gov. Dongan for a reaffirmation of its ancient liberties and privileges, including the monopoly. In 1684, the Duke of York ordered that it be given a monopoly of flour bolting and packing so as to protect that product's quality and that it be the exclusive port so as to facilitate customs collections; the overseas trade monopoly was not mentioned then nor when the city was chartered in 1686. Thus the monopoly seems to have become a dead letter by 1683 or 1684. However, in 1690, the Leislerian Assembly granted everyone the right "to transport where they please directly... anything their places afford," but this probably referred to the Long Islanders' long-standing opposition to New York's exclusive port privileges. Brodhead, *Hist. of N. Y.*, II, 336, 353, 391; N. Y. C.'s petition, Nov. 9, 1683, Duke of York to Dongan, Aug. 26, 1684, O'Callaghan, ed., *N. Y. Col. Docs.*, III, 337-38, 348-49; Commissioners of Statutory Revision, *The Colonial Laws of New York from the Year 1664 to the Revolution* (5 vols., Albany, 1894), I, 181-95, 218; O'Callaghan, ed., *Cal. Hist. Mss.*, II, 124, 164.

5. Holyoke to Livingston, Oct. 20, 1680, Van Cortlandt to Livingston, June 24, 1681 (Dutch), Brockholls to Livingston, June 3, 1682, Livingston-Redmond Mss. Livingston purchased £40 of textiles from Royse; 368 florins of tobacco, rum, and sugar from Wendel; £57 of molasses, sugar, pewter, and candlesticks from Bueno; and 443 florins of beer from Rykman. Bills and accts. with Royse (Sept. 16, 1681), Wendel (May 24, 1681-Mar. 12, 1683/4), Bueno (Oct. 29, 1684), Rykman (June 23, 1680-June 15, 1681), *ibid.*

law, Brandt Schuyler. If Livingston had been trading directly with the Iroquois, it is unlikely that he would buy furs from other Indian traders. Livingston was very successful as a merchant in Albany. His operations expanded rapidly after his marriage, and within two years he was the creditor of a number of his fellow townsmen. By June 1681, more than 15,000 florins were owed to him.[6]

With his greatly improved stature, Livingston did not hesitate to call his debtors to account. He sued several recalcitrant debtors in the years 1680-82, and in none of these cases was he defeated. In August 1681, when he learned that John Palmer had not sent £10 to Boston as promised, he wrote him an "unhandsome letter." Palmer delayed replying seven months, and then used Livingston's earlier reputation as an excuse for his own procrastination—"I presume you forgott how longe you lay in... debt, and what a deale of trouble I had before I could get my money ... but these things are gone and past." [7]

An important facet of Livingston's commercial activities was the assistance he received from his wife. The Dutch *vrouw* of colonial New York was often an accomplished businesswoman, and Alida was no exception. Whenever her husband was away from Albany on public or private business, she skillfully managed his affairs. In November 1680, when he went to New York City to confer with Sir Edmund Andros, she reported that she had rejected offers to sell the pigs they were raising at Kinderhook because the animals had not yet reached full growth, and two years later, in Livingston's absence, she negotiated the sale of flour from his stores.[8] This aid became increasingly important as Livingston's public services expanded and took up more and more of his time.

During the first years of his marriage, Livingston's political duties were limited to the Albany area. Most of his tasks as town clerk, secretary of Rensselaerswyck, and unofficial secretary to the commissioners for Indian affairs were clerical and routine in nature. However, he performed one function which hinted of the future—he advanced

6. "Excyse Book of Albany Begunn the 30 Octo 1678," Schuyler to Livingston, Nov. 21, 1681 (Dutch), Livingston's "*Lyste van Shuldenaars Getracken nyt myn Groot Boeck*," June 1, 1681, *ibid.*
7. Palmer to Livingston, Mar. 16, 1681/2, *ibid.*; Van Laer, ed., *Court Minutes*, III, 20-1, 33-34, 105-6; Van Laer, ed., *Early Records*, II, 169.
8. Alida to Robert Livingston, Nov. 16, 1680, and Oct. 24, 1682 (Dutch), Livingston-Redmond Mss.

funds on the governor's order and transmitted fees to the colony's secretary.[9]

But it was not until he had obtained the post of sub-collector of the excise for Albany that he became more deeply involved in government finance. There is no official record of Livingston's appointment to this office, but it undoubtedly occurred in November 1680, shortly after the Duke of York's investigator, John Lewin, arrived. As a part of the general overhaul of governmental machinery, Van Cortlandt and Peter Delanoy were ordered to audit the accounts of Richard Pretty, then sub-collector. They found that he owed the Duke 1,659 florins, and he was ordered to pay it to Livingston "who was present at the Examining of the Same." [10]

The sub-collectorship, normally an arduous task, was a responsibility which Livingston may well have regretted undertaking at that time. The abnormal conditions which resulted when the secretary, governor, and collector departed for England made the whole matter of customs' duties a *cause célèbre* in New York. As the Duke's personal property, the colony was ruled by his governor and Council. There had never been a true popular assembly, though the *vox populi* had been consulted on occasion under Dutch rule. Nevertheless, there had always been an inarticulate demand for a legislative assembly and, now that the colony was left in the charge of the incompetent Commander-in-Chief Anthony Brockholls, the dissidents struck at the Duke's most vital nerve—his purse.[11]

Late in 1674, the Duke had established a schedule of customs duties for a three-year period, and Governor Andros had renewed it for another three years. Before a third renewal could be effected, the colony was in the throes of Lewin's investigation. When the Court of Assizes met, Governor Andros ordered "the continuing all as then settled," but did not specifically mention customs duties. This oversight had serious consequences for the colony and vastly complicated Livingston's task as sub-collector.

The controversy erupted in both New York City and Albany in

9. Nicolls to Livingston, June 20, 1679, *ibid.;* "Accompt of Charges...April 25-June 7, 1679," Leder, ed., *Livingston Indian Records*, 58-59.

10. Van Cortlandt and Delanoy to Pretty, Nov. 11, 1680, Livingston-Redmond Mss.; Van Laer, ed., *Court Minutes*, III, 154.

11. Brodhead, *Hist. of N. Y.*, II, 336, 353; Andrews, *Colonial Period*, III, 106-7, 110, 112.

1681, when merchants refused to pay duties because the schedule had expired. Brockholls and the Council ruled that they did not have authority to extend the schedule without specific orders from the Duke, and their pusillanimity created "a colonial revolution." Several New York City merchants started civil suits against Collector William Dyer for illegally restraining their merchandise. When the courts ruled against him, Samuel Winder of Staten Island charged the collector with high treason. Persistent in their incompetence, Brockholls and the Council committed Dyer for trial by the next Court of Assizes, "a Strange proceeding," as one of Livingston's correspondents wrote, "not only to ruine his Royall Highness Interest but reflect upon his person & Authority & possibly ... produce as Strange an Effect which Cannot be foreseen." [12]

Dyer was charged with high treason for having levied taxes in the Duke's name, for the Duke's benefit, but without the Duke's authority. By depriving the Proprietor of sorely needed revenue under the guise of upholding his authority, the merchants emphasized their desire for a legislative assembly: such a situation could not exist under a government which included popular representation. When Dyer appeared before the Court of Assizes, which supported the merchants' position, he challenged its jurisdiction and was remanded to England for trial. There, his accuser failed to appear, and the charge was dropped. [13]

In Albany, Livingston also experienced difficulty in executing his office of sub-collector, though he fortunately avoided being charged with high treason. In July 1681, he brought a tavern keeper to trial before the Albany magistrates for failing to pay the excise for 1680 and the first half of 1681. The tavern keeper was ordered to pay the 1680 excise, but no mention was made of the sum demanded for the first half of 1681. Livingston's authority to collect the excise for 1681 had been reinforced, or so he thought, by an order Brockholls had received from Sir Edmund Andros on August 17 to assume the functions of receiver-general of the Duke's revenues. Livingston therefore brought suit against John De Lavall for 1,020 florins due on

---

12. Brodhead, *Hist. of N. Y.*, II, 263, 272, 312, 344-45, 351-52; Edmund B. O'Callaghan, *Origin of Legislative Assemblies in the State of New York, including titles of the Laws passed previous to 1691* (Albany, 1861), 13; John West to Livingston, June 6, 1681, Livingston-Redmond Mss.

13. Andrews, *Colonial Period*, III, 101n, 110n.

510 gallons of rum he had imported into Albany and retailed there. At the trial, De Lavall readily admitted the facts, but demanded to know for whom and by what right Livingston presumed to collect taxes. The defendant began a lengthy diatribe—are we not, he demanded, "considered to be free born subjects of the King? ... By which act ... were we made otherwise?" [14]

These questions were far too difficult for the jury to answer. Their unanimous verdict was that they could find no provision in the laws for payment of such an excise, "but if the order of the Governor must be considered law, then the defendant is guilty." The magistrates were equally timorous, and they referred the matter to Brockholls and the Council. The commander-in-chief decided to wait, writing Livingston a few months later: "As for the Excyse you write that none will pay it, I desire you to Keepe as neare an account of it as you possible can who the importers are and quantities for I expeckt dayly orders from England Concerning it and question not but they must assuredly pay it." [15]

Brockholls' infuriating habit of waiting for someone else to bail the government out of its difficulties did nothing to replenish the colony's depleted treasury. In order to maintain the all-important garrison at Albany, the commander-in-chief turned to private individuals. One was Thomas Ashton, the former sheriff and coroner of New York City, who procured goods for the government from Albany merchants, giving his own bills on the colony in return. Livingston was a creditor of Ashton's and after the latter's death in May 1682, he wrote Brockholls about the redemption of his bills by the government. The commander-in-chief replied evasively, "What you have disbursed for the Garrison by his bills will bee time enough to peruse when I come to Albanie myself which [I] hope will bee Very Speedilie." But Brockholls was almost hopelessly incompetent and mislaid Livingston's account: "doe not know wher at present to find it," he wrote, and "therefore desire you by the very first ... to Send it [to] me." [16] Considering Livingston's dogged persistence in

14. Van Laer, ed., *Court Minutes*, III, 139, 153-54, 201; Brodhead, *Hist. of N. Y.*, II, 354.

15. Van Laer, ed., *Court Minutes*, III, 201-2; Brockholls to Livingston, Jan. 13, 1681/2, Livingston-Redmond Mss.

16. O'Callaghan, ed., *Cal. Hist. Mss.*, II, 78; Brockholls to Livingston, June 3, Sept. 26, 1682, Livingston-Redmond Mss.

money matters, it may be safely assumed that a second account was forwarded and repayment was eventually made.

A degree of harmony was finally achieved in the government when William Penn arrived in New York City in the last months of 1682. On the day after his arrival, the Quaker, dismayed at the disunity in the proprietary of his friend, the Duke of York, brought together the officials and the dissidents and "perswaded all Partys to lett fall their Animositys, which they promest." Calling attention to the Duke's appointment of a new governor and promise of the long-desired assembly, he admonished the New Yorkers that it was now their duty to find ways "to maintain their charge in consideration of the priviledges the duke had . . . assured them they should enjoy." [17]

As Penn predicted, the new governor, Thomas Dongan, arrived within a year; a legislative assembly was convened, and Brockholls' mismanagement was ended. Livingston, of course, lost no time in winning the new executive's favor, both in the matter of land grants and government posts. Within two months after Dongan's arrival, Livingston received a new commission as sub-collector of the excise at Albany at a salary of £50 per annum.[18]

Dongan was sorely pressed by the diminution of governmental revenue caused by his predecessor's maladministration, and the taxes levied by the new assembly were not enough to solve the problem. Dongan therefore employed several other devices to raise funds. He increased the quitrents due the government by renewing land patents, engaged in a controversy with the Jersey proprietors over their establishment of Perth Amboy as a free port, and reorganized the customs collections in the colony.[19]

When the governor visited Albany in July 1686, he altered Livingston's commission as sub-collector of the excise, fixing the salary at 5 percent of the collections. Under the previous arrangement, Livingston's annual salary from November 1683 to July 1686 had

17. William Penn to Blathwayt, Oct. 21, 1682, Blathwayt Papers, VII, Col. Wmsbg. The letter is dated "21-8bre: 1682," but Blathwayt endorsed it "21: Nov: 1682."

18. Wheeler B. Melius, ed., *Index to the Public Records of the County of Albany, State of New York 1630-1894: Grantors* (14 vols., Albany, 1902-7), VIII, 4685; Lucas Santen's receipt to Livingston, Nov. 4, 1684, Livingston-Redmond Mss.

19. Dongan's report on N.Y., Feb. 22, 1686/7, O'Callaghan, ed., *N.Y. Col. Docs.*, III, 392-93, 401-6.

equalled about one-seventh of his collections. Little wonder that Dongan insisted upon replacing the flat fee with a percentage arrangement. He was shrewd enough to realize that one way to increase governmental revenue was to give the collectors a personal stake in their own diligence. More significant than Livingston's compensation, however, was his increasing importance as a fiscal agent of the government. Since Livingston collected public funds, the governor naturally turned to him for advances to meet current expenses. Often, Livingston expended nearly half of his receipts on the governor's order prior to the end of the fiscal year.[20]

Livingston's public duties required his almost continuous presence in Albany. As sub-collector, he had to be on hand to prevent and prosecute evasion of the tax.[21] His more routine posts—town clerk and unofficial secretary to the commissioners for Indian affairs—required that he personally record legal documents and translate the speeches made at the Iroquois conferences. This entailed a great deal of paper work and encroached heavily upon his time, but he was not unmindful of the varied benefits accruing from public service, and he seized every chance to strengthen and expand his hold on his offices. Such an opportunity occurred when the Albany burghers suggested to Governor Dongan that the town be incorporated. They had long desired the advantages of a charter, and in 1676 they instructed Livingston, as town clerk, to prepare a memorandum to be used in discussions with the governor.

Most of the points in Livingston's memorandum dealt with the internal machinery and land rights of the proposed municipal government. Four points, however, illustrated the motives behind the move for incorporation: the fur trade was to "be Reputed & Esteemed as a Peculiar Priviledge" of the town; Albany was to be made a "body Politique"; some means was to be found "to Stop the Patroons [i.e., the Van Rensselaers'] designs who will much Infringe upon the Toune"; and the governor was not to issue hunting licenses "which tends to the Ruine of the Toune" by interfering with the fur trade. This was to be wrung from the governor by a reminder that repairing

20. "Account of the Revenue of the Excyse at Albany . . . Anno 1683 to the first of October 1700," and Receipts of Lucas Santen, Nov. 4, 1684 and Mar. 25, 1687, Livingston-Redmond Mss.
21. Melius, ed., *Records of Albany County: Grantors,* VIII, 4685-86.

the fort was "a Voluntary act of the Inhabitants." Indeed, "it must be used as a urgent argument." [22]

Although nothing came of the proposal at this time, the burghers' desire for a charter was gratified ten years later by Governor Dongan. When the Duke of York became James II in 1685, New York was converted from a proprietary to a royal colony. This gave a pretext for issuing new charters and patents to New York City, Albany, Rensselaerswyck, Hempstead, Kingston, and other towns and manors in the years 1686-88. Dongan, of course, had no hesitancy about issuing them because it permitted him to increase the quitrents due the government and, at the same time, to receive handsome fees as his perquisite. The negotiations for the Albany charter were conducted by Livingston and his brother-in-law Peter Schuyler. On July 21, 1686, they paid a fee of £300 to Thomas Coker for the governor's account, having borrowed £83 of that on their own notes at 10 percent interest. Five days later, they returned to Albany and exhibited the charter which was proclaimed "with all the joy and acclamations imaginable." [23]

The two negotiators received not only the "thanks of the magistrates and burgesses," but were appointed by the charter itself to offices in the municipality—Peter Schuyler as mayor, and Robert Livingston as town clerk, clerk of the peace, and clerk of the Court of Common Pleas. Livingston's salary as town clerk had been £15 a year, but it was now raised to £20 in consideration of his "diverse services." Governor Dongan expressed the hope that Livingston's various offices might now "afford him a competent maintenance." [24]

Government positions, of course, accounted for only a small portion of Livingston's income. His commercial activities were expanding throughout the 1680's, and he had already begun to reach for the ultimate in mercantile success—a direct trade with London. Most of New York's overseas trade was in the hands of London exporters

22. "*Ontwerp van Propos wegende Charter, 1676*," Livingston-Redmond Mss.

23. Bernard Mason, "Aspects of the New York Revolt of 1689," *N.Y. Hist.*, 30 (1949), 174-75; Thomas Coker's receipt, July 21, 1686, Livingston-Redmond Mss.; Joel Munsell, ed., *The Annals of Albany* (10 vols., Albany, vols. I-IV, 2nd edn., 1869-71; vols. V-X, 1st edn., 1854-59), II, 82-83, 95.

24. *Col. Laws of N.Y.*, I, 206; Munsell, ed., *Annals of Albany*, II, 82-84, 86; Dongan's report on N.Y., Feb. 22, 1686/7, O'Callaghan, ed., *N.Y. Col. Docs*, III, 401.

who operated through local factors in the colony.[25] To become one of that elite group, an ambition not easily achieved, was a true measure of the mature and responsible merchant.

Livingston's interest in the London trade was first evidenced by a small purchase of textiles and lawbooks, shipped on his risk, from John Harwood in 1683. The terms of this correspondence, which continued until the Londoner's death two years later, were described by Livingston: "I made an overture to him to send over a Cargo on his Riske out and home & I would allow him 14 or 15 percent[;] that was 6 percent Interest 4 percent Assurance out & 4 percent home being Peaceable times, but the old gent answerd he could not doe that under 20 or 25 percent."[26] Harwood was no stranger to the New York and New England trade, and his refusal to grant credit to Livingston, except at exorbitant rates, was customary.[27] Livingston's reputation had been established in New York, but it had not yet reached London.

When the elder Harwood died in 1685, his son, Jacob, took over the business and proposed the establishment of a "mutual correspondence" with Livingston. However, the New Yorker had already written to another London merchant, John Blackall, for that purpose. Livingston had even persuaded his mother-in-law, Margaret Schuyler, to ship a bundle of furs to Blackall for sale, for which the Londoner promised "to retaliate the same kindness to you as it lies in my way." Before Livingston could follow this up, he received £442 worth of goods from Harwood. This consignment, sent on Livingston's risk, had not been requested and, ironically enough, arrived on the very same vessel that carried Blackall's response to Livingston. Whether or not he had done it intentionally, Harwood most effectively eliminated Blackall's competition. Livingston now had a plenitude of hats, stockings, duffels, blankets, and other haberdashery.[28]

When Livingston attempted to dispose of these goods at Albany, he

25. Curtis P. Nettels, *The Money Supply of the American Colonies Before 1720* (Madison, 1934), Univ. of Wisc., *Studies in the Social Sciences and History*, XX, 74.

26. Harwood's invoice, May 10, 1683, "Memorandum of Robert Livingstons Case with Jacob Harwood," c. Nov. 1695 (hereafter cited as "Memo Livingston's Case"), Livingston-Redmond Mss.

27. Samuel Maverick to Sec. of State, Oct. 16, 1667, extract of letter to Harwood, Sept. 3, 1673, O'Callaghan, ed., *N.Y. Col. Docs.*, III, 106, 205-6.

28. Harwood's invoice, Mar. 19, 1686/7, "Memo Livingston's Case," c. Nov. 1695, Blackall to Livingston, Jan. 1, 1686/7, Livingston-Redmond Mss.

found that the Indian traders were overstocked because of the erup-
tion of hostilities between the French in Canada and the English in
New York. This conflict focused on a rivalry for control of the Iroquois, the fur trade, and eventually the continent itself. It continued,
either as open warfare or an uneasy truce, until the French were
finally driven from the continent in 1763. In its initial stages in the
1680's it consisted of efforts by both sides to win the allegiance of the
Iroquois. In this endeavor, the English had a definite advantage: they
could offer the Indians more desirable goods at lower prices. English
woolen textiles—duffels and stroudwaters—were preferred by the
Iroquois to French luxury textiles; English rum was cheaper than
French brandy and probably just as potent. Frontenac bemoaned the
fact in 1681 that beaver brought one-third to one-half more at Albany
than at Montreal, and six years later the governor of Montreal bitterly
denounced the English for using this trade advantage to "intrigue"
among the Indians.[29] This economic advantage was a definite factor
in the retention of Iroquois support by the English.

The interrelationship of trade and imperial policy was of tremendous significance. Thomas Dongan was one of the first to visualize the
immensity of the stakes and make constructive use of England's advantages. To Dongan, the fur trade was more than just a profitable
business; it was a means of winning England a new empire. The nation
that had Iroquois support would hold an important advantage over
its rival.[30]

Robert Livingston shared Dongan's vision. As unofficial secretary
to the commissioners for Indian affairs, he was more intimately acquainted with the problems of dealing with the Iroquois than almost
any other colonial. As early as 1678, he had sent information on
Indian activities to Sir Edmund Andros.[31] Now, he was ready to
offer information, advice, and aid to Dongan.

One of the governor's most difficult problems was the Caughnawaga, or Praying, Indians. Primarily Mohawks and Oneidas who had
been converted to Catholicism and had moved to Canada in 1668,
these Indians not only worked to convert the other Iroquois, but made

29. McIlwain, ed., *Wraxall's Abridgment*, lxi-lxii; Frontenac to Louis XIV, Nov. 2,
1681, De Callieres to De Seignelay, Nov. 1687, O'Callaghan, ed., *N.Y. Col. Docs.*, IX,
146, 370. See also list of prices, 1689, *ibid.*, 408-9.
30. Andrews, *Colonial Period*, III, 122.
31. Andros to Livingston, Dec. 4, 1678, Livingston-Redmond Mss.

any attack upon Canada especially perilous because of the unwilling-
ness of the Mohawks and Oneidas to fight their kinsmen. Dongan attempted to weaken the French by bringing the Caughnawaga back
to New York, offering them English priests and lands. The former he
hoped to get from his master, James II, a practicing Catholic;[32] the
latter he got from Livingston.

In July 1686, Livingston released his one-seventh share of the
Saratoga patent to the Crown for the exclusive use of any Caughnawaga who might return to the English fold. Should a settlement be
made, Livingston's recompense was to be determined by two appraisers. If no settlement were made, the land reverted to Livingston.
Unfortunately, Dongan's efforts in this direction bore no fruit. But
Livingston's services went beyond making his land available. On
several occasions, he forwarded reports of the latest French activities
to Dongan, who relied upon him to supervise the renovation of the
Albany fort, to expedite tax collections in Dutchess County, and to
donate the use of his Manor as a temporary haven for the women,
children, and old men of the Iroquois so that the warriors could gird
themselves for battle unencumbered by concern for their families.[33]

However, Livingston's most important public service was the lending of money and goods. The imminent prospect of a French attack
required reinforcement of the Albany garrison and the presentation
of gifts to the Iroquois as a token of New York's good faith. Defense
preparations involved great outlays from the colony's treasury, but
it was, as Dongan reported two years earlier, in a "tottering condition." In the first two years of his administration, he had relied upon
one unnamed person to borrow £3,500 from the inhabitants for the
government.[34] In 1687 and 1688, Dongan relied on Robert Livingston.

Livingston was able to support Dongan's plans because he had
received a sudden flood of goods from London. When he acknowledged receipt of Jacob Harwood's shipment of £442 worth of merchandise on August 15, 1687, Livingston promised to repay the

32. Petition of 1686, O'Callaghan, ed., N.Y. Col. Docs., III, 418-19.
33. Livingston's "Release to the King–Expired & Null," July 20, 1686, Livingston-
Redmond Mss.; Livingston to Dongan, Sept. 2, 5, 1687, O'Callaghan, ed., N.Y. Col.
Docs., III, 480-81; "Cal. Council Minutes," N.Y. State Lib., Bulletin 58, 54, 87.
34. Gov.'s Council Minutes, Sept. 7, 11, 1687, N.-Y. Hist. Soc., Collections, 2 (1876),
389-91; Dongan to King, Sept. 30, 1685, W. N. Sainsbury et al., eds., Calendar of State
Papers, Colonial Series, America and West Indies, Preserved in the Public Record
Office, 1574-1733 (40 vols., London, 1860-1939), XII, no. 387.

Londoner within a year and offered him interest in the meantime. He also urged that another such cargo be sent "since a good Trade with the Indians was expected next year." He hoped that a lucrative commerce with the Ottawa Indians would be developed by the Macgregory expedition, but the French captured that trading party, and the outbreak of hostilities between the French and the Iroquois dashed Livingston's hopes.[35]

Harwood, of course, was unaware of this. He simply followed Livingston's suggestion and sent a cargo, valued at £547, on the New Yorker's risk in November 1687. Not sharing his father's cautious attitude, Harwood soon rushed three more shipments on his own risk to Livingston. Received in New York between November 1687 and November 1688, these cargoes were valued at more than £1,000. This was a fantastically large sum—all told, over £2,000—to entrust to a colonial merchant about whom Harwood could have known very little. Since Livingston's returns during the four years from 1685 to 1689 amounted to only £331, it was no wonder that Harwood expressed some concern in July 1688. "I think I have don my partt in order to a Correspondency," he stated; "I hope you will not be laking on your partt for returns, then there may be a Torrantt of business betweene us." [36]

Livingston took advantage of Harwood's indiscretion in shipping merchandise so readily. At a time when defense expenditures rapidly mounted, there was a serious shortage of both ready cash and governmental revenue. Dongan resorted to borrowing to make ends meet and, since coin was not available, he accepted goods. Livingston willingly placed his surplus stores at the governor's disposal, advancing more than £2,000 between August 11, 1687 and June 1, 1688.[37]

These advances were made on the governor's personal credit. In all probability, Dongan had intended that this loan, as well as those made by others for similar purposes, would be repaid out of future tax revenues. But before he could effect this, he was displaced as

35. "Memo Livingston's Case," c. Nov. 1695, Livingston-Redmond Mss.; Leder, ed., *Livingston Indian Records*, 136-37.
36. "Memo Livingston's Case," c. Nov. 1695, "Account of Sales of Mr. Jacob Harwood's goods," Sept. 5, 1694, Livingston's account with Meriwether, Aug. 1695, Harwood to Livingston, July 11, 1688, Livingston-Redmond Mss.
37. Minutes, N.Y. Council, Apr. 30, 1688, V, 228, N.Y. State Lib.

governor of New York by King James II's new commission and instructions to Sir Edmund Andros as governor general of the Dominion
of New England.

This all-embracing union, founded in 1685, now included New
York. On the one hand, it signaled the genesis of a new imperial
concept—realization of the need to centralize colonial control in an
age of imperial warfare; on the other, it climaxed a bitter behind-
the-scenes power struggle between Thomas Dongan and Sir Edmund
Andros. Both realized that New York could not stand alone against
the French in Canada. Dongan had proposed the expansion of his
government to include Connecticut, the Jerseys, and Pennsylvania,
relying "upon his great interest at Court" to achieve this. But Sir
Edmund's friends—Edward Randolph and William Blathwayt—were
more influential. New York was annexed to the Dominion and
Dongan lost his job. "Highly dissatisfied at the Sudden Change as
he calls it," he nevertheless planned to remain in New York where
he had "Laid out his Estate in purchasing Land & houses." [38]

The continued presence of a former governor with friends among
the colony's aristocrats could prove most embarrassing to his successor, so a plot was hatched to force Dongan to leave New York.
Since his accounts for the disbursement of £6,400 during his administration had not yet been approved, he presented them in September 1688 to the Council, and that body, taking its cue from
Randolph who considered the expenditures extravagant, refused to
examine them, looking upon itself "as no way obliged to audite his
accounts." Dongan was bitter; Sir Edmund's "private malice against
him was the sole Cause why the account was not passed." Randolph
warned Blathwayt that "you will receive at Court high recrimina-
tions from Colonel Dongan against his Excellence Especially because

38. James II's commission of Apr. 7, 1688, and instructions to Andros, Apr. 16, 1688,
Dongan's report on N.Y., Feb. 22, 1686/7, O'Callaghan, ed., *N.Y. Col. Docs.*, III, 537-
50, 391-93. Randolph alleged that Dongan wanted to expand his government because
"he has so squeezed the people of New York That they are hardly able to live."
Randolph to Blathwayt, Nov. 23, 1687, Blathwayt Papers, I, Col. Wmsbg. He later
wrote that "the true ground [of Dongan's dissatisfaction] arises from his being disa-
pointed of his great expectation of being Governor of New England." Randolph to
Blathwayt, Oct. 2, 1688, *ibid.* See also Randolph to Blathwayt, Aug. 19, 1688, *ibid.* For
a full discussion of the Dominion, see Viola F. Barnes, *The Dominion of New England: A Study in British Colonial Policy* (New Haven, 1923).

the Councill has not thought fitt to raise so great a Sum & pay It him without once questioning it." [39]

Blocked by Sir Edmund's Council, Dongan turned to the deputy auditor, Stephanus Van Cortlandt. Randolph quickly advised Van Cortlandt that he did not have the authority to approve Dongan's accounts. Since that did not wholly satisfy the deputy auditor, Randolph urged Blathwayt to procure direct orders to that effect from the Lords of the Treasury. This put Van Cortlandt in an awkward position. While he certainly owed favors to Dongan, he did not wish to offend those now in power. He explained his position to Auditor General Blathwayt by saying that he was not certain whether he had "Run to fast in auditing . . . the accounts or that I now walke to slow in scrupling to audite." If Blathwayt upheld Randolph, the accounts would be referred to England, and Dongan would have to leave New York. [40]

These schemes to force Dongan from the scene left Livingston in financial difficulty. As he reported to Jacob Harwood, there were "great discords between governors Dongan & andross So that I could not gett my money." [41] But Andros and Randolph would only create more difficulties for themselves by alienating Livingston, and they might possibly lose the Schuylers' support and even Van Cortlandt's. Thus, when Livingston turned to him for advice and aid, Randolph proved very helpful in directing Livingston's animus against Dongan rather than Sir Edmund and himself.

Randolph and Livingston conferred in New York City in August 1688. Since Dongan's accounts were being referred to the Lords of the Treasury in London, they decided that Livingston could either obtain repayment directly from Dongan, or else initiate action in London to prevent the disbursement of any funds to the former governor until Livingston's claims were settled. Randolph prepared the way for the latter course by writing to John Povey, secretary

39. Randolph to Blathwayt, Sept. 12, 1688, Blathwayt Papers, I, Col. Wmsbg. A recent study of Randolph is Michael Garibaldi Hall's *Edward Randolph and the American Colonies, 1676-1703* (Chapel Hill, 1960).

40. Randolph to Blathwayt, Oct. 7, 1688, *ibid.;* Van Cortlandt to Blathwayt, Oct. 23, 1688, *ibid.,* II; Andros to Blathwayt, Oct. 4, 1688 (2 letters), *ibid.,* IV. Van Cortlandt's qualms adequately served the purposes of Andros and Randolph. In return for his hesitation, the governor general recommended his appointment as a receiver or collector in New York.

41. "Memo Livingston's Case," c. Nov. 1695, Livingston-Redmond Mss.

to the Board of Trade, advising him of the claims and commenting, "tis a just debt . . . . [and] its very uncertain how or where this money may bee ordered to be paid." He also told Povey that Livingston had transmitted copies of all relevant papers to Jacob Harwood, and he asked the secretary to notify the London merchant of any attempt by Dongan to have his accounts passed by the Treasury.[42]

Dongan knew of these meetings and he was disturbed by the web of intrigue being spun around him. When Livingston went to speak with him about the debt in March 1688/9, he did so with trepidation. The former governor, he admitted, "is much offended at me: I wish I knew how to act cautiously in it." However, Livingston, too, was disturbed. It was whispered about town that Dongan had hired a vessel in which to sail to England, only to change his mind at the last moment. "Whatever the designs he has is unknown," lamented Livingston; "some suspects he will goe to Maryland after he has secured his estate & so leave his creditors to console his absence."

Randolph urged Livingston to harass Dongan by bringing a court action against him. "If he will not by faire means comply & give me security than I must arrest him or attach his estate," Livingston reluctantly agreed; "It is a great hardship I am putt to & that for all my estate that I have in the world. . . . I have ventured to doe Colonel Dongan a kindness but he ill requites it. I know not but he may be more calm now. Pray keep this quiet." [43]

Livingston was spared the ordeal of prosecuting the former governor—a not uncommon occurrence in colonial New York—when the two men reached an agreement on May 1, 1689. Possibly the volatile Irishman had been soothed by the charming Scotsman. Whatever the reason, they agreed that Dongan would make a part payment of £312 in cash and secure the balance of £2,172 by a mortgage on the Manor of Castletown, Staten Island, a property purchased by Dongan two years earlier. If Livingston received the balance by May 1, 1694, the mortgage would be canceled; if not, the land was

42. Livingston to Randolph, Sept. 1, 1688, Randolph to Povey, Oct. 3, 1688, Robert Noxon Toppan and Alfred T. S. Goodrick, eds., *Edward Randolph: including His Letters and Official Papers from the New England, Middle, and Southern Colonies in America* (7 vols., Boston, 1898-1909), IV, 234-35, VI, 267-68. Randolph's original letter is in Blathwayt Papers, I, Col. Wmsbg.

43. Livingston to Randolph, Feb. 18, Mar. 22, 1688/9, Toppan and Goodrick, eds., *Randolph,* IV, 260-62.

his.[44] The plans of Sir Edmund and Randolph were maturing satisfactorily. Dongan now had a personal interest in clearing his accounts and going to England.

No one could have realized, however, that more momentous events would soon overshadow these machinations. The "Protestant Wind" which carried William of Orange to Torbay would become a whirlwind in the New World, smashing the plans of lesser men. The Glorious Revolution, the collapse of the Dominion of New England, and the Leisler Rebellion in New York were the dominant themes of the next few years. Livingston's financial involvement with the government, his political alliance with Andros and Randolph, and his family connections within the colony determined his attitude toward these events on the immediate horizon.

44. Blathwayt to Treasury Lords, Feb. 27, 1692/3, William A. Shaw, ed., *Calendar of Treasury Books Preserved in the Public Record Office* (25 vols., London, 1904-50), II (Part IV), 1514. Dongan's mortgage to Livingston, May 1, 1689, Misc. Mss. Staten Island, N.-Y. Hist. Soc.

PART TWO

Years of Political Upheaval
1689-1710

CHAPTER IV

New York in Rebellion

THE SO-CALLED Leisler Rebellion, which played so important a role in Livingston's career, was composed of a myriad of economic, political, and social factors. Economics and politics provided the basic discontent; social unrest determined the leadership. Most of the problems which initiated the movement were not new; some extended back as far as the English reconquest of New York in 1674.

The colony's economic problem was threefold: monopolies, depression, and taxes. The monopoly of flour bolting and packing and the exclusive port privileges given to New York City always piqued other areas of the colony. The Hudson River farmers, with a limited market for their grain, were at the mercy of a small group of New York City millers. The Puritans of Long Island, prohibited from trading directly with Connecticut across the Sound, were supposed to route their goods through New York City at added expense. Albany's fur trade monopoly was another point of contention, particularly irritating to the farmers west and north of that city who were legally prohibited from trading with the Iroquois passing by their doorsteps.

A prolonged depression from 1676 to 1695 compounded the unrest created by these monopolies. The assessed valuation of real and personal property in New York City declined from £100,000 in 1676 to £75,000 in 1685 and £52,000 in 1695. Simultaneously, the price of wheat, a good index of prosperity in a "bread basket" colony, dropped from 4s 6d a bushel in 1673 to 4s in 1680 and 3s in 1688. Coupled with depressed prices was a sizable increase in the tax load in the late 1680's made necessary by the increasing hostility of the French.[1]

Monopolies, depression, and higher taxes were a formidable list of grievances at any time. As long as a means existed to discuss and possibly alleviate them, discontent could be safely channeled. But when that means—the Assembly established in 1683—was eliminated at the time James II ascended the throne, only a spark was necessary to set off a violent explosion. The colony's absorption into the Dominion of New England made the situation more explosive by confirming the end of the Assembly. The government was put in the hands of Governor General Sir Edmund Andros, Lieutenant Governor Francis Nicholson, and the Dominion Council of forty-two, of whom only eight were New Yorkers.

Nothing could have been more frustrating to the artisans and middle-class merchants suffering from the economic difficulties of the time; the Assembly had been their only hope of redress, even though they did not control it. To the aristocrats, whose personal political power was tremendously enhanced by the Dominion, final dissolution of the Assembly was no great loss. Although they probably controlled that body, it was a potential threat to their dominance. Now, the New Yorkers on the Dominion Council, a cross-section of the colony's aristocracy and English officialdom, were not only influential in determining their own future, but New England's as well.[2]

Robert Livingston found little in this new arrangement to disturb him. He was not a member of the Council, but his interests were well protected. He was on good terms with several of its members, including Frederick Philipse, Edward Randolph, and Stephanus Van Cortlandt. Among his close friends was James Graham, attorney general of the Dominion. If anything else were required to wed Livingston's interests firmly to the new government, he was greatly dependent upon Sir Edmund's favors in securing repayment of the advances he had made in Dongan's time.

There were, however, some would-be aristocrats in New York

1. Mason, "New York Revolt of 1689," *N.Y. Hist.*, 30 (1949), 169-74.
2. Royal instructions to Andros, Apr. 16, 1688, O'Callaghan, ed., *N.Y. Col. Docs.*, III, 543-44.

who did not share Livingston's enthusiasm for the Dominion and its officials. A social schism had emerged by 1689, and once the spark of rebellion was ignited, this cleavage determined the character and complexion of the movement's leadership. Jacob Leisler, who had been ostentatiously rejected by the aristocracy (as personified in his wife's relatives), assumed the unquestioned leadership of the mob at the opportune moment.

Certain parallels existed between the careers of Leisler and Livingston. Both arrived in the New World seeking their fortunes, married socially prominent widows, and inherited, through their wives, claims on valuable estates. There the similarities ended. The differences, primarily of emphasis and attitude, were of greater consequence. While Livingston quarreled mainly with his wife's family in the Old World, Leisler quarreled with relatives in the New. Although Livingston's dispute over Nicholas Van Rensselaer's estate was settled without anyone suffering real loss, Leisler's fight over Govert Loockermans' estate resulted in a bitterness that eventually brought him to a traitor's grave.[3]

Perhaps the outstanding difference between the two men was Leisler's pugnacity and religious fanaticism. As early as 1675, he had engaged in a heated theological quarrel with Domine Van Rensselaer over the interpretation of the Calvinist doctrine of original sin. This battle, which rocked the colony even involving Governor Andros, was typical of Leisler's fanaticism and was a portent of the future.[4]

Through a chain of events set in motion in 1689, Leisler found the opportunity to repay those who denied him social acceptance. The opportunity was the "soe strange news" that William of Orange had landed in England at the head of an invading army. These tidings reached Nicholson and the three councilors in New York City—Nicholas Bayard, Stephanus Van Cortlandt, and Frederick Philipse—on March 1, 1688/9. In less than two months, New Yorkers heard an even stranger report that Sir Edmund Andros and most of his aides had been seized in Boston and cast into prison.

This was a crisis of magnitude, for Lieutenant Governor Nicholson was empowered to assume the governor general's duties with a quorum of five councilors only in the event of Sir Edmund's death or

3. Purple, *Genealogical Notes on Leisler*, 5-7.
4. Leder, "The Unorthodox Domine," *N.Y. Hist.*, 35 (1954), 168-74.

absence from the Dominion. Though incarcerated, Sir Edmund was neither dead nor absent, and only three councilors were available in New York. Circumstances thus substituted a *de facto* government for a *de jure* one. Whatever authority the government now had must be based on popular support, but such a foundation did not exist and Nicholson was not the man to build it. The pent-up discontent of the people spilled over, beginning in Suffolk County and rapidly spreading to Westchester, Queens, and New York counties.[5]

Nicholson, by his own words, destroyed his last vestige of authority. Unrest in New York City reached such a fever pitch by May 30 that he feared for his life if he walked the streets unattended. Speaking to a militia officer, he declared that he would not endure the situation—he would sooner "sett the town in fyre." Within half an hour, the city was in arms, the militia deserted, and the fort passed into the hands of the rebels. Nicholson and his councilors were wholly repudiated; in their place emerged a new *de facto* government. At first, the militia captains took control; then, a Committee of Safety was formed; and, finally, Jacob Leisler was appointed commander-in-chief.[6]

The issue which crystallized public support for the new government was an unrealistic dread of a Catholic plot. Many honestly believed that Sir Edmund Andros and his officials were either Catholics or, at the very least, Catholic sympathizers. For proof, they merely recalled the bacchanalian rejoicing of those men when they learned of the birth of a son to Catholic James II.[7] By displacing his Protestant half-sisters in the line of succession, this child promised the continuance of a Catholic dynasty. Many New Yorkers feared a return to the days of "Bloody" Queen Mary.

While the Albany burghers, including Livingston, mourned the fall

5. N.Y. Council Minutes, Mar. 1, 1688/9, May 4, 1689, N.Y.C. Convention Proceedings, May 6, 1689, N.-Y. Hist. Soc., *Collections*, 1 (1868), 241-42, 253, 278; Andros' royal commission, Apr. 7, 1688. Andros' royal instructions, April 16, 1688, Nicholson to Lords of Trade, May 15, 1689, Van Cortlandt to Andros, July 9, 1689, O'Callaghan, ed., *N.Y. Col. Docs.*, III, 538, 542, 543, 575, 591.

6. N.Y. Council Minutes, June 6, 1689, Hendrick Cuyler's deposition, June 10, 1689, N.-Y. Hist. Soc., *Collections*, 1 (1868), 270-71, 293; Leisler to Gov. at Boston, June 4, 1689, Leisler's commission, Aug. 16, 1689, O'Callaghan, ed., *Doc. Hist. N.Y.*, II, 3, 14-15; Bayard's "Narrative of Occurrences," Dec. 13, 1689, O'Callaghan, ed., *N.Y. Col. Docs.*, III, 640.

7. See the description given in Randolph to Blathwayt, Oct. 2, 1688, Blathwayt Papers, I, Col. Wmsbg.

of Andros, they wasted little sympathy on Nicholson. He had been far too timid for them. In May 1689, when Livingston brought him the burghers' request that the members of the Macgregory expedition, the "Traders of Ottawaw," be permitted to attack the French, Nicholson replied that such action "is not safe for the government." [8] This opinion was ventured at a time when hostilities between the French and Iroquois had already occurred. Later, when he could no longer cope with the situation, Nicholson violated the Crown's instructions and decamped for England. [9]

The lieutenant governor's departure left Leisler as the claimant to his powers, but the Albany leaders, Livingston and Schuyler among them, had too much at stake to entrust their affairs to such a firebrand. They well remembered that Leisler was far from diplomatic, and the slightest disruption of the delicate personal relations between the Iroquois and the burghers would bring disaster to the town. The Indians were the colony's sole bulwark against the French, and their allegiance had to be retained at all costs. If the malcontents flocking to Leisler's banner acquired control over Albany, the burghers might also lose their fur trade monopoly. To fill the vacuum created by Nicholson's flight, the town leaders created a Convention composed of local military and civil officials. They subsequently resolved on August 1 to keep affairs firmly in their own hands pending orders from the new sovereigns, William and Mary. They also demonstrated firmness in their dealings with New Englanders who sought Iroquois aid against the attacks of the Algonquian tribes. When Massachusetts sent three agents to the Five Nations, the Albany Convention insisted that the proposals first be discussed with a committee of its members, one of whom was Livingston, before the New Englanders could proceed to a treaty with the Iroquois.

The Albany burghers' ability to retain control depended upon their adroitness in rebuffing Leisler's efforts to bring about the town's subjection. One issue which he could use to stir up public opinion was the burghers' reliance upon commissions issued in James II's name for their authority. On October 25, the Convention decided to remove

8. N.Y.C. Convention Proceedings, May 24, 1689, N.Y. Council to Albany Magistrates, May 24, 1689, N.-Y. Hist. Soc., *Collections*, 1 (1868), 267, 285-86.

9. Standing order, Apr. 27, 1688, W. L. Grant and James Munro, eds., *Acts of the Privy Council of England, Colonial Series, 1613-1783* (7 vols., London, 1908-12), II, 109; Van Cortlandt to Andros, July 9, 1689, O'Callaghan, ed., *N.Y. Col. Docs.*, III, 595.

all doubts about its adherence to the Glorious Revolution and ordered all town officers to take an oath of allegiance to William and Mary. Among those who did so was Livingston.[10]

Both the Leislerians in New York City and the Convention in Albany were in complete accord on the immediate and fundamental issues: support of William and Mary, opposition to the French in Canada, and detestation of Roman Catholicism. To both, the Glorious Revolution was essentially a conservative movement, but they differed in what they wanted to conserve. The Leislerians wanted the *status quo* as it existed in pre-Dominion days; the Convention wished the *status quo* as it existed under the Dominion. Given New York's political experience, however, the differences were more of emphasis than of substance.

In this controversy, Livingston stood firmly against Leisler. The Albany Convention proposed a subscription for maintenance of the town's defenses, offering only a promise that repayment would be recommended to the new governor. Of the £367 subscribed, Livingston gave £50, the largest single contribution. Indeed, it was Livingston's financial support that, for a time, enabled the Convention to maintain its independence of Leisler. On October 28, eight town officials signed a bond pledging to repay him if the new governor did not. A week later, probably after the officials realized that they had pledged their entire personal fortunes, an order was entered in the town's records to guarantee reimbursement to Livingston out of the county revenues.[11]

The Convention's resolve was soon put to the test by Leisler's key lieutenant, Jacob Milborne, who arrived in Albany on November 8 in command of a company of New York City militia, determined to bring about the town's submission. Invited to address the Convention, Milborne exhibited his native arrogance by turning instead to the "Common People in a long oration with a high Stile & language telling them That now it was in there power to free themselfs from the Yoke of arbitrary Power...of the Illegall King James." After he

10. Albany Convention Records, Aug. 1, Oct. 25, 1689, O'Callaghan, ed., *Doc. Hist. N.Y.*, II, 80, 104; Van Cortlandt to Andros, July 9, 1689, O'Callaghan, ed., *N.Y. Col. Docs.*, III, 596; Albany Convention Records, Sept. 4, Oct. 25, 1689, Munsell, ed., *Annals of Albany*, II, 114-15, 122; Leder, ed., *Livingston Indian Records*, 147-48.
11. Albany Convention Records, Sept. 17, Oct. 28, Nov. 4, 1689, Munsell, ed., *Annals of Albany*, II, 118-20, 127, 129.

finished his oration, the Convention concluded that "Milborne Designs the Subversion of the government."

If he could not turn the people against the burghers by oratory, Milborne hoped to tempt the Convention into voluntary submission. As an inducement to capitulation, he promised to leave the militia company he commanded as a supplement to the garrison. Although the town's defenses were woefully inadequate, Albany already had a promise of aid from Connecticut so Milborne's offer was not tempting. Realizing this, he turned to violence to gain his ends. Marching his troops up to the fort, he read an ultimatum. But some Iroquois standing nearby threatened to fall upon him and his men at the first sign of hostility, so he retreated. On November 16, he withdrew to New York City, leaving his troops behind under Captain Abraham Staats' command. Nine days later, Captain Jonathan Bull and eighty-seven officers and men arrived from Connecticut and were "extremely well accepted." [12]

The Convention had won the first round, but Leisler soon received added strength from an unexpected source. On December 8, a royal messenger arrived with a letter from the Privy Council to "Francis Nicholson Esqre. Their Majestys Lieutenant Governor and Commander in Chief of the Province of New York, and in his absence to such as for the time being take care for preserving the Peace and administring the Lawes in their Majestys Province of New York in America." Nicholson was gone. It was no longer a question of legality, but of who was now "preserving the Peace and administring the Lawes." The former members of the Dominion Council still in New York City, Van Cortlandt and Bayard, claimed they were legally entitled to the letter; Leisler claimed he was, since he had accepted the responsibilities it mentioned. Two days later, Leisler forcibly proved his point to the messenger and received the document.[13]

Leisler now believed that the Crown had legally recognized him

12. Albany Convention Records, O'Callaghan, ed., *Doc. Hist. N.Y.*, II, 92-93, 97-98, 113-14, 117, 122, 124-32.

13. William III to Nicholson, etc., July 30, 1689, Bayard to Nicholson, Dec. 10, 1689, O'Callaghan, ed., *N.Y. Col. Docs.*, III, 606, 633; De Riemer's deposition, Feb. 24, 1690/1, N.-Y. Hist. Soc., *Collections*, 1 (1868), 326. In all probability, Leisler was entitled to receive the letter, for he was "doing as much as anyone to preserve the peace"; Andrews, *Colonial Period*, III, 127-28.

as lieutenant governor, and he followed the explicit instructions given in the missive—"to take upon you the Government . . . Calling to your assistance . . . the Principal Freeholders and Inhabitants." The Council of his adherents represented several important New York families. Men such as Peter Delanoy, Samuel Staats, Gerardus Beekman, Thomas Williams, and William Lawrence were not of the rabble. Like Leisler himself, they were prospective aristocrats who were not yet fully accepted as such.[14]

Leisler firmly advised the Albany Convention of his new-found authority by issuing orders to the militia, preparing new commissions for justices of the peace, and ordering new elections. Upon receiving these commands, the Convention was dubious of their authenticity. Where, it asked, was this royal commission? Captain Staats, Leisler's sole representative in Albany, could not produce a copy since Leisler had not permitted its publication. The Convention, therefore, flatly refused to submit to him "till orders come from his Majesty King William for the same, which never hath been hither to showne."[15]

The Convention went further and had Livingston draft a letter on January 20 to the new governor "when he comes." In this, the burghers expressed their longing to be delivered "from these Troubles Confusions & Distractions occasioned by Captain Jacob Leisler & his adherents." Examining his usurpations in detail, they warned of dire consequences if he gained control of Albany. Livingston forwarded this document to Bayard, Van Cortlandt, and Philipse with instructions to place it in the new governor's hands as soon as he landed, little realizing how long they were to wait.[16]

Even more than they feared Leisler's ambitions, however, the Albany burghers dreaded a French attack. When the blow fell, however, it was aimed at Schenectady, not Albany. In the late evening of February 9, nearly 200 French and Indian attackers swept down upon Schenectady, massacring sixty-two people, carrying off another twenty-seven, and burning all but five or six buildings. The survivors

14. William III to Nicholson, etc., July 30, 1689, O'Callaghan, ed., *N.Y. Col. Docs.*, III, 606; Charles M. Andrews, ed., *Narratives of the Insurrections, 1675-1690* (N.Y., 1915), 340*n*.

15. Leisler to Albany Convention, Dec. 28, 1689, Albany Convention Records, Jan. 11, 12, 1689/90, O'Callaghan, ed., *N.Y. Col. Docs.*, II, 51, 144-49.

16. Magistrates, etc., of Albany to the Gov., Jan. 20, 1689/90 (draft), Livingston-Redmond Mss.

fled eastward, bringing alarming rumors that 600 Frenchmen and Indians were marching on Albany. Though the people were near panic, the Convention remained calm. The only way to end the menace was to counterattack and insure "that Quebec may be taken by water in the Spring." The Convention wrote to the governors of Massachusetts, Connecticut, and Virginia, and to the military and civil officers of New York City—still refusing to recognize Leisler as lieutenant governor—to seek immediate assistance in this project.[17]

But Leisler was not idle. The Schenectady massacre convinced him that Albany must pass into his hands. The town could not stand alone, and its loss would open the entire colony to enemy attack. He believed that Albany's resistance to him had been bulwarked by the Connecticut militia stationed there, and he sought either control or removal of that company. On February 21, he commissioned Johannes Vermilye, Benjamin Blagge, and Jacob Milborne as agents to secure Connecticut's acquiescence in his plans. To these demands, the Connecticut officials responded unfavorably, pointing out that the Albany burghers were better acquainted with the Iroquois than Leisler: he should give "little alteration or interruption . . . to those in authority there."[18]

At about the same time, the Convention decided to send out its own agents, unanimously selecting Livingston to visit Connecticut and Massachusetts. Even before Leisler learned of this mission, he unleashed his hatred of Livingston, who, he asserted, was responsible for Albany's lawless rejection of his authority. Because Livingston, "by the Instigacon of the Devill did utter the Malice of his heart in saying that . . . a parcell of rebells were gone out of holland to England," Leisler ordered his arrest for defaming William of Orange and "other high Crimes" which remained unspecified.[19]

But Livingston was unaware of these charges as he made preparations for his trip. In any event, he had enough on his mind. At five

17. Leisler to Coode, Mar. 4, 1689/90, Albany Convention Records, O'Callaghan, ed., *Doc. Hist. N.Y.*, II, 183, 157-59.

18. Governor's Council Minutes, Feb. 16, 1689/90, Leisler to Vermilye, Blagge, and Milborne, Feb. 21, 1689/90, N.Y. Commissioners to Gov. Treat, Feb. 24, 1689/90, Allyn to N.Y. Commissioners, Feb. 24, 1689/90, *ibid.*, 71-76. See also Kiliaen Van Rensselaer's statement, N.-Y. Hist. Soc., *Collections*, 1 (1868), 328.

19. Albany Convention Records, Feb. 27, 1689/90, Leisler to Blagge, Mar. 1, 1689/90, O'Callaghan, ed., *Doc. Hist. N.Y.*, II, 171-72, 200; Munsell, ed., *Annals of Albany*, II, 192-93.

o'clock in the morning of March 3, his wife gave birth to their fourth son, Gilbert. But the proud father had little time for rejoicing; on the same day, he prepared his will and received his commission from the Convention. On the next day, he and his fellow agent, Gerrit Teunise, received detailed instructions for their mission. In Connecticut, they were to secure orders to keep Captain Bull's troops in Albany, enlist another fifty "Briske young men or more" for duty, and obtain 100 barrels of pork or beef. After finishing in Hartford, they were to go to Boston and make similar requests. In both places, they were to impress upon the New Englanders the need to destroy French power at its source by a naval attack on Quebec. To cover all contingencies, the Convention gave the agents *carte blanche* "to act & doe in our Behalf ... whatever you shall juge expedient & needful." [20]

When Livingston and Teunise appeared before Governor Robert Treat and his Council in Hartford on March 11, they were joined by Thomas Garton of Ulster County. Livingston took the leadership, adhering closely to their instructions. However, Governor Treat preferred getting Massachusetts' views before doing anything himself, promising to consult further after receiving Governor Simon Bradstreet's reply. [21]

In the meantime, Leisler learned of Livingston's mission and wrote to Bradstreet and Treat on March 5 to denounce "this rebell Livingstone," charging that his mission was only a pretext to avoid arrest for his "crymes." Leisler accused Livingston of playing a prominent role in Albany's resistance to his authority, an indisputable fact, and of being considerably indebted to the Crown, a complete falsehood. The two governors were advised that Daniel Teneur and Benjamin Blagge were en route with a warrant for Livingston's arrest.

Teneur arrived in Hartford on March 12 and presented the warrant to Governor Treat who viewed it rather dimly, especially since it was so vague, "no time place or yeare mentioned." The governor agreed to take Livingston into custody for trial in Hartford if someone would stand security for his prosecution and for damages should

20. Livingston, *Livingstons of Livingston Manor*, 68; Livingston's will, Mar. 3, 1689/90, Livingston-Redmond Mss.; Livingston's commission & instructions, Mar. 3, 4, 1689/90, Munsell, ed., *Annals of Albany*, II, 196-99.
21. Connecticut Council Minutes, Mar. 11, 1689/90 (true copy), Livingston-Redmond Mss.

he be proven innocent. This, of course, was not what Leisler wanted, and he must have been very displeased when John Allyn, secretary of Connecticut, sent him this rebuff.[22]

Though unable to apprehend Livingston, Teneur won an order from Treat for the removal of Captain Bull's troops from Albany. Connecticut did not want to get involved in New York's factional disputes, nor did its leaders want its soldiers used as pawns. The withdrawal, of course, was a great victory for Leisler. With its defenses weakened, Albany's ability to resist him was considerably lessened.

Livingston remonstrated against the removal and pleaded for an additional 200 men for Albany. He warned of the consequences of Leislerian control of that outpost—"they of New Yorke, whatever they pretend, are not able to maintain that . . . territory without a considerable supply." His main concern was not the defeat of Leisler's schemes, but defeat of the greater enemy, France. The English, he predicted, cannot "expect any peace or tranquility, so long as the French of Canada be not subdued." [23]

Unable to get any definite commitments from Connecticut, Livingston and the two other agents proceeded to Boston. Arriving there on March 17, they immediately recounted Albany's "disgust" with Leisler's proceedings. Their reception, however, was little short of hostile; the people of Massachusetts were more sympathetic to Leisler than those of Connecticut. This apparent enigma was explained a little later by a Bostonian who wrote that Leisler's actions, "being soe like our pattern, we cannot but love our own Bratt." [24] While both New York City and Massachusetts had overthrown duly constituted authority, Albany and Connecticut, as best they could, had merely filled governmental vacuums created by others.

Before Livingston could expound his case to the Massachusetts authorities, Leisler's agent, Blagge, arrived and Livingston found himself "disregarded." There was even talk of imprisoning him. But he promptly printed the treaty by which the Iroquois agreed to support

22. Leisler to Bradstreet and Treat, Mar. 5, 1689/90, Munsell, ed., *Annals of Albany*, II, 203-4; Treat's declaration, Mar. 12, 1689/90, Allyn to Leisler, Mar. 1689/90, O'Callaghan, *Doc. Hist. N.Y.*, II, 188-89. See also *ibid.*, 186.

23. Livingston's memorial to Treat, Mar. 12, 1689/90, Livingston-Redmond Mss. See also *Cal. State Papers, Col.*, XIII, no. 2763; O'Callaghan, ed., *N.Y. Col. Docs.*, III, 692-94.

24. Allyn to Winthrop, Mar. 18, 1689/90, Winthrop Papers, X, 50, Mass. Hist. Soc.; Francis Foxcroft to [Blathwayt], Apr. 16, 1691, Blathwayt Papers, V, Col. Wmsbg.

the Albany Convention and "managed his affairs with such discretion
... [that] he walked the streets more chearfully." [25] The treaty took
the wind out of Blagge's sails since Massachusetts could ill afford to
antagonize the Iroquois and open its western borders to Indian attack.

When the Albany agents finally appeared before the General
Court on March 20, there was little likelihood of getting any aid.
They saw no reason, therefore, to be modest. After requesting 500
men, an engineer, £500 worth of goods, and ministers to counteract
the Jesuits, they announced: "There is neither pleasure nor satisfaction to be in office in such times . . . Wee have exhausted [ourselves]
for the publick . . . Wee fear such changes as Mr. Leysler is now
about . . . Our interest and Dependence is chiefly in the welfare of
Albany." [26]

It was all to no avail. Bradstreet replied that Albany must capitulate
to Leisler. If there was to be any retribution for Leisler's "hard or
unreasonable measures," it would have to await a settlement from
England. Further, Massachusetts could not help with men or supplies
because she was devoting her full energies to the naval attack on
Canada.[27]

After conferring with John Borland, a fellow Scot and a Boston
merchant, Livingston wrote to two English officials. To the Earl of
Nottingham, secretary of state, he explained Albany's predicament,
the outrages committed by the French, and the importance of sending
a new governor at once "to Put a Period to these distractions." He
also sent documents which described developments in the colony since
Nicholson's departure.[28] Livingston also wrote to Robert Ferguson
of the Excise Office in London. Ferguson was a mysterious intriguer
of Stuart England, and has remained an enigma ever since. A participant in numerous plots against James II, he was exiled to The Netherlands where he played a role in William of Orange's invasion of
England. While in exile in Amsterdam in the 1680's, he had boarded

25. "Benjamin Bullivants Journall of Proceedings from the 13 Feb. to the 19th of
May [1690 in Boston]," Mass. Hist. Soc., *Proceedings*, 1st ser., 16 (1879), 105; N.-Y.
Hist. Soc., *Collections*, 2 (1876), 165-76.

26. Memorial of Livingston, Teunise, and Garton to Mass., Mar. 20, 1689/90, O'Callaghan, ed., *N.Y. Col. Docs.*, III, 695-97.

27. Bradstreet to Albany Convention, Mar. 25, 1690, Livingston-Redmond Mss.;
letter to Dudley, Apr. 1, 1690, Public Record Office, London, CO 5: 855, no. 416
(hereafter cited as PRO).

28. Livingston to Nottingham, Mar. 27, 1690, Livingston-Redmond Mss.

with Livingston's brother-in-law Andrew Russell, and it was there that he had met John Borland.[29]

Presuming on this involved chain of friendships, Livingston poured out his woes to Ferguson. Not only did he emphasize the concern he felt for the future of the English colonies if the French were not destroyed, but he also called attention to his expenditures for the public. He told Ferguson that Jacob Harwood possessed copies of all documents pertaining to the loan to Dongan, and requested whatever aid Ferguson could offer. Borland's cover letter, cautious in supporting Livingston's vilification of Leisler, recommended that Ferguson "doe any kindness for Mr. Livingston you Can In his oune particular affaires. . . . Mr. Livingston is a stranger to my self but my Intimat acquaintance with his friends In Holland oblidges me to serve him." [30]

As Livingston started back to Albany to deliver the news that Massachusetts would not send help, he learned that the town, fearing an immediate attack by the French, had surrendered to Leisler. Three commissioners—Johannes De Bruyn, Johannes Provoost, and Jacob Milborne—had been appointed by Leisler to control Albany. On March 22, they ordered Livingston, who was still in Boston, to turn over all papers and records to their newly appointed town clerk, Johannes Cuyler. At the same time, the commissioners began collecting depositions attesting to Livingston's "treasonable" activities.[31]

Richard Pretty, appointed sheriff of Albany County by Leisler, made the first attack on Livingston by alleging that he had denounced William of Orange as the leader of a "Parcell of rebells" who would end "as Monmouth did." [32] Leisler's commissioners collected additional depositions but each one seemed to dilute Pretty's charge. As the facts emerged, Livingston had merely translated James II's declaration against William for the benefit of several non-English inhab-

29. "Robert Ferguson," *Encyclopaedia Britannica* (24 vols., Chicago, 1947), IX, 172; Borland to Ferguson, Apr. 1, 1690, PRO, CO 5: 1081, no. 117 (Lib. Cong. transcripts).
30. Livingston to Ferguson, Mar. 27, 1690 (draft), Livingston-Redmond Mss. See also O'Callaghan, ed., *N.Y. Col. Docs.*, III, 698-99.
31. "Bullivants Journall," Mass. Hist. Soc., *Proceedings,* 1st ser., 16 (1879), 105-6; Commission to De Bruyn, Provoost, and Milborne, Mar. 4, 1689/90, O'Callaghan, ed., *N.Y. Col. Docs.*, III, 702-3; Leisler's Commissioners to Livingston, Mar. 22, 1689/90, O'Callaghan, ed., *Doc. Hist. N.Y.*, II, 194; Munsell, ed., *Annals of Albany,* II, 208.
32. O'Callaghan, ed., *Cal. Hist. Mss.*, II, 189; Pretty's deposition, Mar. 25, 1690, O'Callaghan, ed., *N.Y. Col. Docs.*, III, 747. Pretty probably disliked Livingston because of the treatment he had received in 1680 when Livingston and his friends had ousted him as sub-collector of Albany.

itants. Thus James, not Livingston, had defamed William. Despite the weakness of their evidence, the commissioners forwarded all the depositions to Leisler. They also complained that the town's financial records were missing; Livingston had absconded, and his wife denied any knowledge of the location of his papers. The commissioners concluded that these "were reasons numerous enough to secure said Livingston." Leisler thought so too, for he denounced Livingston as that "malefactor charged with treasonable crymes." [33]

Livingston had no desire to join Nicholas Bayard and William Nicolls in the prison of the New York City fort, so he remained in Connecticut. He advised the General Court at Hartford of his fruitless negotiations at Boston and of Albany's surrender. Even though the burghers had chosen to ignore the "sundry enormities committed by Captain Leysler," he cautioned Connecticut's leaders against allowing Leisler's "undecent carriage" to diminish their resolve to crush the French—"there is no medium left, we must destroy or be destroyed." [34]

As an exile, there was little that Livingston could do personally to aid in destroying the French. He could and did write to influential persons in England and the colonies, and he spurred the Connecticut authorities on to greater efforts. In a letter to Sir Edmund Andros, who had returned to England, Livingston discussed the Schenectady massacre, placing the full blame on Leisler who had so "bygotted" the villagers that they failed to take any precautions. He reminded Sir Edmund of his expenditures for the government and hoped "that his Majestie may send orders to settle and pay all thos arrears; else I am undone." [35]

Livingston also corresponded with Fitz-John Winthrop of New London, thus beginning a friendship which was symbolic of the relationship between their fathers in the 1630's. To his new friend, Livingston passed along word of events taking place in Albany, Boston,

33. Various depositions, Apr. 1, 1690, Commissioners to Leisler, Apr. 2, 1690, Leisler to Bradstreet, Apr. 7, 1690, O'Callaghan, ed., *Doc. Hist. N.Y.*, II, 205-7, 227; Munsell, ed., *Annals of Albany*, II, 216-18.

34. Leisler to Coode, Mar. 4, 1689/90, Leisler to Melyn, Jan. 24, 1689/90, O'Callaghan, ed., *Doc. Hist. N.Y.*, II, 182, 62; Livingston to Conn. officials, Apr. 11, 1690, "Correspondence Between the Col. of N.Y. and Conn." (transcripts), N.-Y. Hist. Soc. See also O'Callaghan, ed., *N.Y. Col. Docs.*, III, 705-6.

35. Livingston to Andros, Apr. 14, 1690, O'Callaghan, ed., *N.Y. Col. Docs.*, III, 708-10.

and Hartford. He confided that he was proud to have incurred Leisler's wrath; he had "been as great a Stickler against him as any & ever will be to any Such usurper as he." "My frinds both at home and here," he added, "advise me to Stay till a Setlement Comes."[36]

The wisdom of Livingston's voluntary exile soon became evident. Leisler's commissioners in Albany issued an order against him as "one that hath defrauded his Majestie of his dues and rights and broken the trust reposed in him." Since Livingston had not appeared to answer the charges against him, Sheriff Pretty was ordered to seize all his lands, houses, goods, and chattels. In New York City, Leisler seized a cargo of his rum and sugar that had just arrived from Barbados.[37]

Winthrop sympathized with Livingston, and the understanding which developed between them eventually resulted in the former's appointment as commander of the land expedition against Canada. An intercolonial conference was held at Leisler's call in New York City at the beginning of May. Connecticut, Plymouth, Massachusetts, and New York were represented, and each agreed to supply a specific number of troops.[38] Before the Connecticut delegates set out for New York City, Livingston gave them an extensive memorandum stressing the necessity for a naval assault on Quebec. The land expedition could only "facilitate the Enterprise"; indeed, if the sea attack failed, it would be "in Vain to Speak of subdueing Canida by Land." But the land expedition was an important element in the campaign, and Livingston warned that its control should not fall into Leisler's hands; this was a joint responsibility and each colony must have an equal voice. Nevertheless, the conference decided, probably at Massachusetts' insistence, to permit Leisler to name the commander. The Connecticut authorities were not entirely pleased and, under Livingston's prodding, made their dissatisfaction vocal. Livingston warned Governor Treat that Leisler intended to appoint Jacob Milborne and added: "If Mr. Milbourn have any command there, no good can be ex-

36. Livingston to Winthrop, Apr. 15, 1690, Winthrop Papers, XIV, 154, Mass. Hist. Soc.

37. Order of Leisler's Commissioners, Apr. 14, 1690, Leisler's Commissioners to Sheriff Pretty, Apr. 30, 1690, Leisler to Commissioners, Apr. 30, 1690, O'Callaghan, ed., Doc. Hist. N.Y., II, 218, 225, 238; Munsell, ed., Annals of Albany, II, 224-25.

38. Leisler's circular letter, Apr. 2, 1690, Agreement of delegates, May 1, 1690, O'Callaghan, ed., Doc. Hist. N.Y., II, 211, 239-40; "Diary of Samuel Sewall, 1674-1729," Mass. Hist. Soc., Collections, 5th ser., 5 (1878), 317n, 318.

pected." Livingston's admonitions roused John Allyn, secretary of Connecticut, to write Leisler on May 25, protesting Milborne's unfitness for the command and suggesting Fitz-John Winthrop for the post, an idea which probably originated with Livingston. Allyn's attitude, and that of Treat for whom he spoke, pleased Livingston.[39]

Soon, even more heartening news came from another quarter. Francis Nicholson, erstwhile lieutenant governor of the Dominion, had been appointed lieutenant governor of Virginia and had taken up his post there. Livingston was overjoyed, not because of Nicholson's good fortune, but because it signified "how our massienello's [i.e., Leisler's] Proceedings are Received at Home." It was already common knowledge that a new governor had been appointed for New York, and Livingston hoped that he would arrive soon.[40]

Livingston was then in New London, visiting Winthrop, who assured him that he was "willing to goe & Serve his king & Country to the utmost." Winthrop agreed with Livingston's analysis of affairs at Albany, observing that Peter Schuyler's "interest with your owne & the gentlemen at Albany will firmly settle" the Anglo-Iroquois alliance. When Livingston returned to Hartford, he continued to agitate for his friend, even suggesting to Governor Bradstreet that "great Dislike" had been shown of Milborne and that Winthrop's appointment "would be to every bodyes Content." The Iroquois' "blood being hott," all that was necessary was a capable leader such as Winthrop.[41] His and Allyn's importunities had the desired effect. On June 20, Leisler gave way and consented to the appointment of "that excellent person Major Generall Winthrop." By July 3, the new commander

39. Livingston's Memorandum, Apr. 22, 1690, Livingston to Treat, May 9, 1690 (draft), Livingston-Redmond Mss.; Livingston to Treat, May 13, 1690, O'Callaghan, ed., *N.Y. Col. Docs.*, III, 729-30; Allyn to Leisler, May 25, 1690, O'Callaghan, ed., *Doc. Hist. N.Y.*, II, 253.

40. Livingston to Nicholson, June 7, 1690, Livingston to Bradstreet, June 7, 1690 (drafts), Livingston-Redmond Mss. Both Nicholson and Sloughter sought the N.Y. governorship. The former was supported by the Duke of Bolton to whom he had once been a page; the latter was sponsored by the Marquess of Carmarthen and the merchants trading to N.Y., one of whom was Livingston's correspondent, Harwood. Carmarthen to Nottingham, Sept. 11, 1689, Hist. Mss. Comm., *Report on the Manuscripts of the Late Allen George Finch, Esq., of Burley-on-the-Hill, Rutland* (2 vols., London, 1922), II, 245; Petition of merchants, 1689, O'Callaghan, ed., *N.Y. Col. Docs.*, III, 651-52.

41. Livingston to Bradstreet, June 7, 1690 (draft), June 18, 1690, Livingston-Redmond Mss.; Winthrop to Livingston, June 16, 1690, Mass. Hist. Soc., *Collections*, 5th ser., 8 (1882), 305-6.

was on his way to Hartford to confer with the officials there, and Livingston intended to wait upon him. There will be "little Readiness & order at Albany," he warned, "till your honor comes there." [42]

News that Livingston's youngest daughter, Johanna, was "very ill with a kinde of Consumption and tis thought is not long of this world" quickened his natural desire to return home. Winthrop then proved his friendship: when the commander entered Albany with the Connecticut contingent on July 21, Livingston was in his entourage. Leisler raged that this was a plot by Livingston and Allyn either to destroy the expedition or to overthrow him. Leisler demanded Livingston's surrender, but Winthrop kept him under his personal protection, using his home as his headquarters. However, when Winthrop set off for Canada on July 28, Livingston returned to the safety of Connecticut after arranging that his wife and children join him. [43]

The expedition against Canada was a complete failure. The army advanced to Wood Creek, near Lake Champlain, then turned back. Winthrop and his officers blamed the inadequacy of supplies, particularly canoes, the loss of troops because of smallpox, and the lack of Iroquois support. But Leisler was furious at Winthrop; the commander had "lived in open adulteries" and was "a toole fitt for the wicked purposes that... [Allyn] & Livingston had contryved." [44] Livingston's exile was even more necessary now because, in Leisler's eyes, he was responsible for the failure of the Canada expedition as well as other "crimes." To Leisler, every misfortune, however unintentional, was a plot directed at himself and the Protestant cause with which he identified himself.

While safe in Hartford, Livingston received the disheartening news that the naval attack on Quebec had also failed. "It lookes dark and sorrowful upon us," John Allyn concluded. But one ray of hope shone through this gloom. Word reached Boston that Henry Sloughter, New York's new governor, had left England some ten weeks before

42. Leisler to Treat, June 20, 1690, O'Callaghan, ed., *Doc. Hist. N.Y.*, II, 265; Livingston to Winthrop, July 3, 1690, Winthrop Papers, XIV, 154, Mass. Hist. Soc.

43. John Tuder to Livingston, June 21, 1690, Livingston-Redmond Mss.; Leisler to Shrewsbury, Oct. 20, 1690, O'Callaghan, ed., *N.Y. Col. Docs.*, III, 752; Leisler to John Stedman, July 31, 1690, N.Y. Colony Mss., Box I, N.Y. Pub. Lib.; Livingston, *Livingstons of Livingston Manor*, 68.

44. Allyn to Leisler, Sept. 1, 1690, Leisler to Allyn, Sept. 30, 1690, O'Callaghan, ed., *Doc. Hist. N.Y.*, III, 288-89, 300-2.

and was expected in the colony "any day." The suspense was finally broken on February 1, 1690/1, when Livingston learned that three vessels of Sloughter's convoy had entered New York harbor. The report said that the governor's ship had been separated from the others near Bermuda, but a deputy governor had safely arrived in company with the Council president, a general to command a Canada expedition, and 100 "Red Coats." [45] Much of this was wishful thinking: the only officials who arrived were Joseph Dudley, ranking member of the Council, and Captain Richard Ingoldesby of the foot company.

Moreover, neither Dudley nor Ingoldesby had any authority until Sloughter proclaimed his own commission. Since Leisler had as much or more authority than they and also controlled the fort in New York City, they were helpless. But in Connecticut, Livingston felt that his star was in the ascendant. He optimistically reported that "Leyslers faction hang ears Prodigiously." Even though "wake & feeble," he intended to go to New York City to witness Leisler's fall.[46] His enthusiasm was dampened when he learned of the true situation. Nothing had changed in New York City: Dudley, Ingoldesby, and the royal troops were being reviled as "king James his men, Papists & Catholics . . . here to cut off the protestant party." [47]

Livingston's spirit fluctuated with the news he received. Tidings from Jacob Harwood buoyed him considerably. In addition to regular commercial news, the Londoner expressed the hope that "all those things [committed by Leisler] will be prevented, & accomodated upon the arrivall of Governor Sloughter who goes with this, he is my very good ffriend, as likewise his Secretary mr Clarkson the Bearer hereof." Even before he left England, Sloughter had concluded that the Leislerians were a "rabble." For that reason, when he finally arrived and demanded the fort from Leisler, he refused to show any proof of his authority. In turn, Leisler refused to surrender until it had been thrice demanded. When the gates were finally opened, the

45. Allyn to Livingston, Nov. 18, 1690, Livingston-Redmond Mss.; Johannes Kerfbyl to Abraham De Peyster, Nov. 20, 1690, De Peyster Papers, 1695-1710 (Dingman Versteeg translations), N.-Y. Hist. Soc.; Livingston to Winthrop, Feb. 2, 1690/1, Winthrop Papers, XIV, 155, Mass. Hist. Soc.
46. Royal Commission to Ingoldesby, N.-Y. Hist. Soc., Collections, 1 (1868), 299; Livingston to Winthrop, Feb. 2, 1690/1, Livingston to Dellius, Feb. 2, 1690/1 (Dutch), Winthrop Papers, XIV, 155, Mass. Hist. Soc.
47. Dudley to Blathwayt, Mar. 17, 1690/1, Blathwayt Papers, IV, Col. Wmsbg.

new governor had Leisler and his aides clapped into jail to await trial.[48]

Livingston learned of all this on March 23, a few days after the events had occurred. It made him all the more anxious "to Inform our Governor of all Transactions." Despite his illness, he and his family left Fairfield, Connecticut, the next day. When Livingston arrived in New York City on April 2, he learned that the Leislerian leaders were standing trial for treason and murder. As he put it, matters were "somewhat Composed & Settled." [49] Though not a participant in the proceedings, nothing could have pleased him more than the sentences meted out by President Joseph Dudley of the Court of Oyer and Terminer. Leisler, Milborne, and six of their associates were to be "hanged by the Neck and being Alive their bodys be Cutt downe to the Earth that their Bowells be taken out and they being Alive burnt before their faces that their heads shall be struck off and their Bodys Cutt in four parts." [50]

Many of the staunch anti-Leislerians, including Livingston, feared that the prisoners would be reprieved. There has been great controversy over the means used to persuade the governor to sign the death warrants, especially since he had been reluctant to do so at first. It has been suggested that his concurrence was won only by means of liquor, bribes, or both. But the executions took place two days after the warrants were signed, and forty-eight hours seems time enough for any man to recover from the effects of even seventeenth-century whisky.[51] As for bribery, there was little need of it. Sloughter admittedly despised all Leisler stood for, and his closest advisers were anti-Leislerians. Livingston had suffered a year's exile and intolerable vilification, and Bayard and Nicolls had been imprisoned for a year. The governor could not very well resist the pressure of the anti-

48. Harwood to Livingston, Oct. 18, 1690, Livingston-Redmond Mss.; Sloughter to Lords of Trade, Oct. 20, 1690, *Cal. State Papers, Col.*, XIII, 169; Lawrence H. Leder, "Captain Kidd and the Leisler Rebellion," N.-Y. Hist. Soc., *Quarterly*, 38 (1954), 52.

49. Livingston to Winthrop, Mar. 23, 1690/1, April 23, 1691, Winthrop Papers, XIV, 156, Mass. Hist. Soc.

50. Lawrence H. Leder, ed., "Records of the Trials of Jacob Leisler and His Associates," N.-Y. Hist. Soc., *Quarterly*, 36 (1952), 431-57. The sentences are on p. 454.

51. For the controversy over the means used to persuade the governor to sign the warrants, see William Smith, *The History of the Late Province of New-York, From Its Discovery to the Appointment of Governor Colden, in 1762* (2 vols., N.Y., 1829), I, 103-4. Smith repeats the story in the letter of the Dutch Church to the Classis of Amsterdam, Oct. 21, 1698, N.-Y. Hist. Soc., *Collections*, 1 (1868), 406.

Leislerians for the deaths of the two leading rebels, the minimum blood sacrifice which would appease them.[52]

On May 17, 1691, Leisler and Milborne, his son-in-law, were led to the scaffold. Before they paid the supreme penalty, not so much for the crimes they had committed as for the enemies they had made, they were permitted to make last statements. Leisler, in what may have been his finest moment, urged his followers "in our graves with us to bury all malice, hatred & Envy." Milborne, spying Livingston in the crowd of onlookers, turned to him and solemnly charged: "You have caused the king that I must now die. but before gods tribunal I will implead you for the same." [53]

52. Bayard wrote: "I have had severall times the promise from his Excellency that he would not reprieve them without the advice of the Council, which if it be left to them I am assured that Justice will not be delayed." Nicolls was particularly bitter over the delay, blaming it on Joseph Dudley whom he alleged was responsible for the acquittal of Peter Delanoy and Samuel Edsall at the trials. He wrote: "The Usuall Sentence for Treason was pronounced . . . but they are all safe and well, and the fear of a reprieve . . . gives . . . universall discontent. . . . The source of all these and other our evils is attributed to the President Dudley, whose actions demonstrate on all Occasions his affection & assiduous care for those of Leislers ffaccon, which tho he has not the Courage to own bare fact, Yet itts manifest and apparent to all that are not very dimsighted." Bayard to Blathwayt, May 6, 1691, Nicolls to Blathwayt, May 7, 1691, Blathwayt Papers, VII, XV, Col. Wmsbg.

53. Sloughter to Blathwayt, July 1691, O'Callaghan, ed., *N.Y. Col. Docs.*, III, 789. For Leisler's and Milborne's death speeches, see O'Callaghan, ed., *Doc. Hist. N. Y.*, II, 379-80.

CHAPTER V

Public Finance and Factional Politics

AFTER RETURNING from his exile in Connecticut, Robert Livingston rapidly resumed his prominent place in New York life. At the age of thirty-six, he had an impeccable social position, an excellent mercantile reputation, a baronial estate, a devoted and capable wife, four sons, and a daughter. Moreover, he had developed an intimate relationship with the dominant political faction in New York and England—the Tory, or Court, Party.

Politics in New York after the Glorious Revolution were not, as often suggested, merely a division between Leislerian and anti-Leislerian, but rather a mirrored reflection of developments in the mother country, although a time lag often existed. Great influence was exerted in New York's affairs by the dominant clique in imperial politics—William Blathwayt, John Povey, and Edward Randolph—as the volume of correspondence from the colony's officials to Blathwayt testified. The political picture in New York was further complicated by the imperfect nature of party mechanisms. There were factions within factions, particularly among the anti-Leislerians, or Tories. Largely an internal conflict of personalities, it was the age-old story of power's corrupting influence. Livingston began on the best of terms with this group, gradually drifted away, and dramatically split with them in 1695.[1]

1. On the relationship between New York and English politics, see Herbert L. Osgood, *The American Colonies in the Eighteenth Century* (4 vols., N.Y., 1924), I,

Livingston's early intimacy with the Tories was symbolized by his attitude toward Governor Sloughter; he found him "a verry Courteous good human gentleman, not morross nor high, neither a Courtier but a Plain Country Gentleman, [who] means well for the Countrys Interest & his Masters honour." When the governor journeyed to Albany late in May 1691, he bestowed a great honor on Livingston by accepting his hospitality. Only one thing caused the Albany merchant misgivings—he had "not a Cup of Stale Beer for his Excellency" because the brewer had failed to fill his order. But the governor apparently forgave this oversight, for he was so thoroughly pleased with Livingston that he confirmed him in his local Albany offices, recommended him to the Lords of Trade in the Dongan matter and conferred the "Commissaries Place" on him. Since Sloughter gave "better assurance of payment than Colonel Dongan did," Livingston gratefully accepted this office.[2]

The commissary was responsible for victualing all royal troops stationed in the colony. The soldiers were paid, fed, and clothed by the British Treasury on the basis of muster rolls, and whenever the prospects of prompt repayment seemed good, the office of commissary was eagerly sought. But even the normal delays between expenditures in New York and repayment from London made it necessary that the post be given to a local merchant who could advance his own funds. It was a risky business, for no one could foretell the length of the delay.

Whitehall authorized the commissary to spend 5 pence a day per man, and this amount was occasionally supplemented by the Assembly. The difference between this allowance and the actual cost was part of the victualer's profit. It was obvious, of course, that the profit was, to use a later governor's phrase, "pinch'd out of the poor soldiers bellies." British Redcoats were undoubtedly the most abused soldiers in the New World, but the fault lay not so much with the victualers as with the system that made them necessary.[3]

---

228. Gertrude Ann Jacobson, *William Blathwayt: A Late Seventeenth Century English Administrator* (New Haven, 1932), 122-23, 304, gives a radically different view, placing the emphasis on English reactions to New York developments.

2. Livingston to Winthrop, Apr. 23, June 3, 1691, Winthrop Papers, XIV, 156, 157, Mass. Hist. Soc.

3. New York was the only continental colony in which British troops were stationed continuously throughout its history under the British flag. Stanley M.

Since Livingston was charged with victualing troops in both New York City and Albany, he included Stephanus Van Cortlandt as a partner. According to the contract, made retroactive to March 25, 1691, they paid Sloughter 10 shillings a year per man, "his part of the Profitts of the Supply of the forces." [4] Today, this would be graft; then, it was the governor's legitimate perquisite.

Livingston had now inextricably involved himself in government finance. Defense expenditures were steadily mounting in this period of imperial warfare, but the ordinary revenue was inadequate to meet them, the Assembly's special taxes were very difficult to collect, and the government had not yet developed the technique of modern deficit financing. Instead of public borrowing on its own credit, the government relied upon the credit of a few private individuals, such as Livingston, paying exorbitant rates for the privilege. [5]

As long as Henry Sloughter remained governor and Livingston was in his favor, all went well. Livingston secured acknowledgments of the government's indebtedness to him through the issuance of warrants which were liens against funds either in the collector's hands or to be received by him. Normally, these were immediately redeemed in cash, but in a period of crisis they were far more easily secured than redeemed. A critical scarcity of bullion and coin in the colony complicated tax collections. Payment in kind was a means of circumventing the difficulty, and Livingston suggested that the government utilize it. He had borrowed grain from the local brewers to feed the Albany garrison, and he proposed that Ulster County, delinquent in its tax payments, be ordered to deliver to him 1,000 bushels of wheat and

Pargellis, "The Four Independent Companies of New York," *Essays in Colonial History Presented to Charles McLean Andrews by His Students* (New Haven, 1931), 97-99, 105-6; J. W. Fortescue, *A History of the British Army* (13 vols., London, 1910-30), I, 320; Bellomont to Lords of Trade, Oct. 17, 1700, O'Callaghan, ed., *N. Y. Col. Docs.*, IV, 720.

4. Van Cortlandt's and Livingston's deposition, May 26, 1691, PRO, CO 5: 1042, no. 7i (Lib. Cong. transcripts); Livingston to Winthrop, June 3, 1691, Winthrop Papers, XIV, 157, Mass. Hist. Soc.

5. The "revenue" consisted of regular fund-raising devices such as import and export duties, liquor excise, quitrents, fines, etc. The "taxes" were special levies upon property and were used to meet deficits. "This was very regularly the condition during the war." Osgood, *Colonies in the Eighteenth Century*, I, 240-41. On credit arrangements, see Sloughter's order on Livingston, June 11, 1691, N. Y. Col. Mss., XXXVII, 163b, N. Y. State Lib.; "Accompt of Money Disbursed by Robert Livingston," Aug. 12, 1691, Livingston-Redmond Mss.

300 of peas in lieu of cash. With this, he could repay the brewers and provide for the troops' future needs.[6]

Livingston found such expedients useful as long as King William's War continued. They became essential after the sudden death of Governor Sloughter on July 23, 1691. Without a lieutenant governor, there was a serious problem regarding Sloughter's successor. Under normal circumstances, the Council, acting under the presidency of its senior member, should have assumed the executive functions. But Dudley, the senior councilor, was absent, and he was viewed with disfavor by the dominant anti-Leislerian elements. Therefore, three days after Sloughter's death, the Council resolved to confer full executive power upon a commander-in-chief, naming Richard Ingoldesby to the post.

Ingoldesby's appointment was a gross violation of the recently enacted statute for quieting disorders, which recognized that the granting of executive authority over the colony was an irrevocable royal prerogative. The Council action was more manifestly treasonable than Leisler's earlier assumption of the lieutenant governorship, for Leisler had violated no law while the Council certainly did so.[7] But the councilors were not bothered by such a consideration: Ingoldesby was very useful as a symbol around which most of the Tory faction could rally. Its leaders felt certain that "had they not perswaded the Major to take possession of the ffort they had been altogether by the Ears." No one member was willing to acquiesce in another's elevation to the chief executive's office, but all were able to agree on a compromise. However, the real power was wielded by Graham, attorney general and Assembly speaker. He was, according to Randolph, "in Effect Governor Councill and Assembly too"; though Ingoldesby strutted, the words he spoke were Graham's.[8]

Livingston must have been saddened by Sloughter's death, but Ingoldesby's appointment caused him no anxiety. When he presented his accounts for audit in August, the highly favorable report issued by the Council committee—Bayard, Graham, and Minviele—was, for all practical purposes, a reaffirmation of his close political bonds with the

6. Livingston's petition, c. June 1691, N. Y. Col. Mss., XXXVII, 158, N. Y. State Lib.
7. Osgood, *Colonies in the Eighteenth Century*, I, 230. Capt. Hicks of H.M.S. *Archangel* refused to recognize Ingoldesby's authority. "Cal. of Council Minutes," N. Y. State Lib., *Bulletin 58*, 66.
8. Randolph to Blathwayt, Aug. 16, 1692, Blathwayt Papers, II, Col. Wmsbg.

Tories. He received warrants for more than £350 for miscellaneous expenses, and his and Van Cortlandt's victualing account, not due for another three weeks, was approved in advance for £689.[9]

Livingston relied on Van Cortlandt for the difficult and sometimes impossible task of redeeming the warrants. In one instance, when Livingston needed ready cash, Van Cortlandt obtained £110 in coin by giving £119, presumably in warrants on the colony. Despite such difficulties, Livingston continued to use his own credit for the government; by October, he had incurred a debt of £312 with one Schenectady merchant alone.[10]

Livingston found himself involved more heavily in the government's support in October 1691 by the need to strengthen the Albany garrison. One hundred and fifty militiamen were called to active duty, and the victualing profits attracted the attention of three Albany merchants—Kiliaen Van Rensselaer, Levinus Van Schaick, and Dirk Wessels—who asked for the contract. Ingoldesby and the councilors were amenable, but they were unable to offer a substantial cash advance with which to begin, and the merchants withdrew. Van Cortlandt notified Livingston that "it was quickly said then that we have to do it, which will be very difficult for us since we have no provisions and have not yet received a stuiver" from London for the royal troops' subsistence.

Indeed, discouraging reports had been received from London. Sloughter had appointed a Dr. Cox, presumably Dr. Daniel Coxe, a proprietor of West Jersey, as his agent in London to receive and transmit payments from the British Treasury. In October 1691, Van Cortlandt heard a rumor that "Dr. Cox absents himself and it was being said that he has been broken." He was uncertain of its authenticity, but "if it is true, we cannot expect any cargo from the Court and will have to do without our money even longer."

Though little could be done about affairs in London, something had to be done in New York. The archaic system of farming out tax collections had made them a mockery. Collector Chidley Brooke was ostensibly responsible for supervising the local collectors, but Van

9. N. Y. Council Minutes, Aug. 27, Sept. 3, 1691, VI, 49, 50, N. Y. State Lib.

10. The warrants therefore sold at an 8 percent discount. Van Cortlandt to Livingston, Oct. 5, 1691 (Dutch), Livingston-Redmond Mss.; Acct. Bk. of [Johannes Glen (?)], 1682-95, 15 (Dutch), N.-Y. Hist. Soc.

Cortlandt found that if he wished to redeem his warrants, he had to do the collecting himself. He had little success and warned Ingoldesby and the Council that "if they do not see to it that money comes in, we cannot provide for the garrison." [11]

By mid-November, Van Cortlandt was desperate: "I never in my life had so much trouble to get money together as these days." He had gone to Staten Island to prod the local collectors, but "did not get anywhere." As a result, he was again forced to purchase coin at an 8 percent loss in order to secure supplies for the troops and cash for Livingston. Nor was Livingston idle. Ingoldesby and the councilors soon felt the pressure he exerted for relief. In December, he secured a certificate from Albany's civil and military officials which urged that the debt to him for supplying the garrison be repaid out of the tax receipts. Collector Brooke promptly authorized Livingston to receive certain revenues from Albany and Ulster Counties in repayment of some disbursements, but the amounts involved were relatively small. [12]

Lacking financial support from London for victualing, Van Cortlandt decided to present his case to William Blathwayt. The victualers, he explained, had been assured of reimbursement and "Encouraged againe to provide provisions for the two [royal] companies ... when others would not undertake it ... upon promise it should be paid to one Dr. Cox who was to send over Effects [i.e., merchandise] for the payment of said Companies. But since wee Understand that said Dr. Cox hath absented him selfe and agreed with his Creditors for his Debts, which hath soe much Discouraged the people here that hardly any person will give Creditt for the Victualling and Cloating off said Soldiers." For the colony's safety, as well as the victualers' relief, Van Cortlandt begged Blathwayt to intercede. [13]

The usual transatlantic delays meant that several months would pass before Blathwayt could act, but Livingston and his partner needed

11. Van Cortlandt to Livingston, Oct. 5, 28, 1691 (Dutch), Livingston-Redmond Mss.; Van Cortlandt to Blathwayt, Jan. 7, 1691/2, Blathwayt Papers, II, Col. Wmsbg.
12. Van Cortlandt to Livingston, Oct. 5, 28, Nov. 15, 1691 (Dutch), Livingston-Redmond Mss.; Albany's officials to Ingoldesby, Dec. 30, 1691, O'Callaghan, ed., *N. Y. Col. Docs.*, III, 816. In two years, Livingston received £309. "Account of Money Receivd ... of Ulster, January 1692-March 1694," "An Account of Money Receivd at Albany anno 1692 & anno 1693," Livingston-Redmond Mss.
13. Van Cortlandt to Blathwayt, Jan. 7, 1691/2, Blathwayt Papers, IX, Col. Wmsbg.

immediate action. David Jamison, clerk of the Council, was doing his best to secure compliance with the tax laws, writing each county three times. When these efforts failed, Livingston finally went to New York City and presented his accounts for audit on March 17. Six weeks later, he won an order for "payments to the gentlemen who advanced money for the troops at Albany."[14]

While Livingston was absent from home, his wife distributed provisions to the troops and Iroquois. Alida was very worried about the situation on the Albany frontier. "Families leave here with every sloop," she reported; "the enemy will find an open door as the places above have been deserted." Economic conditions were so bad in Albany that she suggested to her husband, "if you intend to stay there [i.e., New York City], then look for a good employ also, for here is nothing to do."[15]

The Council soon found a "good employ" for Livingston. When two hundred militiamen were ordered to reinforce Albany, he was asked to become their victualer. He promptly rejected the offer, complaining that "he had Expended his whole Estate" and "Could not see which way he can in a Short time be reimbursed." The Council persisted, and its "earnest request" and a pledge of funds finally swayed him. The councilors agreed to use their personal credit to secure £300 at 10 percent interest as his advance.[16]

Livingston returned to Albany with the expedition and presumably spent the next few months in supplying the garrison. Once again, however, the government's inability to provide financial support prompted him to seek aid. He wrote to James Graham, who replied: "You must be your own freind, & every body will oblidge you for it is money makes the man." Of more importance was Graham's news that "Colonel Dongan is at Last gone for England." He warned Livingston, "you will now doe well to use your Interest at home that no money should be paid [to Dongan] untill he gives Security to pay the debts here." Following this suggestion, Livingston sent his London

---

14. Jamison to Livingston, Feb. 28, 1691/2, Livingston-Redmond Mss.; N. Y. Council Minutes, Mar. 17, 1691/2, VI, 76, N. Y. State Lib.; N. Y. Council Minutes, Apr. 27, 1692, *Cal. State Papers, Col.*, XIII, no. 2206.

15. Alida Livingston to Robert Livingston, Apr. 7, 1692 (Dutch), Livingston-Redmond Mss.

16. N. Y. Council Minutes, May 7, 12-14, 1692, VI, 92, 94-97, N. Y. State Lib.

correspondent a petition to the Treasury Lords and a power of attorney.[17]

Livingston also turned to Councilor Nicholas Bayard for assistance in collecting for his victualing services, but the official replied that when the accounts were given to the Council, "there was so much to be done that it was referred to the next Council day." These delays continued, and the only hope that Bayard could offer was that there had been a slight improvement in tax receipts because of the imprisonment of several delinquent collectors. "It is unreasonable," he added, "that you should incur any loss for your trouble." [18]

Van Cortlandt and Graham, in the meantime, urged Ingoldesby to take immediate action. On August 19, the former advised Livingston to go to New York City "so you may get the first order and receive the first money that comes in." The trip was unnecessary: Livingston learned three days later that his accounts had been passed, and Van Cortlandt promised to send the money to Albany as soon as possible.[19]

More effective support for the victualers was expected as the result of the appearance of Edward Randolph in New York City on August 12. Randolph, a dedicated fanatic, was on one of his perennial tours of inspection for Blathwayt, and he prepared a report for his superior which was a valuable commentary on New York's politics and Livingston's relationship with the Tories. The leading political figures in the colony, Randolph declared, fell into one of three categories: they were either "Insiped Wretches unworthy of their Majesties favour," men undeserving of positions of authority because they had no estates in the colony, or men whose loyalty to the Crown was exceeded only by his own. In the first category, he placed John Lawrence and Thomas Johnson; in the second, Joseph Dudley, William Pinhorne, and Richard Townley—all members of the Council. Among those who "heartyly espoused their Majestys Interest," Randolph listed Councilors Van Cortlandt, Bayard, Minviele, and Philipse, and Attorney General Graham. As new councilors he suggested Peter Schuyler, Charles Lodwick, Lewis Morris, and Robert Livingston, "a man of a Great Estate at Albany and well known in all Matters of this Gov-

17. Graham to Livingston, July 2, 1692, Harwood to Livingston, Apr. 25, 1692, Livingston-Redmond Mss.

18. Bayard to Livingston, July 8, 1692 (Dutch), *ibid.*

19. Van Cortlandt to Livingston, Aug. 10, 1692, with postscripts of Aug. 19, 21, 22 (Dutch), *ibid.*

ernment." However, he cautioned that Dongan "will be of another opinion because he [i.e., Livingston] would not be bubled by him." [20]

Randolph's praise confirmed the closeness of Livingston's alliance with the New York Tories. According to Graham, Randolph had written in Livingston's "favor in Dongan's matter, & also to recommend you to be one of the Councill, which he doubts not but he shall obtaine. I have seen all the Letters wherein the Services you have done . . . are not forgott." Because a new governor was daily expected, Livingston was urged "to hasten down upon your own private Concerns." On August 25, Livingston was in New York City where he received from Jacob Harwood several commercial documents, some merchandise, and two letters. Harwood's missives contained comments on two passengers who arrived on that same ship—Sir Edmund Andros, governor-designate of Virginia, and Benjamin Fletcher, governor-designate of New York.[21]

Sir Edmund, who planned to spend the summer in New York, was an old friend of both Livingston and Harwood, but Fletcher was an unknown element. The London merchant felt certain, however, that Sir Edmund, "being your very good ffriend," would influence Fletcher "to Serve your Interest to the utmost of his Power." But Harwood added a word of caution: do not "trust the Publique too ffar; ffor People cant get what they Creditt ffor here, & I am afraid worse with you."

Livingston must have been pleased with his prospects. A successful conclusion to the Dongan affair seemed imminent, and with Sir Edmund's help, the new governor was quickly convinced of the urgency of the victualers' situation and the need to straighten out the colony's finances. Fletcher called a new Assembly, issued warrants for the victualers of the militia, and ordered an audit of Livingston's accounts. By October 10, warrants for £368 were issued for the Albany militia's subsistence.[22]

20. Randolph to Blathwayt, Aug. 16, 1692, Blathwayt Papers, II, Col. Wmsbg.
21. Graham to Livingston, Aug. 23, 1692, Livingston's acct. of goods shipped to Harwood, Nov. 8, 1690, Invoice of goods shipped by Harwood, Apr. 12, 1692, Meriwether to Livingston, Mar. 18, 1691/2, Livingston-Redmond Mss.; Andros to Blathwayt, Sept. 6, 1692, Blathwayt Papers, IV, Col. Wmsbg.
22. Harwood to Livingston, Apr. 23, 25, 1692, Livingston-Redmond Mss.; Fletcher to Blathwayt, Sept. 10, 1692, O'Callaghan, ed., N. Y. Col. Docs., III, 846; N. Y. Council Minutes, Sept. 12, 1692, Cal. State Papers, Col., XIII, no. 2464; N. Y. Council Minutes, Oct. 10, 1692, VI, 133, N. Y. State Lib.; Receipts to Livingston from Bickford and Schuyler, Oct. 7, 1692, N. Y. Col. Mss., XXXVIII, 204a, 204b, ibid.

Livingston pressed his advantage by importuning the governor for further payments. Fletcher sent him £105 in warrants together with a caustic note pointing out that he had given him first consideration in money matters and that he needed "Noe remembrancer in Things that are Just and can bee effected." The governor's last phrase—"can bee effected"—was the crux of his relationship with the victualer. All too often, Livingston desired settlements that were just, but impossible. At this time, he was annoyed because the councilors who had audited his claims had been unwilling to consider those which antedated Governor Sloughter's arrival. Furthermore, they rejected his charge of a 5 percent commission on his expenditures for Ingoldesby's recent Iroquois conference, and they refused to substitute an annual salary of £50 for the 10 percent commission he received as sub-collector of the excise at Albany. He urged Fletcher to use his influence to have these decisions reconsidered.[23]

In response to Livingston's request, a Council committee composed of Van Cortlandt, Bayard, and Brooke, ruled on November 3 that he should receive £46 due him from Andros' administration out of the excise arrears; that his claim for a 5 percent commission should be rejected because he was a public official and "Should do that Service gratis"; and that he should get his annual salary of £50 as sub-collector beginning March 28, 1691. Within a week, these claims were settled by warrants for £202.[24]

Graham reported that Livingston's affairs had been handled with "suitable dispatch," but he bitterly grumbled that he met with only "bantering promises" when he applied for his own salaries.[25] This, too, was Livingston's problem. The expenses of King William's War, which bore most heavily on New York, were depleting the govern-

23. Fletcher to Livingston, Oct. 26, 1692, Livingston-Redmond Mss.; Livingston's petition to Fletcher, Nov. 1, 1692, N. Y. Col. Mss., XXXVIII, 217, N. Y. State Lib.
24. N. Y. Council Minutes, Nov. 3, 7, 11, 1692, VI, 142, 143, 145, N. Y. State Lib.; Report of Van Cortlandt, Bayard, and Brooke, Nov. 3, 1692, N. Y. Col. Mss., XXXVIII, 217, ibid. Another petition which Livingston had signed on behalf of the officers and soldiers employed in the 1687 expedition for their arrears of pay and subsistence was referred to the Assembly for its consideration. Petition of Willett, Tuder, Jackson, Lockhart, and Livingston, Nov. 2, 1692, N. Y. Council Minutes, Nov. 7, 1692, ibid., 221a, 221b.
25. Graham to Livingston, Nov. 25, 1692, Livingston-Redmond Mss. Randolph reported that Graham "is reduced to great necessityes his place of Atturney General being rather a Charg then profitt." He suggested that the posts of chancellor and receiver-general in Maryland might be more attractive to Graham. Randolph to Blathwayt, July 14, 1693, Blathwayt Papers, II, Col. Wmsbg.

ment's coffers faster than they could be refilled. An audit of defense expenditures since Sloughter's arrival was ordered in January 1692/3; it showed that in less than two years, more than £10,800 had been spent from the ordinary revenue and special taxes. This, of course, did not include borrowed money which had not yet been repaid.[26] As a result, warrants became unsecured promises to pay, with no one able to forecast when the collector could redeem them. Fletcher complained that he could borrow money, but only at 10 percent interest, and he could see "no prospect of paying the principal." The situation became so desperate that three councilors finally offered to supply the militia "out of their private estate, upon the security of the garrison." [27]

No matter how the money was obtained, the troops had to be maintained on the frontier; otherwise, a fate worse than bankruptcy awaited the colony. Possibly as a means of encouraging Livingston's continuance as victualer, the Council ordered £818 in warrants issued to him on April 8 for previous troop expenditures from October 1, 1692, to May 1, 1693. Since a large item in the victualer's account was for bread, the counties of Ulster and Dutchess were ordered to pay their taxes to him in wheat. A few days later, he received another £258 in warrants.[28]

But there was a vast difference between warrants and cash-in-hand which disturbed Livingston, as he informed Fletcher, pointedly telling him that he had spent more than £2,140 for frontier defense. With "the Coffers of the Treasury being Empty," he had not been repaid, a particularly distressing fact because £835 of his expenditures represented goods obtained on credit from local merchants "who press him now very hard for their money." Livingston insisted that his creditors had to be satisfied. Fletcher passed the problem on to the Council, which resolved that "the frontier is the first thing to be regarded" and all money must be devoted to that. If Livingston insisted upon repay-

26. New York's *total* revenue from all sources took a precipitous drop: 1687–£5,162; 1692–£3,371; 1693–£2,972; 1694–£4,333; and 1695–£3,601. Bellomont to Treasury Lords, May 25, 1698, *Cal. State Papers, Col.,* XVI, nos. 50 li, 50 lii. See also N. Y. Council Minutes, Jan. 31, 1692/3, *ibid.,* XIV, no. 44; "An Account of the Charge of Albany," c. Feb. 1692/3, N. Y. Col. Mss., XXXVIII, 192, N. Y. State Lib.

27. Fletcher to Blathwayt, Mar. 8, 1692/3, and N. Y. Council Minutes, Feb. 17, 1692/3, *Cal. State Papers, Col.,* XIV, nos. 179, 101.

28. N. Y. Council Minutes, Apr. 8, 13, 1693, VI, 186, 189, N. Y. State Lib.

ment, he was welcome to try collecting delinquent taxes on Long Island.[29]

Despite the irregularity of this proposition—tax collecting was Brooke's responsibility—Livingston accepted the challenge after outlining the situation's seriousness. On Long Island, he impressed local officials with the urgency of collecting back taxes and secured more than £1,000 of the £1,711 owed by Kings, Queens, and Suffolk counties. When he returned to New York City, the Council had no alternative but to allot most of that money to him.[30]

At the suggestion of Peter Schuyler, Livingston returned to New York City in July to give the governor information about an impending French attack on the Iroquois. His lengthy memorandum concentrated on the "Secret Intregues" of the Jesuits and the need to destroy their influence among the Five Nations.[31] During the next few months, while Livingston was seemingly preoccupied with Albany's defenses, the governor made some headway in clearing the Crown's indebtedness to the Livingston-Van Cortlandt partnership for victualing the royal troops. For the expenditures in that service from March 1691 to September 1693, Van Cortlandt reported, Fletcher gave complete satisfaction, but for their other disbursements, particularly those made during the Dominion, "nothing is paid." A special tax of £1,513 had been levied for that purpose, but the "Extraordinary Condition of the Government required that said Money should be Imployed to pay the Charges of his Excellency three Voyages to Albany and the Jorney to Philadelphia." Livingston's disappointment must have been assuaged somewhat by word that the militia's victualing account—£817 for the period to November 1, 1693—had been passed by the Council.[32]

A month later, even better news arrived: in London, Jacob Har-

29. Livingston to Fletcher, Apr. 14, 1693 (draft), Livingston-Redmond Mss.; N. Y. Council Minutes, Apr. 14, 1693, *Cal. State Papers, Col.*, XIV, no. 274.
30. Livingston to Council, Apr. 26, May 14, 1693, and Livingston's accts. of "moneys received" and "arrears of taxes due," May 27, 1693, N. Y. Col. Mss., XXXIX, 48, 52, 61, 62, N. Y. State Lib. He received a warrant for £884. N. Y. Council Minutes, May 27, June 8, 1693, VI, 201, 207, *ibid.*
31. Schuyler to Fletcher, July 25, 1693, O'Callaghan, ed., *N. Y. Col. Docs.*, IV, 47; Leder, ed., *Livingston Indian Records*, 170-72.
32. Albany Common Council Minutes, Sept. 12, 1693, Munsell, ed., *Annals of Albany*, II, 249; Livingston's petition, Sept. 17, 1693, N. Y. Col. Mss., XXXIX, 95, N. Y. State Lib.; Van Cortlandt to Blathwayt, Sept. 30, Oct. 30, 1693, Blathwayt Papers, IX, Col. Wmsbg.; N. Y. Council Minutes, Dec. 14, 1693, VII, 37, N. Y. State Lib.

wood had finally collected Livingston's money from Dongan. He had waited until Dongan returned to London in the summer of 1692, and then searched for him in order to discuss some concerted action to clear the accounts before the Treasury Lords. Dongan, however, was not to be found. Harwood then turned to Povey in accordance with Livingston's instructions, but Povey proved to be as difficult to deal with as Dongan was elusive. When pressed by Harwood, Povey declared that Dongan "was A great man, . . . & if I [Harwood] went to meddle with him the Court would protect him."

Unable to obtain satisfaction from either Dongan or Povey, Harwood entered a caveat and seconded it with a petition to the Lords of the Treasury. But, he complained, "Dongan offered Povey £300: & Blathwate £1,000: to get his accountts passed, & they influenced all the under Clerkes" so that the petition was pigeon-holed for five weeks. Finally, Harwood turned to a friend who engaged the Chancellor of the Exchequer's interest. Through him, Harwood claimed, the petition was finally brought forth and read. Blathwayt then suggested that there was no need to pay Harwood as Livingston's agent because Dongan had already given Livingston security in the form of a mortgage on property in New York. Nevertheless, the Treasury Lords referred the petition to Blathwayt for a full and formal report.

Things then began to move quickly. According to Harwood, the petition's referral to Blathwayt "brought Dongan to me & So nettled Blathwayt & Povey when they See I should have the money, & they not finger it, that I was forced to run up to Westminster four days in the week three times a day, & when Dongan & I had agreed was at last forced to trouble Mr. Chancellour, to Call for Blathwayt Report, he would not give it in of himself." Blathwayt reluctantly recommended payment but proposed that the debt should be discounted 30 percent in order to equate the New York pound with the pound sterling, and that tallies should be issued against the royal customs for the sum of £1,670 sterling with 6 percent interest until they were redeemed. Harwood had gotten Livingston his money, but he also created a rift between Livingston and the Blathwayt-Povey-Randolph faction that was to develop into full-blown enmity.[33]

33. Harwood to Livingston, Aug. 22, 1693, Livingston-Redmond Mss. According to official records, Blathwayt received the petition on Feb. 11, 1692/3. Sixteen days later he submitted his report, noting that Dongan's "accounts are not sufficiently

In New York, however, Livingston continued on good terms with Fletcher. A cessation in Anglo-French hostilities had encouraged the Assembly to assert its rights by labeling the grants that it made a "voluntary gift" of the people. By mimicking the British House of Commons, the Assembly hoped to elevate itself to a co-equal, if not a dominant, branch of government. These tactics were anathema to Fletcher and the Tories, and Livingston sympathized with the governor. "I blush to think," he exclaimed, "how base people are growne ... never were people more generous than they were to a papist Governor [i.e., Dongan] who never did nor designed them any good, & now when the Heavens has blest us with a Governor of our owne religeon, we know not what pretence to make to shuffel it off." [34]

Livingston's unusually effusive comments were not motivated by any ulterior design, for he had already commented to Harwood that he "thought of laying aside publique matters; and so follow trade wholly." The London merchant was delighted, and Livingston even suggested that they join in building several vessels for the transatlantic and coastal trades. Harwood was noncommittal, but Livingston's brother-in-law, Peter Schuyler, was willing to participate in such a proposal. They entered a joint venture to construct a brigantine and two sloops at Albany; the keels were laid in November 1693, and Livingston supervised much of their construction and outfitting until the vessels were completed in October 1694 at a cost of £501. [35]

---

vouched," and that it was customary to refer such cases back to the colony of origin. However, since Dongan's mortgage would soon fall due, and since Livingston's portion had been certified by Van Cortlandt, Blathwayt's deputy, "it will be a present relief ... if his Majesty shall order payment ... to said Livingston." The New Yorker was to deliver up the mortgage and agree to "stand obliged" with Dongan if any discrepancy were later found. Harwood gave Dongan a £500 indenture to make good any discrepancy and to get him his mortgage. Treasury Lords to Blathwayt, Feb. 11, 1692/3, Blathwayt's report, Feb. 27, 1692/3, Shaw, ed., *Cal. Treasury Books*, X, 46, IX, 1514; Indenture between Harwood & Dongan, May 24, 1693, Harwood's bond to Dongan, 1693, Livingston-Redmond Mss.

34. Livingston to Fletcher, Feb. 14, 1693, O'Callaghan, ed., *N. Y. Col. Docs.*, IV, 97-98.

35. Harwood to Livingston, Mar. 30, 1694, "An Account of Money Disbursed by Robert Livingston for the Materialls and Workmanship of three New Vessels," Nov. 20, 1693-Oct. 12, 1694, Campbell to Livingston, Apr. 9, 1694, Livingston-Redmond Mss. This was not Livingston's first venture into shipbuilding. In 1690, he was Van Cortlandt's partner in the *Margriet* carrying rice and slaves on her voyage to Madagascar, Barbados, and Virginia. Livingston's share of the expenses was 4,591 florins; his net profit was 1,745 florins. "*Rek van Ship de Margriet van Madakasker naer Barbados & nae Virginia,*" 1690, *ibid.* Livingston also had a one-fourth interest in the brigantine *Orange.* See below, pp. 93-94.

Factors beyond Livingston's control thwarted his desire to retire from public service. He had subsisted the four militia companies in Albany to May 1, 1694, and, probably as the only way to recover his money, was authorized on May 5 to go to Westchester County to "hasten the respective Collectors . . . in with the arrears." On May 14, the governor announced that Livingston had agreed to continue as victualer. He was to receive 6d a day for each soldier from May 1 to November 1, 1694, and 5d from the latter date to May 1, 1695. If he wished to "leave off," he promised to give three months' notice.[36]

Livingston's return to public affairs may have resulted from Fletcher's use of a polite form of blackmail on him. The government was still heavily in debt—as of February 1693/4, in the amount of £7,890 —and a large portion of that money was owed to Livingston. On the day after the new victualing agreement was announced, Livingston received warrants for nearly £2,300, most of it for militia expenditures to May 1, 1694. Also, the government gave him more adequate support than before—all public money in Collector Brooke's hands on May 21 was to be turned over to Livingston, and the sub-collector of New York City was to pay all tax arrears to him.[37]

This new victualing engagement proved to be short-lived; Livingston gave notice to "leave off" by September 1. This second resolution to quit public affairs was prompted by his decision to go to England. There were several problems which could only be settled in the seat of empire and by the fall of 1694, he had made up his mind to undertake the voyage. Although Livingston had received warrants for repayment of his money, the perennial difficulty in redeeming them remained unchanged. As long as King William's War continued, there was little prospect of getting the more than £4,200 he claimed unless the royal treasury footed the bill or he received orders forcing the New York authorities to give his claims priority.[38]

36. Receipts of Schuyler's, Phipps', Matthews', and Ingoldesby's militia companies, May 1, 1694, Brooke to Livingston, May 5, 1694, ibid.; N. Y. Council Minutes, May 14, 1694, VII, 66, N. Y. State Lib.

37. List of govt. debts., Feb. 9, 1693/4, N. Y. Col. Mss., XXXIX, 135, N. Y. State Lib.; N. Y. Council Minutes, May 15, 1694, VII, 67, ibid.; N. Y. Council Minutes, May 21, 1694, Cal. State Papers, Col., XIV, no. 1057; Brooke to N. Y. C. sub-collector, May 23, 1694, Livingston-Redmond Mss.

38. N. Y. Council Minutes, Sept. 1, 21, 29, 1694, VII, 90, 95, 97, N. Y. State Lib.; Statement of Livingston's case, Sept. 19, 1695, O'Callaghan, ed., N. Y. Col. Docs., IV, 132-37.

Harwood's activities in securing tallies from the royal treasury also necessitated Livingston's presence in London. Harwood had stirred up antagonism against Livingston which could only be removed through personal meetings with Blathwayt and Povey. Equally important was the question of what had happened to the tallies. In August 1693, Harwood had blamed England's economic depression for the fact that "no man will advance any money upon talleys at present," but he promised to hold them until they could be sold at a "very easy discompt if not for nothing." Seven months later, they were still unsold; as late as December 1694, he was still promising a final settlement. This procrastination must have made Livingston suspicious, for the tallies were liens on the royal customs duties and bore 6 percent interest until redeemed. Three thousand miles from England, they seemed like gilt-edged securities.[39]

Livingston was also indirectly concerned in an attempt to secure a parliamentary reversal of the convictions of the leading Leislerians for treason and murder. Although this, by itself, would not have necessitated his being in London, it was, in view of his own role in the Rebellion and Milborne's dying words, an added reason for going. By October 11, he had begun his preparations for the perilous mid-winter Atlantic crossing. He gave his nephew and namesake detailed instructions for collecting the excise at Albany, renewed his last will and testament, and drew up a power of attorney for his wife "dureing his absence being now bounde (if God will) for England." Within a week he left for New York City.[40]

Once in the colony's capital, Livingston presented a memorial to the governor requesting a complete audit of all his accounts. He then

---

39. Harwood to Livingston, Aug. 22, 1693, Mar. 30, Dec. 13, 1694, Livingston-Redmond Mss.; Harvey E. Fisk, *English Public Finance From the Revolution of 1689* (N.Y., 1920), 96-97. Harwood's delay in converting the tallies to cash was justified by Britain's chaotic public finance. "All payments were delayed ... some of the nation's earlier creditors were not paid at all." Andrews, *Colonial Period*, IV, 278-79.

40. Jacob Leisler, Jr., and Abraham Gouverneur to House of Lords, c. Mar. 1694/5, Leo F. Stock, ed., *Proceedings and Debates of the British Parliament respecting North America* (4 vols., Wash., D. C., 1924-37), II, 113-15; Instructions appended to "Account of the Excyse at Albany," Mar. 25-Oct. 11, 1694, Livingston-Redmond Mss. Robert Livingston, Jr., was usually referred to as "the nephew" and was the son of James Livingston. He was sent to N. Y. in Aug. 1687 by Harwood. Harwood to Livingston, Aug. 12, 1687, *ibid*. See also Livingston's will, Mar. 3, 1689/90, confirmed Oct. 12, 1694, and letter of attorney to Alida Livingston, Oct. 12, 1694, *ibid.*; Ingoldesby to Fletcher, Oct. 18, 1694, O'Callaghan, ed., *N. Y. Col. Docs.*, IV, 114.

prepared a lengthy memorandum of things to do "before I goe off." In addition to the payment of local debts, he had to prepare his victualing accounts with Van Cortlandt, arrange the shipment of furs to London on the *Daniel,* and forward various goods to Albany. He also completed the last-minute arrangements for the sailing of his two new sloops, one to Newfoundland and the other, the *Mary,* to Roanoke. Finally, he sought letters of recommendation from several merchants and officials.[41]

Three weeks later, the methodical Livingston drew up a second memorandum. This time, the unfinished tasks dealt with commercial matters—preparing invoices, building a dock at his New York City home (previously bought from William Kidd), arranging the maiden voyage of the brigantine *Robert,* which he and Schuyler owned, and buying supplies for his own voyage.[42]

Both Governor Fletcher and Collector Brooke considered Livingston's imminent departure newsworthy. Each not only warned Blathwayt to expect him, but cautioned that he was involved in a most important admiralty case—the seizure of the brigantine *Orange* for illegal trading with the French. The governor believed that this case was "the first of that nature," and that the verdict would be appealed to London. "One Mr. Leviston who will attend youe," he notified Blathwayt, "is an owner of this Vessell and Indefattigable solicitor." [43] The governor, of course, knew whereof he spoke.

But Fletcher's comments were mild in comparison with Chidley Brooke's. Livingston "will be very sollicitous against me in this affair," he predicted, "he having a Considerable part in the Brigantine as owner &c & all the rest of the owners his relations." Warming up to his subject, the collector went on to charge that Livingston was "one that wants not craft or Assiduity to carry on his designes, & put a fair Gloss upon the foulest Actions where his Intrest is Concern'd." The *Orange*'s illegal trading, he continued, had made possible the French invasion of Jamaica during the previous summer.

41. N. Y. Council Minutes, Oct. 20, 1694, VII, 102, N. Y. State Lib.; "Memorandum of what I am to doe before I goe off the 21 Octob 1694," Livingston-Redmond Mss.
42. Livingston's memorandum, Nov. 14, 1694, Livingston-Redmond Mss. He had bought the house from William and Sarah Kidd in June 1693. Commissioners of Records, *Index of Conveyances Recorded in the Office of Register of the City and County of New York: Grantees* (20 vols., N.Y., 1857-64), vol. "L," 219.
43. Fletcher to Blathwayt, Nov. 19, 1694, Blathwayt Papers, VIII, Col. Wmsbg.

The *Orange*'s seizure was the second major rift between Livingston and the Tory faction. The brigantine was owned equally by Livingston, Peter Schuyler, Hendrick Van Rensselaer, and Cornelius Jacobs, the master. Having sailed for Jamaica in November 1693, Captain Jacobs intended to navigate the Windward Passage between Porto Rico and Hispaniola. However, a storm allegedly forced the ship into Port-de-Paix on Hispaniola's northwest coast. There, the French had boarded her and seized vessel and cargo as enemy property.

For some unexplained reason—Brooke charged collusion—the French governor had restored the ship and one-fourth of the cargo with the provision that the merchandise be traded for French goods. According to Brooke, the *Orange*'s outbound cargo was valued at £1,000. Thus, after the French seizure, only £250 of the cargo remained. Yet, when she returned to New York, she brought back over £1,500 worth of linen, salt, and bills of exchange. Even in those days, a 500 percent return on a shipment was extraordinary.[44]

In July 1694, Attorney General Graham had brought a criminal action for trading with the enemy against Captain Jacobs. Graham's close friendship with Livingston—along with that of the grand jury's foreman, William Kidd—may have been the reason why "no Evidence for the King could be had," and the jury dropped the charge. But the collector was not satisfied, and in October he had instituted a civil suit against the vessel under the Navigation Acts. Stephen Delancey, foreman of the petit jury, handed in a verdict for the Crown; William Nicolls, attorney for the defense, obtained an arrest of judgment; and the court agreed to hand down its decision in April 1695.[45]

Brooke's charges may have been perfectly correct. Although the Crown's evidence has since been destroyed, one document survives which casts some doubt on the collector's libel of the *Orange*. According to the captain's accounting of the voyage, the four owners made a net profit of £61, not £500 as the collector alleged. It is possible that this accounting was falsified to hide the illegal trading,

44. Brooke to Blathwayt, Nov. 24, 1694, PRO, CO 5: 1038, no. 94 (Lib. Cong. transcripts); Accts. of Brigantine *Orange*, 1694, and Deposition of Right & Eames, Apr. 26, 1694, Livingston-Redmond Mss.

45. Paul M. Hamlin and Charles E. Baker, eds., *Supreme Court of Judicature of the Province of New York, 1691-1704* (3 vols., N.Y., 1959), I, 163-64; "Minutes of the Supreme Court of Judicature, April 4, 1693, to April 1, 1701," N.-Y. Hist. Soc. *Collections*, 45 (1913), 59, 61-63, 65, 68, 73; Report of Customs Commissioners, Aug. 28, 1695, PRO, CO 5: 1039, no. 10 (Lib. Cong. transcripts).

but another serious rift had developed between Livingston and the Tories.[46]

Fletcher's and Brooke's hostility towards Livingston, however, was not shared by James Graham or Stephanus Van Cortlandt. Both still held Livingston in high esteem and gave him enthusiastic letters of introduction to Blathwayt. According to Graham, Livingston was "a gentleman that hath not only been Serviceable in that Station [i.e., Indian affairs] but Likewyse in the Support of the government haveing been Seldom Since the warr in Less disburse for their Majestys Service than £2,000." He even attempted to heal the breach caused by Harwood—"the misconduct of his Correspondent... I pray may not be Imputed to him Especially Since to my Knowledge his orders was not to move one Step in that matter but as directed by Mr. Povey." Though less effusive, Van Cortlandt's comments followed the same pattern.[47]

On December 4, Livingston received his clearance from David Jamison, clerk of the Council, certifying that "he hath published his intended voyage according to Law and that no person hath made any claims nor entered any protest." Having put his affairs in order, Livingston and his eldest son, John (baptized Johannes), boarded the *Charity* on December 9. On the following day, the ship headed its bow out into the Atlantic and commenced a most unlucky voyage.[48]

46. The evidence was destroyed in the N. Y. State Library fire of 1911. Accts. of Brigantine *Orange*, 1694, Livingston-Redmond Mss.
47. Graham to Blathwayt, Nov. 24, 1694, Van Cortlandt to Blathwayt, Dec. 3, 1694, Blathwayt Papers, X, IX, Col. Wmsbg.
48. Jamison's certificate of clearance, Dec. 4, 1694, and "Journall of our voyage to England in the Charity who Lost her Rudder and was drove ashore in Portugal," Livingston-Redmond Mss. Written partly in English and partly in Dutch, the latter sections of the journal were translated and the whole typed by Arnold J. F. Van Laer. His typescript will be used and cited as "Livingston Journal."

CHAPTER VI

Journey to the Seat of Empire

THE WIND WAS fair and the sea calm as the *Charity* left Sandy Hook on December 10, 1694. A routine crossing was expected by Robert and John Livingston, the six other passengers, and the captain and crew; but when only one day out the vessel ploughed into a powerful Atlantic storm which lasted intermittently for nearly three weeks. Both Livingston and his son became "quite sick," the water casks stored on deck "sprang leaks and went to pieces," and most of the sails were shredded by the gale-like blasts. The greatest disaster of all occurred on January 3 when the waves knocked off the *Charity*'s rudder.[1]

Without a rudder, the ship "drifted whither it pleased God." She had taken on so much water that her two pumps could "hardly keep the ship afloat," and when the storm finally abated, the cargo had shifted and the vessel was listing badly. To prevent her from capsizing, the main topmast was cut down, and the two guns on the larboard side were jettisoned. Water-logged and listing, without sails, rudder, or adequate supplies, the *Charity*'s future was grim indeed.

During the next five months, the passengers and crew faced four basic problems: navigating towards a landfall, husbanding their water,

1. Portions of this chapter have appeared in Lawrence H. Leder, "Robert Livingston's Voyage to England, 1695," *N. Y. Hist.*, 36 (1955), 16-38. The account of the voyage and the "grand tour" is based upon the Van Laer typescript of Livingston's Journal, Livingston-Redmond Mss.

stretching their food supply, and simply living with one another under great tension. Failure to resolve any one of those meant disaster for the twenty-five souls on board.

Their first thought was to head the stricken vessel for the West Indies by sailing a southeasterly course. Attempting to maneuver into the wind so as to utilize the few sails they had patched together, they tried several makeshift rudders—trailing two lengths of cable, dragging a cable with tackle attached, and using the fore-topmast with two planks spliced to it—but "all means that are employed to steer the ship are fruitless."

Their means of reckoning and their measurement of distance from land was extremely crude. Until February 7, they still hoped to reach the West Indies, but they were then 100 leagues from their goal, or so they thought, and drifting further away each day. Therefore, they decided to head the *Charity* eastward "in the hope that God may be so merciful as to let us reach the coast of France, or Ireland, or to get into the path of a ship."

Rationing their potable liquids was a life or death matter for the passengers and crew. On January 6, the supply was inspected, and they learned that there was little beer, "which was quite sour," and only 100 gallons of water. Upon rechecking five days later, their complacency, if any, was rudely shattered when they found their water supply was down to twenty gallons for twenty-five people.

Rain, which had first brought them misery, now became their salvation. All available barrels were placed on deck, and everyone was assigned a place where, with all imaginable utensils, he could catch rain water. Despite these efforts, the shortage finally drove the crew to drinking salt water and even bilge water. Death by thirst was only averted by taking advantage of occasional rains and by careful rationing.

A problem which nature's bounty did not resolve so readily, however, was that of making a five weeks' food supply last for five months. The captain and passengers had separate provisions from those of the crew. When the crew finally reached the end of its patience on May 2, the hidden stores of the captain, Livingston, and the mate were raided. Although Livingston lost a two-pound piece of smoked beef, he was almost as upset about losing the pillow case in which it had been secreted. The captain lost some oysters, ginger, and tamarinds, while the mate forfeited his five pots of marmalade.

These robberies, justified or not, illustrated another problem—living with one another under unnatural tensions. The task was not made easier, if Livingston may be believed, by the type of men in the crew. To him, the sailors were "an exceedingly godless lot of people," though he later noted that they "now begin to come diligently to prayer." They were also a careless lot, and Livingston condemned them for wasting scarce supplies. He also abhorred their profanity, for which they "will not be rebuked," and their uncivilized habits, such as eating raw bacon.

But Captain Lancaster Syms' control over his crew was strong enough to put down several mutinies. On March 4, "there was a conspiracy among the crew to attack the people in the cabin for the cider, but it was discovered. The arms were brought into the cabin. They deny it. Some time ago there was one Haman [i.e., James Hayman, a seaman], who also had a wicked design. He was tied up and confessed that the devil had such power over him that he intended to blow up the captain, so that they put the powder in the cabin." Three days later, there was another conspiracy to "murder the passengers and run away with the ship and cargo."

These difficulties had a profound effect upon Livingston. He became more deeply religious than ever before. After a month of aimless drifting in the mid-Atlantic, he made a "covenant with God not only to improve my former sinful ways, but to renounce them completely." Hearkening back to his father's greatest sermon text, he beseeched God "that He might take away my stony heart and grant me an heart of flesh." At first, it would seem that he tried to bargain with the Almighty: "If God delivers me...I promise upon my return to my family to give 100 pieces of eight to the church at Albany and, if we salvage any thing from this ship, to use all that I have therein for purposes of Christian charity and to satisfy those whom I may in any way have defrauded." But he soon realized that his fortune meant nothing, that he and his poorest shipmate were destined for the same fate or the same salvation— "O what would one not give now to be on land a humble servant; how much money would one not give now!"

Livingston's prayers and exhortations were finally answered on

April 25, when the mate sighted Cape Roca, Portugal. Though the aimless wanderings of the *Charity* had ended, the ship lay off a sandy beach awaiting a Portuguese tug to tow her in. When fresh supplies were brought on board on April 29, the passengers and crew had a sumptuous feast of dried fish, goat meat, bread, and wine.

On May 8, the battered ship was brought to rest before the fort in Pederneira harbor. A day later, Livingston and the other passengers thankfully debarked. He went to the governor's house, paid his respects, and received that official's promise of "all the assistance in his power." An offer to lodge at the home of Manuel d'Almeyde, "master carpenter of the King," was accepted by Livingston and his son.

This was the beginning of a new adventure for the Livingstons; few New Yorkers had ever made a "Grand Tour" of Portugal and Spain. Many strange sights greeted this Protestant voyager in Catholic lands, and had his shell of Calvinism not been so staunchly constructed, his views might have been mellowed somewhat by what he saw. Instead, his comments reveal a man torn between fascination for the strange and new, and repugnance for that which he had been taught since childhood to despise.

During his stay in Pederneira, Livingston went sightseeing, was entertained by the governor, wrote to his family and friends, and settled affairs with Captain Syms. He eagerly visited the local church, but shunned a Catholic religious procession. At the governor's home, he had an evening of "music on the harp and guitar and dancing by the girls in the Portuguese fashion," but was disappointed that his only refreshment was "a glass of wine and water."

Livingston collected whatever he could salvage of his goods and, with his son and Richard Lesley, another of the *Charity*'s passengers, set off in a small coastal vessel for Lisbon. After sailing for twenty-four hours, they landed at Cascaes, a town at the mouth of the Tejos River, and then went upstream to Lisbon. Livingston soon found "one R. Williams" who had a vessel bound for London, and arranged passage for himself and his son. However, the owner failed to wait as promised, and Livingston was forced to remain in Lisbon a little longer.

While in the Portuguese capital, he visited "the country seat of a great Lord, which was very pleasant, with all sorts of fruit, a vinyard, etc., and fine waterworks." His sightseeing finally included a Catholic religious procession; the streets, he reported, were "full of people and all the nobility in their coaches. Many holy wooden images were carried and then came what they call their sacrament." True to his Calvinist upbringing, he concluded that "it was no pleasure for me to see that the people are so blind."

When Livingston learned that a Frenchman had a ship bound for England, he sought passage on it. After extensive negotiations for a French pass, Livingston learned that the shipowner wanted £10 apiece for himself and his son. He discussed this with the English ambassador and concluded that it would be cheaper to go by mule to Coruña on Spain's northwest coast and there take the packet boat to Falmouth, England.

Astride their mules, hired at half price, Livingston, his son, and Richard Lesley left Lisbon on the afternoon of June 22. The country-side through which they passed varied from "a fruitful Countrey, many olive Trees," to "barren morish." Livingston was most intrigued by the convents and monasteries, especially the riches contained in them. He visited the monasteries of Alcobaça and Santiago, and made extensive lists of the "Rarityes." But the inhabitants, particularly the Spaniards, were to Livingston "a wicked, superstitious, Poor, Proud, beggarly People."

In typical tourist fashion, Livingston complained about the enter-tainment received by wayfarers in Portugal and Spain. At one inn, he reported, "the Entertainment...was but mean as is most upon this Road & no fruit for money." At another, his meal was "a little fish miserably dressed." When Livingston and his companions got to the inn at Caldas de Rays, they were given "bad entertainment... being taken up with 2 drunken Priests that were whoremongers."

After arriving in Coruña on July 9, Livingston secured from the English consul a request to the captain of the packet boat that because of their losses and ill fortune the party be given free passage to England. Five days later, Livingston and his party went aboard, and the last leg of the voyage began. Livingston arrived in Falmouth at nine o'clock on the evening of July 16. From there, he and his son journeyed by horseback to Exeter, where they took a coach to London, sharing it with a Mrs. Carter. A short while later, William Carter, the lady's husband, joined them; he promised Livingston "to bring me acquainted with my Lord Bellomont, governor of N. England." Having been warned that the road to London was frequented by highwaymen, Livingston sent his belongings ahead by courier, keeping a minimum of cash on his person. His foresight was rewarded when the coach was stopped and robbed at Hounslow Heath, just outside London. Livingston lost only thirteen shillings.

The seven months' travail finally ended at four in the afternoon of July 25, when Livingston's coach entered London. The government was seething with political intrigue, and his first job was to determine upon whom he could or could not rely, a rather delicate task to which Livingston's personality was well adapted.

The London in which Robert Livingston found himself in July 1695 was the seat of empire and the fountainhead of political intrigue. The Tories, dominant in Parliament and Cabinet after 1690, were gradually being eased out, and party feeling became more and more rancorous as time wore on. By March 1693/4, both secretaries of state were Whigs, and though Parliament retained a Tory complexion until October 1695, it, too, was rapidly changing.[2]

This shift, well under way by the time Livingston arrived, was prompted by William III's growing dissatisfaction with the Tories' apathy toward the French War, criticism of his Dutch favorites, and constant correspondence with James II, the "king across the water." With the scent of victory strong, the Whigs were eager to push their advantage, and deal the Tories a death blow. Their weapon—tarring the Tories with the brush of corruption, bribery, and extortion—was not new, but it served admirably to send their enemies scurrying with "blasted characters." As Macaulay once put it, "whispers which, at another time, would have speedily died away and been forgotten, now swelled, first into murmurs, and then into clamours."[3]

Livingston's only business with the government, as even his enemies admitted, was to secure reimbursement of his expenditures on behalf of New York.[4] He had no intention of getting involved in the Whigs'

2. O'Callaghan, ed., *N. Y. Col. Docs.*, III, viii; George Macaulay Trevelyan, *England Under the Stuarts* (London, 1949), 432; Jacobsen, *Blathwayt*, 141.

3. Maurice Ashley, *England in the Seventeenth Century* (London, 1952), 181-82; Thomas Babington Macaulay, *The History of England from the Accession of James II* (5 vols., N. Y., n.d.), V, 22-23.

4. Povey to Fletcher, Dec. 1695 (draft), William Blathwayt Papers, BL 215, Henry E. Huntington Library and Art Gallery.

campaign; indeed, he had come armed with letters of introduction to Blathwayt from two prominent members of the Tory faction in New York. Yet, he was well aware that his purpose would only be frustrated were he to sail against the political tides.

Livingston had to face three basic political facts: Queen Mary, the Tories' bulwark, was dead; King William was in the Low Countries; and the Crown's powers were in the hands of seven Lords Justices, of whom six were Whigs and only one a Tory. Moreover, Blathwayt, to whom he would normally have turned, was abroad. Had that official been in London, he might have kept Livingston from joining the Whigs, because his power was diminished, not destroyed. But he was not available, and his deputy, John Povey, was not as influential at Whitehall.[5]

These circumstances, combined with a chance meeting with William Carter on the road from Exeter to Salisbury, pushed Livingston into the Whigs' arms. This encounter had great significance, for Carter promised to introduce him to the Earl of Bellomont, a leading Whig who was being officially mentioned as New York's next governor by mid-July 1695.[6] Livingston was never one to pass up an opportunity to ingratiate himself with a new governor, and Bellomont's friendship would be a guarantee of future political preferment.

Soon, Livingston met other important Whigs. After settling himself in London, he was visited by Fitz-John Winthrop, now Connecticut's agent to Whitehall, whom Blathwayt and the Tories viewed with a scornful eye. When this old friend called on Livingston, they "took a walk in moore fields."[7] Though their topic of conversation

5. The Whig Lords Justices were Somers, Pembroke, Devonshire, Dorset, Shrewsbury, and the Archbishop of Canterbury; the Tory was Godolphin. Macaulay, *History of England*, V, 35; Jacobsen, *Blathwayt*, 140.

6. Shrewsbury, on July 16, 1695, wrote to William III: "The committee of plantations have advised...that no salary can be depended on from New England [for Bellomont]; so that he must either have subsistance out of your majesty's exchequer, which is an ill precedent, or the expedient we have projected must take, which has no other hardship or difficulty, that the removing Colonel Fletcher, who has been there four years, and by many much disliked." William Coxe, ed., *Private and Original Correspondence of Charles Talbot, Duke of Shrewsbury, with King William, the Leaders of the Whig Party, and other Distinguished Statesmen* (London, 1821), 94.

7. Livingston Journal (Van Laer typescript), 75. To Blathwayt, Winthrop was "a Great Coward & hopes to be made therefore Governor of that Colony [i.e., Conn.] as his Neighbour S[ir] W P[hips] they both deserve a wooden sword rather than to be honoured beyond their meritt." Blathwayt's note on extract of letter from Graham to Randolph, Oct. 11, 1693, Blathwayt Papers, II, Col. Wmsbg.

was not disclosed, they probably discussed the intricacies of London politics. There was much about such matters that the New Yorker could learn from his older and more experienced friend. After Livingston and Winthrop went to the Exchange on July 30 "to be welcomed," the New Yorker walked to Whitehall and visited another Whig, counselor-at-law Robert West. His immediate purpose was to learn whether Thomas Neale intended to honor several bills of exchange. West gave him "little encouragement" on this score, but he must have given him sage advice about financial dealings with Whitehall.

Although Livingston appeared at the Plantation Office on the following day, he was not yet ready to prosecute his claims. Instead, he continued to make important political contacts. Along with Robert West and a Captain Browne, he went to Thistleworth, twelve miles from London, to renew acquaintance with Thomas Dongan, former governor of New York. It may be safely assumed that the English political situation was not neglected in their conversations.

Two days later, Livingston visited the prospective governor of New York, Bellomont, "but he was not at home." The interview finally took place on August 10; Livingston only noted in his journal that they had "a long conference," and that he "exhibited to him the Leysler affair." Since the Earl was a staunch Whig and firmly believed in Leisler's and Milborne's complete innocence, and since Parliament had already reversed the attainders and convictions of the leading Leislerians, Livingston must have excused away his now embarrassing participation in the Rebellion.[8]

Livingston then laid the final plans for his appearance before the Lords Justices. On August 11, he met with Philip French, Giles Shelly, and William Carter, and all four went to Chelsea, presumably

8. Livingston Journal (Van Laer typescript), 75-76, 78. Bellomont was reported to be "one of the committee of parliament to inquire into the trials of Leisler and Milborne, and [he] told Sir Henry Ashurst those men were murdered and barbarously murdered." Thomas Hutchinson, *The History of Massachusetts from the first settlement thereof in 1628, until the year 1750* (2 vols., Salem, 1795-97), II, 103n. Bellomont was a member of Commons from Droitwich Borough, Worcestershire, from Mar. 20, 1689/90 to Oct. 11, 1695. House of Lords, *Return of the Names of Every Member returned to serve in each Parliament from the year 1696 up to 1876....Also, Return, from so remote a Period as it can be obtained, up to the year 1695. Part I: Parliaments of England, 1213-1702* (London, 1879), 570. Parliament passed the reversal of the attainders and convictions on Apr. 30, 1695. Stock, ed., *Proceedings and Debates of Parliaments*, II, 131.

to discuss strategy. According to Povey, Livingston and Bellomont agreed on a plan of action, and Carter, as the Earl's friend, may have been responsible for coordinating the stories of the witnesses who were to appear in his behalf.[9]

On August 22, Livingston submitted a petition to the Lords Justices for redress without which, he claimed, he would not only be "disabled to carry on his trade of a Merchant, but must be totally ruind." He requested repayment of £2,917 from various New York revenues. Then, he asked for restitution of ten barrels of gunpowder seized by Leisler in 1689, a salary for the secretaryship for Indian affairs which he "hath for Twenty years...Executed...but never received any Salary, or other recompense," and a royal commission for his local offices in Albany for which he had never received more than £70 a year in salaries and fees.[10]

Never one to ignore an advantage, Livingston played on the Lords Justices' sympathies by describing his misfortunes at sea. Embroidering the truth a bit, he stated that he had been "reduced to a pint of water and litle Cocoa-Nut a Day for Seventeen Weeks." But he was also diplomatic; recognizing the Crown's great expense because of King William's War, he "waives all expectation of being reimbursed here." His case was referred to the Lords of Trade for a full report.[11]

When Livingston appeared before the Lords of Trade six days later, he made a subtle change in his story. In order to justify orders requiring Governor Fletcher to pay him his money, he suddenly charged that without compulsion "he had no hopes of relief in New York *by reason of Coll: Fletcher's proceedings there,* for the proof whereof he produces divers witnesses." What prompted this sudden attack on Fletcher? Previously, Livingston had conceded that Fletcher had diverted all available revenue to frontier defense. However, he could not ask the Crown to countermand those orders simply because he wanted his money. If he wanted orders to force Fletcher

9. Livingston Journal (Van Laer typescript), 79; Povey to Fletcher, Dec. 1695 (draft), Blathwayt Papers, BL 215, Huntington Lib.

10. Livingston to Lords Justices, Aug. 22, 1695, "The Case of the Petitioner Robert Livingston," Aug. 22, 1695, PRO, CO 5: 1039, nos. 9 i, 9 ii (Lib. Cong. transcripts), and copies in Livingston-Redmond Mss. Unless otherwise stated, all references to money in this chapter will be in New York pounds.

11. "The Case of...Livingston," Aug. 22, 1695, PRO, CO 5: 1039, no. 9 ii (Lib. Cong. transcripts); Order of Lords Justices, Aug. 22, 1695, *Cal. State Papers, Col.,* XIV, no. 2018.

to pay him, he had to find a much better reason, and the opportunistic Livingston seized the evolving English political pattern as a device which he could utilize.

Livingston undertook to convince the English authorities that New York's revenue had been withheld, not for frontier defense, but by an avaricious official who was lining his own pockets. Thus he alleged that type of crime against Fletcher which had proved so effective in destroying the reputations of the Tory chieftains in London. In doing so, he not only followed the Whig pattern, but he performed a valuable service for the Whigs who desired the New York governorship for Bellomont and who therefore had to discredit Fletcher. In return, Livingston could expect favorable consideration of his claims.

When he reappeared before the Lords of Trade on August 28, Livingston brought witnesses to substantiate his charges against Fletcher. These men—Philip French, William Kidd, Samuel Bradley, John Albrough, and Joseph Davies—alleged that the governor had intimidated Assembly elections, embezzled public funds, accepted graft, and falsified muster rolls of the royal troops. Livingston relied upon several others—Thomas Jeffrys, Giles Shelly, and Benjamin Bladenburgh—for testimony, but, he reported, they had "gone out of the way to avoid giving evidence." The Lords of Trade promptly summoned the reluctant witnesses.[12]

Fletcher, of course, was not without friends in London. At the same time that Livingston made his charges, Gilbert Heathcote, prominent London merchant and elder brother of New York Councilor Caleb Heathcote, requested that he might appear in Fletcher's behalf if charges had been made against him. His appearance was unnecessary, however, for the reluctant witnesses did more harm to Livingston than to the governor. When examined on September 14, they denied all knowledge of any crime on Fletcher's part. Livingston had "made but Sad Stuff of it," as Povey reported, but he had done his best to blacken Fletcher.[13]

12. Lords of Trade Proceedings, Aug. 28, 1695, O'Callaghan, ed., *N. Y. Col. Docs.*, IV, 127-28 (italics supplied); Lords of Trade Journal, Sept. 2, 1695, and Lords of Trade Order, Sept. 7, 1695, *Cal. State Papers, Col.*, XIV, nos. 2041, 2051.
13. Heathcote to Povey, Aug. 31, 1695, Memorandum of Lords of Trade, Sept. 14, 1695, *Cal. State Papers, Col.*, XIV, nos. 2037, 2056; Povey to Fletcher, Dec. 1695 (draft), Blathwayt Papers, BL 215, Huntington Lib.

Now Livingston claimed his reward. He protested against his former correspondents, Harwood and Meriwether, for allegedly swindling him of £901 sterling by fraudulent charges for procuring and selling the tallies received from the Crown in settling Dongan's debt. Both admitted making such a charge, and Harwood also admitted charging 20 percent "advance," as well as 6 percent interest, on goods sent to New York. This was referred to the attorney general "for his opinion what may be done *by the King* for Mr. Levingston's relief." Livingston next documented his request for a £100 sterling salary as secretary for Indian affairs with a certificate from Thomas Dongan, testifying that he was "a person fitt to be employed in that station, there being none of those parts ... that can speake the languages [i.e., Dutch and English] as he doth." [14]

When the Lords of Trade, on the next day, referred his whole case to John Povey for a full examination and formal report, Livingston was frightened. He wrote to the Lords of Trade and freely poured forth all of his troubles. Harwood and Meriwether had given him nothing but "ill-usage," with the result that he had to defend himself by tactics which he would have preferred not to use. They now threatened him with "tedious and expensive suits" unless he complied "with there unreasonable terms." He pleaded for orders for his repayment and a salary for life "which may not be in the power of our angry Governor to stop or pervert"; otherwise, he would be in "a worse condition" than he had been in twenty years before. [15]

On the same day, Livingston submitted a statement of his case, listing every sum and office that he desired, with proofs for each. The only major difference between this and his initial requests was in the amount of interest he sought. At first, he asked for £868 interest on the sum repaid in tallies, computed at 8 percent from the date the debt was incurred to the date of the tallies' issuance; now, he requested another £634 as 8 percent interest on his other claims. He suggested that this £1,503 should be given him over a two-year period out of the colony's revenues. Thus he asked that New York be burdened with a total debt of £3,553 as well as his annual salaries

14. Lords of Trade Proceedings, Sept. 14, 1695, Dongan's certificate, Sept. 17, 1695, O'Callaghan, ed., *N. Y. Col. Docs.*, IV, 130 (italics supplied).

15. Livingston to Lords of Trade, Sept. 19, 1695, *ibid.*, 131; Lords of Trade Journal, Sept. 18, 1695, *Cal. State Papers, Col.*, XIV, no. 2059.

of £100 sterling as secretary for Indian affairs and £50 as sub-collector at Albany.[16]

Povey, who had no love for Livingston, suggested to the Lords of Trade that the New Yorker was not entitled to £868 interest on the £2,172 already repaid in tallies. However, he intimated that the expenses allegedly incurred by Harwood and Meriwether in procuring and selling them were extortionate. Povey apparently preferred to see Livingston entangled in a hopeless commercial lawsuit rather than have him recover his money from the Crown. To defeat this suggestion, Livingston wrote to one of the Lords and again expressed the hope that the interest "on consideration . . . will appear as reasonable as the principal, which has been allowed to be just." Again, he stretched the truth by solemnly declaring that "All of the sums for which I seek relief, except the £2,172 . . . were paid in specie out of my pocket, and no part of it for goods sold, out of which I could get any profitt." [17]

Povey's effort was not the only roadblock thrown in Livingston's way. His request for a salary as secretary for Indian affairs was challenged on the ground that the post was only useful in wartime, an assumption denied by Livingston. He also denied a rumor that he had protested the proclamation of William and Mary in Albany in 1689. The Lords of Trade ordered all the records brought in; witnesses were summoned, and Livingston swore that he himself had proclaimed the sovereigns but had denounced Leisler's proceedings.[18]

Livingston's friends assured him that such attacks would not damage his case, and felt that they might even be helpful. However, Livingston submitted a request to the Lords of Trade for a quick decision, claiming that his business affairs required his return to New York within three weeks. He apologized because his accounts were not in the customary form, but blandly reminded them that he was "a Stranger to the manner of . . . this Honorable Board, and . . . at too great a distance to rectify that Error now." Besides, after his attacks

16. Statement of Livingston's Case, Sept. 19, 1695, O'Callaghan, ed., *N. Y. Col. Docs.*, IV, 132-35.

17. Povey's extract of Livingston's case, c. Sept. 1695, Blathwayt Papers, BL 216, Huntington Lib.; Livingston to Lord (?), c. Sept. 1695, *Cal. State Papers, Col.*, XIV, no. 2084 viii.

18. Lords of Trade Minutes, Oct. 1, 1695, O'Callaghan, ed., *N. Y. Col. Docs.*, IV, 138.

on Fletcher, he could not hope for any "favor that was necessary to recommend my case." [19]

Livingston's incessant pleadings finally had their desired effect. On October 3, he wrote in his diary: "I have been continually employed at Whithal to obtain my money, or a warrant for the same, . . . and the end of it is not yet, for our side will not allow the Report of the [Lords of Trade] Committee to be handed in until the Earl of Monmouth comes, as it depends mainly on the interest. . . . The Earl of Montague, Romney, and Sir William Trumbull, Secretary of State, and the Bishop of London, it is true, are great friends of mine, but no one takes the matter so to heart as Monmouth." Within a week, Charles Mordaunt, Earl of Monmouth, had apparently returned, for the Lords of Trade recommended that Fletcher be ordered to give him *preferential repayment* of £771 if he was satisfied that the claims were just, and that repayment of £388 be entrusted to the New York Assembly. The claim for £1,503 interest was to be paid from the tax arrears in the colony. They also agreed that Livingston should receive the gunpowder he requested from the royal ordnance in England, and that his annual salary as secretary for Indian affairs was justified. Finally, they suggested that he be authorized to sue Harwood and Meriwether *at the Crown's expense.*[20]

Nothing could have pleased Livingston more. The Whigs had kept their bargain. But the Lords of Trade report was only their recommendation to the Privy Council of which they were a committee. In order to guarantee acceptance of the proposals, Livingston had to perform a greater service for the Whigs than merely dragooning a few reluctant witnesses against Fletcher. He therefore seized upon a scheme that had been discussed in official circles for some time to end piracy in the Red Sea, an action which would also put a handsome profit in the pockets both of the Whig leaders and himself.

Livingston decided to ingratiate himself with the Whig chieftains by arranging a privately financed expedition against the pirates who

19. Livingston Journal (Van Laer typescript), 80; Livingston to Lords of Trade, c. Sept. 1695, PRO, CO 5: 1039, no. 25 x (Lib. Cong. transcripts). Also see O'Callaghan, ed., *N. Y. Col. Docs.*, IV, 137-38; Hist. Mss. Comm., *Report on the Manuscripts of the Marquess of Downshire, Preserved at Easthampstead Park, Berks.* (3 vols., London, 1924-38), I (part I), 437.

20. Livingston Journal (Van Laer typescript), 79-80; Lords of Trade Journal, Oct. 9, 1695, Lords of Trade Minutes, Oct. 10, 1695, *Cal State Papers, Col.*, XIV, nos. 2083, 2085. See also O'Callaghan, ed., *N. Y. Col. Docs.*, III, 633.

had been attacking the Grand Mogul's commerce and thereby embarrassing the East India Company. He lacked only a bold and adventuresome leader, and this was supplied by Captain William Kidd, who had just arrived in London in command of his own armed brigantine, the *Antigua*, "with design to Enter into his Majesties Service if he Can have any Encouragement." Although a stranger in London, Kidd had a letter of introduction to Blathwayt. Because that official was absent from London, Kidd must have been relieved to see Livingston's familiar face.[21]

Livingston, Kidd, and the Whigs had mutually compatible desires. The first wanted to win the Whigs' favor, the second wished to enter the Crown's service, and the latter were anxious to put an end to the Red Sea pirates. Livingston promoted a privateering scheme, Kidd led the expedition, and the Whigs secured royal approval and helped finance it. Although Livingston could not know it at the time, his partnership with Captain Kidd was to be one of the greatest political blunders of the era. •

Since Kidd was too rough and unpolished to court the favor of some of the highest nobles in the land, Livingston served as negotiator. On October 3 he noted that he had discussed final arrangements "with two great personages and satisfied them. They take the Earl of R[omney] into partnership and they are now 4 in number and the business is to proceed. I hope by this my affairs may have a happy ending." Exactly one week later, Kidd, Livingston, and Bellomont, acting as agent for the four "great personages"—Romney, master general of ordnance; Sir Edward Russell, first lord of the admiralty; Sir John Somers, lord keeper of the great seal; and the Earl of Shrewsbury, secretary of state—signed articles of agreement and launched the project.[22]

21. Livingston Journal (Van Laer typescript), 79. On Kidd, Graham declared: "I know him to be very hearty & Zealous for the government, and is a gentleman that has served Long in the fleet & been in many Engagdements & of unquestioned Couradge & Conduct in sea affairs. He is a Stranger at home [i.e., England] which gives birth to the presumption of earnestly recommending him to your Honours favour." Graham to Blathwayt, May 29, 1695, Blathwayt Papers, X, Col. Wmsbg. Blathwayt noted receipt of this on Aug. 30, indicating it had been forwarded to him on the continent.

22. Livingston Journal (Van Laer typescript), 80; J. Franklin Jameson, ed., *Privateering and Piracy in the Colonial Period: Illustrative Documents* (N.Y., 1923), 190*n*.

Under the agreement, Bellomont was to secure commissions for Kidd as a privateer against pirates and French vessels and was to pay four-fifths of the cost of outfitting the *Adventure Galley*. Livingston and Kidd agreed to pay the balance, and Kidd was to command the expedition. The crew was to be hired on a "no purchase no pay" basis, and the vessel was to return to Boston without breaking cargo. Unless Kidd seized lawful prizes before March 25, 1697, Bellomont's investment was to be returned. If prizes were taken, 60 percent of their value was to go to Bellomont, 25 percent to the crew, and the remainder to Livingston and Kidd. If more than £100,000 sterling worth of prizes were captured, the *Adventure Galley* became Kidd's. Bellomont was protected by performance bonds signed by Livingston for £10,000 sterling and by Kidd for £20,000 sterling.[23]

The ship's sailing was delayed, partly by financial difficulties. Robert West suggested that Livingston talk with Sir Richard Blackham, a ne'er-do-well London merchant ever on the alert for questionable enterprises which promised above average profits. On February 7, 1695/6, Livingston and Kidd sold Blackham one-fifteenth of the *Adventure Galley*, one-third of their interest, for £396 13s 4d. In two weeks, the ship was ready to sail.[24]

Once the basic agreements for the venture with Captain Kidd had been signed in mid-October, Livingston turned his attention to Harwood and Meriwether. His claims against them involved three controversial points: the £901 sterling charged for procuring and selling the tallies, the disposition of £700 worth of furs consigned by Livingston to Harwood with directions "not to dispose of the same till further order," and, finally, the charge of 20 percent "advance" on goods shipped to New York, amounting to £480 15s 7d sterling. When Livingston insisted that the tallies be delivered to him, Harwood claimed that he had sold them to Meriwether at a 25 percent discount. The New Yorker also demanded the return of the furs held

23. Articles between Bellomont, Livingston, and Kidd, Oct. 10, 1695, Livingston's and Kidd's performance bonds, O'Callaghan, ed., *N. Y. Col. Docs.*, IV, 762-65.

24. Robt. Livingston to Wm. Livingston, May 9, 1706 (draft), Livingston-Redmond Mss.; Narcissus Luttrell, *A Brief Historical Relation of State Affairs from September 1678 to April 1714* (6 vols., Oxford, 1857), IV, 247, VI, 82; Agreement between Livingston, Kidd, and Blackham, Feb. 7, 1695/6, Livingston's Memorandum, May 13, 1696, Livingston-Redmond Mss.; Kidd's Memorandum, Feb. 20, 1695/6, O'Callaghan, ed., *N. Y. Col. Docs.*, IV, 764.

by Harwood, who was not to "take up any more of my goods which I expect my wife will consign...Shee being ignorant how I am used in this affair." As to the "advance," he was certain that "I doe not know what it means neither did I ever hear of itt." [25]

Five arbitrators were finally appointed to resolve the deadlock, and the three participants signed performance bonds for £2,000 sterling, thereby binding themselves to abide by the arbitrators' decision. Livingston's numerous and detailed memoranda on this matter indicated the seriousness with which he viewed it; "I have...had much trouble with the matter of Harwood," he wrote on October 3, "so that I have become terribly thin." By November 9, however, he had outlined his claims for the arbitrators. He had paid for all goods shipped on Harwood's risk and account except for £8. Similarly, he had paid, except for £175 11s 11d shipped after he left New York, for all goods sent on his risk and account. Whatever balance was due his London correspondent, Livingston conceded, could be deducted from the furs held by Harwood, along with interest.

As for the tallies, Livingston claimed that he was the victim of some rather sharp dealing; Harwood had taken the tallies "in his owne name, but hearing Robert Livingston was to come over...he invents a way with...merriwether to Ballance them." Although they sold at a discount earlier, tallies were close to par value in 1695 because of the restoration of the Crown's credit through the Bank of England's establishment. But Harwood said he had sold the tallies in April 1694 to Meriwether at a discount of £417 10s sterling, or 25 percent. He also listed £483 16s sterling as expenses in originally getting them from the Crown. When he added the 20 percent "advance" on goods shipped against the tallies' value, Livingston was left with only £505 12s 11d sterling out of the original £1,670 sterling. But Harwood had signed a £500 sterling bond to Dongan "to Stand an audite when ever the King pleases." After Livingston reimbursed him for the bond's possible forfeiture, the New Yorker's net had shrunk to £5 12s 11d sterling.

25. Harwood's acct. with Livingston, Apr. 1691-Oct. 1695, Meriwether's and Harwood's sale of furs, Feb. 16, 1694/5-Aug. 19, 1695, Harwood's acct. "given me by Richard Merriwether," Aug. 1695, Livingston's acct. with Harwood, Aug. 1695, Memorandum of Livingston's case with Harwood, c. Nov. 1695, Livingston's acct. with Harwood, Sept. 1695, Livingston-Redmond Mss.

Livingston furiously denounced Harwood's "stock-jobbing." "This is the way," he wrote, he would "be paid by his Trusty agent the Somme of £1670 Sterl: for which he hath been Slaving and Labouring these 20 years past." He demanded the "Tallys Intire, with the Interest," together with the proceeds from his furs which his correspondent retained to his "great damage." [26]

Harwood now argued, since the tallies were issued in his name and since Livingston had authorized him to receive them "to his oune use," that he could do with them what he pleased. But Livingston irately denied that his power of attorney transferred "a property from me without any Consideration paid me by Mr. Harwood... he is in Law but a Trustee." "If he Insists upon the Talleys as his own," Livingston replied, he "is a debtor to me for £1670 and Interest... and ought not to bring the Charges of procureing and discounting 'em to my account." [27]

Despite the possible advantages of such a concession, Livingston stubbornly refused to acknowledge that the tallies belonged to Harwood, and rejected the "Extravagant Charges he reckons for procureing 'em and his selling 'em afterwards," as well as the "sham sale" itself. The whole thing, Livingston charged, had been rigged so that Harwood could repay his personal debt of £1,200 to Meriwether.[28]

The arbitrators handed down their decision on November 22. They tried to effect a compromise by disallowing the tallies' sale and the withholding of £500 sterling against a possible royal audit and by allowing Harwood's charges for procuring the tallies and his 20 percent for "advance." Harwood was to turn the tallies and accrued interest over to Livingston, who was to pay the Londoner £1,047 18s 3½d sterling in full settlement of all claims. Within two weeks, all accounts were settled, but the business relationship be-

26. Livingston Journal (Van Laer typescript), 80; Bonds of Livingston, Harwood, and Meriwether, Nov. 1, 7, 1695, Memorandum of Livingston's case with Harwood, Nov. 9, 1695, Livingston-Redmond Mss.

27. Livingston's case with Harwood and Meriwether "to be presented to the arbitrators," Nov. 11, 1695, Livingston-Redmond Mss.

28. "The Charges of the Talleys," 1693, Livingston's case with Harwood and Meriwether "to be presented to the arbitrators," Nov. 11, 1695, Memorandum of Livingston's case with "J harwood & R m," Nov. 18, 1695, Reasons why the arbitrators should not allow "Harwood's Sham Sale," c. Nov. 1695, *ibid.*

tween Livingston and Harwood, which had lasted more than a decade, came to a sudden and bitter end. However, Livingston apparently bore Meriwether no grudge, for he sold the tallies to him a few days later at a discount, not of £417 sterling, but of £83 sterling.[29]

Livingston was very disappointed by the arbitrators' decision. Because the sale of the tallies and the payment to Harwood more or less balanced each other, he realized little ready cash from the transactions. Thus he found it necessary to seek payment of some of his money from the Crown in London rather than New York.

The King-in-Council had ruled on Livingston's case a day before the arbitration award was announced. Of the principal sums he claimed, £761 were to "be forthwith reimburst... *preferably before all others*" out of the New York revenues, and £388 were to be recommended to the New York Assembly's consideration. His other claims— £1,503 interest, £100 sterling annual salary as secretary for Indian affairs, and confirmation in his local offices—would receive the Treasury Lords' "further consideration."[30]

This delay, which would normally have exasperated Livingston, gave him an opportunity to restate his demands so that he could receive some money in London. Because a large part of the principal he had disbursed was borrowed money on which he had to pay interest himself, he hoped that he would receive interest from the government. Moreover, because "the necessityes of N. Yorke dureing the warr are so great that it will be very difficult to raise the principall ...and impossible to raise the interest out of the Revenue," he hoped that the interest could be paid to him in London.[31]

The Treasury Lords reported to the Privy Council that Livingston's salary as secretary for Indian affairs should be paid him "dureing his life" in "Consideration of the Long and Faithfull Service" he had shown, and that he should be confirmed in his local offices. They

29. Arbitration of Pickering *et al.,* Nov. 22, 1695, Harwood's receipt to Livingston, Dec. 6, 1695, Harwood's and Meriwether's release to Livingston, Dec. 7, 1695, Acct. of "The Morgadge of Coll Dongan," Nov. 29, 1696, *ibid.*

30. Minutes of King-in-Council, Nov. 21, 1695, *ibid.;* Order of King-in-Council Nov. 21, 1695, PRO, CO 5: 1039, no. 27 (Lib. Cong. transcripts); Order of King-in-Council, Nov. 21, 1695, N. Y. Col. Mss, XL, 92, N. Y. State Lib. (italics supplied).

31. Livingston to Treasury Lords, Dec. 1695, O'Callaghan, ed., *N. Y. Col. Docs.,* IV, 139-40.

also agreed that £868 16s—the interest from 1688 to 1693 on the money which the Crown had repaid by tallies—be given to him in London; the remainder of the interest money should come from New York's treasury.[32]

After concluding his affairs more or less successfully, Livingston now awaited the issuance of the formal orders and warrants. His royal commission as secretary for Indian affairs was issued on January 16, 1695/6, and he was confirmed in his local Albany offices. A day later, tallies for £868 (£668 sterling) were ordered, and Fletcher was directed to pay the balance of £634 interest as well as the principal.[33] But several last-minute attempts were made to deprive Livingston of his hard won gains. When he received the royal warrant ordering the governor to pay his claims, he found a stipulation added: such payments were to be made only for what Livingston "should make appear to you [i.e., Fletcher] and our Councill to be justly due to him." [34] That was almost certainly a promise of future trouble.

In a similar manner, Livingston's right to his local offices was challenged. Under the terms of the recently enacted Navigation Law of 1696, the Act Against Frauds, all matters pertaining to the royal treasury were to be in the hands of "native born subjects" of England. Livingston, of course, was a Scotsman, and most of his local offices involved the handling of royal funds. Attorney General Thomas Trever and Solicitor John Hawley were asked for their opinions. Both concluded that the *intent* of the law was to include Scotsmen as Englishmen. Therefore, Livingston could not be deprived of his offices because of his birth.[35]

Though that assault failed, John Povey laid the groundwork for

32. Treasury Lords' Report, Jan. 2, 1695/6, Shaw, ed., *Cal. Treasury Books*, X, 1273-74. It was approved by the King-in-Council on Jan. 16. Minutes of King-in-Council, Jan. 16, 1695/6, Livingston-Redmond Mss.

33. Order of King-in-Council, Jan. 16, 17, 1695/6, PRO, CO 5: 1114, pp. 241, 245-47 (Lib. Cong. transcripts); Royal Warrant, Jan. 29, 1695/6, Shaw, ed., *Cal. Treasury Books*, X, 1294.

34. Royal Warrant, Jan. 30, 1695/6, PRO, CO 5: 1114, pp. 248-50 (Lib. Cong. transcripts).

35. Andrews, *Colonial Period*, IV, 167-68, states that "the Board of Trade... allowed the case...to lie by without decision." "The Opinion of the Atturney Generall and Solicitor upon the Provision...relating to Scotchmen," Jan. 24, Feb. 3, 1695/6, Livingston-Redmond Mss.

another in a letter to Governor Fletcher. He recounted the details of Bellomont's appointment to the Massachusetts governorship, his unhappiness with the prospect of a salary fixed by the Assembly, and his desire to add New York's governorship to his commission since that salary was fixed by royal command. Bellomont's suggestion, according to Povey, was greeted with much dismay by "those who understood the nature of the Country." However, the King's absence "made all things of this Nature sleep." Livingston's arrival, Povey continued, reawakened Bellomont's scheme. The New Yorker had come to London to straighten out his finances, not to attack Fletcher, but he "hapned to Light into hands that thought him extreamly fitt to carry on the designe of Uniting [New York and Massachusetts under Bellomont] by Articles against the Governor of New York which Should break his neck." Povey pointed out that Livingston had appeared at the Plantation Office only to drop out of sight and reappear a month later "at the Head of proving divers Enormities" against Fletcher. The only thing that had blunted Livingston's attack, Povey stated, had been the efforts of "our old freind," presumably Blathwayt.

Povey then hinted at what Fletcher's future relations with Livingston should be. The governor "ought not to seeme to Levingston to know more of the Matter, then what he brings you, and not to Lett him perceive any resentment hereon." Since the question of paying Livingston was left to the governor's discretion, Fletcher might be able to retaliate in that way. However, if he decided to withhold payment, he would have "to find out a good reason at your Perill." Though Povey was unwilling to mention names, Fletcher might "aske Mr. Levingston who was his great Freind here, which I Suppose he'll not Scruple to tell you." Thus forewarned, Fletcher wrote to Blathwayt in July 1696 that "by some chance letters from private friends" he had learned of the attacks made upon him. However, he trusted that the Lords of Trade would not credit such tales until they heard his side. He believed that his emissaries to London, Chidley Brooke and William Nicolls, would vindicate him.[36]

Livingston, completely unaware of this correspondence, was at

36. Povey to Fletcher, Dec. 1695 (draft), Blathwayt Papers, BL 215, Huntington Lib.; Fletcher to Blathwayt, July 13, 1696, O'Callaghan, ed., *N. Y. Col. Docs.*, IV, 165.

Gravesend on May 10, 1696, preparing for his homeward journey.[37] In New York, Fletcher and the Tory element still retained power and Livingston's reward for deserting the Tories and joining the Whigs in England was predictable. He returned as a political outcast and Fletcher's enmity exploded in his face as soon as he reached New York.

37. Livingston to Stockere, May 10, 1695 [*sic*] (draft), Livingston-Redmond Mss.

CHAPTER VII

The Trials of an Apostate

ON AUGUST 2, 1696, Robert Livingston returned to New York after an uneventful voyage from London. Unaware that news of his political apostasy had preceded him, he acted the role of a political innocent when he met the governor in Albany. But Fletcher was too blunt and forthright to hide his feelings. "Our Governor is very much dissatisfyed at me," Livingston reported, "because some witnesses were examined at Court" who "testifyed somewhat reflecting on his Excellency." [1]

Livingston had struck the first blow, but the governor meant to retaliate. About a week after Livingston returned to the colony, a Board of Indian Commissioners was established to conduct the government's negotiations with the Iroquois. Not only did Fletcher purposely exclude Livingston, but he also included a clause to "supersede vacate and make null any former warrant or commission granted in this behalfe." [2] Since Livingston knew more about Anglo-Iroquois

1. Livingston to Shrewsbury, Sept. 20, 1696, Livingston to Romney, Sept. 20, 1696, Hist. Mss. Comm., *Report on the Manuscripts of the Duke of Buccleuch & Queensberry, K.G., K.I., Preserved at Montagu House, Whitehall* (2 vols., London, 1903), II (part II), 405, 406; "Cal. Council Minutes," N. Y. State Lib., *Bulletin 58*, 117; Livingston to Gov. and Council of Conn., Aug. 13, 1696, "Correspondence Between the Col. of N. Y. & Conn." (Mss. transcript), N.-Y. Hist. Soc.

2. Fletcher's commission to Delius, Schuyler, Bancker, and Wessels, Aug. 10, 1696, O'Callaghan, ed., *N. Y. Col. Docs.*, IV, 177.

negotiations than anyone except Peter Schuyler, his exclusion was a direct snub. Even though the governor was willing to risk the board's failure in order to satisfy his personal desire for revenge, this was only a minor example of Fletcher's animus, an omen of Livingston's political ostracism during the ensuing two years.

Fletcher wrote two letters in August to his friend and political ally, Blathwayt. In a formal note, he promised that Livingston, who had presented Shrewsbury's letter, "shall have all right done to him in his just pretensions." However, he added, the councilors, particularly Van Cortlandt, "were much Surprized at his whole proceedings & have beggd leave to remitt . . . a true answer."

In a second, more personal letter, Fletcher expressed his true feelings: the political turncoat's accusations were lies which would "little affect me." The Council had sent two agents to London, and the governor hoped that they "may find as much favor from the Lords as Robert Levingston has Don[e]." They were men of integrity, he continued, while Livingston "will always Adheer to his owne Assertion that hee had Rather Bee Call'd Knave Levingston then poore Levingston." [3]

Livingston soon gave Fletcher an opportunity to retaliate. On September 10, he presented the royal orders, as well as vouchers and proofs, and asked repayment of £760 and referral of his claim for £388 to the Assembly. The governor submitted these matters to the Council, a mere formality, for its members were in complete accord with him. They agreed upon their strategy quickly, and in a few hours the formal report was issued. Heeding Povey's warning "to find out a good reason at your Perill," the Council adroitly avoided violating the letter of the Crown's instructions. They allowed some of Livingston's claims and rejected others, but always with a "good reason." Payment of £490, for which Van Cortlandt had earlier given his certificate, was approved; but an item for £37 was rejected because it was supported only by "severall Small accounts bills & bonds from Some of the officers & soldiers." Since this was not the government's concern, he "must look for his support from his debtors." Similarly, the Council denied a demand for £33 as "an assign-

3. Fletcher to Blathwayt, Aug. 22, 1696 (two letters), Blathwayt Papers, VIII, Col. Wmsbg.; see also PRO, CO 5: 1039, no. 52 (Lib. Cong. transcripts).

ment of one Yetts...from whom he has the benefite of the Law to recover the Same." [4]

These were minor annoyances, however, in comparison with the Council's attitude toward the Crown's order for preferential reimbursement of Livingston's expenditures. After the councilors examined this order in connection with the 1692 law for repaying the government's creditors, they reported that it would be impossible to give anyone preference because the statute "contains certain rules & direccons of payment Your Excellency cannot properly & legally derogate from." Certain sums should and would be paid to Livingston, but he, like anyone else, would have to wait his turn, the king of England notwithstanding.

Technically, the councilors had remained within the limits of their authority, but they overstepped their bounds in handling the royal directive that Livingston's claim for £388 be referred to the Assembly for consideration. They advised Fletcher not to do so until it could be determined "whether Collonel Dongan has Satisfyed Mr. Livingston or not." By this means, they delayed the claim's submission until the last possible moment so as to prevent Assembly action on it.[5]

Although Livingston had tasted his enemies' bitterness, he persisted in placing himself at their mercy. When he presented his royal commission as secretary for Indian affairs, sub-collector of the excise and quitrents, town clerk, clerk of the peace, and clerk of the common pleas, several councilors immediately objected that the "allegacons upon which the grant thereof is founded are false and that he is an aliene borne."

Fletcher and his friends now had an excellent opportunity to besmirch Livingston's reputation and strip him of his offices. The councilors declared that he had been sufficiently rewarded in his public service; as a result "he has attained to a verry comfortable Estate In Soo much that thereby he has raised himselfe from nothing to be one of the Richest men of the province." They then analyzed

<hr>

4. Livingston's petition, Sept. 10, 1696, O'Callaghan, ed., *N. Y. Col. Docs.*, IV, 201-2; "Cal. Council Minutes," N. Y. State Lib., *Bulletin 58*, 118; Report of Committee of N. Y. Council, Sept. 10, 1696, N. Y. Col. Mss., XL, 195 (1), N. Y. State Lib. The report is unsigned.

5. Report of Committee of N. Y. Council, Sept. 10, 1696, N. Y. Col. Mss., XL, 195 (1), N. Y. State Lib.

each of his offices. Quitrent collections had always been the sheriff's
duties, never those of a special officer; the post of secretary for Indian affairs was dismissed with the observation that "there never was
any Such office" and "all that Mr. Livingston can pretend to have
done there was to render from Dutch into English what passed at
the Conferences, which has ... been the duty of the Toune Clerke."
Finally, he was "disabled from executing any place of trust relateing
to the Treasury" because he was "born of Scotch parents in Rotterdam." [6]

Based upon these findings, the Council formally recommended to
the governor that Livingston be suspended from his offices of sub-
collector and secretary for Indian affairs. The latter position, they
urged, he should not exercise "otherwise than by virtue of his office
as Town Clerk of Albany"—in effect, he could do the office's work
but was forbidden to claim either the title or remuneration bestowed
upon him by the Crown.[7] If these decisions stood, Livingston had
labored in vain during his year in London: instead of gaining a salary
of £100 sterling, he lost the £50 salary that he already had; instead
of receiving the money for which he had obtained royal approval, he
got only those sums which probably would have been awarded him
anyway; instead of preferential repayment, he would have to wait
his turn.

Clearly, Livingston had failed to foresee that his attacks on the
governor would have such disastrous results. He knew, of course, that
New York politics were neither refined nor charitable, and that his
desertion of the Tories was a dangerous step. However, he apparently
assumed that Fletcher would either not learn of his apostasy until
after the royal directives were put into effect or, if he did learn of it,
he would not have the temerity to flaunt the Crown's orders. In addition, he probably assumed that the Whigs would quickly extend their
power to New York by replacing Fletcher. Unfortunately for Livingston, none of these assumptions was correct.

Livingston had miscalculated, but why had Fletcher received such
wholehearted support in his retaliatory measures from his councilors,

---

6. N. Y. Council Minutes, Sept. 15, 1696, VII, 217, *ibid.;* Report of Committee of
N. Y. Council, Sept. 15, 1696, N. Y. Col. Mss., XL, 197b, *ibid.;* N. Y. Council Report,
Sept. 15, 1696, O'Callaghan, ed., *N. Y. Col. Docs.,* IV, 203.
7. N. Y. Council Minutes, Sept. 17, 1696, N. Y. Col. Mss., XL, 197a (1), N. Y.
State Lib. See also N. Y. Council Minutes, VII, 218, *ibid.*

including Livingston's brother-in-law Van Cortlandt?[8] They certainly knew that Livingston had the backing of influential politicians in London, that the Whigs had ousted the Tories from Cabinet and Commons, that Blathwayt's influence was daily diminishing, and, as a result, that Fletcher's days as governor were numbered. Aware of all this, why did they persist in supporting Fletcher's persecution of a man who would assuredly become an important lieutenant of the Whig faction once it made its power felt in this corner of the empire?

For one thing, these councilors were political conservatives, ever reluctant to gamble all they possessed on the unknown and untried. At stake were position, prestige, and wealth. The aristocracy's natural timidity had been visible in the Leisler Rebellion when they had hesitated to desert James II until they were certain that William and Mary would not end as Monmouth had four years earlier. Now, in 1696, they were equally hesitant about deserting Fletcher until they were first assured that the Whigs could replace him.[9]

Coupled with the councilors' conservatism was Fletcher's ability to retain their support by offering them lavish rewards. Livingston could only offer a vague probability of future rewards if Bellomont became governor; with Fletcher, there was no need to wait, for the rewards were both immediate and substantial. In the last two years of his administration, he gave his supporters prodigious tracts of land without the least thought of the consequences for the colony. One commentator has suggested that this symbolized his "extraordinarily low level of public morality." The most exorbitant grant, and certainly one of the most politically tempestuous, was the Mohawk patent given to Domine Godfredius Delius, Dirk Wessels, Evert Bancker, Peter Schuyler, and William Pinhorne. They received title to a tract fifty miles long and two miles wide on either side of the Mohawk River.[10]

8. Peter Schuyler, another brother-in-law, was absent from these meetings although he was also a councilor.

9. Bellomont's commission as Gov. of N. Y. was not issued until June 18, 1697. O'Callaghan, ed., *N. Y. Col. Docs.*, IV, 266-73. Definite word of his appointment was not received in N. Y. until May 3, 1697. O'Callaghan, ed., *Cal. Hist. Mss.*, II, 257.

10. Irving Mark, *Agrarian Conflicts in Colonial New York, 1711-1775* (N.Y., 1940), 23-24; "Cal. Council Minutes," N. Y. State Lib., *Bulletin 58*, 115-26; Osgood, *Colonies in Eighteenth Century*, I, 282-83.

These were not the only favors distributed by Fletcher to his co-horts. Offices, salaries, and even official sanction of trafficking with pirates were among the rewards he conferred. It is little wonder, then, that he could report that he had presented Livingston's case to the Council, but refused to be present at the debates "least it should be supposed I influenced them, which I am sure I would not en-deavour tho' he hath done me much wrong. . . . He hath many rela-tives and countrymen here, I will allow them to be Judges." [11] He neglected to add that he had already corrupted the judges.

For the moment, there was little that Livingston could do. Relief would have to come from the Whig leaders in London, but un-happily the wheels of imperial administration turned slowly, and their direction was not always clear to someone 3,000 miles away. Thus, to protect himself, Livingston addressed his complaints, not only to the Whigs, but to Blathwayt who, though a friend of Fletcher, was also a member of the Board of Trade. [12]

Livingston shrewdly appealed to Blathwayt's toryism by claiming that Fletcher's "arbitrary act" established a precedent whereby the governor could overrule Whitehall. If Fletcher had given him the reasons for his suspension from office, Livingston was sure that he could "lay their nakedness open and . . . shew that the Council pro-ceeds more from prejudice than otherwise." He prayed that he would not be "condemned unheard" and concluded with the pointed re-minder that the "noble lords" had "shewn so much greater sense of my services then these here." [13]

To the two Whig chieftains, Shrewsbury and Romney, Livingston took a much stronger tone. He was involved with them in the Kidd venture, and he apparently felt that he could express himself more freely. "The Governor," he began, "was so incensed against me for appearing at the Council board, that he not only vented his rage and fury with great indignation, but has stepped over all his duty to his Majesty." By suspending the royal commission, Livingston informed Shrewsbury, Fletcher "seateth himself in a higher station than your Grace." Indeed, the governor's actions verged on treason, "it haveing

11. The charges against Fletcher, generally accepted by modern scholars, were first made by Peter Delanoy. Delanoy to [Penn], June 13, 1695, Fletcher to Blathwayt, Sept. 18, 1696, O'Callaghan, ed., *N. Y. Col. Docs.*, IV, 221-24, 205.

12. *Ibid.*, III, xv.

13. Livingston to Blathwayt, Sept. 19, 1696, *Cal. State Papers, Col.*, XV, no. 235.

never been known that a subject has questioned his Prince's power." [14]

In New York, Livingston was getting the worst of the battle, but Fletcher's cause was not faring very well in England. The governor had sent Chidley Brooke and William Nicolls to London in 1695 as his agents to secure greater assistance in the war against the French in Canada. Their arrival was delayed until April 1696 because of their capture by French privateers, and this delay was to be fatal to their mission. When they reached London, they requested aid for the colony, thereby giving the Whigs grounds for a renewed attack on Fletcher. The Board of Trade expressed astonishment at Fletcher's inept handling of the colony's relations with its neighbors; "It is almost incredible that his Majestys Governor of New York in the middle of above forty thousand English ... should say as he does, that he has but the four Companies his Majesty sent ... to rely on for the defence of that frontier." It was also extraordinary that "so great a number of English there ... should expect to be wholly supported from England, which hath spent so much blood and Treasure" in the war with France.[15]

The predominantly Whig Board promptly launched a vigorous effort to dislodge Fletcher. He had made important enemies in Pennsylvania, Connecticut, and Massachusetts, and thus lost all chance of getting financial or military assistance from these colonies. Intercolonial cooperation could therefore be achieved only by replacing Fletcher with someone who could command the support of neighboring colonies. Bellomont, because he had already been appointed governor of Massachusetts, was the logical candidate. This Whig strategy had many supporters, among them William Penn, Fitz-John Winthrop of Connecticut, Peter Delanoy of New York, and William Popple, secretary to the Board of Trade. Popple, appointed to his post in July 1696, was an avowed opponent of Blathwayt; his very elevation to this office was viewed as a sign of Blathwayt's declining influence at Court.[16]

14. Livingston to Shrewsbury, Sept. 20, 1696, O'Callaghan, ed., *N. Y. Col. Docs.*, IV, 205.

15. Memorial of Brooke and Nicolls to Lords Justices, May 19, 1696, Livingston-Redmond Mss.; Board of Trade's report on northern colonies, Sept. 30, 1696, O'Callaghan, ed., *N. Y. Col. Docs.*, IV, 227-28.

16. Osgood, *Colonies in Eighteenth Century*, I, 247-52, 260-61; Jacobsen, *Blathwayt*, 298-99.

By December 1696, the campaign against Fletcher gathered speed, and evidence began to pour in to the Board of Trade. Winthrop and Penn testified against Fletcher, and Popple soon informed them that the Board had considered the importance of their testimony and was now anxious to see further proof of Fletcher's iniquity, "which you or any other person can produce . . . such accusations as can be made good will be a very acceptable piece of service to them, from what hand soever it comes." [17]

The governor himself had no idea how badly his affairs were going in England. He only knew that Livingston had sent some additional complaints against him, so he concentrated on that protagonist. "All men know," he wrote, that Livingston "has made a considerable fortune by his employments in the Government, never disbursing six pence, but with the expectation of twelve pence, his beginning being but a little Book keeper, [yet] he has screwed himself into one of the most considerable estates in the province." "A man of such vile principles," Fletcher warned, must be kept "from sucking any more the blood of the Province, for he has been a very spunge to it." [18]

While Fletcher was struggling for his political life, Livingston was effectively excluded from public affairs. In at least one respect, this was a blessing in disguise, for it permitted him to devote his energies to a facet of his career which did not depend upon the governor's favors—commerce. Throughout his entire life, he remained a merchant, although politics frequently dominated his activities. Even while enmeshed in the Whig intrigues in London in 1695-96, he had not forgotten that he was bred to trade. During those hectic days, whenever he had a free moment, Livingston toured the shops of various merchants, inspecting and ordering goods for shipment to New York. Not only did he buy textiles and spices, but he also added to his library, purchasing copies of Machiavelli, Livy, Tacitus, Plutarch, *The Lively Oracles*, *The Gentleman's Calling*, *The Evening's Conference*, and *The State of New England*.[19] Upon his return to

17. Popple to Penn and Winthrop, Dec. 12, 1696, *Cal. State Papers, Col.*, XV, no. 495.

18. Fletcher to Brooke and Nicolls, Dec. 20, 1696, O'Callaghan, ed., *N. Y. Col. Docs.*, IV, 251.

19. Bills of Luke Forster, Sept. 15, 1695, John Baker, Oct. 1695, Roger Lillington, Oct. 9, 1695, Richard Gilbert & Co., Oct. 11, 1695, John Pyke, Oct. 12, 1695, Jeremy Gough & Co., Oct. 21, 1695, Edward Poole, Feb. 7, 1695/6, Livingston-Redmond Mss.

New York in the summer of 1696, he found that his wife had kept affairs in good order. Continuing the intercolonial trade which he had initiated, she had sent goods valued at £60 on the sloop *Mary* to Carolina in September 1695.[20]

Though the evidence is slight, there is a temptation to conclude that Livingston's trade flourished in almost inverse ratio to his withdrawal from public service. On December 31, 1696, various residents of the colony owed him more than 40,000 florins (about £3,200), and £450 were due him from non-residents. About one-third of his debtors came from Schenectady, Esopus, and Livingston Manor, and another fourth lived in the Albany area.[21]

The most important of Livingston's overseas ventures was his London investment of £475 8s 5d in Captain Kidd's *Adventure Galley*. In addition, he shipped two cargoes, valued at £42, to Barbados; two others to London, one consigned to John Blackall and the other to Robert Hackshaw; and another to Levinus Van Schaick of Amsterdam. During the next few years, both Hackshaw and Van Schaick were to figure prominently in Livingston's overseas trade. He had first met Hackshaw in Lisbon in May 1695, and he now channeled most of his English trade through him. On their first transaction in October 1696, Livingston sent him £296 worth of peltry and Jamaica sugar. At the same time, Livingston began a correspondence with Van Schaick, a former Albany resident who had established himself as a merchant in Amsterdam.[22]

The Navigation Acts prohibited a direct trade with Amsterdam, but there was a legal and profitable, although involved, means of carrying on such a commerce. As Van Schaick explained it, each beaver skin imported into England was subject to a duty of 12s sterling. Upon re-exportation to Amsterdam, however, three-fourths of that sum was rebated. Added to these savings was the fact that "so many of the expenses attached to [the sale of] peltry in England are not [encountered] in Holland, so that if you get only as much for your peltry here as in England, it will still be more advantageous for you here." Livingston therefore sent furs to Van Schaick through Hackshaw. In the summer of 1697, he shipped 1,936 florins (about £155)

20. Invoice of goods, Sept. 14, 1695, List of debts in Roanoke, Apr. 26, 1696, *ibid.*
21. "*Lyste Van Debiteurs*," Dec. 31, 1696, *ibid.*
22. Invoice of merchandise, Oct. 15, 1696, *ibid.*; Livingston Journal (Van Laer typescript), 55; Van Laer, ed., *Correspondence*, 24*n*.

worth of peltry to Amsterdam; soon thereafter, Hackshaw sent him returns of £135 worth of textiles, gloves, and laces. In August 1697, furs valued at 2,383 florins (about £190) were forwarded to Van Schaick. In turn the Amsterdam merchant sold the furs and shipped to Livingston ironware, copper, brassware, paint, 1,000 panes of French plate glass, and two cases of the best Mecklenburg china.[23]

The Amsterdam trade went so well that Livingston proposed that he and Van Schaick become partners in a merchant vessel, but the latter was hesitant, preferring to wait until peace eliminated the piracies of wartime. He was also discouraged about the Leipzig market for furs; it was extremely bad because "the fashion in Germany has changed greatly as a result of the scarcity of money."[24]

Although Livingston's trade with Amsterdam stayed within the legal technicalities of the Navigation Acts, he was ready to stray beyond those limits and engage in the illegal French-Canadian trade. Little is known of this except that such a transaction was proposed by "Jan the Frenchman," and that young John Livingston was planning to go to Canada with a mission for the exchange of prisoners. His father had agreed to supply him with the two commodities most desired in Canada—English woolens and pieces-of-eight.[25]

But before Robert Livingston could become involved in the Canadian trade, politics interrupted the scheme. As early as May 1697, it was reported that the Earl of Bellomont would replace Fletcher as governor of New York; in November, Fletcher himself acknowledged it, although he was probably unaware of the low repute in which he was held in London.[26] Livingston looked forward to Bellomont's

23. Van Schaick to Livingston, Sept. 14, 1697 (Dutch), Van Schaick's acct. of sales of Livingston's goods, Aug. 29, 1697-June 26, 1698, Invoice of goods, Sept. 3, 1697, Acct. current between Van Schaick and Livingston, Sept. 10, 1697-May 12, 1699, Van Schaick to Livingston, Aug. 12, Sept. 15, 1697 (Dutch), Livingston-Redmond Mss.

24. Van Schaick to Livingston, Aug. 12, Nov. 17, 1697, Feb. 15/25, 1698 (Dutch), ibid.

25. Alida to Robert Livingston, Mar. 20, 24, 1697/8, Aug. 25, Oct. 2, 1698 (Dutch), ibid.; Andrews, Colonial Period, IV, 354-55, 357.

26. O'Callaghan, ed., Cal. Hist. Mss., II, 257; Fletcher to Board of Trade, Nov. 16, 1697, O'Callaghan, ed., N. Y. Col. Docs., IV, 293. Fletcher's reputation was so blemished that Shrewsbury refused to include in the letter of recall the customary phrase: "The King would take care of him and otherwise employ him for the future." Blathwayt approached William III and secured its inclusion. Shrewsbury to Blathwayt, July 13, 1697, Blathwayt to Shrewsbury, July 19, 1697, Hist. Mss. Comm., Report on the Manuscripts of the Duke of Buccleuch & Queensberry, II (part II), 492, 500.

friendship as his only means of recouping the losses he had suffered at Fletcher's hands, and in January 1697/8, he went to New York City to greet the new governor on his arrival.[27]

Now that Fletcher's departure was merely a matter of time, many people felt free to criticize him sharply for his actions. In Albany, the focal point of discontent was his lavish distribution of public lands to his favorites, particularly the Mohawk grant of two hundred square miles to Delius, Wessels, Bancker, Pinhorne, and Peter Schuyler. Livingston was kept fully informed of events in Albany by his wife. The people, she wrote, were in an uproar "because the minister [Delius] and the mayor [Bancker], who speak for the place, should have a patent for the Maquase country.... They ... summoned the minister and Dirk Wessels to the courthouse and asked them if they wanted to transfer the patent to the town, but they refused ... and threatened to establish a trading company there." The mayor, as Fletcher's appointee, could afford to be obstinate, but not so the popularly elected aldermen who led the opposition to the Mohawk patent. They sent Hendrick Hansen and David Schuyler to meet the new governor and lay their case before him. In addition, they were to ask for the assistance of Livingston and James Graham.[28]

Livingston's mind had not yet been made up on this matter. Most of the patentees were hostile to him, and he had suffered much at their hands. While a nephew, David Schuyler, was a leader of the opposition to the grant, a brother-in-law, Peter Schuyler, was one of the patentees. Moreover, Livingston's own inclination was to side with the aristocracy against the "mob," for not only was he a large landowner, but he had plans of his own to apply to Bellomont for the Onondaga lands just to the west.[29]

Alida Livingston was not at all uncertain, and she chided her husband for his indecision. An application for the Onondaga lands, she warned him, would turn the Albany populace against him. Further pressure was exerted on Livingston by the patentees themselves, who did their utmost to alienate him. Wessels and Delius were circulating

27. Alida to Robert Livingston, Jan. 12, 1697/8 (Dutch), Livingston-Redmond Mss.
28. Osgood, *Colonies in Eighteenth Century*, I, 282-83; Alida to Robert Livingston, Jan. 12, 1697/8 (Dutch), Livingston-Redmond Mss.
29. Alida to Robert Livingston, Jan. 25, 1697/8 (Dutch), Livingston-Redmond Mss. David Schuyler was the son of David Pieterse Schuyler, who, in turn, was a brother of Philip Pieterse Schuyler, patriarch of the Schuyler clan and father of Peter and Alida. Schuyler, *Colonial New York*, II, 458, 461.

stories in Albany that Livingston was not really Bellomont's friend, because they feared that the disorganized hostility to them might find a leader who had the new governor's ear. At the same time, the patentees tried to wean Hendrick Hansen away from the opposition by offering him a plantation within their grant, but he rejected the bribe and retorted his hope "that never in their lives will they possess a foot of it." [30]

The rumor that Livingston had reached a *modus vivendi* with the patentees and had purchased Pinhorne's share of the grant puzzled Alida. She was certain that her husband knew that the patentees were "so much in the hatred of the people that the majority of them do not go anymore to listen to the minister's preaching and say, 'he teaches that they shall not covet and covets for himself.'" [31]

However, Livingston's concern with the Mohawk patentees was temporarily relegated to the background by the arrival of the Earl of Bellomont on April 2, 1698. Livingston was overjoyed to learn that the governor had been instructed "to enquire and examine ... into all ... Levingstons demands ... as into the reasons that have hitherto induced the foresaid Governor [Fletcher] & Councill, to defer their complyance therewithall." [32] After two desolate years of political ostracism, Livingston was about to reap the rewards that had been denied him; he was about to be elevated by Bellomont to the highest councils of government.

30. Alida to Robert Livingston, Jan. 12, 25, 27, 1697/8 (Dutch), Livingston-Redmond Mss.
31. Alida to Robert Livingston, Feb. 8, 22, 1697/8 (Dutch), *ibid.*
32. Royal instructions to Bellomont, Aug. 31, 1697, O'Callaghan, ed., *N. Y. Col. Docs.*, IV, 291.

CHAPTER VIII

Bellomont and the Moderates

NEW YORK's political heritage during the 1690's was one of bitterness and violence, whose roots extended back to the Leislerian upheavals, and whose character was sharpened by the life-or-death power inherent in high office. Political leaders, including Livingston, had to stand with one extreme faction or the other, with the Tories or anti-Leislerians on the one hand or with the Whigs or Leislerians on the other. As long as the Rebellion's major personalities kept their hatreds alive and allowed themselves to be used by corrupt governors, the dominant *motif* in the colony's politics was the lack of a middle ground.

The first real opportunity to dispel the unwholesome aura surrounding New York's politics occurred when Richard Coote, Earl of Bellomont, arrived as governor in April 1698. At first, he remained somewhat aloof from the colony's factionalism, although his sympathies certainly lay with the Leislerians whom his predecessor had maltreated. Under his influence, therefore, a small handful of moderates emerged, men who renounced both extreme factions, who trimmed their sails to meet the shifting political breezes.

There is no reason to believe that these moderates consciously sought to be a third force in politics; rather, it was likely that circumstances determined their positions—this was certainly the case with Robert Livingston. He had broken completely with the Tories, but it was inconceivable for him to join hands with his most bitter enemies, the Leislerians. Though he probably considered himself a Whig, he would undoubtedly have added the qualifying adjective: moderate.

Not so easily discernible are the attitudes of others who became moderates, such as Stephanus Van Cortlandt, Peter Schuyler, and James Graham, but they also deserted the extreme Tory faction and joined Livingston in the as yet uncharted middle ground between the two embattled factions. Van Cortlandt and Schuyler had been very close to Fletcher during the height of his power, but both now found it more advantageous to serve Bellomont. Their decision may have been simply a means of protecting their own interests; perhaps, since both were Livingston's brothers-in-law, he influenced them. Regardless of the way in which they rationalized their positions, they definitely made themselves useful to the new governor. Van Cortlandt supplied derogatory information about Fletcher, Schuyler gave Bellomont the benefit of his influence with the Iroquois, and both aided in victualing the royal troops after others refused to perform that service. Graham was also very close to Livingston and may have been influenced by his friend's attitude. He, too, served Bellomont by supplying information which could be used against Fletcher's associates and by bridging the gulf between the extreme Whigs in the Assembly, where he was speaker, and a basically moderate executive.

As long as Bellomont remained moderate, he found these men helpful in accomplishing his major objective in New York: to root out the tangled undergrowth of graft and corruption which had been nourished by Fletcher.[1] Moreover, since they had cut their ties with the extremists, they were also useful to Bellomont in his less successful attempt to eliminate the factionalism which plagued the colony. Indeed, the first year of Bellomont's administration was to be the moderates' best time.

The new governor detested Fletcher, and he soon learned that Livingston shared his attitude. When Livingston chanced to meet the former governor, Fletcher denounced and threatened him: "Sirrah or villain I am now out of Commission and a private man & you are the occasion of all the mischeif & I will be revenged of you & I wish I may find you with a Sword by your Side." Livingston's conquests

1. For his reforming zeal, see Bellomont's report to the Bd. of Trade, May 8, 1696, O'Callaghan, ed., *N. Y. Col. Docs.*, IV, 302-6.

were not by the sword. He sought the Earl's protection and urged, "if Colonel Fletcher have anything to object to me that he may do it by a due course of law, & not terrify me by his threatening expressions." [2]

Bellomont promptly ordered his predecessor to appear on April 16 and prove his charges against Livingston. The futility of such a performance was obvious, and Fletcher did not press his accusations.[3] Having thus been vindicated, although in an indirect manner, Livingston assisted the governor in collecting evidence to send Fletcher back to England for trial.[4]

Livingston, Van Cortlandt, and Graham furnished Bellomont with information about the former governor's extravagances, his neglect of the colony's defenses, and his mishandling of public funds. Livingston supplied a memorandum on the decline of Albany's population between 1689 and 1697. Although King William's War was the real cause, Bellomont could argue that Fletcher's ineptness magnified the war's result. Livingston and Van Cortlandt, who had victualed the royal troops, also provided evidence of Fletcher's insatiable greed, recounting the story of the annual perquisite of ten shillings per soldier demanded by the governor. When the victualers protested that they could not pay it without further depriving the soldiers, Fletcher secured an additional allowance for them from the Assembly so that they could continue the payment.[5]

Livingston also ingratiated himself with the new governor when he and Graham uncovered a "plot" against Bellomont; it implicated Nicholas Bayard and Chidley Brooke, two of Fletcher's most intimate associates. Bellomont received the report that "Sundry persons

2. Bellomont to Blathwayt, Nov. 14, 1698, Blathwayt Papers, VIII, Col. Wmsbg.; Livingston to Bellomont, Apr. 7, 1698, PRO, CO 5: 1040, no. 58 (Lib. Cong. transcripts). See also *Cal. State Papers, Col.,* XVI, no. 359.

3. Livingston's petition, Apr. 9, 1698, Bellomont's order, Apr. 13, 1698, N. Y. Col. Mss., XLII, 9, N. Y. State Lib.; Bellomont to Bd. of Trade, June 28, 1698, O'Callaghan, ed., *N. Y. Col. Docs.,* IV, 331.

4. Before the Board of Trade, Fletcher testified: "I cannot be ignorant that there are two scotchmen [i.e., Livingston and Graham] gott into Credit who are my mortall enemies, men that are able not only to trouble a Province, but to turne it upside down; and if these men can by successive complaints keep me under prosecution they have their ends." Fletcher to Bd. of Trade, Dec. 24, 1698, O'Callaghan, ed., *N. Y. Col. Docs.,* IV, 450.

5. "Memorandum to Enquire," 1698 (Livingston's draft), Livingston-Redmond Mss.; Livingston's return of Albany inhabitants, Apr. 19, 1698, *Cal. State Papers, Col.,* XVI, no. 381; Van Cortlandt's and Livingston's certificate, Nov. 3, 1698, PRO, CO 5: 1041, no. 21 xiii (Lib. Cong. transcripts)—originally prepared June 10, see *ibid.,* no. 7 i; Bellomont to Bd. of Trade, Nov. 8, 1698, O'Callaghan, ed., *N. Y. Col. Docs.,* IV, 423.

... had Conspired together to disturb the Peace," and took it seriously
enough to transmit it to the authorities in London. Bellomont was
grateful for Livingston's aid, and word soon spread throughout the
colony that the Albany merchant was again a power in politics. The
Albany Common Council, still fighting the Mohawk patentees, recognized his status by appointing him one of its agents to seek that grant's
cancellation.[6]

Ironically, the political changes being wrought by Bellomont led to
a renewal of strife between Leislerian and anti-Leislerian, much to the
governor's dismay. He ordered new Assembly elections, but neglected
to replace Fletcher's sheriffs, with the result that the Tories won
control of the legislature. So heated were the contests, Edward Randolph reported, that "they can hardly be kept from shedding blood."
Ever prudent, Alida Livingston cautioned her husband not to become
"involved with either side." "I hope," she urged, "that you will stick
to your own affairs and not meddle with anything but your own business." [7]

Although Livingston apparently kept out of the elections, he did
help the governor. Indeed, if he wanted to receive his money and
regain his offices, he had to court Bellomont by gathering evidence
against Fletcher and by making his financial resources available to
the government. On May 1, he was named victualer of the royal
troops, sharing the contract for the three companies in Albany with
Peter Schuyler, while Van Cortlandt supplied the one in New York
City.[8]

In return, Bellomont recommended Livingston for the highest post
that a colonial could normally hold—a seat on the governor's Council.
According to his instructions, Bellomont was to retain Fletcher's
councilors, an impossible situation because it meant that those who
had profited most from maladministration would be able to thwart all
efforts at reform. Within two months after his arrival, therefore,

6. Graham's and Livingston's certificate, Oct. 27, 1698, PRO, CO 5: 1041, no. 12
xxix (Lib. Cong. transcripts); Common Council Minutes, May 7, 1698, Livingston's
and Jan Janse Bleeker's commission, May 10, 1698, Munsell, ed., *Annals of Albany*,
III, 28-30.

7. Osgood, *Colonies in Eighteenth Century*, I, 277; Randolph to Blathwayt, May 12,
1698, Blathwayt Papers, II, Col. Wmsbg.; Alida to Robert Livingston, May 17, 19,
1698 (Dutch), Livingston-Redmond Mss.

8. "Generall Account of Victualling his majesties forces," May 1, 1698-Nov. 1,
1700, Livingston-Redmond Mss.; Affidavits, May 1, 1698, *Third Annual Report of
the State Historian of the State of New York* (N.Y., 1898), 464-70.

the governor suggested to the Board of Trade six new names for appointment to the Council. Only two of them could be classed as Leislerians; the others were either moderates or mild Tories.[9] The governor was the prisoner of no faction, but a moderate trying to strike a political balance.

Despite the close relationship between Livingston and Bellomont, the governor had not yet formally restored Livingston to his offices or settled his accounts as outlined in the Crown's directives. "I am astonished," Alida informed her husband impatiently, "that you write that they are so idle there ... the assembly does not accomplish much but discords." Preoccupation with the Assembly, which was controlled by the Tories, may well have been the reason for Bellomont's neglect of Livingston's claims. The governor had urged moderation upon the Assembly's leaders, but without effect, and he finally dissolved that body after a month.[10]

With that out of the way, he took up the problem of Livingston's claims. In mid-June, he asked the councilors—the same men who had so bitterly denounced Livingston for nearly two years—to consider Livingston's case. They were now somewhat wary and reported that they "had nothing further to offer against him," adding that "it was not proper for them to sit as judges" on charges which they had originally made. They even agreed that he was "the fittest person to be entrusted with the business of victualling." Since neither Fletcher nor the Council was willing to substantiate their charges, Bellomont informed the Board of Trade that Livingston's monetary claims were "justly due to him and ought to be discharged here." He also endorsed Livingston as "a person fitt and capable" of executing the offices granted by the royal commission of 1696.[11]

The reticence of Fletcher and the councilors in this affair and the Tories' obstructionism in the Assembly seemingly convinced Bellomont that he had to rely upon moderates and Whigs. In his second

9. Bellomont's royal instructions, Aug. 31, 1697, O'Callaghan, ed., *N. Y. Col. Docs.*, IV, 284. The Leislerians were Staats and De Peyster; the others were French, William Beekman, Adolphus Philipse, and Livingston. Bellomont to Bd. of Trade, May 28, 1698, *Cal. State Papers, Col.*, XVI, no. 472 vi.

10. Alida to Robert Livingston, June 13, 1698 (Dutch), Livingston-Redmond Mss.; Osgood, *Colonies in Eighteenth Century*, I, 277-78.

11. N. Y. Council Minutes, June 16, 1698, *Cal. State Papers, Col.*, XVI, no. 578; Bellomont to Bd. of Trade, June 28, 1698, O'Callaghan, ed., *N. Y. Col. Docs.*, IV, 331-32. See also O'Callaghan, ed., *Doc. Hist. N. Y.*, III, 634-35.

list of recommendations for appointment to the Council, he renewed his earlier suggestions with the exception of two Tories, Philip French and William Beekman, replacing them with James Graham and John Corbile (or Kerfbyl), a moderate and a Leislerian, respectively.[12]

Bellomont had already illustrated his resolution to rely on moderates and Whigs by appointing Livingston as manager of his expedition to Albany to meet with the Iroquois in June.[13] In Albany, the Mohawk grant to Delius, Wessels, Bancker, Pinhorne, and Peter Schuyler had aroused a deep and bitter hostility toward Fletcher; it was not only a serious economic threat to Albany's fur trade, but also a strategic threat to the whole colony, since it weakened Anglo-Iroquois relations. "Instead of sending around everywhere to attract the Indians back again," wrote Mrs. Livingston, "they were chasing them away, and the Indians say, if that continues, they will then go and live in Canada." When the Mohawk sachems therefore urged Governor Bellomont to cancel Fletcher's grant of their lands, he listened to their appeal, concluded that the patent "appears from the Records to be an Infamous Cheat & most Iniquitous Imposition," and promised to write to the London authorities for its cancellation.[14]

Since the patent had been engineered by Fletcher's Indian commissioners for their own benefit, Bellomont dismissed them, appointing Robert Livingston and Peter Schuyler in their stead. Although Schuyler had been a member of Fletcher's board and a participant in the patent, Bellomont retained him because he was "the most popular man . . . with the 5 Nations." The governor neither trusted nor liked him, however, and relied on Livingston to keep a watchful eye on his brother-in-law.[15]

Livingston's and Schuyler's appointment came at a critical time. Although King William's War was ended by the Treaty of Ryswick in September 1697, Indian affairs, more than ever before, became a

12. Bellomont's memo, July 13, 1698, *Cal. State Papers, Col.*, XVI, no. 672; Bellomont to Bd. of Trade, Oct. 17, 1700, O'Callaghan, ed., *N. Y. Col. Docs.*, IV, 726.

13. N. Y. Council Minutes, June 9, 1698, VIII, 48-49, N. Y. State Lib. See also "A List of Warrants Issued by Richard Earle of Bellomont," in "New Netherlands, Oldest New York, and the Colonial Government," N.-Y. Hist. Soc.

14. Osgood, *Colonies in Eighteenth Century*, I, 282-83; Alida to Robert Livingston, Feb. 8, 22, 1697/8 (Dutch), Livingston-Redmond Mss.; McIlwain, ed., *Wraxall's Abridgment*, 30.

15. Bellomont's instructions to Schuyler and Livingston, Aug. 1, 1698, *Cal. State Papers, Col.*, XVI, no. 822 i; Bellomont to Somers, Mar. 7, 1699/1700, Harley Papers, XXXVI, fol. 84, British Museum.

vital concern of the government because intertribal Indian warfare between New York and Canada continued unofficially. The Iroquois were still the key to the continent, and the English and the French vied for control over them. The French strategy was to stir up war between the Iroquois and the western tribes allied with the French so that the Five Nations could secure peace only by submitting to France.

Only two things welded the Iroquois to the English—a good trade, and a knowledge that the English, should a full-scale war erupt, would assist them with arms and men. French intrigue made it essential that the royal troops in New York be maintained at full strength. The colony's delicate relations with the Five Nations gave added significance, therefore, to the problem of provisioning the royal troops. The old system, in use since Dongan's time, had proven inefficient, dangerous, and costly. Even though the government had paid 10 percent interest to the victualers, they were often dissatisfied at the delays in clearing their accounts in London, and an alternative method of supplying the troops had to be found.

Livingston proposed a new victualing arrangement to Bellomont on August 25, suggesting that Sir William Ashurst, the governor's agent in London, should "Imploy annually at least 1500 or 2000 £ Sterling in the Purchasing of Such goods & merchandice as [is] . . . Suteable for this market . . . & Consign the Same to Such Person or persons your Lordship Shal judge fitt, for the disposing of the Said goods to the best advantage this market will afford."

Livingston stressed two major advantages of his plan. Not only would it facilitate the victualing and eliminate borrowing at high interest rates, but it would also make a handsome and perfectly legitimate profit for the governor. The annual expense of victualing 400 men at 5½ d a day each, he noted, was £3,345 in New York currency; adding 10 percent interest made the cost £3,680. However, if the agent used £2,090 for trade goods and insurance in London, the investment would bring about £4,000 in the New York market, more than enough to cover the cost of victualing. Since the Crown allocated £2,830 sterling for that service, and since only £1,587 sterling would be required under the new system, the governor would make an actual profit of £1,243 sterling. These profits, of course, would be those normally received by a merchant.[16]

16. Livingston's memorial to Bellomont, Aug. 25, 1698, Livingston-Redmond Mss.

Though foolproof on paper, the plan contained several flaws. There were the inevitable risks facing the merchant—loss of vessel and cargo, or collapse of the market for a particular commodity. If any of these catastrophies occurred, the governor would be forced to revert to the old method of borrowing. But that might be more difficult because the merchants would certainly not appreciate the Crown's competition in the sale of goods. Nor would the Crown be likely to favor the King's representative soiling his hands with commerce. As a result, although Bellomont suggested the idea to his London agent, nothing came of it.[17]

Livingston certainly had no cause for complaint about the treatment he received from Bellomont, but there were others who thought less highly of the governor. Edward Randolph, certainly no friend of Bellomont, reported that some of the leading merchants were exceedingly discontented, but he admitted that "all the noise and crye they make . . . is not against his Lordship's person, but against the Act of Parliament [to prevent frauds and regulate abuses in the plantation trade] which his Lordship is sworn to observe, and should his Majesty send another Governor tomorrow, as carefull as his Lordship in relation to their trade, they would be as Mutinous as they are now." [18]

Council members Nicholas Bayard, Gabriel Minviele, Thomas Willet, and John Lawrence led the opposition to the governor's reforms. They were testy and perverse, he wrote, "always caballing and contriving to make the government uneasy to me." By September 1698, Bellomont had had enough of their "caballing" and, without awaiting royal approval of his proposed councilors, summarily dismissed the "perverse" members. At the same time, he dismissed Richard Townley, though for non-residence and non-attendance rather than obstructionism, and Frederick Philipse, now in his seventy-third year, decided that this was the opportune moment to retire from public life.

Having swept out the Tory extremists, Bellomont replaced them with Abraham De Peyster, Samuel Staats, Robert Walters, and Robert Livingston. The Council was now almost evenly divided between moderates and extreme Whigs. The first three of the new councilors were avowed Leislerians, Walters being a son-in-law of the martyred

17. Bellomont to Ashurst, Oct. 12, 1698 (Livingston's draft), *ibid.*
18. Randolph to Blathwayt, Sept. 12, 1698, Blathwayt Papers, II, Col. Wmsbg.

Leisler. Livingston was a moderate, as were the hold-over councilors —Van Cortlandt, Schuyler, and William Smith.

Livingston's inclusion in the Council was not an afterthought by the governor, who was most effusive in his praise: "The Government has no small obligation to Mr. Livingston, for were it not for him, the four Companys here had deserted long since, there having been due for their subsistence in Colonel Fletcher's time near £2500, which so far discouraged the then victuallers and others, that I find nobody willing to subsist the companies but Mr. Livingston, who purely to serve the government... did undertake it." Livingston immediately pressed his advantage and secured warrants for more than £890 in repayment of a wide variety of disbursements during Fletcher's and Bellomont's administrations.[19]

Developments in London, however, foreshadowed future financial difficulties for the victualer and the governor. Thomas Weaver, New York's agent to Whitehall, reported that the royal troops in the colony had not "received a farthing of subsistance since January twelve-month." Because the whole expense of victualing had been charged against "Lord Bellomont's credit with the victuallers," Weaver pleaded with the London authorities for funds.[20]

The British Army was then in a deplorable condition. After the Treaty of Ryswick ended King William's War, Parliament expressed its dislike of standing armies by cutting the forces to 7,000 men and then hesitating to vote it any funds. As a result, pay arrearages amounted to more than £2,000,000 sterling. In New York, the royal troops faced an even more awkward situation; the paymaster-general had reportedly forgotten to include them in his annual estimates to Parliament, and they were simply "cutt off" from two years' pay.[21]

Fortunately, this news had not yet reached the colony. Bellomont and the victualers only knew that no money was forthcoming: the reason remained a matter of speculation. The governor assumed at first that his agent, Sir William Ashurst, had been negligent, and sent

19. Bellomont to Bd. of Trade, Oct. 21, 1698, O'Callaghan, ed., *N. Y. Col. Docs.*, IV, 399-400; N. Y. Council Minutes, Oct. 6, 1698, VIII, 67-68, N. Y. State Lib.; N.-Y. Hist. Soc., *Collections*, 2 (1876), 439-41; "Accounts of the Revenue of the Province of New York," Apr. 2, 1698-Apr. 2, 1699, Phillipps Mss. (photostats), N.-Y. Hist. Soc.

20. Weaver to Treasury, Oct. 12, 1698, *Cal. State Papers, Col.*, XVI, no. 1039 i.

21. Pargellis, "Four Independent Companies of New York," *Essays to Andrews*, 105-6; Bellomont to Bd. of Trade, Feb. 28, 1699/1700, O'Callaghan, ed., *N. Y. Col. Docs.*, IV, 608-9.

him a sharply worded message. Weaver, the colony's agent, was striving to get money for the troops' support, pleading with William Popple, secretary to the Board of Trade, for the use of his influence. He even applied directly to the Board, but to no avail.[22]

Unaware of events in London, Livingston continued to work closely with Bellomont. In April 1699, he participated in the Council's debates on Iroquois relations. The Five Nations, under great pressure from the French and the western tribes, were seriously thinking of adopting a policy of neutrality. In an effort to dissuade them from such a step, the Council and Assembly recommended that John Schuyler and Johannes Bleeker should attend an Iroquois conference at Onondaga.[23]

But this proposal was only a temporary expedient, and Livingston decided to draft a master plan for future action by the New York government. On April 12 he submitted to Bellomont a comprehensive report based on his extensive knowledge of Anglo-Iroquois relations. Since the French were instigating continual warfare between the Iroquois and "the far Indians," Livingston suggested that first priority be given to establishment of a general peace under British auspices. He proposed that a delegation of 200 Christians, 300 or 400 Iroquois, and all of the Far Nations' prisoners being held by the Iroquois be sent to the western tribes. On their way, they could implement a secondary aspect of British policy by erecting a fort at Wawyachtenok, modern Detroit, to control the fur trade of the west. Then, after a general peace had been concluded, several sachems from the Far Nations should be brought back to Albany to ratify the peace. There, they would see "the plenty and cheapness of goods" which will encourage them "to bring all their trade thither." [24]

Bellomont agreed that utilization of England's economic advantage was the best means of destroying French influence among the western tribes, but he did not feel that New York was the proper colony to

22. Bellomont to Ashurst, Oct. 12, 1698 (Livingston's draft), Livingston-Redmond Mss.; Weaver to Popple, Dec. 10, 1698, Weaver to Bd. of Trade, Dec. 20, 1698, O'Callaghan, ed., *N. Y. Col. Docs.*, IV, 437, 451.

23. *Journal of the Votes and Proceedings of the General Assembly of the Colony of New-York....1691 ... 1765* (2 vols., N.Y., 1764-66), I, 99 (hereafter cited as *Assembly Journal*); *Journal of the Legislative Council of the Colony of New-York.... 1691...1775* (2 vols., Albany, 1861), I, 124 (hereafter cited as *Legis. Council Jour.*).

24. Livingston's memorial to Bellomont, Apr. 12, 1699, O'Callaghan, ed., *N. Y. Col. Docs.*, IV, 500-1; *Cal. State Papers, Col.*, XVII, no. 250 ix.

undertake this. When he sent Livingston's memorial to the Board of Trade, he suggested that the Carolinas were more conveniently located for the experiment. However, both were in complete accord in urging "the finding out, now in time of peace, a trade with those remoter Indians." Perhaps, if both had agreed on the means, the end might have been achieved; but there was to be no real implementation of the idea for two decades.[25]

Livingston's intimate concern for the colony's welfare did not cause him to lose sight of his own affairs. On May 4, he reminded the governor and Council of the royal directive to refer his claim for £388 to the Assembly's consideration. Bellomont, once it was called to his attention, placed it before the Assembly, which promised to "take the same into their Consideration." But the Leislerians who had won control of the legislature earlier that year had no intention of facilitating Livingston's collection of the money, and they referred the claim to two committees and then put it aside.[26]

The perverted pleasure derived by the Leislerians in tormenting Livingston notwithstanding, the governor needed his services. He reminded the Assembly of the royal directive, but Livingston's claim was simply referred "untill another time." Thoroughly annoyed, Bellomont blasted the legislators for paying so little deference "to his Majestys order in Council concerning a Debt due Mr. Livingston." Unwilling to alienate the governor, particularly over so small a matter, the Leislerians quickly capitulated. The Assembly asked the governor to issue warrants for £388 to Livingston, who was to surrender all documents pertaining to his claim. On May 15, the governor and Council passed the necessary warrants.[27]

Sure of Bellomont's desire to please him, Livingston produced still another royal order, which directed the New York government to pay him 8 percent interest on the money he had previously advanced for the public. Livingston had wisely withheld this from Fletcher until favorable action seemed more predictable. The Council promptly

25. Bellomont to Bd. of Trade, Apr. 13, 1699, O'Callaghan, ed., *N. Y. Col. Docs.*, IV, 488. See below, Chaps. XV-XVII.
26. N. Y. Council Minutes, May 4, 1699, *Legis. Council Jour.*, I, 136; N. Y. Assembly Minutes, May 5, 10, 11, 1699, "Journal of the General Assembly, 1698-1705," 55, 57-58, N.-Y. Hist. Soc.
27. N. Y. Assembly Minutes, May 12, 13, 1699, "Journal of the General Assembly, 1698-1705," 59, 61-62, N.-Y. Hist. Soc.; N. Y. Council Minutes, May 15, 1699, VIII, 109, N. Y. State Lib.

appointed a committee to determine the amount of interest due Livingston. Two weeks later, his claims for salary arrears as sub-collector of the excise were presented to the governor and Council. The clerk of the Council reported that Livingston's annual salary had been £50, that no payments had been made since May 28, 1691, and that the arrears were £281.[28]

Patience was proving a most rewarding virtue. Livingston had received most of his money, his offices had been restored to him pending royal approval of Bellomont's action, his post of victualer had been renewed, and he had been elevated to the governor's Council. These rewards were adequate compensation for the indignities he had suffered at Fletcher's hands. But dark clouds were gathering on the horizon, and the harmonious relations between Livingston and Governor Bellomont were to deteriorate gradually as a result of William Kidd's activities in the Red Sea, Bellomont's campaign to vacate the extravagant land grants in the colony, and the hopeless financial muddle of the British Army at the turn of the century.

Although the Leislerians made some modest political gains during Bellomont's first year, the governor was determined to prevent them or the handful of moderates from dominating the machinery of government. Maintenance of this delicate political balance called always for great acumen and often for swift action, and only Bellomont's personal intercession prevented its disruption.

The governor faced just such a situation in May 1699, as he was about to leave for a visit to Massachusetts. The Assembly had prepared a memorial recounting Leisler's last days and bitterly denouncing the administrations of Sloughter, Ingoldsby, and Fletcher as iniquitous. In part, this was an honest expression of grievances, but it was also a scheme to force James Graham's resignation as speaker. Because he had been intimately associated with all three administrations, he could either sign the memorial and denounce himself, or resign. Bellomont could not afford to lose his services, so he rescued Graham, just before the vote was taken on the memorial, by elevating him to the Council.[29]

Once Bellomont left for Boston on May 16, however, he could no

28. N. Y. Council Minutes, May 16, 1699, VIII, 114, N. Y. State Lib.; Barne Cosens' certificate, May 31, 1699, Livingston-Redmond Mss.
29. N. Y. Assembly Minutes, May 16, 1699, "Journal of the General Assembly, 1698-1705," 62-65, N.-Y. Hist. Soc.

longer protect the New York moderates. Instead, he entrusted affairs to his wife's cousin, Lieutenant Governor John Nanfan, who probably had the same intentions as the governor but not the same abilities. Perhaps the only politicians desirous of preserving the political equilibrium were the moderates, who were completely dependent upon executive protection. If either extreme group, Whigs or Tories, became dominant, the moderates would be ostracized and persecuted. The Whigs hated them because they were tainted with Leisler's blood; the Tories hated them because of their attacks upon Fletcher and his friends.

Despite their contrariety of aims, the Leislerians and the anti-Leislerians both sought to separate Bellomont from the moderates, and both believed they had found their opportunity when Captain William Kidd arrived off Oyster Bay, Long Island, in June 1699.[30] To the Tories, it was a chance to embarrass Livingston and Bellomont while proving the governor's vaunted anti-piracy campaign a hollow mockery. To the Whigs, it was also an opportunity to embarrass Livingston, but they believed that Bellomont would prove his rectitude beyond a doubt and thereby confound his enemies.

Caught in the middle of these schemes, of course, was Captain Kidd. Although he had failed to end piracy in the Red Sea, he had been successful as a privateer, capturing several merchant vessels, including the rich Moorish prize, *Quedah Merchant*. For these acts, the British Admiralty charged him with piracy. In reality, Kidd was no pirate: every vessel he had captured was a legal prize which, when challenged, flew the French flag and presented a French pass. But some of them happened to belong to the Grand Mogul whose feelings were far from assuaged by legal technicalities. Kidd's mission, designed to alleviate the difficulties of the East India Company, increased rather than decreased them, and when the British Admiralty circulated orders to the colonial governors for the apprehension of pirates, his name was prominent on the list.[31]

Although Kidd's innocence is well established today, there was plenty of room for doubt in 1699. His actions after he returned to America did little to dispel the charge that he had turned pirate. He

30. Dunbar Maury Hinrichs, *The Fateful Voyage of Captain Kidd* (N.Y., 1955), 129.
31. For the vessels encountered by Kidd, see *ibid.*, 175-79; Osgood, *Colonies in Eighteenth Century*, I, 540-41.

arrived in the sloop *St. Anthony*, rather than the *Adventure Galley;* most of the treasure he had brought back was secreted in the West Indies; and he was noticeably reluctant to enter New York harbor, preferring instead to anchor off Oyster Bay and hold clandestine meetings with his friends. Moreover, he made no effort to communicate with his two partners, Livingston and Bellomont.[32]

The governor had already made up his mind about Kidd. He firmly intended to carry out the orders to apprehend and return him to England for trial. In Bellomont's eyes, there was only one thing that could vindicate his partner—proof that he had been "forced by his men against his will to plunder two Moorish ships." Livingston, on the other hand, had little opportunity to get involved in Kidd's fate at this time. On June 8, Nanfan ordered him to attend an Iroquois conference in Albany, where he remained until the sixteenth. Meanwhile, James Emott—friend and countryman of Kidd, and a lawyer—joined the captain on the *St. Anthony*, and they sailed for Boston. There, it was generally believed, Emott would petition Bellomont for Kidd's pardon.[33]

The Leislerian position was clear. Samuel Staats, one of their leaders, hoped that the governor would act "with all circumspection, for the opponents are already beginning to brag, and say, now it will soon be seen in what manner My Lord will protect the pirates." This hope was soon realized. Kidd arrived in Boston on June 28, fully expecting a friendly welcome. Bellomont exercised the greatest caution in dealing with him, and finally lured him to his doom with promises of fair treatment and false expressions of belief in his honesty and innocence. Kidd was hailed before the Massachusetts Council on July 3, and five days later, Bellomont reported his *coup* to the Board of Trade. He felt certain that Kidd had turned pirate and "would not so much as speak with him but before Witnesses, I thought he lookt very guilty, and to make me believe so he and his friend Levingston (Who Posted hither

32. The only thorough analysis of Kidd's voyage is Hinrichs, *Voyage of Captain Kidd, passim.* An excellent discussion of Kidd's trial is in Richard B. Morris, *Fair Trial* (N.Y., 1953), 33-68.

33. Bellomont to Bd. of Trade, May 15, 1699, *Cal. State Papers, Col.*, XVII, no. 384; [Nanfan] to Livingston, June 8, 1699, PRO, CO 5: 1042, no. 40 xxxi (Lib. Cong. transcripts); Conference Minutes, June 12-16, 1699, *Cal. State Papers, Col.*, XVII, no. 740 xxxii; Wendell to De Peyster, June 19, 1699, De Peyster Papers (Versteeg translation), N.-Y. Hist. Soc.

from Albany upon news of Captain Kidds designe of coming hither) and [Duncan] Campbell... began to Juggle togeather and Imbezle some of the Cargo." [34]

Livingston's dash to Boston could have been prompted by only one thing—somehow, he had learned of Bellomont's intentions and, as the governor later reported, was badly frightened. He had good cause for alarm; if Kidd had violated the agreements signed in London in 1695, Livingston's bond for £10,000 sterling was forfeited. According to the governor, Livingston approached him in a "peremptory manner," demanded the return of the bond and the articles of agreement, and told him that "Kidd swore all the oaths in the world, that unless... [the governor] did Immediately Indemnify Mr. Levingston... he would never bring in that great ship [i.e., *Quedah Merchant*] and Cargo, but that he would take care to Satisfy Mr. Levingston himselfe out of that Cargo." [35]

Livingston's bluff, if such it was, failed. Kidd was committed to prison by order of the Massachusetts Council, and Livingston and Campbell were summoned to be "severally examined" about "Imbezelments, Concealments and disposals" made by Kidd. Under oath, Livingston admitted that he and Campbell had each been given a Negro boy and that Campbell had received 100 pieces-of-eight.[36] Since Bellomont pursued the matter no further, he was apparently satisfied that this was the full extent of all "Imbezelments" by Livingston and Campbell.

Bellomont's behavior was intricate and perhaps devious but almost totally predictable. He had to disassociate himself thoroughly from Kidd, but he could not dispense with Livingston's services in victualing and Indian affairs. At the same time that he publicly implicated Livingston in Kidd's activities by his letter to the Board of Trade, he privately pleaded with Chancellor of the Exchequer Somers for per-

34. Staats to De Peyster, July 3, 1699, De Peyster Papers (Versteeg translation), N.-Y. Hist. Soc.; Bellomont to Bd. of Trade, July 8, 1699, Blathwayt Papers, V, Col. Wmsbg. See also PRO, CO 5: 860, fols. 62, 64; Hinrichs, *Voyage of Captain Kidd*, 130-31.

35. Bellomont to Somers, Mar. 7, 1699/1700, Harley Papers, XXXVI, fol. 84, British Museum.

36. Mass. Council Minutes, July 7, 12, 1699, PRO, CO 5: 787, pp. 222, 224; Livingston's deposition, July 12, 1699, *ibid.*, 860, no. 64 xv. For printed versions, see Morton Pennypacker, "Captain Kidd: Hung, not for Piracy But for Causing the Death of a Rebellious Seaman Hit with a Toy Bucket," *N. Y. Hist.*, 25 (1944), 501, 529.

mission to return Livingston's bond.[37] Thus, Livingston's safety depended on his usefulness to the governor. Whatever one might have thought of Bellomont's political maneuvering, his rejection of Kidd and his rebuff to Livingston did prove him to be a consummate politician. He vindicated himself, cleared his partners in London, confounded his enemies in New York, and increased Livingston's dependency.

The Leislerians rejoiced, for the news, as Samuel Staats exulted, "has absolutely put me at ease, for to see his [i.e., Bellomont's] enemies totally disappointed in their so frivolous, positive assertions causes me the greatest satisfaction." Still another cause for elation on the part of the Leislerians was the report that Fletcher had been completely disgraced in London. He had been censured for his aid to pirates, mismanagement of the revenue, and general maladministration of the colony. For the Leislerians, this defeat of one of their bitterest enemies cleared the way for attacks upon the Tories who had stood by him.[38]

Of all the Tories, Nicholas Bayard was probably the man most detested by the Leislerians, who charged him with having influenced Sloughter to sign Leisler's and Milborne's death warrants. Anticipating these charges, Bayard fled to England early in Bellomont's administration and wisely realized "that it will not be safe for mee to return to New York, unless I can obtain here from the Lords something to be my protection." The Leislerians then turned to Domine Godfredius Delius, an avowed friend of Fletcher. When summoned to appear before the lieutenant governor and Council, he also decided to go into hiding.[39]

This pattern alarmed Livingston, for he, too, was a likely candidate for Leislerian vengeance. But other things were worrying him at this time. He did not know the nature of Bellomont's private correspond-

37. Bellomont's original letter has apparently disappeared. In a later one he stated that he desired "your Lordship this last Sumer in one of my Letters to order me to give him [i.e., Livingston] his bond and articles with the consent of the other Lords." Bellomont to Somers, Mar. 7, 1699/1700, Harley Papers, XXXVI, fol. 84, British Museum.

38. Staats to De Peyster, July 17, 1699, De Peyster Papers (Versteeg translation), N.-Y. Hist. Soc.

39. N. Y. Assembly Memorial, May 16, 1699, "Journal of the General Assembly, 1698-1705," 63, N.-Y. Hist. Soc.; John to Abraham De Peyster, June 26, 1699, De Peyster Papers (Versteeg translation), ibid.; Bayard to Povey, June 25, 1699, Blathwayt Papers, VII, Col. Wmsbg.

ence with Lord Somers, and so he still feared the forfeiture of his
£10,000 sterling bond. In addition, the governor's recently announced
policy towards New York's large landowners made him even more
uneasy. Ordered by the Crown to vacate his predecessor's extravagant
land grants, Bellomont accepted the idea enthusiastically and suggested that there were other grants, equally extravagant, which antedated Fletcher and should receive similar treatment. He included the
lands of William Smith, Frederick and Adolphus Philipse, Stephanus
Van Cortlandt, Henry Beekman, Peter Schuyler, Kiliaen Van
Rensselaer, and Robert Livingston. These, he noted, "I have neither
time nor strength to breake . . . but if your Lordships will send over a
good Judge or two and a smart active Atturney Generall, I will God
willing . . . breake all these Extravagant Grants."

This issue broadened the rift between the Leislerians, who supported the governor's policy because none of them had had an opportunity to acquire princely estates, and the moderates, who opposed
it because all of them possessed great tracts of unsettled lands. A law
to vacate the Fletcher patents easily passed the Leislerian-controlled
Assembly, but met with great opposition from the moderates on the
Council. Bellomont, who broke the tie vote on the Council, was not
surprised that those who have "unmeasurable grants, fancie I shall
push at them the next time, so they are equally angry." [40]

Bellomont was determined to carry his land policy to its logical
conclusion, but even he admitted the impossibility of doing so without aid from London. He told the Board of Trade that, if they wanted
him to end the land grants, they had to send him "a peremptory order
from the King so to do." It was his desire to be impartial and break all
grants above 2,000 acres in size, but the Assembly did not have the
"courage to go through with a businesse of that kind." The more he
considered the problem, the more Bellomont became convinced that
he could never get the bill passed in New York. [41] The moderates,
however, only knew that the governor's determination was unaltered.
This threat and the Kidd fiasco were Livingston's most immediate
problems, but they were by no means his only troubles.

Although Livingston had received no money to repay his advances

40. Bellomont to Bd. of Trade, May 3, Apr. [i.e., May] 27, 1699, O'Callaghan, ed.,
N. Y. Col. Docs., IV, 514, 510.
41. Bellomont to Bd. of Trade, July 22, Aug. 24, 1699, *ibid.*, 535, 553.

for the subsistence of the royal troops, he continued to use his own funds and credit in this service. But the victualers soon reached the breaking point—there was a limit to their credit. By the summer of 1699, their attitude was summed up by a lieutenant of one of the companies, John Riggs: "His Lordship hass beene kind to mee in words but . . . that will butter no Parsnips." Bellomont warned that unless the arrears were paid, "the Victuallers will be broke (they tell me they are out of pocket £7000) and the soldiers turned a-grazing." But despite Sir William Ashurst's best efforts to get money in London, he regretfully reported to Bellomont that "there is no expectation of receiving any of your arrears, there being no manner of fund or provision made for them." Bellomont's first thought upon learning that the arrears had been "cutt off" was to keep the news from the victualers at all costs. "I am forc'd to keep this to myself," he declared, "not daring to communicate it to the Officers . . . nor to the Victuallers, for it would set them a madding." [42]

So successful was the governor in keeping his secret that even Lieutenant Governor Nanfan, who was also a captain of one of the companies, knew nothing of it. He had to rely on Livingston for news about when the pay and subsistence might be expected. Livingston, in turn, got his information from Van Cortlandt and it was disheartening. "We will not receive our money in the spring," Van Cortlandt warned, and "we will be in the greatest financial difficulty we have ever been in." [43]

The entire financial structure of the colony was most unsteady. Traffic with the pirates, a major source of New York's specie, had been effectively halted by Bellomont's anti-piracy campaign; there was a scarcity of coin, and the colony found itself on the brink of an economic depression. [44] Livingston's expenditures in the government's behalf, other than the victualing, had been repaid in warrants, and he now turned them over to Van Cortlandt for collection. Although he was collector and receiver general of New York, Van Cortlandt found

42. Riggs to Livingston, Sept. 23, 1699, Livingston-Redmond Mss.; Ashurst to Bellomont, Aug. 13, 1699, Bellomont to Bd. of Trade, Sept. 8, 1699, *Cal. State Papers, Col.,* XVII, nos. 14 xvi, 769 xiv; Bellomont to Bd. of Trade, Jan. 5, 1699/1700, O'Callaghan, ed., *N. Y. Col. Docs.,* IV, 601. The arrears covered a period of twenty-seven months prior to Mar. 25, 1700.

43. Van Cortlandt to Livingston, Jan. 15, 1699/1700 (Dutch), Livingston-Redmond Mss.

44. Nettels, *Colonial Money Supply,* 205, 207.

it impossible to redeem the warrants. The customs duties were being paid in scrip rather than cash, and the collector could not even pay the governor's salary. His comment, a not unfamiliar one, was: "Happy are those who have nothing to do with the government." [45]

Sorely beset by this assortment of afflictions—Kidd, land grants, victualing, and lack of specie—Livingston and his friends eagerly grasped at any solution, no matter how tenuous. There were rumors that Kidd had secreted £8,000 in gold in New York City. "If that could be secured," Graham suggested, "it might ease you of your bonds." But the only honest advice he could give Livingston was to curry favor with Bellomont and be patient. Servility and patience, in the light of the rumor then circulating, seemed to be of dubious value. Brandt Schuyler reported that "My Lord Cornbury tries to get this government, and it is believed that he will succeed." John Riggs repeated the story, adding a comment that probably typified the moderates' attitude: "Wishe for a governor but no more Lords." [46]

Beset with difficulties, Livingston chose the seclusion of his Manor to the perplexities of New York politics. He concentrated on the construction of his manor house and refused to get involved in the current political controversies. With a note of genuine envy, Van Cortlandt commented that peace and quiet was something which Livingston would "experience only when you eat, sleep, and awaken at your ease in Roeloff Jansen Kill, released from the common troubles." [47] If Livingston hoped to isolate himself midway between Albany and New York City and become a gentleman farmer, he failed to reckon with the plans and ambitions of the Leislerians. They had neither forgotten nor forgiven his role in the Leisler Rebellion and its bloody aftermath, and they were eager to repay him in kind. The weakest chink in Livingston's armor, as they soon realized, was his financial involvement with the government.

45. Van Cortlandt to Livingston, Jan. 15, 1699/1700 (Dutch), Livingston-Redmond Mss.
46. Graham to Livingston, Jan. 16, 1699/1700, Schuyler to Livingston, Jan. 16, 1699/1700 (Dutch), Riggs to Livingston, Jan. 16, Feb. 12, 1699/1700 (Dutch), *ibid.*
47. Van Cortlandt to Livingston, Jan. 15, 1699/1700 (Dutch), *ibid.*

CHAPTER IX

Bellomont and the Leislerians

DURING THE FIRST three months of 1700, Livingston remained
on his manor, studiously avoiding any direct contact with
the New York government. According to Bellomont, he had "fallen
into a fit of Melancholy...resolving to meddle no more with
business." He and his wife were "frightened out of their wits" about
their liability in the Kidd venture, the governor continued, and even
James Graham reported that Alida had a "great uneasiness in her
bosom." [1] However, Captain Kidd's fate was only one aspect of Livingston's fears. Victualing, the colony's precarious finances, and the
Leislerians' appetite for revenge all contributed to his desire to avoid
any further financial entanglement with the government.

The Leislerians' mode of attack soon became obvious. Lieutenant
Governor Nanfan moved that the Council issue £800 in warrants to
Livingston as his 8 percent interest on the money he had loaned the
government. Although this was in accord with the Treasury Lords'
directive, the Council could not reach a decision. When Bellomont
was told of their hesitancy, he referred Nanfan to the Crown's instructions; but this only confused matters because the orders merely
directed the governor to determine why Fletcher had previously failed
to repay Livingston. At the Council hearing, Van Cortlandt pointed

1. Bellomont to Somers, Mar. 7, 1699/1700, Harley Papers, XXXVI, fol. 84, British
Museum; Graham to Livingston, Mar. 18, 1699/1700, Livingston-Redmond Mss.

out that the governor had already conducted such an investigation and had reported Livingston's case favorably. However, the Leislerians on the Council were curious as to Fletcher's reasons for withholding payment. They asked Matthew Clarkson and David Jamison, both aides of Fletcher, to produce the former governor's report. Van Cortlandt did not know whether the Leislerians had read those documents, but he learned that Samuel Staats had queried Jamison about the matter. It was most peculiar, Van Cortlandt wrote Livingston, that Staats "shows himself to be very zealous to nose through your affair thoroughly." [2]

Livingston's withdrawal from public affairs was very disconcerting to Bellomont. "I am in a great perplexity about the Indians," he confessed; "everything happens to fall out most unluckily to Cross and distract all my measures for keeping our 5 Nations of Indians steddy to us." He admitted that Schuyler was the most popular figure among the Iroquois, but "he is not a man of head, nor can I depend on him, he being of Fletcher's faction." To retain control of Indian policy, Bellomont had to balance Schuyler's interest with Livingston's. If the governor intended to use Livingston, he had to repair the breach which had developed in their relations. He again pleaded with Lord Somers for permission to return Livingston's bond and articles of agreement. Upon reflection, Bellomont now acknowledged that "Mr. Livingston when he was here was heartily troubled and ashamd at Kidd's villanous behaviour, ... he had no design of harm to us but was deceived as well as we." [3]

Another cause of Livingston's "melancholy" was the more than £7,000 which he and Schuyler had spent and the approximately £3,000 which Van Cortlandt had expended for victualing. Although the governor thought the claims reasonable, there was no prospect of repayment, and he warned the Board of Trade, "If those 3 men knew what Sir William Ashurst writ to me of the four Companies being cutt off all their Arrears ... it wou'd make 'em quite desperate." Bello-

2. Van Cortlandt to Livingston, Feb. 7, 1699/1700 (Dutch), Livingston-Redmond Mss.

3. "Mr. Livingston is married to Schuyler's sister, yet they [Livingston and Schuyler] love not one another, and Livingston having much the advantage of t'other in point of understanding I put him into the management of the 5 Nations to ballance the other's Interest and the Influence he has on them." Bellomont to Somers, Mar. 7, 1699/1700, Harley Papers, XXXVI, fol. 84, British Museum. Cadwallader Colden later supported Bellomont's evaluation of Schuyler. N.-Y. Hist. Soc., *Collections*, 1 (1868), 199-200.

mont was himself desperate; his reputation was at stake and his whole
political structure threatened to collapse. As a last resort, he turned to
William Blathwayt, his old enemy, for help. "Most of the Lieutenants
had starv'd before this time had I not lent 'em money out of my own
pocket. Colonel Courtland Colonel Schuyler and Mr. Livingston will
be entirely ruin'd if they be not very speedily satisfied for victualling
the Companies. I desire your friendship," he begged Blathwayt, "in
setting these things on a right foot." [4]

The first step in setting things "on a right foot" was taken in London, but it dealt with Livingston's association with Kidd, not with
victualing. Bellomont had been criticized in Parliament for his role in
Kidd's commission, but had been "acquitted with great applause for
his Conduct and the Lord Justices has sent him Thanks for prudent
administration." Almost immediately, this unexpected report placed
Livingston's role in a new light. The governor "being Released from
all imputations in that matter," James Graham wrote Livingston, so
"you must [be] in Consequence." Bellomont stated that "your Bond
shall never hurt you," Graham added, so that "you may sett your mind
at rest upon that matter"; indeed, this news from London has "regain[ed] you well wishers who Now change their notes and believe
you a good man." [5]

Although the threat of the Kidd affair fizzled out with little harm,
Livingston still faced formidable financial problems. There were
rumors that the victualing money had been paid in London, and Van
Cortlandt was inclined to believe them, but he acutely observed that
"that does not help us as long as we do not have it." He was so disgusted with the victualing contract that he was ready to give it up,
but he reluctantly agreed to continue until November 1700. Van
Cortlandt bore the brunt of the demands made by the victualers' creditors, but the only assets he had at his disposal were the unredeemable
warrants issued to Livingston and himself for their non-victualing disbursements. The customs duties were bringing little cash into the
treasury because the importing merchants were paying the levies with
warrants which the collector then retired. [6]

---

4. Bellomont to Bd. of Trade, Feb. 28, 1699/1700, O'Callaghan, ed., *N. Y. Col. Docs.*,
IV, 608-9; Bellomont to Blathwayt, Mar. 5, 1699/1700, Blathwayt Papers, VIII, Col.
Wmsbg.
5. Graham to Livingston, Feb. 20, Mar. 18, 1699/1700, Livingston-Redmond Mss.
6. Van Cortlandt to Livingston, Mar. 7, 22, 1699/1700 (Dutch), *ibid.*

Before Bellomont could assist the victualers, he was forced to call upon Livingston's services once again. The New Englanders feared an Indian war and suspected that the Iroquois were involved. In this delicate situation, the governor turned to his two stalwarts in Indian relations, Schuyler and Livingston. Although both were disgruntled about the victualing situation, they placed the colony's welfare above their personal grievances, at least for the moment. Bellomont warned them that the Indian troubles were being fomented by the governor of Canada, who was "as deep in the design as his Jesuits," and proposed that French artifices could be counteracted if Livingston, Schuyler, and Hendrick Hansen would confer with the sachems at Onondaga, the central council fire of the Iroquois.[7]

Livingston had apparently recovered from his earlier despondency by April 6 when he received formal instructions from the governor in Albany. The conference at Onondaga was to be a preliminary to a meeting with the Iroquois scheduled in Albany on August 10, and Bellomont appointed Livingston and Abraham De Peyster as agents to supply the presents for the Indians at the latter council. The governor would have preferred to give that patronage to De Peyster alone, but he was "obliged to Mr. Livingston, and would not willingly put any slight upon him."[8]

Although Livingston agreed to participate in the preliminary Indian negotiations, he did not support the governor's evaluation of the basic problem. He strongly doubted that the Iroquois were involved in any plot or that French intrigues were responsible for arousing the New England Indians. "The English to the Eastward," he believed instead, "are too Rigid and jealous of their Indians, and keeping them so in aw[e] does rather Exasperate them then keep them under." Despite this disagreement, Livingston joined Schuyler and Hansen and left for Onondaga on April 9. They quickly learned that the various tribes distrusted the English and were circulating rumors which diminished English prestige. Two Mohawk sachems repeated a story that the French intended to build forts in Iroquois territory and that the English were too weak to stop them; it was also whispered that the

---

7. Graham to Livingston, Mar. 29, 1700, *ibid.*; Bellomont to Commissioners of Indian Affairs, Mar. 21, 1699/1700, *Cal. State Papers, Col.*, XVIII, no. 345 xi.

8. Bellomont to De Peyster, Apr. 5, 1700, Frederick De Peyster, *The Life and Administration of Richard, Earl of Bellomont, Governor of the Provinces of New York, Massachusetts and New Hampshire, From 1697 to 1701* (N.Y., 1879), xiv-xv.

English intended to disarm the Five Nations and then destroy them. Both rumors were vigorously denied by the agents who, to prove their good will, told the sachems that Bellomont would meet them in Albany on August 10 to settle all matters.[9]

Having completed a round trip of 540 miles through territory only rarely traversed before by white men, Livingston, Schuyler, and Hansen returned to Albany on May 2. Livingston's formal report pointed out that the Iroquois were "much dejected and in a staggering condition." Quick action was needed to prevent their desertion to Canada, and the three agents endorsed the governor's plans to build a fort and send missionaries among the Indians.[10] In addition to his official report, Livingston prepared a personal analysis of Anglo-Iroquois relations for the governor. The Mohawks "are grown weake," he announced, not only because of the war's effects, but because of French intrigues since the peace. More than two-thirds of them had gone to Canada where they were "kindly Received," fed, clothed, guarded, and instructed by Jesuits. To frustrate the French, Livingston suggested that the Five Nations be resettled. The Mohawks should be moved closer to Albany, a fort built to protect them, and a minister sent to instruct them. He also urged that the Oneida and Onondaga be relocated nearer Albany.

"It is morally impossible," Livingston argued, "to Secure the 5 Nations to the English Interest any longer without building forts & Secureing the Passes that lead to their Castles." The governor also subscribed to this idea, but he disagreed about the number of forts and their locations. Bellomont wished to build a series of them, beginning with one at Onondaga. Now that Livingston had first-hand geographical knowledge of the area, he pointed out the inadequacy of such a location: it would defend only one Indian castle and would be virtually impossible to reach in time of war. He proposed instead a fort between Lake Ontario and Lake Oneida, just west of the site of modern Oswego. This was the main route between Canada and the Iroquois' territory; a fort there "Secures all the 5 Nations from the

9. Livingston to Bellomont, Apr. 18, 1700, PRO, CO 5: 861, no. 31 xiv; Negotiations of Livingston, Schuyler, and Hansen, Apr. 9-May 2, 1700, O'Callaghan, ed., *N. Y. Col. Docs.*, IV, 654-56.

10. The exact route is given in Leder, ed., *Livingston Indian Records*, 175-76. See also Livingston to Bellomont, May 3, 1700, Livingston, Schuyler, and Hansen to Bellomont, May 3, 1700, O'Callaghan, ed., *N. Y. Col. Docs.*, IV, 647, 653.

french at once." [11] But two decades were to elapse before a royal governor acted upon this suggestion.

Together with these documents, Livingston sent a personal plea to Bellomont; he had been forced to advance the expedition's full cost, £170, which he could not spare because of the victualing situation. A few days later, he also sent his eldest son, John, to Massachusetts to give the governor the latest information about the Indians. Bellomont told him that he expected news from London any day, but when vessels arrived, there were no letters for the governor. Bellomont was greatly disturbed: he "could not tell what for to thinck of it." But, as a Captain Green explained, letters addressed to him might have been placed on board ships bound directly for New York, not Boston.[12]

If so, one was probably the disheartening letter written by the Board of Trade on April 11. The Board notified the governor that the four companies of royal troops had been reduced from 400 men to 200, that arrears of pay and subsistence were authorized only for the period from March to December 1699, and that, insofar as the earlier period was concerned, the troops in New York were "in the same Case with all the rest of the land Forces who by an Act past this Session of Parliament are to be paid by Debentures upon forfeited Estates in Ireland." Since those properties had become "a popular subject of declamation" in English politics and were grossly overvalued, this news did nothing to relieve the situation in New York.[13]

But the letter contained more cheerful news for Livingston; whether it was fully revealed to him is unknown, but he must have gotten some hint of it. The Board announced that Customs Commissioner Benjamin Overton had presented Bellomont's favorable report on Livingston's case to them and they had recommended that it be laid

11. "Observations made by Robert Livingston," Apr. 1700, Livingston-Redmond Mss.

12. "An Accompt of the Charges advanced by Robert Livingston," PRO, CO 5: 1044, no. 1 viii (Lib. Cong. transcripts); Information of Robert Livingston, Jr., Abraham and David Schuyler, May 9, 1700, Livingston, Schuyler, and Hansen to Bellomont, May 11, 1700, O'Callaghan, ed., *N. Y. Col. Docs.*, IV, 662, 653-54; John Livingston's "Gurnell of my Gurney from Albany to Baston," May 11, 1700, Livingston-Redmond Mss.

13. Bd. of Trade to Bellomont, Apr. 11, 1700, O'Callaghan, ed., *N. Y. Col. Docs.*, IV, 630-35. The forfeited Irish estates were being used by the Tories in Parliament to embarrass King William who had granted these lands to his favorites. The Tories proposed their confiscation and sale so that the public debt might be repaid. Gilbert Burnet, *Bishop Burnet's History of His Own Times* (6 vols., Oxford, 1833), IV, 404-5, 436-39.

before King William. The Board also recommended that the governor's program to eliminate the large landed estates in the colony be shelved temporarily.[14]

Livingston's financial difficulties remained unsolved, however, and he turned in desperation to his old friend Graham for advice. Graham calmed his suspicion that there might be something more than administrative inefficiency behind his monetary problems. After considering Livingston's circumstances carefully, he concluded that "the delay you meet with in not receiving your money . . . proceeds from Accident more than design. . . . His Lordship is so Engaged in the Intrigues of State that he forgetts that matter which would be the only means to Suport his reputation and Enable those freinds who ar hearty in his Service to Stand by him for whatever value he may put upon these L[eislerians] he will find at a push & in time of business that he is mistaken. . . . Your hand is in the Lyons mouth, so you ought not to draw back. . . . My Lords Integrity wil apear as Clear as the Sunshine." Graham's optimism and unbounded faith in Bellomont apparently convinced Livingston, at least temporarily, that his fears were groundless.[15]

When the governor returned to New York City from Boston at the end of July, Livingston gave him a disturbing account of the condition of the royal troops. "Some of the inhabitants of Albany who are now here,"—in other words, Livingston—had reported that the soldiers were in a shameful state. "Those parts of 'em which modesty forbids me to name, are expos'd to view," Bellomont wrote, and "the women forced to lay their hands on their eyes as often as they pass by 'em." This not only embarrassed the troops and the ladies, but it degraded the Crown in the Iroquois' eyes.

The officers and soldiers were "dissatisfied," Bellomont continued, and the victualers "like distracted men." To make matters worse, there were many who would "rather nourish than endeavour to extinguish the flames" of discontent. One of the many rumors then circulating in New York, he observed, claimed that he had received the subsistence money but had converted it to his own use "and car'd not what became of them, whether they starv'd or no." To Secretary of

14. Bd. of Trade to Bellomont, Apr. 11, 1700, Aug. 21, 1699, O'Callaghan, ed., *N. Y. Col. Docs.*, IV, 635, 547. See also Bd. of Trade Journal, Oct. 5, 1699, *Cal. State Papers, Col.*, XVII, no. 843.

15. Graham to Livingston, June 8, 1700, Livingston-Redmond Mss.

State Vernon, the governor confessed that "truly I am almost at my wits end; and have the most uncomfortable time of it that ever any man had." [16]

Non-payment of the victualing account was most frustrating, for it threatened the political balance of power so carefully constructed by Bellomont, and the governor could do nothing to rectify the situation. But there were other ways in which he could mollify the moderates, especially Livingston. He issued nearly £400 in warrants to him for several small expenditures on behalf of the Indians, gave him £922 in bills of exchange when he learned that the subsistence up to June 9, 1700, had been paid, placed him in complete charge of the finances of the commissioners for Indian affairs, formally recognized his commission as secretary for Indian affairs, and gave him warrants for £715 as salary arrears for that office.[17]

In return for his generosity, the governor expected a full measure of devotion and loyalty. When it was not forthcoming, he began to find fault with the moderates. Livingston, for example, refused to reveal the name of the man allegedly responsible for warning pirates with £500,000 in treasure away from Long Island. Bellomont was angry because of the loss of this specie and, unable to find the actual culprit, directed his anger at Livingston. Peter Schuyler also came in for his share of barbed criticism. While conferring with the Iroquois at Albany, the governor learned that his Indian commissioners, Schuyler in particular, made a practice of entertaining the sachems at their homes and charging the expenses to the Crown. Schuyler, Bellomont reported, "studies to make himself popular by that means . . . to serve himselfe and gratifie his own vanitie."

The moderates' opposition to the governor's land reform program further aggravated him. "Till these grants of land have had their doom," he warned, "these people are irreconcileable." He singled out four grantees for special notice—the moderates Smith, Schuyler, Van Cortlandt, and Livingston. Since Graham, another councilor, was "a

16. N. Y. Council Minutes, July 16, 1700, VIII, 157, N. Y. State Lib.; Bellomont to Bd. of Trade, July 26, 1700, Bellomont to Vernon, July 29, 1700, O'Callaghan, ed., *N. Y. Col. Docs.*, IV, 687-88, 697.
17. N. Y. Council Minutes, Aug. 3, 7, Sept. 12, 1700, VIII, 161, 163, 165, N. Y. State Lib.; "Generall Account of Victualling . . . at Albany from Primo May 1698 to Primo November 1700," and "List of 21 warrants for my Sallary from the 25 of March 1696 to the 25 of June 1700," Sept. 14, 1700, Livingston-Redmond Mss. See also Leder, ed., *Livingston Indian Records*, 180-83.

friend to the Grantees," they "have five of the eight Councilors." The
final rupture between the governor and the moderates was brought
about by the victualing. Bellomont accused Van Cortlandt of giving
the soldiers in New York City inadequate provisions, while Livingston
in Albany had "pinch'd an estate out of the poor soldiers bellies." The
governor canceled the victualing contract and began paying the men
in cash every Saturday so they might fend for themselves and no
longer be at the mercy of unscrupulous contractors.[18]

In Bellomont, there was a streak of the fanatic, and he often struck
out wildly at those whom he suspected of standing in his way.[19] The
soldiers probably had been supplied with "sad provisions," but the
victualers could offer them nothing else because Bellomont had exhausted their credit—he still owed Livingston more than £1,600. His
own credit was not much higher, for the merchants refused to honor
the bills of exchange which he sold to get cash to pay the troops. The
governor suspected that this resulted from a conspiracy between the
victualers and the merchants, and he proposed to his London correspondent that the only way to circumvent the conspiracy was by
sending goods to New York rather than bills of exchange, an idea
originally suggested by Livingston.[20]

Bellomont was so annoyed at Livingston that he revived the charge
of his complicity in Kidd's alleged piracies. Restatement of this charge,
which the governor himself had once refuted in a letter to Somers,
was typical of his vindictive attitude toward the moderates. On October 28, he removed Graham from his post as recorder of New York
City and in his place appointed Abraham Gouverneur, the arch-Leis-
lerian who had also replaced Graham as speaker of the Assembly.[21]

Although disillusioned with the moderates, Bellomont was willing
to call upon their services in a critical situation. On October 28, a
company of royal troops, just arrived from Ireland after a harrowing

18. Bellomont to Lds. of Admiralty, Oct. 15, 1700, Bellomont to Bd. of Trade, Oct.
17, 1700, O'Callaghan, ed., *N. Y. Col. Docs.*, IV, 711, 714-25.
19. "You know how much his Lordship humor has Intangled him into Incon-
veniencys." Graham to Livingston, June 8, 1700, Livingston-Redmond Mss.
20. Bellomont to Bd. of Trade, Oct. 17, 1700, O'Callaghan, ed., *N. Y. Col. Docs.*,
IV, 723. See also Nettels, *Colonial Money Supply*, 192.
21. "We were all of us Strangers to Kidd, but employed him on Mr. Livingston's
recomendacon of his Bravery and honesty." Bellomont to Vernon, Oct. 18, 1700,
O'Callaghan, ed., *N. Y. Col. Docs.*, IV, 760. See also N. Y. Council Minutes, Oct. 26,
1700, Blathwayt Papers, VIII, Col. Wmsbg.

twelve weeks' passage, mutinied in protest against the maltreatment they had received and because they had not yet been paid. When they were finally quelled by the militia, they were imprisoned and the governor convened a court-martial for their trial. Livingston and three other members of the Council—Van Cortlandt, De Peyster, and Walters—were appointed as judges, along with three military officers. The court condemned a large number of the soldiers as mutineers, but the governor pardoned all but four ringleaders. When the judges pronounced the sentence of death on those four men, they unanimously appealed to Bellomont for a reprieve until the King's pleasure could be known.

Perhaps the judges remembered all too well an earlier sentence of death which had been precipitously executed; the consequences of the Leisler affair were an indelible part of New York's life. Whatever their reasons, the judges used three basic arguments for a reprieve: the law under which the soldiers were tried had been passed a day before the event; the legislation had not yet received royal approval; the current English practice was to pardon a first offense against a new law. Disgusted with the timidity of the judges, Bellomont reprieved two of the condemned men, but the other two paid the supreme penalty for their drunken misconduct.[22]

Bellomont's reaction to the court-martial was an important indication of his state of mind. Determined to make an example of the unfortunate soldiers, he ridiculed both Leislerians and moderates for seeking a reprieve. Recurring and prolonged attacks of gout probably account for his fanaticism and seemingly contradictory actions. For example, on November 7, he paid £470 to Livingston on the victualing account, but six days later removed him from the office of subcollector of the excise at Albany. Livingston was deprived of this office at the instigation of the Leislerian members of the Council, who contended that excise collections were more profitable for him than the government. Bellomont concurred and accepted their recommendation that the post be awarded to the highest bidder.[23]

22. Lawrence H. Leder, ed., " 'Dam'me Don't Stir A Man'; Trial of New York Mutineers in 1700," N.-Y. Hist. Soc., *Quarterly*, 42 (1958), 265-83.

23. De Peyster, *Earl of Bellomont*, 71; "Generall Account of Victualling...at Albany from Primo May 1698 to Primo November 1700," Livingston-Redmond Mss.; Bellomont to Treasury Lords, Nov. 23, 1700, O'Callaghan, ed., *N. Y. Col. Docs.*, IV, 776. See also Graham to Livingston, Dec. 3, 1700, Livingston-Redmond Mss.

Encouraged by their successful attack upon Livingston, the Leislerians struck again, utilizing an act passed on November 8 "for appointing and enabling Commissioners to examine, take and state the publick Accounts of this Province." The commissioners, all Leislerians appointed by the Assembly, immediately entered a caveat against payment of the £800 interest on the money Livingston had advanced the government. Although they gave no reasons for their action, Bellomont blocked the payment.[24]

Livingston was not the only moderate to become the target of the governor's wrath. He branded James Graham, a former favorite, a "false tricking" man who had not "a freind in this Province but Mr. Livingston, who has not quite so much cunning as he." If Stephanus Van Cortlandt had not died on November 25, he, too, would have borne his share of abuse; instead, Mrs. Van Cortlandt suffered the obloquy.[25]

No longer shielded by the governor, Livingston retreated temporarily from politics to domestic affairs. A family matter of vital importance—the marriage of his eldest son, John—received most of his attention. As lord of Livingston Manor, a prominent merchant, and an important public official, the father was deeply concerned about his heir's selection of a wife, especially since John had always been something of a problem for his parents. In 1698, when a lad of eighteen, John had "his eye" on Jacob Rutsen's daughter, ten years his senior. The age difference upset his mother and father almost as much as the report that the young lady "had followed the army all her life." Horrified by the thought of such a match, Alida warned John that he could expect nothing less than disinheritance if he continued the affair. This, plus a stern warning from his father, convinced John of the error of his ways. "He knew very well what would happen to him," his mother concluded triumphantly; "he was not crazy enough to throw himself away." [26]

Now, in November 1700, John Livingston's roving eye had lighted upon another, though much more suitable, young lady. Mary Win-

24. *Col. Laws of N. Y.*, I, 430-31, 441-43; Bellomont to Treasury Lords, Nov. 23, 1700, O'Callaghan, ed., *N. Y. Col. Docs.*, IV, 777.

25. Bellomont to Popple, Nov. 29, 1700, Bellomont to Customs Commissioners, Nov. 26, 1700, O'Callaghan, ed., *N. Y. Col. Docs.*, IV, 813, 779; N. Y. Council Minutes, Feb. 19, 1700/1, Blathwayt Papers, VIII, Col. Wmsbg.

26. Alida to Robert Livingston, June 24, 1698 (Dutch), Livingston-Redmond Mss.

throp was the only child of Fitz-John Winthrop, governor of Connecticut and descendant of the leading Puritan family of New England. Besides a most proper family background, she was an heiress and
her father was an old family friend. Despite the advantages for each
family, however, both showed some reluctance to permit the marriage.
The Winthrops and Livingstons were on approximately the same social level, and perhaps neither family wished to appear overanxious
about taking the first step toward such a union.

Rumors that Fitz-John Winthrop's own marriage had not been entirely legal or proper caused Robert Livingston some concern. If they
were true, then Mary Winthrop bore the mark of the bar sinister.
Robert Livingston's negotiations with the Winthrops were conducted
by Duncan Campbell, who did his best to dispel Livingston's doubts
about Mary's parents. They were "man and wife Although itt was
not so publick att first . . . as itt is now," Campbell asserted, and Livingston "need not scruple giveing your consent to your son to marey
so vertious & sober [a] young lady." Winthrop, he added, "is more
or as much desarring to see his daughter welle settled and marryd as
you can be to settle youre Son." Mary's father promised to will her
his entire estate and "to put in a stock in mony Equall with what you
Shall doe for your Son to begine a trad." [27]

If Winthrop were eager to marry his daughter to John Livingston,
he hid it well, announcing to his old friend, "I was much Surprized
when I understood your Sons Affection to my Daughter." Although
he regretted that the parents had not first had an opportunity to discuss it, he promised, "if it shall please God to open a way for their
further proceeding, I shall be wholy guided by His Providence." John,
who had inherited his father's trait of pleading a cause with stubbornness and exaggeration, won his parents' consent after a dramatic appeal: "If They and you Should be So Chruell, I would Reather Chuse
to Dey then to Leave her, for She is the onely one in all the Worald
to me . . . to be Parted a Sunder . . . would Sartenly Breack both our
heardts." Both sets of parents gave their blessings to the wedding, which
took place in the spring of 1701.[28]

27. Campbell to Livingston, Dec. 2, 1700, ibid.
28. Winthrop to Livingston, Dec. 9, 1700, John to Robert and Alida Livingston,
Dec. 10, 1700, Journal, Jan. 1-3, 1700/1, ibid.; Florence Van Rensselaer, The Livingston
Family in America and Its Scottish Origins (N.Y., 1949), 81.

After this blissful interlude, Livingston returned to the realities of New York politics. The balance of power on the Council had shifted by the end of January in favor of the Leislerians. Bellomont appointed Thomas Weaver to succeed the recently deceased Van Cortlandt, and Graham was incapacitated with "violent pains in my belly" and soon died.[29] The Leislerians therefore controlled Council and Assembly, and the governor was most receptive to their suggestions.

With the moderates no longer able to interfere, the Leislerians began to press their attack against Livingston. They selected his weakest point—his financial involvement with the government—and formally resolved that his salary as sub-collector should be discontinued since the Albany excise had been farmed out. Furthermore, the councilors "were of opinion that his Excellency could not regularly order" payment of Livingston's salary as secretary for Indian affairs "till his Majesty's pleasure be known." Therefore, the collector was directed not to honor the £715 in warrants given to Livingston for those salary arrears.[30]

The death of Richard Coote, Earl of Bellomont, on the morning of March 5, 1700/1, interrupted these attacks, but only temporarily. Lieutenant Governor Nanfan was absent in Barbados, and the only councilors available were the four Leislerians. They immediately appointed De Peyster as president pending the return of either Nanfan or William Smith, the eldest councilor. At the same time, they summoned Councilors Smith, Schuyler, and Livingston to attend their deliberations.[31]

Bellomont's experiment in political moderation was the first attempt to apply the Enlightenment concept of a balance of power to New York politics, but it failed completely. As the Leislerians prepared to drown their grief over the loss of the governor in the sweet draught of revenge, the pattern of factional politics moved inevitably toward bitterness and violence.

29. "Cal. Council Minutes," N. Y. State Lib., *Bulletin 58,* 152; Graham to Livingston, June 8, 1700, Livingston-Redmond Mss.; "Abstracts of Wills ... 1665-1707," N.-Y. Hist. Soc., *Collections,* 25 (1893), 100-1.

30. N. Y. Council Minutes, Jan. 27, 1700/1, Livingston-Redmond Mss.; N. Y. Council Minutes, Jan. 30, 1700/1, *Cal. State Papers, Col.,* XIX, no. 114.

31. N. Y. Council Minutes, Mar. 5, 1700/1, VIII, 211, N. Y. State Lib.

CHAPTER X

The Leislerians Triumphant

B Y THE SPRING of 1701, the distinction between moderate and Tory had become meaningless. Bellomont's capitulation to the Leislerians' constant pressure, as well as the deaths of Graham and Van Cortlandt, had made the position of the handful of moderates untenable. Those who had formerly placed their reliance upon Bellomont's personal protection realized that they now needed a more formidable and substantial sanctuary. Only by seeking the protection of the Tories could the moderates avert the loss of their reputations, their fortunes, and, as it developed, even their lives. During the ensuing year, this was driven home to Livingston, one of the chief targets of Leislerian vengeance.

Since De Peyster, Staats, Walters, and Weaver were the only councilors in New York City on March 5, 1700/1, the reins of government passed into their hands after Bellomont's death. The first problem which these Leislerians faced was not new—securing subsistence for the royal troops. The simplest solution would have been to request Livingston and Schuyler to resume victualing, but that would have acknowledged the value of their previous services. Instead, the Leislerians turned to Hendrick Hansen and Peter Van Brugh for money and pledged the excise duties of Albany and Ulster Counties for repayment.[1]

1. N. Y. Council Minutes, Mar. 5, 6, 1700/1, *Cal. State Papers, Col.*, XIX, no. 210; Nettels, *Colonial Money Supply*, 193.

Livingston, Schuyler, and Smith, although a minority on the Council, were still entitled to a voice in the government, and they were duly summoned to New York City.[2] William Smith was the first to appear at the Council board and, as the eldest in length of service, he automatically became president. The Leislerians did not dispute his title, but his claims to pre-eminence were bitterly controverted. He insisted that the governor's powers, in Nanfan's absence, devolved upon him personally and not upon the Council as a whole. But the Leislerians considered the president to be only a presiding officer and not the chief executive; by a four to one vote they decided that executive functions were to be exercised by a majority of the entire Council. Legally, as the Board of Trade eventually decided, the Leislerians were correct.

When the Council majority proposed recalling the Bellomont Assembly to solve the colony's pressing financial problems, Smith refused to sign the necessary order, and the Council majority ruled that he "was obliged to join and sign with them whatever the majority approved." Smith's position was unenviable, and he announced that his family affairs were "in such disorder as necessarily requires his immediate going into the country," thereby utilizing a convenient excuse for leaving a difficult situation.[3]

While Smith was on Long Island, Livingston and Schuyler arrived from Albany. They were immediately summoned to the Council, but failed to appear or return any answer. Three days later, when the invitation was renewed, Livingston replied with a question: had President Smith returned as yet? Neither Livingston nor Schuyler intended to appear until Smith was seated in the chair.[4]

The Leislerians wanted Livingston and Schuyler present, not because they valued their counsel, but because they needed their prestige. There was a simple yet effective weapon which could be used

2. Their continuance as councilors was a matter of chance; if Bellomont had lived a few more weeks, he would have suspended all three. Bayard to Sir Philip Meadows, Mar. 8, 1700/1, O'Callaghan, ed., *N. Y. Col. Docs.*, IV, 849; Walters, Weaver, De Peyster, and Staats to [Champante], May 19, 1701, Rawlinson Mss. A, CLXXII, fol. 124, Bodleian Lib., Oxford Univ. (Lib. Cong. transcripts); Livingston to Blathwayt, May 23, 1701, Blathwayt Papers, BL 149, Huntington Lib.

3. N. Y. Council Minutes, Mar. 13-15, 1700/1, Bd. of Trade to Nanfan, Aug. 20, 1701, *Cal. State Papers, Col.*, XIX, nos. 248, 755.

4. N. Y. Council Minutes, Mar. 21, 24, 1700/1, VIII, 221-22, N. Y. State Lib.

to compel their attendance. In the preceding November, an act had established commissioners to audit public accounts. Although Bellomont had expressed grave doubts whether the commissioners "be very capable or skillfull in accounts," they had the proper political orientation, and their report charged Livingston and Schuyler with receiving large sums of public money for which they refused to account.[5] Since the Council was to judge these charges, it now became imperative for Livingston and Schuyler to appear in Council to defend themselves. On March 31, they came forward to read a remonstrance against the Leislerians' assumption of executive power. The majority would not "suffer it to be entred in the Councill book," however, because it supported Smith's claim to sole executive authority. Charges and countercharges were exchanged until April 1, when President Smith returned.

The question of reconvening the hold-over Bellomont Assembly was revived, and Livingston, Smith, and Schuyler argued that since no one could exercise a veto power, the Assembly could not meet. According to the Leislerians, Smith could not veto laws because he was president in name only. The Council could not do it because they would then have a double veto—once as the legislative upper house and once as the governor in commission. The argument was irrefutable, but the Leislerians ignored it, called the Assembly into session, and refused to permit the minority dissent to be entered in the records.[6]

Livingston viewed these controversies as a prelude to the re-enactment of the tragic drama played a decade before. He expressed his fears to Fitz-John Winthrop: "Our government here being much out of frame, our parties being more divided I think than eleven years ago, so little has my Lords administration contributed to our union. The Councell, Assembly, & indeed the whole Province, divided & in a foment." This was the death-knell of moderatism; in a life and

---

5. Such legislative commissions with primarily political purposes were typical of the period. Burnet, *History*, V, 4-6, 61. See Bellomont to Bd. of Trade, Oct. 17, 1700, O'Callaghan, ed., *N. Y. Col. Docs.*, IV, 721.

6. *Assembly Journal*, I, 113; "Remonstrance of Peter Schuyler and Robert Livingston," Mar. 31, 1701, "Peter Schuyler & Robert Livingston approval of Col. Smiths Paper," Apr. 14, 1701, Livingston-Redmond Mss.; N. Y. Council Minutes, Apr. 1, 8-9, 14, 1701, *Cal. State Papers, Col.*, XIX, nos. 296, 318, 337.

death struggle, safety is not found by standing between the contenders.[7]

The Leislerians made it clear that they had no intention of reconciling their differences with the moderates by the new report of the commissioners of accounts submitted on April 18. Their chief complaint was that neither Livingston nor Schuyler had accounted for public funds they had received. They informed the Assembly that Livingston had received the greatest sums and suggested that "by his Accounts the greatest Frauds are committed." The Assembly therefore recommended that the commissioners proceed against Livingston according to law.[8]

The sole hope of the moderates now lay in England. On April 30, Livingston, Schuyler, and Smith jointly prepared for the Board of Trade a narrative of events since Bellomont's death. After recounting the bitter debates about the Assembly's meeting, the trio warned that the Leislerians planned to pass "severall acts of private consequence, to the publick disquiet of this Province." The villain of the piece, they said, was Thomas Weaver, "a person of a turbulent spirit & very violent." In an effort to forestall the Leislerians, Livingston refuted the old charge about his involvement in embezzling Kidd's loot. At his request, Smith wrote a lengthy explanation of that affair which was sent to the Board of Trade. A supporting deposition from Duncan Campbell was also transmitted to the Board, along with a statement of the money owed by the government to Livingston, £2,858.[9]

No matter what his own personal problems were at the moment, Livingston retained a deep interest in the colony's welfare. In the midst of the Leislerian persecution, he prepared for the Board of Trade a series of observations on New York's difficulties. His analysis of the seriousness of French influence among the Iroquois generally supported Bellomont's earlier evaluations. But he was strikingly original and far in advance of his own time in his discussion of the diffi-

7. Livingston to Winthrop, Apr. 14, 1701, Mass. Hist. Soc., *Collections*, 6th ser., 3 (1889), 67.
8. *Assembly Journal*, I, 112-13.
9. Three of N. Y. Council to Bd. of Trade, Apr. 30, 1701, Smith to Bd. of Trade, May 10, 1701, O'Callaghan, ed., *N. Y. Col. Docs.*, IV, 857-61, 869; Campbell's deposition, May 3, 1701, and "The account of money due to Robert Livingston," c. May 1701, PRO, CO 5: 1046, nos. 14 ii, 14 iii (Lib. Cong. transcripts).

culties and usefulness of the royal troops and in his examination of the English colonies' defensive problems.

The basic problem of the royal troops, Livingston suggested, was that their remuneration was 40 percent less than that of soldiers in England. Instead of being paid in pounds sterling, the soldiers received the colony's local currency, pound for pound. Since the New York pound was worth 30 percent less than the pound sterling, and because the governor's bills of exchange were discounted, the soldiers exposed to the greater dangers received a smaller reward than those safe in England. Moreover, the cost of clothing, food, and drink was twice as high in New York as in England. Livingston had no illusions about the royal troops' usefulness. Two companies of sixty men each on the frontier, he candidly stated, "have been of little more service to the country than the bringing of so much money from England for their subsistance to be spent amongst us." Indeed, "the Merchant of New York has no better way of making returns, especially in time of warr, when there is no risque in bills of exchange." "Soldiers from Europe," he continued, "cannot fight in the woods here, according to the manner of fighting in Europe." The problem of the soldiers' pay was partially resolved on the very day these observations were written. The troops were notified that the Crown had authorized a 10 percent deduction from their pay instead of the previous 30 percent.

Perhaps Livingston's most interesting suggestions dealt with making the troops more effective and remedying the neglect of frontier defenses. He suggested that soldiers be seated as frontier farmers, an English counterpart of the French *coureurs du bois*. He advised that 200 troops be sent to New York every two years and, after a brief period of service, be discharged, given land, and encouraged to settle. Once they spent a few years "fowling and hunting along with our youth and the Indians," he promised, "they will have learnt perfectly to understand the woods." Livingston believed that fortifications could be erected in the Iroquois country only through intercolonial cooperation. This could not be obtained voluntarily, and he suggested the establishment of three super-colonies: one consisting of Virginia, Maryland, North and South Carolina; another of western Connecticut, New York, the Jerseys, Pennsylvania, and Delaware; and the third of eastern Connecticut, Massachusetts, Rhode Island, and New

Hampshire. Then with authority centralized, cooperation in military and financial matters would be assured.[10]

Although Livingston spent considerable thought on his long-range report on imperial policy, New York's politics received most of his attention. The local situation was made more complex by the return of Lieutenant Governor Nanfan from Barbados on May 19. Although Smith's claim to executive authority and the legality of reconvening the Assembly were now hypothetical questions for Crown lawyers to consider at their leisure, no one was certain which side Nanfan would support. Indeed, on the same day that Nanfan returned, the Leislerians submitted an explanation of their conduct to John Champante, the colony's London agent, so that he might defend them "if anything should be imputed amiss in our conduct in opposition to Smith Livingston & Schuyler." They alleged that Livingston had "persuaded & prevailed on" Bellomont to sign unauthorized warrants, that he had been "very false to his trust" as sub-collector, and that he was involved in Kidd's piratical schemes. For these reasons, they asserted, Bellomont intended to suspend him from the Council, but had died before he could do so.[11]

Like the Leislerians, Livingston was uncertain about Nanfan, and he, too, wrote to an English official—Blathwayt. "Haveing Lost my very good ffrinds Mr. graham and . . . Colonel Cortlandt," a discouraged and perplexed Livingston returned to the Tory fold and sought Blathwayt's advice and assistance. All that he wanted was the payment of the money rightfully due him. After that, he told Blathwayt, "I long for a retirement, and . . . I should be glad to see any person better qualified to enjoy all my offices." It was most unfortunate that "no care is taken on the part or behooffe of this province to undermine their [i.e., the French] designs . . . It greeves me to See how much time is Spent, and how many heads are imployed in contriving to promote faction." Recounting the injustices he and his friends had suffered at the Leislerians' hands, Livingston commented that "it can

10. Livingston to Board of Trade, May 13, 1701, O'Callaghan, ed., *N. Y. Col. Docs.*, IV, 870-75.
11. N. Y. Council Minutes, May 19, 1701, *Cal. State Papers, Col.*, XIX, no. 459; Walters, Weaver, De Peyster, and Staats to [Champante], May 19, 1701, Rawlinson Mss. A., CLXXII, fol. 124, Bodleian Lib. (Lib. Cong. transcripts).

never be expected that his Majestie will be well Serv'd abroad if others receive the Like treatment as I have had." [12]

Nevertheless, financial conflicts between Livingston and the Leislerians continued. The commissioners of accounts constantly pressed Livingston and finally submitted a report to Nanfan on June 17. Under threat of jail, Livingston had finally been persuaded to show them the accounts of the Albany excise, but he refused to reveal "in what Way and Manner, and to whom" the money had been paid. He also denounced the law under which they operated and announced that "he did not think himself obliged to give any other accounts." This, the commissioners claimed, left them in a quandary—if they could not force Livingston to account "for above *Twenty Thousand Pounds* received," how could they insist that others account for lesser sums? [13]

Although others were being called to account by the commissioners, Livingston felt that their actions against him were persecution, and he decided to go to England for relief. His plans were changed, however, by Nanfan's urgent request for help in negotiating with the Iroquois. Instead of making a personal appearance in London, Livingston sent the Board of Trade a detailed analysis of his financial grievances: he wanted £3,412 as reimbursement of his expenditures, his salary arrears, and interest on both sums.

Livingston owed a large amount of money to various New York City merchants and, fearing that they "are like to teare me to pieces," he took refuge in Albany. Onzeel Van Swieten, one of them, wrote a very sharp note and chided him for breaking his promise to meet with his creditors by secretly departing for Albany. "You are thoroughly aware," Van Swieten reminded him, "that your notes have been absolutely refused by the Collector, so I ask you to order that money may be on hand here in time, and not leave me hanging as a reward for a friendship which I have been good enough to show you in this matter." [14]

12. Livingston to Blathwayt, May 23, 1701, Blathwayt Papers, BL 149, Huntington Lib.

13. *Assembly Journal*, I, 119.

14. Livingston to Bd. of Trade, June 21, 1701, O'Callaghan, ed., *N. Y. Col. Docs.*, IV, 883-84; "An account of money due to Robert Livingston," June 21, 1701, PRO, CO 5: 1046, no. 21 i (Lib. Cong. transcripts); Van Swieten to Livingston, June 24, 1701 (Dutch), Livingston-Redmond Mss.

While holding off his creditors, Livingston remained active in politics. Nanfan, caught between the two factions, had accentuated their animosity by dissolving the hold-over Bellomont Assembly and ordering new elections. Jamison was very frank in urging Livingston to campaign for the anti-Leislerians: "It will concern you to be active at Albany ... You must expect better quarter at the hands of our people than the others."

Livingston agreed to work for the anti-Leislerians and asked Jamison for "arguments about the Election." "The difficulty," he replied, "is to finde Such as will be taking with the people, that which is most likely to prevail with them is the Saving of therr money." Despite their efforts, however, the anti-Leislerians lost control of the Assembly by a narrow margin.[15]

Before the new Assembly met, Livingston participated with Lieutenant Governor Nanfan at a conference in Albany with the Iroquois, who requested that "our Secretary Robert Livingston may be sent to ... the great King of England to acquaint how that the French of Canada incroach upon our territories." "Wee fear if he does not goe," they added, "this will be only read and layd aside and forgott." Nanfan failed to respond, and an Onondaga sachem repeated the demand two days later. When asked if a letter would not do as well, the Indians replied in unison: "It was concluded by all the Five Nations that our Secretary Robert Livingston should goe to the King." The lieutenant governor, somewhat taken aback, promised to consider their request.[16]

Until the full implications of the Indians' demand were realized by the Leislerians two months later, other matters occupied people's attention. In July, a new chief justice, William Atwood, and a new attorney general, Sampson Shelton Broughton, arrived from England, arousing curiosity about which side of the factional dispute they

15. O'Callaghan, *Cal. Hist. Mss.*, II, 284; Jamison to Livingston, June 28, July 7, 15, 1701, Livingston-Redmond Mss. See also John Riggs to Livingston, July 6, 1701, *ibid.*; Osgood, *Colonies in Eighteenth Century*, II, 54-55.

16. Minutes of Iroquois conference, July 19, 1701, O'Callaghan, ed., *N. Y. Col. Docs.*, IV, 905-8. At least one scholar has been puzzled by this incident, interpreting it first as the result of Livingston's intrigues, thereby accepting the Leislerian thesis, and then as something most meaningful to the Indians and thus not an imposition by Livingston or anyone else. In either case, Livingston's influence with the Iroquois sachems was apparently greater than has been generally acknowledged. Osgood, *Colonies in Eighteenth Century*, I, 475-76, II, 55-56.

would support. In August, the newly elected Assembly convened, and Livingston returned to New York City. For a very short time, it appeared that his fortunes were changing. Nanfan wrote to the Board of Trade about the Iroquois conference and felt himself "obliged in justice to certify . . . that he [i.e., Livingston] hath been a very great help to me in all this Negotiation for which . . . there being no person in . . . Albany so capable and well qualifyed as he is." [17]

The lieutenant governor's favor, however, could not prevent the Leislerians from carrying out their attack upon Livingston. The commissioners of accounts submitted another report to the Assembly on August 28 and demanded that he be committed to jail. If his defiance went unpunished, the commissioners "Conceived it to be against our Oaths to proceed rigorously against other Persons, when we could not force Mr. *Livingston*." The Assembly and Council appointed a special committee to consider the commissioners' complaint; it recommended that an act should be passed to confiscate Livingston's "real and personal Estate for so much Debt to the Crown as he can be charged with," unless he accounted for the funds. On the next day, a Saturday, the Assembly required Livingston to present his accounts "before Wednesday next" or else the bill would be introduced. [18]

Livingston appeared before the commissioners on Monday, and declared "that for what Money he received for the King, he had given an Account already; and as for what he had received from the King, he desired to know his Charge, and in a reasonable Time he would discharge the same." The commissioners insisted that he turn all records over to them, so that they could compare his accounts with those of the king. Clearly, the commissioners were overstepping their authority by passing judgment on matters which had already been approved by the Treasury Lords and the Privy Council. Despite their impertinence, Livingston announced that he was "willing to give all the Satisfaction imaginable, and has begun to transcribe all the particular Accounts for 17 years last past." Because he had been delayed by public duties in Albany and New York City, he asked

---

17. Riggs to Livingston, July 25, 1701, Livingston-Redmond Mss.; *Assembly Journal*, I, 115; Nanfan to Bd. of Trade, Aug. 21, 1701, O'Callaghan, ed., *N. Y. Col. Docs.*, IV, 901.

18. *Assembly Journal*, I, 119-21; *Legis. Council Jour.*, I, 159.

that the commissioners send someone to his quarters to see just what he had accomplished and to report on the time he would need to complete the task.

Livingston's cooperative attitude was not what the commissioners had expected. Apparently, they wanted to condemn him for obstructing their investigation, but they could not do so if his time in the government's service prevented him from casting up his accounts. Perplexed, they turned to the Assembly for advice. If Livingston's offer of cooperation was merely a ruse to delay the accounting until a new administration took over, he did not fool the Leislerians. The Assembly quickly and unanimously resolved that "the Pretences made this Day by *Robert Livingston* . . . are frivolous; . . . *Livingston* hath wholly disobeyed the Act of Assembly . . . and that therefore this House cannot agree to give any further Time." When a conflict existed between the Leislerians' plans and the facts, the latter gave way to the former. The bill to confiscate Livingston's estate was accordingly introduced.[19]

Never ready to accept defeat without a struggle, Livingston appealed to Nanfan and the Council on September 2 for relief from this unwarranted oppression, claiming that he had "immedeatly Sett to worke to make a Collection of all his accounts with the government whatsoever." He had already submitted the Albany excise accounts and had "made a beginning" on the other "numerous prolix & difficult" records. Although he had been delayed by his public duties, he "never did refuse" to render his accounts.[20]

Livingston's plea to Nanfan and the Council fell on deaf ears, and the Assembly proceeded with the confiscation bill. Livingston now poured out his woes to Blathwayt: "Our people that would be Zealous for the Publik Intrest have been so discountenanc'd and frown'd upon of Late, that matters look with an ill aspect, the factions now more blown up then ever since the arrivall of our Cheiffe Justice [Atwood], and if we gett not a moderate Impartiall governor this Province will run all into Confusion & distruction, for all peoples Study is now how to be reveng'd of their neighbour." "All what I have in the world," he continued, "is in the hands of the Publick, & except I gett some Speedy relieff, I shall be Crushed to peeces." This

19. *Assembly Journal*, I, 120-21.
20. Livingston's petition, Sept. 2, 1701, Livingston-Redmond Mss.

was "bad Incouragement for any to follow my example, & Launch out their Estates for the Kings service." Not one to underplay his hand, Livingston warned, "people are more ready to cutt an others throat." [21]

Revenge remained uppermost in the thoughts of the Leislerians, and Livingston could not keep them from their plans. The confiscation bill made some progress in September, but the Assembly's attention was diverted by an opportunity to attack Livingston on another score. When Nanfan presented a copy of his earlier negotiations with the Iroquois, the assemblymen immediately took a deep interest in the Indians' wish to have Livingston sent to England as their agent. Their request and his personal preference coincided so completely that the suspicious Leislerians asked whether the Indians' proposal was mere coincidence or a diabolical plot by Livingston to avoid the legislative retribution planned for him. The Assembly asked the Council to join with it in investigating the matter.[22]

When Livingston appeared before the joint committe, the members informed him of their suspicions that he or his agent had "prevailed [on] and influenced" the Iroquois. The committeemen were unable to find any evidence to support the charge, so they asked "if he thought it not proper for him to take a voluntary Oath...in order to clear himself from the Censure therein." As the committeemen probably expected, Livingston "thought it not worth his while to do the same." The Assembly, after first approving the initial reading of the bill to confiscate his estate, went into a committee of the whole to consider this new issue.

It was becoming obvious that the Leislerians, instead of seeking the truth, were looking for a means to punish Livingston for his political views. When he refused to take the oath, he gave them an opportunity to charge him with contempt. If he had taken it, he would probably have opened himself to a charge of perjury, which, even if untrue, would have been difficult to disprove. The committee of the whole resolved, despite a total lack of evidence, that the Iroquois' request "had been procured by Persons disaffected to the Peace of this Government...that the *Indians,* have been imposed

21. Livingston to Blathwayt, Sept. 3, 1701, Blathwayt Papers, BL 217, Huntington Lib.
22. *Assembly Journal,* I, 124-25; *Legis. Council Jour.,* I, 160.

upon by Mr. *Livingston,* or his Agents, with his Privity and Consent."
It was thereupon ordered that a recommendation be sent to the lieutenant governor for Livingston's suspension as secretary for Indian
affairs pending his formal removal by the Crown. The Assembly
adopted the recommendation of the committee of the whole on
September 13, and Speaker Abraham Gouverneur then presented two
requests to Nanfan: first, only Lawrence Claese should be permitted
to translate at Indian conferences, thereby eliminating Livingston's
influence; and second, since Livingston had tampered with the sachems, he should be suspended from his office and his misconduct
reported to England.[23]

There is no evidence that Lieutenant Governor Nanfan actually rejected the Assembly's requests, but he apparently ignored them. He
certainly realized the value of Livingston's services in Indian affairs,
and he had found nothing improper in the Iroquois negotiations conducted jointly with Livingston in the previous July. Thus, as late as
November, Livingston was still acting as secretary for Indian affairs.[24]

Frustrated in their attempt to deprive Livingston of this office, the
Leislerians turned with renewed vigor to the bill to confiscate his
estate. The commissioners of accounts presented a computation of
the sums with which he could be charged: £3,413 for the Albany
excise from 1683 to 1700, £13,656 for various warrants he had received from 1690 to 1701, and other items for which they could not
find specific amounts. All these sums were included in the bill which
was given its second reading on September 17.

At this precise moment, Nanfan elevated Livingston to the "High
Court of Chancery," probably to indicate his reaction to Leislerian
pressure. But this in no way influenced the Assembly, which, on the
day after Livingston's elevation, read the confiscation bill for the
third time and sent it on to the Council. The Assembly's persistence
angered Livingston, and he hopefully presented his case to the lieutenant governor. He informed Nanfan that he had completed his
accounts and presented them to Rip Van Dam, one of the commis-

23. *Assembly Journal,* I, 126, 127; *Legis. Council Jour.,* I, 161-62; Smith, *History of New York,* I, 139.
24. See note of Sept. 22, 1701 appended to journal of Bleeker and Schuyler, O'Cal-
laghan, ed., *N. Y. Col. Docs.,* IV, 920; Nanfan to Livingston, Sept. 26, 1701, Leder, ed.,
Livingston Indian Records, 184; Nanfan to Schuyler, Nov. 3, 1701, Livingston-Redmond Mss.

sioners, whom he asked to notify the Assembly of his compliance. Van Dam did so, but the Assembly "did not only refuse to make entry of this in their publick minutes but did proceed to passe the said Bill." Livingston insisted that his money should be repaid, that "this vigorous proceeding" against him should cease, and that his protest be entered in the Council minutes. His demands were rejected, however, and the councilors gave the confiscation bill its first reading two days later.[25]

Realizing the futility of any further appeals to the Council, Livingston retired to Albany, but was kept fully informed by David Jamison of events in New York City. In October, the decision finally came: "Just now I came from hearing the bills read off where I find your bill is passed but the 25th of March given to bring in your account." As Jamison reported, the confiscation bill had been amended before passage upon Nanfan's insistence. Livingston was to receive another six months in which to comply and to answer under oath all questions concerning his accounts before the Supreme Court.[26]

Although Livingston was a chief target, he was not alone in experiencing the Leislerians' wrath. As a group, the anti-Leislerians were taking a severe drubbing and, like Livingston, they fought back with all their strength. Jamison coordinated the counterattack, and Livingston aided the movement in Albany. Jamison reported that hotly contested elections in New York City had "Strangly Shaken" Leislerian unity and he urged Livingston to "pray stirr your Self." To defeat the Leislerians, he added, "money must be had to justify our right. *we desire none of them hurt but to prevent their mischeif & plague to us and our property.*"[27] Considering both the prevailing pattern of New York's politics and the source of this magnanimous statement, it is clear that a basic change was occurring. The dominant viewpoint, to which the Leislerians still subscribed, was that political power should be used to destroy the party or faction out of office.

25. *Assembly Journal*, I, 128-29; N. Y. Council Minutes, Sept. 18, 20, 1701, VIII, 276, N. Y. State Lib.; Livingston's petition to Nanfan, Sept. 20, 1701, Livingston-Redmond Mss.; *Legis. Council Jour.*, I, 163.

26. Jamison to Livingston, Oct. 1701, Livingston-Redmond Mss.; *Legis. Council Jour.*, I, 164-65; *Assembly Journal*, I, 136; *Col. Laws of N. Y.*, I, 462-65.

27. Jamison to Livingston, Oct. 20, 1701, Livingston-Redmond Mss. (italics supplied).

That was gradually losing favor among the anti-Leislerians who now began to view political power more as a means of protecting the emoluments and profits of office and less a tool of revenge. Another decade and a half would elapse before the idea became firmly rooted, but Jamison's statement indicated that the seed had been planted.

There was little hope in October 1701 that the Leislerians would share Jamison's sentiments. Indeed, they were too busy fighting among themselves to adopt a moderate attitude toward their real enemies. Their discontent was caused by the Assembly's passage of an address praising Nanfan, Atwood, and Weaver in which it was made to appear that the lieutenant governor was the "fool or tool," while the chief justice and collector were "the helmsmen." Abraham Gouverneur "fretts & frys," Jamison gleefully reported, while Samuel Provoost and Abraham De Peyster "are very furious." [28]

The anti-Leislerians gloated over their enemies' discomfiture and organized a party treasury to support their political campaign.[29] Nicholas Bayard was preparing a set of addresses to the King, Parliament, and Lord Cornbury, the new governor, and Jamison hoped that Livingston would "be alert to receive & forward" those papers. By mid-November Livingston had circulated copies of Bayard's addresses among the Albany burghers, who authorized eight of their number, including Livingston, to sign the official copies in their behalf. Because "the Season of the year and our private affares will not admitt of our going to New Yorke," those eight men in turn authorized four residents of New York City to sign for the City and County of Albany.[30]

Cornbury was now expected almost any day, and John Riggs told Livingston that the new governor would make great changes. Richard Ingoldesby, who "is in greatt favor with my Lord," was accompanying him, as was Daniel Honan, Fletcher's former private secretary. Riggs was certain that Cornbury "has a true carrecter of this please, and that you will have as great an alteration in your Council as my

28. Jamison to Livingston, Oct. 28, 1701, *ibid.*
29. Rip Van Dam, Onzeel Van Swieten, and Stephen De Lancey were "trustees for the receiving keeping and delivering what is collected for publick [i.e., party] Services." *Ibid.*
30. Livingston *et al.*, "Our Power to 4 Gentlemen at N: York to Sign the 3 Peticons," Nov. 13, 1701, *ibid.*

Lord Bellomont meade"; according to rumors, the new councilors would all be staunch anti-Leislerians. This news was confirmed by several others, one of whom evaluated the new governor as "a Very well humourd affable Gent [who] takes great paines to Informe himselfe both of the Country & people & has Mr. W[eaver]s character truly painted." Cornbury was assured of the Crown's support because "Most or all of the knott of Lords whereof the E[arl of] B[ellomont] was one are Removed & Dead." [31] The "Tory Saturnalia" had begun in England, and the Whig ministry was now suffering the barbed attacks of the Tories.[32]

Just as Livingston's hopes began to rise, he found himself the victim of a new Leislerian onslaught. A great misfortune had befallen his son John, his son-in-law Samuel Vetch, and their vessel, the sloop *Mary*.[33] On the evening of November 25, "two expresses" came to New York City from Montauk, Long Island, and "officiously give an account... of a Wreck drove up on Sunday last at High water. No sort [of person] on board... the hatches & Cabbin door open." On board had been found twenty-five casks of brandy and French wines, and a journal kept by Samuel Vetch.[34]

The *Mary*'s misadventures began when Fitz-John Winthrop and Robert Livingston agreed to "put in a stock in mony" so that the young bridegroom, John Livingston, might "begine a trad." Taking this gift, John entered a partnership with his brother-in-law, Vetch, and John Saffin of Boston to buy the *Mary*, outfit her, and begin a profitable but illegal trade between Quebec and the English ports of Boston, New London, and New York. The sloop left New York City on April 26, 1701, with 475 gallons of rum, sailed to New London, and headed for Canada on June 13 with a ton of wool. Fitz-John Winthrop was uncertain about the wisdom of the undertaking: "I

31. Riggs to Livingston, Nov. 22, 1701, Bayard to Livingston, Nov. 24, 1701, Jamison to Livingston, Nov. 24, 1701, Sharpas to Livingston, Nov. 24, 1701, *ibid.*

32. Trevelyan, *England Under the Stuarts*, 384-85.

33. See G. M. Waller, *Samuel Vetch: Colonial Enterpriser* (Chapel Hill, 1960), 58-65, and Edmund B. O'Callaghan, ed., *Journal of the Voyage of the Sloop Mary, From Quebeck, Together with an Account of her Wreck off Montauk Point, L. I., Anno 1701* (Albany, 1866), xi-xii.

34. Jamison to Livingston, Nov. 25, 1701, Livingston-Redmond Mss. Vetch's journal was the basis for O'Callaghan's *Journal of the Voyage*, but he suggested erroneously that John Maher, the mate, was its author (p. ix).

know not what to think of their desyne," he told Robert Livingston, "but hope you did well understand it before hand." [35]

When the *Mary* left Quebec, she carried about £1,000 worth of brandy, white wine, and claret. Half of it was landed in Boston where "it was all Seased" by customs officials; the remainder was discharged at Morrisania, the home of Lewis Morris, for fear of Leislerian hostility. On her second voyage to Canada, the *Mary* carried £1,400 worth of cargo, leaving New London on September 16 "with out Entring or Clearing," because there had been rumors that she might be seized. Now, Fitz-John Winthrop had more confidence in his son-in-law's plans: "I have heard but a litle of their next proceeding but believe tis well laid." But Livingston's next report informed him that the sloop had been cast ashore as a wreck and that Collector Weaver had seized the brandy, wines, furs, and dry goods acquired by Vetch in Quebec. Everyone knew that the vessel belonged to the Livingston-Vetch-Saffin partnership, and one informant reported that Nanfan, Atwood, and Weaver "have been very privat this morning in their consultation" about appropriate action against the owners.[36]

Fate had presented the Leislerians with another opportunity to strike a blow at Livingston. Atwood immediately began legal proceedings to have the *Mary* and her cargo condemned for violation of the Navigations Acts, and he promised that the owners would not "come off so easily upon the seizure [as] at Boston." Although the Admiralty Court proceedings have not survived, John Livingston wrote on December 22: "This day wee heave had a admerelty cort here and they have Condemned Slope and Cargo which is worthe or at Lest was worth when shee came a Shore at Mountack Two Thousand Pound New England money. I hope that wee are all Sensebell that the Almighty God gives and takes." [37]

35. John to Robert and Alida Livingston, June 17, 1701, Winthrop to Livingston, June 26, 1701, Livingston-Redmond Mss.; "Accounts and Balance Sheets of Collector Weaver," June 1701-July 1703, Liber XXX, Register's Office, N. Y. County Hall of Records.

36. John to Robert Livingston, Aug. 24, 1701, Winthrop to Livingston, Sept. 16, 1701, John to Robert Livingston, Sept. 16, 1701, Robert Watts to Livingston, Nov. 26, 1701, Livingston-Redmond Mss. John hoped that the goods seized in Boston would be returned, that "wee Shall have favor Shoed us there because my Eunckell is Gudge of the admerelty there." John to Alida Livingston, Aug. 24, 1701, *ibid*.

37. Atwood to Bd. of Trade, Dec. 29, 1701, O'Callaghan, ed., *N. Y. Col. Docs.*, IV, 931; John to Alida Livingston, Dec. 22, 1701, Vetch to Alida Livingston, Dec. 25, 1701,

Shortly after the *Mary*'s condemnation, the Leislerians learned of Bayard's addresses to the King, Parliament, and Cornbury. Because these were efforts to discredit Nanfan, Atwood, and Weaver, the lieutenant governor and Council charged Bayard with being the head of the "factious party" engaged in a "conspiracy to raise sedition and mutiny here and to defame the Administration of the Government." Although Livingston had signed these addresses, the Leislerians were interested only in the movement's leaders, Bayard and Alderman William Hutchins. In their attempt to destroy Bayard, they resorted, ironically enough, to a law enacted in 1691 for the purpose of their own suppression. Bayard was tried for treason, convicted, and sentenced to suffer the same fate that had befallen Leisler and Milborne eleven years before. Only by indirectly admitting his guilt, something Leisler and Milborne had stubbornly refused to do, did Bayard win a reprieve until the King's pleasure could be known.[38]

As the probable date of Cornbury's arrival neared, the Leislerians resumed their attack on Livingston. On March 23, 1701/2, the commissioners of accounts submitted a report on his financial transactions with the government and, three days later, presented a series of questions to be put to him before the Supreme Court. When Livingston failed to furnish answers, the Council on April 15 ordered the sequestration of his estate. Even then, it seems that someone interceded in Livingston's behalf, because only his New York City property was seized. The confiscation law contained no geographical limits, and Chief Justice Atwood's warrant referred to his property "within our said Citty and County of New York which with all other the lands Tenements and hereditaments goods and Chattels of . . . Livingston . . . are confiscated and fforfeited to us." Escheator General Barne Cosens for some unknown reason apparently read into this warrant limitations which prevented him from seizing the Albany, Saratoga, and Livingston Manor properties.[39]

Livingston-Redmond Mss.; N. Y. Col. Mss., XLVI, 120-21, 124-29, 132-35, 138, N. Y. State Lib. (so badly obliterated in the fire of 1911 as to be unreadable).

38. Nanfan and Council to Bd. of Trade, Jan. 20, 1701/2, Petition of Protestants of N. Y. to William III, Dec. 30, 1701, O'Callaghan, ed., *N. Y. Col. Docs.*, IV, 942, 933-40; Samuel Bayard to Adderley and Lodowick, Jan. 29, 1701/2, *Cal. State Papers, Col.*, XX, no. 343 viii; Osgood, *Colonies in Eighteenth Century*, II, 58-60.

39. N. Y. Council Minutes, Apr. 15, 22, 1702, VIII, 336, 340, N. Y. State Lib.; Livingston's petition to Cornbury, June 8, 1702, Atwood's writ, Apr. 21, 1702, Living-

But nothing could be done to save Livingston's seat on the Council. On April 27, Nanfan removed him, citing Livingston's complicity in the Kidd affair, his fraudulent management of the Albany excise, his contempt of the law requiring him to account, and his failure to obey calls to Council meetings. Removal from the Council, according to William Atwood, was the least punishment Livingston deserved. That "busy Scotchman," he charged, had planned to use physical force to free Bayard and Hutchins if the Leislerian-controlled government attempted to execute them. Also, Livingston had procured from Lieutenant Governor Treat of Connecticut a "Threatning letter" addressed to Nanfan.[40]

Livingston must have been exasperated by his inability to express himself freely and forcefully on the Leislerians and their actions, but he was not willing to share Bayard's prison cell. Other anti-Leislerians apparently felt the same way, and copies of a poem entitled "A Satyr Upon the Times" were passed among them.[41] Written in heroic couplets, this vitriolic verse blasted the Leislerians' characters. Of Bellomont, the poet wrote:

> Twas gold (that curst Tempter) that did bribe
> The grand Ringleader of this hellish Tribe
> great by his Title Vile in every action
> He's gon but has entailed a Curse on's faction

Portraying Bellomont's successor, Nanfan, as "a fawning sychophant . . . ," the satirist's doggerel denounced the lieutenant governor:

> Cunning and Rogue enough to embroyle mankind
> Devout he Seems as tho Religion was
> His aim, but gold would make him go to Mass.

---

ston-Redmond Mss. When the confiscation was nullified, the Council ordered the restoration of Livingston "to his quiet and peaceable possession of his Estate reall and personall in the City of New York Confiscated." N. Y. Council Minutes, Feb. 2, 1702/3, IX, 164, N. Y. State Lib.

40. N. Y. Council Minutes, Apr. 27, 1702, VIII, 341, N. Y. State Lib.; Nanfan's reasons, Apr. 27, 1702, O'Callaghan, ed., *Doc. Hist. of N. Y.*, III, 629-30; "Case of William Atwood, Esq.," N.-Y. Hist. Soc., *Collections,* 13 (1881), 256-57, 310; Treat to Nanfan, Mar. 27, 1702, Livingston-Redmond Mss.

41. "A Satyr Upon the Times," 1702, Livingston-Redmond Mss.

Chief Justice Atwood likewise felt the sharp edge of the pen, "vennom'd as adders Teeth":

> A Crafty Knave deliver'd from a jayle
> To be a Statesman here, who'll never fail
> The Laws to turn and wind, wher's Interest Sways
> And overrule the barrmen as he pleases
> He's proud as Lucifer tho poor as job
> greedy as Cibernis mercilesse as the mob
> Feirce as a Lyon in's Judiciall Chair
> But when he's out as Timorous as a hare

The "other Villans on the Stage," the poet added, were Abraham Gouverneur, "a gogle Eyd Serpent from Batavia Sprung," and Abraham Staats, "a Low Duch Quack no better than an asse." "As for the rest o the Scoundrells," the anti-Leislerians predicted, "let em wait the approaching Change and then lament their fate."

CHAPTER XI

In New York and London:
A "Most Unhappy Supplyant"

Edward Hyde, Lord Cornbury, entered the government of New York on May 3, 1702, and was sworn in at "the house of the sick Chief Justice," William Atwood. And well may Atwood, leader of the Leislerians, have been mentally disturbed, if not physically ill, over the transfer of government: in Cornbury's entourage were Livingston, Vesey, French, Wenham, and Jamison. The new governor quickly gave the Leislerian councilors notice that they could not expect his friendship by declining their dinner invitation in favor of one at which French and his friends "openly appeared masters of the Feast."

But the governor was not given to rash actions, and he allowed the Leislerians to retain their offices for over a month in accordance with the royal instructions he had received. Nevertheless, Livingston, who was apparently in frequent attendance on Cornbury during May, was encouraged. In a letter to Fitz-John Winthrop, he noted that "the last week has past without doing any businesse but Receiving the Congratulatory Complements from persons of all Ranks & from all Places Especially those of the English Party who my Lord declares he never could have beleeved they had been so much abused if he had not come upon the Spott to Receive Information." It was generally believed that the "2 grand Incendiaries," Weaver and Atwood, would soon be ousted along with the other Leislerian councilors. "My Lord," remarked Livingston, "is Extream hearty to Redresse all greevances & we must Reckon it a duble mercy that god has been Pleased to send him at this juncture." As soon as Cornbury obtained sufficient evidence, he preferred charges against Councilors Atwood, Weaver, De Peyster, Staats, and Walters. He also removed Atwood as chief justice, replacing him with William Smith, and he ousted Weaver from the collector's office, substituting a commission consisting of Caleb Heathcote, Thomas Wenham, and Peter Fauconnier.[1]

The governor's actions, although belated, opened the way for a full examination of Livingston's affairs. He had already reported optimistically that "My Lord has directed me to have Copys of all papers that Relates to my bussinesse mannaged by my adversaries... which I shall soon answer to their Shame & Reproach." In a petition of June 8, Livingston related the methods by which the Leislerian commissioners of accounts had persecuted him. They forced him to give an accounting of all public money he had received for seventeen years, even though he was "Principall Creditor of the government," and his accounts were carefully audited before he was given any money. To clear his name, he asked the governor to appoint competent commissioners to examine his case. Two days later, his petition was read by the governor and Council and referred to a committee of Van Dam, Broughton, and Beekman. Six disinterested merchants were asked to join the councilors in auditing Livingston's transactions with the government.[2] This was what Livingston had hoped for, but the committee did little or nothing for the next few months.

In the meantime, Cornbury held a conference with the Iroquois in Albany in mid-July. The sachems repeated their earlier request that Livingston be sent to England to represent them before the Queen, and Cornbury must have been impressed with the merchant's reputa-

1. "Cal. Council Minutes," N. Y. State Lib., *Bulletin 58,* 168, 170; "The Case of William Atwood, Esq.," N.-Y. Hist. Soc., *Collections,* 13 (1881), 285; Livingston to Winthrop, May 18, 1702, Winthrop Papers, XIV, 157, Mass. Hist. Soc. See also Mass. Hist. Soc., *Collections,* 6th ser., 3 (1889), 93-94.
2. Livingston to Winthrop, May 11, 1702, Winthrop Papers, XIV, 158, Mass. Hist. Soc. See also Mass. Hist. Soc., *Collections,* 6th ser., 3 (1889), 91; Livingston's petition to Cornbury, June 8, 1702, Livingston-Redmond Mss. The merchants were Thomas Noel (N. Y. C.'s mayor), Matthew Ling, Lawrence Reade, John Cholwell, Robert Lurting, and Johannes Kip. Order of N. Y. Council, June 10, 1702, *ibid.*

tion among the Indians. Perhaps that was why he appointed Livingston one of the senior judges of a special court to try four Negroes for murdering a River Indian.[3]

However, Livingston's financial problems remained unsolved, and he continued to press Cornbury. On September 12 he presented a memorial about the victualing debt for the royal troops, asserting that he had Bellomont's certificate acknowledging that £1,196 were due him; he had applied to the Countess Bellomont for relief, but had "never Received one farthing." He owed most of the £1,196 to local merchants, and had had to borrow money at 10 percent interest to satisfy them. Cornbury was asked to intercede with the English authorities for repayment of the principal and 8 percent interest which, by December 31, 1702, would amount to £393.[4]

Three months earlier, Livingston had requested the appointment of a Council committee to audit the Albany excise, a task which Van Cortlandt had left unfinished at the time of his death. The accounts were referred to the customs commissioners, who finally submitted a report on September 30. Livingston was cleared completely except for the trifling sum of £55, which he claimed as a part of his salary. This was the first step in clearing away the mass of charges and insinuations built up by the Leislerians. Livingston's other accounts, which had been cited in the sequestration of his estate, were still in the hands of the committee of councilors and merchants. Because of a virulent plague in New York City, the government had moved to Jamaica, Long Island, and the councilors could not meet with the merchants. Cornbury therefore enlarged the committee by adding the customs commissioners and authorized the committee to proceed with any one of the six governmental members and four of the merchants. Within two weeks, the committee submitted its report.[5]

This elaborate analysis of Livingston's financial transactions with

3. Iroquois conference minutes, July 19, 1702, O'Callaghan, ed., *N. Y. Col. Docs.*, IV, 988; N. Y. Council Minutes, Aug. 5, 1702, IX, 68, N. Y. State Lib.

4. Livingston's memorial to Cornbury, Sept. 12, 1702, Livingston-Redmond Mss. Livingston owed £1,225 at 10 percent interest to Philip French, Onzeel Van Swieten, John Barbarie, Isaac Marquis, Margaret Van Schaick, Jean Pero, Daniel Crommelin, and Margaret Schuyler. He also owed £619 without interest to Jacobus Van Cortlandt "and Sundry other Persons." "Account of what Robert Livingston ows," Sept. 1702, *ibid.*

5. Livingston's petition to Cornbury, June 30, 1702, N. Y. Council order, June 30, 1702, Wenham and Fauconnier's report, Sept. 30, 1702, *ibid.*; N. Y. Council Minutes, Sept. 12, 1702, IX, 79, N. Y. State Lib.

the government not only cleared him completely from all the Leislerians' imputations, but concluded that he had "been undeservedly
molested & disquieted . . . he haveing made it plainly appear unto us,
that in the time wherein they Charge him with the Said Sum [of
£17,069], he has Charg'd the government with the Sum of £17,650."
Thus he was still owed £581 on these old accounts. Although the
Council tabled this report for further consideration, the report must
have buoyed Livingston, Meanwhile, a new Assembly had been
elected which consisted principally of Bellomont's enemies. It immediately repealed all the laws enacted under Nanfan's administration, including the one confiscating Livingston's estate.[6] Chances
seemed good that Livingston's name would soon be fully cleared.

But Livingston's optimism faded as delay followed delay. The September report of the committee of councilors and merchants was referred in December to another committee for further examination
and another report. By the end of the year, a disillusioned Livingston
reported to Fitz-John Winthrop: "After all I beleeve [I] shall have no
Releefe here . . . I see Plainly its to delay me & weary me out, they
not being designed to part with any money, knowing that as soon I
have my quietus I will then make my demands." [7] Livingston's analysis of Cornbury's dilatory tactics was most accurate. His claims against
the colony—exclusive of the victualing which was a debt of the
Crown—amounted to about £3,000, and its payment would put a
sizable dent in the New York treasury, making it very difficult for
Cornbury to indulge himself with the government's funds as he
planned. Indeed, from Livingston's viewpoint, there was little about
Cornbury's administration that was an improvement over Nanfan's
regime.

"I am Sometimes of the thought," Livingston confided to Winthrop, "if I could sell what I have I would Leave the government."
But in spite of the gloom which enveloped him, the habits of a lifetime were not easily broken. "Since I have Staid so Long," he concluded, "I am Resolv'd to see the Issue, whether they will doe it or

6. Report of Wenham et al., Nov. 24, 1702, Livingston-Redmond Mss.; N. Y. Council Minutes, Nov. 24, 1702, IX, 136, N. Y. State Lib.; Smith, History of New York, I,
150; Col. Laws of N. Y., I, 524.

7. N. Y. Council Minutes, Dec. 1, 1702, IX, 147, N. Y. State Lib.; Livingston to
Winthrop, Dec. 29, 1702, Winthrop Papers, XIV, 159, Mass. Hist. Soc. See also Mass.
Hist. Soc., Collections, 6th ser., 3 (1889), 116-17.

not, because I may have the better Plea, if I should be obligd to visit whitehall again." [8] Finally, the long relayed report by the Council committee on the report of the committee of councilors and merchants was submitted. Livingston was completely exonerated from all charges of financial manipulation, and all his accounts were endorsed. He expected the long-desired *quietus* from the governor, although he feared that his enemies might recommend that Cornbury refer him to the Queen. The governor took his time, but he finally issued the *quietus* on February 2, 1702/3, restoring Livingston "to his quiet and peaceable possession of his Estate reall and personall in the City of New York." Livingston then presented his claims against the government which totalled £2,774, plus interest. The Council summoned him to explain this more fully and, on February 18, the matter was referred to a committee for a full examination and report. [9]

Since Cornbury and his cohorts were determined to pay little or nothing to the government's creditors, it took the committee only two days to reach a decision. It allowed one of Livingston's claims—the £262 advanced for incidental expenditures on behalf of the Albany fort and the Iroquois. All of his other claims were rejected on technical points. The only solace Livingston could have found in the report was the admission that he had met with "unjust treatment" at the hands of the Leislerian-controlled government. When the report was submitted to the Council, no action was taken, perhaps because its reasoning was too specious even for Cornbury and his friends. Unable to secure a copy of the report, Livingston waited two weeks, then petitioned Cornbury, repeating the whole story of the persecutions he had undergone, and begging for some detailed information about the report. The governor finally gave an oral opinion on it, but Livingston realized the necessity of reducing such statements to writing, and he continued to bother Cornbury. After several applications, the governor agreed to ask the Council for permission to present

8. For descriptions of Cornbury, see Smith, *History of New York*, I, 146, and Osgood, *Colonies in Eighteenth Century*, II, 63; Livingston to Winthrop, Dec. 29, 1702, Winthrop Papers, XIV, 159, Mass. Hist. Soc. See also Mass. Hist. Soc., *Collections*, 6th ser., 3 (1889), 116-17.

9. Report of Broughton *et al.*, Jan. 7, 1702/3, Livingston-Redmond Mss.; Livingston to Winthrop, Jan. 27, 1702/3, Winthrop Papers, XIV, 159, Mass. Hist. Soc.; N. Y. Council Minutes, Feb. 2, 12, 18, 1702/3, IX, 164, 172, 176, N. Y. State Lib.; "An Account of Moneys due to Robert Livingston," Feb. 8, 1702/3, in "Historical Documents and Autograph Letters," Myers Mss., 274, N. Y. Pub. Lib.

his opinion in writing, but when the Council adjourned, Livingston learned that nothing had been done.[10] By now, it was clear that the sybaritic Cornbury had no intention of allowing anyone other than himself and his closest intimates to manipulate the colony's finances. He had his own uses for whatever funds he could wheedle out of the Assembly, and these did not include the payment of £3,000 to Livingston.

Disappointed and distracted, Livingston decided to carry his case to England and he made hasty plans for his second trip abroad. On June 2, 1702, he sailed from New York City on the *Thetie*. Compared to his first voyage, it was comparatively uneventful. On July 8, after sighting the Isle of Lundy and heading for Bristol, the *Thetie* was stopped by a French privateer and ordered to surrender. After a brief skirmish, the small vessel capitulated. The privateer, Livingston reported, "used us very Barbarously." The sloop was redeemed by the passengers for £450, but the privateer's captain robbed them and set them adrift in the *Thetie*. Fortunately, Her Majesty's frigate *Rye* appeared on the horizon, the privateer beat a hasty retreat, and the man-of-war went off in pursuit.

Thus began Livingston's second visit to the seat of the empire. After landing at Clovally, Devonshire, on July 9, he wrote to the Board of Trade: "I make haste to wait upon your Lordships to give an account of the affairs of our province." [11] But there was no need for the haste; the next three years were to be a painful lesson in the virtues of patience.

London in July 1703 had not changed greatly in appearance since Livingston's visit eight years earlier but there were some significant political alterations. Governmental control had passed from the Whigs' hands into those of the Tories, and the focus of political controversy had shifted from acceptance of the Revolution Settlement of 1688 to questions of its direction and the way in which it should be modified. International affairs were becoming increasingly important

10. Report of Lawrence *et al.*, Feb. 20, 1702/3, Livingston-Redmond Mss.; N. Y. Council Minutes, Feb. 20, Mar. 22, 1702/3, IX, 179, 194, N. Y. State Lib.; Livingston's petitions to Cornbury, Mar. 5, 19, 1702/3, Misc. Mss. Robert Livingston, N.-Y. Hist. Soc.

11. Robert Livingston's letter of attorney to Alida Livingston, Oct. 12, 1694, and confirmation of Apr. 30, 1703, Livingston to Bd. of Trade, July 9, 1703, Livingston-Redmond Mss.

as a result of Queen Anne's War which lasted for all but fourteen months of that monarch's reign.[12]

Indeed, Livingston's immediate concern in England was not finance but the international rivalry between France and England in America. He first turned to the problems of frontier defense, stressing the rapidly degenerating position of the Iroquois. They have "fought our Batles for us," he argued pointedly, "& been a Constant Barrier of defense," but the prolonged war had depleted their ranks and made them "very dispirited." For two years they had pressed him "to come over & give your Lordships an account of their condition." Livingston considered them as the key to Canada and he offered his "humble opinion" that security for the colonies could only be achieved by taking Canada. This "might be done with Less Charge to the Crown," he continued, "than has been Lately Expended at one French Island"; a few frigates, a bomb-ketch, an English regiment, and a party of colonial militia were all that was necessary. Once conquered, Canada should be retained, "for the French will other wise in time grow . . . formidable by Setling behind all the English Plantations." [13]

Having done all he could for the moment to sharpen the Board of Trade's focus on frontier defense, Livingston turned to his personal affairs. Since his fortunes were adversely affected by the death or political eclipse of the Whig Lords with whom he had allied himself in 1695-96, he had to court a powerful group of Tory ministers. Not all of them were unknown to him, however; Auditor General Blathwayt, a member of the Board of Trade, Lord High Treasurer Godolphin, and Charles Mordaunt, Earl of Peterborough and Monmouth, were old acquaintances. Despite these friends, Livingston was to find his task in London a hard one: after a year, he declared that "its a miserable thing to Solicite the Treasury for money at this juncture." [14] His claims drew him through a tortuous maze, but his ability to carry them from one office to another is mute testimony to his competence and persistence in both finance and politics.

12. Ashley, *England in the Seventeenth Century*, 193-210; Trevelyan, *England Under the Stuarts*, 389-91.
13. Livingston to Bd. of Trade, Aug. 10, 1703, Winthrop Papers, XV, 131, Mass. Hist. Soc.; O'Callaghan, ed., *N. Y. Col. Docs.*, IV, 1067-69.
14. Livingston to Winthrop, May 7, 1705, Mass. Hist. Soc., *Collections*, 6th ser., 3 (1889), 292.

Livingston's demands were complex but he patiently compiled a statement of each of the sums for which he sought reimbursement. First, there were the claims which the New York government should have paid: £875 sterling salary arrears as secretary for Indian affairs, £147 sterling interest on that sum, £679 sterling interest authorized by the Crown in 1696, £262 sterling interest on the victualing from May 1, 1698, to March 25, 1699 (the principal to be repaid by debentures on the forfeited Irish estates), and £53 sterling salary as commissary of the forces for a year and a half. In addition to this total of £2,016 sterling, he made a direct claim on the Crown for £252 sterling for victualing expenditures from December 25, 1699, to April 25, 1700, as well as £79 sterling interest thereon. Later, he also requested £394 (New York) for miscellaneous disbursements on behalf of the Albany garrison.[15]

Livingston first sought information on the payment of the arrears of the troops' pay and subsistence which were to be settled by debentures on the Irish estates. He then obtained the acquiescence of the parliamentary commissioners to state the debts of the army in a proposal that each captain of the companies in the colony should appoint his own agent to receive the debentures rather than allow Cornbury to handle them. After that, he sent powers of attorney in his own name to two of the captains for completion. The next step was to get the government to issue the debentures, and Livingston, on behalf of all the officers and victualers concerned, petitioned the parliamentary commissioners for an accounting. Only partial muster rolls existed for the period, and the commissioners insisted first upon a royal warrant directing them to draw up the account. When Livingston asked the Earl of Ranelagh, paymaster general of the army, for such a warrant, he referred the matter to Auditor General Blathwayt. After some delay, Ranelagh finally issued a "State of ther Pay . . . Pursuant to Such Muster Rolls as he had," which was transmitted to the parliamentary commissioners.

According to Ranelagh, no more than £500 sterling had been paid to the troops from December 1696 to March 1699; many of the muster rolls were either lost at sea during the war or "refuzd to

15. "The Case of the Petitioner Robert Livingston," Apr. 13, 1704, "Vouchers and Prooffs of Robert Livingstons Debt of £2016," Apr. 13, 1704, Livingston-Redmond Mss. See below, pp. 196-97.

be received by the comisary [and] were Returnd to the Post officers where they were destroyd as wast paper." Livingston asked the parliamentary commissioners to accept Ranelagh's estimates, make a report to the next session of Parliament, and secure relief for the victualers and officers.[16]

Concurrently with these negotiations, the Board of Trade took heed of Livingston's proposals for promoting the English interest among the Iroquois. He was directed to apply for missionaries to the Bishop of London, who referred him to the Society for the Propagation of the Gospel in Foreign Parts. Livingston prophesied to the society that the redemption of the Iroquois from "this Slavery to Popish Priests would ... most effectually tend to the Glory of God, and the Peace, Trade and Credit of the *English*." The society was impressed with the possibility of converting the heathen Indians and asked Livingston to appear in person and explain the scheme. He did so, and won the society's support for Domine Lydius of Albany and their recommendation that additional clergymen be sent to New York. Two men were found by December, but the society did not have sufficient funds to support them, and Queen Anne's assistance was requested.[17]

At the same time that Livingston encouraged the society to expand its work among the Iroquois, he undertook some missionary work in his own behalf among the members of Parliament. When the Mutiny Act of 1703 was being debated, he saw an opportunity to settle some of his own problems by having two specific clauses included in that law. With the aid of William Lowndes of the Treasury, sections fifty-six and fifty-seven were incorporated into the Mutiny Act; they were, in effect, private bills for Livingston's benefit. Section fifty-six dealt with the arrears of pay and subsistence of the royal troops in New York from 1691 to 1699, ordering the Earl of Ranelagh to compute the pay in accordance with the troops' establishment and whatever muster rolls existed, and to transmit that data to the parliamentary commissioners who were to pay the debts with deben-

16. Livingston's notes on "a Power to be given by a Captain to Receive the ... debentures," Aug. 25, 1703, *ibid.*; Memorial of Fletcher *et al.*, Oct. 14, 1703, Winthrop Papers, XV, 132, Mass. Hist. Soc.

17. Livingston to Bd. of Trade, Dec. 18, 1703, O'Callaghan, ed., *N. Y. Col. Docs.*, IV, 1074; Livingston's memorial quoted in [John Chamberlayn], *An Account of the Society for Propagating the Gospel in Foreign Parts, Established by the Royal Charter of William III. With their Proceedings and Success* (London, 1706), 43-45.

tures. This removed the lack of muster rolls as a stumbling block to Livingston. Section fifty-seven, which dealt with the surplusage of 30 percent deducted from the soldiers' pay, could not have more effectively aided Livingston if his name had been inserted into the terminology. The parliamentary commissioners were directed to certify to the paymaster general the amount in that fund, and debentures were to be issued against it "unto such Person or Persons whom Her Majesty shall judge to be duly intituled thereto." [18]

Livingston's path was now clear and his plan obvious. In April 1704 he petitioned Queen Anne for payment of £2,016 sterling, because the funds from which he should have been satisfied had been "applyed to defraying the Contingent Charges of the said forces." Since the Queen could grant the 30 percent fund to whomever she judged "to be duly intituled thereto," and since it amounted to £2,498 sterling, it could be used to settle Livingston's claim. For victualing from December 1699 to April 1700, he requested £252 sterling from the pay which Ranelagh was to compute under section fifty-six of the Mutiny Act, and £79 sterling interest on that debt from the 30 percent fund. [19]

The Queen referred the detailed statement of Livingston's case and his collection of "vouchers and prooffs" to the Lord High Treasurer for consideration and a report. [20] This, of course, was only routine procedure; the success of Livingston's application depended upon his personal contacts and political influence. Although little is known of his maneuvers, one of his letters to his wife affords a glimpse into what really happened when his case was presented to the Queen:

The Earl of Peterborough took me in his coach and delivered my request to the Earl of Nottingham, Secretary of State, who immediately went to the Queen and had the matter referred to the Lord Godolphin, High Treasurer. The above mentioned Earl took me along last Thursday to the Lord High Treasurer and spoke for me and gave him my request and the Queen's order, who has referred my affair to the Earl

18. "If I cannot get it [the money] out of the 30 percent which I obtained with so much trouble in the Parliament then I can never expect a stuiver." Robert to Alida Livingston, Apr. 29, 1704 (Dutch), Livingston-Redmond Mss.; Livingston to [Lowndes], June 2, 1707, PRO, Treas. 1: 102, pp. 134-35; 2 and 3 Anne, c. 17, *The Statutes of the Realm. Printed by Command of His Majesty George III* (12 vols., London, 1810-28), VIII, 293-94.

19. Livingston's petition to Queen Anne, Apr. 13, 1704, Livingston-Redmond Mss.
20. Order-in-Council, Apr. 13, 1704, *ibid.*

of Ranelagh and Mr. Blathwayt. What they will now do with it, time will tell. I do my very best every day to make friends, and save no trouble or expenses. What the result will be, God only knows.[21]

Charles Mordaunt, Earl of Peterborough and Monmouth, had befriended Livingston eight years before and was doing so again. His friendship was vital because he was a close associate of the Churchills, a member of the Tories' inner councils, and a favorite of Queen Anne. Livingston also sought aid from other influential figures. "Mr. William Penn is my good friend and takes much trouble for me," he told his wife, adding that "the Viscount Teviot of our name is here and will help me." Alida was very impatient for her husband's return and apparently scolded him for delaying so long in England, for he replied: "Now, my love, I cannot but do my best. I am so tired every night from walking that I cannot sleep well."

Livingston's opposition came mainly from William Blathwayt. The auditor general, he told his wife, "seemed inclined to delay me and write to New York when I spoke with him last. I said I have everything I need from New York and will never take any orders on New York ... I do not intend to leave here before I have my money, for I know nothing will be done in New York, and I will be anxious until we have reached an even keel again." Livingston's decision not to trust his fate to Cornbury was based upon past experience; never again would he permit a rapacious governor to deny him the fruits of his labor.[22]

A month later, Blathwayt and Ranelagh reported to Godolphin on Livingston's petition, dividing his claims in two categories—military and civil. The former included everything but his salary arrears as secretary for Indian affairs and the interest on that money. These claims, they agreed, should be paid by the Crown except for the £262 sterling interest on victualing expenditures and the £79 sterling interest on the unpaid interest. Under the heading of "civil" claims, Ranelagh and Blathwayt listed Livingston's salary arrears of £875 sterling as secretary for Indian affairs and the interest on that sum of £147 sterling. These items, they concluded, should be referred to

21. Robert to Alida Livingston, Apr. 29, 1704 (Dutch), *ibid*.
22. Colin Ballard, *The Great Earl of Peterborough* (London, c. 1929), 12, 98-100; Robert to Alida Livingston, Apr. 29, 1704 (Dutch), Livingston-Redmond Mss.

Cornbury and the New York Council "with Directions to Return a Speedy answer to your Lordship on every Particular Relating to the Petitioners office." [23]

Although grateful for this preliminary approval of the issuance of £984 sterling, Livingston still insisted upon the payment of his other claims. He argued that the 30 percent fund was appropriate for this purpose because the money originally intended for his salary had been diverted to military uses. When Godolphin referred this matter back to Blathwayt and Ranelagh, they approved the additional payment of £262 sterling interest on the victualing out of the 30 percent fund. They also agreed that the £252 sterling for unpaid victualing expenses and the £79 sterling interest on that sum should be given him once Godolphin made some provision for the soldiers' pay for that period. [24]

Although Livingston was gradually securing official approval of his claims, three important ones remained unsettled: the victualing account, the salary arrears, and the interest on each sum. Since the Mutiny Act established procedures for clearing these debts, Livingston urged that the paymaster general compute the pay and subsistence of the four New York companies under the law's terms and that Godolphin query the attorney general about the legality of paying the salary arrears as secretary for Indian affairs out of the 30 percent fund. On August 11, Attorney General Edward Northey ruled that the Queen could use the 30 percent fund to repay moneys advanced by the New York government for the troops, in default of remittances from England. [25]

With the chief legal obstacle out of the way, Livingston naively assumed that his claims would be paid as readily as they had been approved. Eager to return home, he had the Earl of Peterborough deliver

23. Lowndes to Ranelagh, Apr. 29, 1704, Livingston-Redmond Mss.; Ranelagh's and Blathwayt's report, June 1, 1704, PRO, Treas. 64: Misc. 38 (Blathwayt Journal, II), 332-37 (Lib. Cong. transcripts).

24. Livingston to Godolphin, July 12, 1704, Lowndes to Ranelagh and Blathwayt, July 17, 1704, Certificate of Commissioners to State Army Accounts, June 29, 1704, Livingston-Redmond Mss.; Ranelagh's and Blathwayt's report, July 25, 1704, PRO, Treas. 64: Misc. 38, 338-40 (Lib. Cong. transcripts).

25. Livingston to Godolphin, July 31, 1704, Lowndes to Atty. Gen., Aug. 8, 1704, "Livingstons Case Stated to the atturney Generall & Sent to him ... this 9 of August by my Lord Treasurer," Livingston-Redmond Mss.; Livingston to Winthrop, Aug. 10, 1704, Mass. Hist. Soc., *Collections*, 6th ser., 3 (1889), 254; Atty. Gen. Northey to Godolphin, Aug. 11, 1704, O'Callaghan, ed., *N. Y. Col. Docs.*, IV, 1125.

a letter to Godolphin which asked the Lord High Treasurer to give immediate consideration to the attorney general's report. "Severall ships bound for Neue York are ready to Sail," he added almost impatiently, "and I am in hopes of going in one of 'em if this businesse were dispatchd." But it was a case of hurry up and wait. A month later he notified Godolphin that he had seen the draft of a warrant for his payment out of the 30 percent fund according to which he was to receive £123 instead of £875 as salary arrears for the secretaryship. Someone had decided that he was to be paid only for the period from the date of his commission to his suspension by Governor Fletcher; his right to the remainder was "to be referred back to the Consideration of the governor and Councill of New York."

This was the last thing that Livingston wanted. He cited Bellomont's report that his suspension was unjust and again pointed out that he had continued to perform the office's duties despite the suspension. Cornbury and the Council had also acknowledged this when they asked the Crown to specify the fund to be used for payment of the claim. Since no new issue had arisen, Livingston argued, there was little likelihood of a change in their position, "but the Petitioner and his private affairs must Suffer a great Detriment by waiting here 12 months longer for their answer." [26]

Godolphin apparently ignored this plea, for Livingston wrote to him again on October 12, declaring that he was "the most unhappy Supplyant that ever applyd to the Treasury for Relief." He left his family, he reminded the Lord High Treasurer, "Exposd to a Cruel & vigilant Enemy on the fronteers" and undertook a "dangerous Voyage of 1000 Leagues" in the hope of getting relief in England so that he could "pay every body, & Sitt down quietly, & end my days in Some ease after a 30 years fateague & Hurry of publik Bussinesse." He was determined, he concluded, "to goe home with the Virginy fleet which is to sail in December next." But Livingston could not sway Godolphin. When a royal warrant was signed on October 19, Ranelagh was directed to issue debentures for £679 for the interest first authorized in 1696, £53 sterling for eighteen months' salary as commissary of the royal troops, and £262 sterling as interest on the re-

26. Livingston to Godolphin, "deliverd by my Lord Peterborrow," Aug. 20, 1704, Livingston to Godolphin, Sept. 24, 1704, Livingston-Redmond Mss.

paid victualing expenditures. However, no mention was made of the salary arrears or the unpaid victualing debt.[27]

After a month had elapsed, Livingston again wrote to Godolphin, who had refused to budge from his position that the 30 percent fund could only be used for military purposes. Livingston now sought to prove that the secretaryship had a military nature. The Iroquois had "no Established Civill Polity" and all negotiations between them and the English, therefore, were "only upon military Occasions as fighting our Batles, guarding our Frontiers, & Offensive and Defensive Leagues, for which they receive Money, Arms, Ammunition, Cloaths, & Provisions... through my hands." Thus payment of his salary arrears, Livingston concluded with tortured logic matching the Lord High Treasurer's, could not be a "misaplication of that money."[28]

While arguing about the "military" character of the secretaryship, Livingston also made efforts to get payment for the victualing expenditures made during the period for which there were no muster rolls. He asked one of the comptrollers of the army to clear the accounts of the four companies from December 25, 1699, to April 25, 1700, offering the victualing accounts witnessed by the company commanders instead of muster rolls. The official machinery of government had been set in motion, and Livingston now awaited the results. The comptrollers of the army reported that no money had been paid the four companies during the period in question, and Livingston turned to Godolphin to request that payment be made before the accounts were made up; otherwise, he could not return to America.[29]

Livingston brought still another matter to the Privy Council's attention when he petitioned for the formal removal of the suspension from the secretaryship imposed by Governor Fletcher. The request was referred to the Board of Trade, and he was asked to submit a "memorial of what he desires." On January 5, 1704/5, he asked for restoration to the office, payment of the salary arrears out of the 30

27. Livingston to Godolphin, Oct. 12, 1704, *ibid.*; Royal warrant, Oct. 19, 1704, Shaw, ed., *Cal. Treasury Books*, XIX, 381-82.
28. Livingston to Godolphin, Nov. 23, 1704, Livingston-Redmond Mss.
29. Livingston to Sir Joseph Tredenham, Dec. 13, 1704, Rawlinson Mss. D, CMXVI, fol. 176, Bodleian Lib. (Lib. Cong. transcripts), copy in Livingston-Redmond Mss.; Tredenham and Moore to Godolphin, Jan. 4, 1704/5, Livingston to Godolphin, Jan. 4, 1704/5, Livingston-Redmond Mss.

percent fund, and an order that his salary in the future "be paid out of her Majesties Quitt Rents arriseing in that Province." In turn, the Board of Trade reported on January 10 that he had "a just Pretence to his said Salary, which we apprehend, the Revenue of New York... will not be able to Satisfy," and that his suspension should be formally lifted by Queen Anne. Within twenty-four hours, the Queen-in-Council signed an order lifting the suspension, ordering payment of the salary arrears, and directing Cornbury to readmit Livingston to the office "without further Delay." [30] Evidently, Livingston's friends had greater influence with the Board of Trade and Privy Council than with the Treasury, because the prompt handling of this matter stands in marked contrast to the hairsplitting and delays which accompanied the Treasury's action on his financial claims.

Livingston's success on one front led him to renew his petition to Godolphin about the victualing debt on January 19, but the Lord High Treasurer demanded proof that he had advanced funds for subsisting the four companies. Livingston promptly supplied receipts, certificates, and official reports as "infallible proofs," then marked time for nearly two months. On March 16 he finally returned to Godolphin's office to obtain his salary arrears for the secretaryship. Since the Queen had ordered payment, the Lord High Treasurer finally prepared a warrant for that purpose on March 17. [31]

Complete reimbursement now seemed within Livingston's grasp, and he outlined his prospects in a letter to Fitz-John Winthrop. "As to my own Concerns," Livingston wrote, "I find its no easy matter to dispatch matters at Court now." Godolphin's warrant for payment of his salary arrears had encountered "some opposition by Mr. Taylor one of the Clerks of the Treasury, Mr. Loundes being sik." By April 30, Lowndes apparently recovered, for the royal warrant was signed. However, it provided for the payment of only £670 sterling, for as Livingston now learned, his commission had been terminated by the death of William III on March 8, 1701/2. This was an unex-

30. *Journal of the Commissioners for Trade and Plantations* (14 vols., London, 1920-37), I, 75, 78, 80 (hereafter cited as *Journal Bd. Trade*); Livingston to Bd. of Trade, Jan. 3, 1704/5, Bd. of Trade's report, Jan. 10, 1704/5, Order-in-Council, Jan. 11, 1704/5, O'Callaghan, ed., *N. Y. Col. Docs.*, IV, 1124-27.
31. Livingston to Godolphin, Jan. 19, 1704/5, "Proofs of Robert Livingston Claim for 252: 9: 1 Sterling," Jan. 19, 1704/5, Livingston to Godolphin, Mar. 16, 1704/5, Livingston-Redmond Mss.; Royal warrant, Apr. 30, 1705, Shaw, ed., *Cal. Treasury Books*, XX (Part II), 237.

pected development, and it became clear to Livingston that he could not get the rest of the salary arrears without a new royal order. On May 3, he petitioned Sir Charles Hedges, secretary of state, for a new commission for all of his offices except that of sub-collector of the excise, which had been farmed out, and for payment of his salary from March 8, 1701/2, the date of the last payment.

Although Livingston had made much progress in clearing his accounts he continued to find "great opposition here." He told Winthrop a month later that "tho I durst not Suspect our governors Intrest because of haveing letters of Recommendation from him to his father [the Earl of Clarendon], yet I am inform'd it was from that Corner it came." It was the Treasury clerks who were causing him trouble with his salary arrears and the victualing. If he could get those sums, he stated, "I would scarce trouble my self with the Publik further, for its a miserable thing to Solicite the Treasury for money at this juncture."

Having done all that he could at the moment to expedite his affairs, Livingston turned to other matters. In a letter to Winthrop he stressed Connecticut's need for a permanent agent in London to protect itself against a concerted attack then being made against proprietary and corporate colonial charters. "I am not to direct, only to advise you as a frind, and a well wisher tho of another Collony," he told Winthrop, adding: "I would not have you So much as mention that I give you any advice about the matter because People are apt to make a wrong Construction and Interpretation upon any thing now a days." Since Blathwayt and the Board of Trade were in the vanguard of these attacks, Livingston certainly did not want word of his correspondence with Connecticut officials to reach the wrong ears.[32]

After his close confinement to London for two years on personal and colonial affairs, Livingston broke away in the summer of 1705 for a quick trip to his native Scotland. The main reason for his trip was to see his son Robert, Jr., who was enrolled at the University of Edinburgh. At the same time, he probably looked forward to visiting with the remnants of his family—his widowed sisters, Janet Russell

32. Livingston to Winthrop, Apr. 7, May 7, 1705, Mass. Hist. Soc., *Collections*, 6th ser., 3 (1889), 285-88, 292; Livingston to Hedges, May 3, 1705, Livingston-Redmond Mss.

and Barbara Miller, their children, and the children of his two dead brothers. He probably arrived in Edinburgh sometime in July, because his name appears in the Town Council minutes for August 3. Conferring on him the same honor given to his grandfather, father, and brother, the citizenry made him a "burgess and Guild brother, *gratis*, by act of Councill." [33] The reasons for this honor are not indicated in the records, but a wealthy man returning to his birthplace is rarely neglected by his less adventuresome or fortunate countrymen, and Livingston had unquestionable social, political, and economic status in New York.

Just when Livingston left Scotland is unknown, but he was probably in London in time for the issuance of his new royal commission on September 29. This confirmed him in all his offices—secretary for Indian affairs, town clerk, clerk of the peace, and clerk of the common pleas—but the secretaryship's salary was to be paid out of the colony's revenue rather than the quitrents.[34]

Now, only three claims remained to be settled. Two were demands previously presented for payment from the 30 percent fund—£252 sterling for victualing and £350 sterling salary arrears as secretary from Queen Anne's accession. But the third was a new one: Livingston now asked that £394 (New York), advanced for the Albany garrison, be repaid in the colony "out of the customs and Excyse of such goods as he shall Import into or Export out of . . . new york." These three matters were referred to Godolphin on October 22 with orders to "give such Directions therein for the Petitioners Relief, as his Lordship shall think fitt." An unusual procedure, this meant that the Lord High Treasurer's decision would be final. Blathwayt was asked to report on the salary arrears and miscellaneous disbursements,

---

33. Livingston to Winthrop, May 7, 1705, Mass. Hist. Soc., *Collections*, 6th ser., 3 (1889), 292. The wills of Livingston's brothers and brothers-in-law made no mention of him. Letter of June 29, 1955, to the author from Mr. C. T. McInnes, Curator of Historical Records, H. M. General Register Office, Edinburgh. Bartholomew Fleeming, the Rev. John Livingstone, and William Livingstone had been honored as burgesses and guild brothers. Quoted from Edinburgh Roll of Burgesses in letter of June 27, 1955, to the author from Dr. C. A. Malcolm, Librarian, Society of Writers to H. M. Signet, Edinburgh. Livingston was admitted "in the most ample form." Quoted from Edinburgh Town Council Minutes in letter of July 26, 1955, to the author from the Deputy Town Clerk, City Chambers, Edinburgh.

34. Livingston's royal commission, Sept. 29, 1705, O'Callaghan, ed., *N. Y. Col. Docs.*, IV, 1158.

and the comptrollers of the army were requested to give their opinion on the victualing.[35]

The comptrollers concluded that the claim for victualing should be paid to Livingston and charged to the subsistence of the four companies. However, they refused to authorize payment of the £79 sterling interest on that sum until the accounts were adjusted. Livingston took an oath on November 30 that the money was actually owed to him, and a royal warrant was issued two weeks later which directed Ranelagh to prepare debentures for the principal sum. Blathwayt took no action on the matters referred to him, however, and a second referral had to be made a month later. When he finally responded, he gave a partial reason for the delay. He agreed to payment of £350 sterling salary arrears out of the 30 percent fund, but he strongly objected to paying the £394 (New York) in the way that Livingston had proposed. Upon further consideration, Livingston withdrew the request, preferring to rely on the ordinary course of payments in New York rather than suffer further delays.[36]

With Blathwayt's report in hand, Livingston began to conclude his affairs in London while awaiting the issuance of the debentures. Most of his remaining time in England was spent in commercial pursuits, an activity he never neglected. He remained a merchant at heart no matter how deeply he might be immersed in politics. Indeed, his entire career reflected this dual interest, with the emphasis shifting from commerce to politics and back again in accord with prevailing conditions at any given time. After several years in London, he had had his fill of political intrigue and, distrusting Cornbury, he had no intention of getting involved with the government on his return home. He decided to place even greater emphasis on the mercantile aspect of his career. Throughout his stay in England, he invested whatever money he received from the Crown in cargoes which were shipped to his wife so that she could clear the debts he "had contracted for the publik service." To Fitz-John Winthrop, he wrote: "I wish

35. Livingston's petition to Queen Anne, Oct. 22, 1705, Order-in-Council, Oct. 22, 1705, Livingston-Redmond Mss.; Treasury to Blathwayt, Oct. 22, 1705, Treasury to Army Comptrollers, Oct. 31, 1705, Shaw, ed., *Cal. Treasury Books*, XX (Part II), 447, 454.
36. Tredenham and Moore to Godolphin, Nov. 13, 1705, Livingston's oath, Nov. 30, 1705, Lowndes to Blathwayt, Dec. 19, 1705, Livingston-Redmond Mss.; Royal warrant, Dec. 12, 1705, Shaw, ed., *Cal. Treasury Books*, XX (Part II), 500; Blathwayt to Godolphin, Jan. 29, 1705/6, PRO, Treas. 64: Misc. 38, 423-25 (Lib. Cong. transcripts).

those 2 Ships may arrive Safe, will putt my wife in a Condition to pay everyone their own, and enable us to goe on with our Trade, which if we had minded, and not been Concern'd for the Publik would have been some hundreds in our way." [37]

Because the Crown's payments did not always coincide with the sailing of the spring fleet to America, Livingston often bought goods on credit. His extensive use of credit can be documented by a comparison of the dates and values of his shipments with those of the royal warrants he received. In 1704, he made four shipments to his wife valued at £1,051 sterling. These were sent in March and July, but the royal warrant to pay for them was not forthcoming until October 19, when he was given £994 sterling. Similarly, three shipments were made in March and April 1705 for £933 sterling, but the warrant was issued in the latter month for £670 sterling, a lesser sum than he had expected. This pattern suggests that Livingston's credit reputation with the London merchants was good. By the prompt repayment of their advances, he must have enhanced his reputation. For example, James Douglas consigned £690 sterling worth of textiles and ironware on his own "Propper account and Risque" and Livingston soon found his business solicited by his Scottish cousins, with whom he had had no previous contacts of a business or personal nature.[38]

By May of 1706, Livingston had completed his public and private business and prepared to return home on the *Unity*. Since the vessel could not sail until the convoy was ready, the captain put into Gravesend to permit the passengers to buy additional supplies. When Livingston went ashore on May 6, he was immediately seized by the sheriff of Kent. Once again, Captain Kidd's spectre stalked the land to disturb Livingston's composure. Sir Richard Blackham, a silent

---

37. "I have not yet received any decision on Mr. Blathwayt's report to the Lord Treasurer about the £355 sterling of my salary during the Queen's time," Livingston wrote his wife, "but as soon as the Lord Treasurer finishes some private matters he will order the amount paid. I have left a power of attorney here with Col. [Charles] Lodwick.... There is still £113 due to me for interest on the 4 months' provisions... which cannot be obtained until the accounts of that time are made up." Robert to Alida Livingston, May 10, 1706 (Van Laer translation), Livingston-Redmond Mss.; Livingston to Winthrop, May 7, 1705, Mass. Hist. Soc., *Collections*, 6th ser., 3 (1889), 292.

38. Invoices, Mar. 30, July 12, 1704, Mar. 31, Apr. 20, 30, 1705, Jan. 15, Mar. 15, 1705/6, Apr. 13, 1706, Livingston's notes on "Copy of the Certificate for the Arrears," c. 1706 (hereafter cited as Livingston's notes), Livingston-Redmond Mss.

partner in the Kidd venture, now brought a civil suit against Livingston, demanding £700 sterling as the return of his investment with interest. Blackham had attempted to sue Livingston a year earlier but had failed because he could not produce the agreement between Kidd, Livingston, and Bellomont, under which the terms of the voyage were established. Livingston was lodged, at his own expense, in the Sign of the Saracenshead, Gravesend, until he could arrange bail. At the suggestion of his cousin, William Livingston, he asked to be transferred to Fleet Prison where he would be under Chancery Court jurisdiction and could then win his freedom on the grounds of false arrest. This was done by a writ of habeas corpus, and Blackham then offered to settle the dispute for £170. To speed his departure from England, Livingston agreed to these terms, and the necessary documents were signed in London on May 10.[39]

More than a month elapsed before Livingston returned to the *Unity,* which was then lying off Plymouth awaiting a convoy. Not until early July, nearly three years after his arrival, did Livingston begin his journey to New York, and it was September 16 when he arrived at Sandy Hook.[40]

39. Livingston to Macmorran and Key, May 7, 1706, Sheriff of Kent's warrant, May 6, 1706, Livingston to Norton, May 7, 1706, William Livingston, Sr., to Robert Livingston, May 8, 1706, Livingston to Robert West, May 9, 1706, Key to Livingston, May 10, 1706, Sheriff of Kent's warrant, May 10, 1706, Sir Richard Blackham's release, May 10, 1706, Livingston to Patience, May 11, 1706, Livingston-Redmond Mss.
40. Key to Livingston, June 28, 1706, Livingston's "List of my things to be Sent a Shore," Sept. 16, 1706, *ibid.*

CHAPTER XII

End of an Era:
Cornbury, Lovelace, and Ingoldesby

As the first decade of the eighteenth century drew to a close, a basic change occurred in New York's politics; the Leisler Rebellion was no longer the touchstone. Neither Leislerians nor anti-Leislerians had produced a successful program, and new issues began to break across the old alliances. Intermarriage of the leading families, the deaths of the Rebellion's participants, and the beneficial influence of time caused memories to fade. In place of the past bitterness, there evolved a new party and factional system. These changes were inevitable, but the catalyst which quickened them was Edward Hyde, Lord Cornbury, whose mismanagement did much to unite the previously estranged leaders of the colony's factions. Undeniably the worst governor who ever administered, or maladministered, New York, Cornbury was "a spenthrift, a 'grafter,' a bigoted oppressor, and a drunken, vain fool," according to one scholar, and his administration "wrought the empire distinct damage." [1]

1. Beverly McAnear, Politics in Provincial New York, 1689-1761 (unpublished doctoral dissertation, Stanford University, 1935), 127-29, 225-44, 1000-2; Charles Worthen Spencer, "The Cornbury Legend," N. Y. State Hist. Assn., *Proceedings*, 13 (1914), 309-10, 319. See also Smith, *History of New York*, I, 164; "Continuation of Colden's History of the Five Indian Nations," N.-Y. Hist. Soc., *Collections*, 68 (1935), 362.

Livingston was in no way beholden to Cornbury when he returned to New York. He had wisely secured the payment of most of
his money in London, and he waited on the governor in mid-October
1706 for only one thing—recognition of the royal commission for his
several offices. The wisdom of his plan was soon demonstrated, for
Cornbury had no intention of even recognizing the commission. Had
he done so, Livingston could have claimed his £100 sterling salary as
secretary for Indian affairs, and the rapacious Cornbury had other
uses for public funds. Therefore, he used the pretext that he and the
Council first had to compare Livingston's commission of 1706 with
that of 1696.[2]

Cornbury would have preferred to relegate the document to official oblivion, but Livingston was too shrewd and persistent to be
ignored. Now, just as in 1696, he took up the duties of his office
despite the governor's attitude, because the secretaryship was to play
an important role in his future plans:[3] Who was in a better position to
share in the profits of the Iroquois fur trade? Livingston's reputation among the Indians was good; he had gone to England as their
spokesman, at least in part, and had secured two missionaries for them.
He now planned to capitalize on their friendship, thereby reconciling
the concepts of public service and private profit. But Livingston did
not wish to be burdened by his routine duties as town clerk of
Albany. His younger son, Philip, was approaching his majority and
he wished to provide him with a foothold in politics. This office had
been Robert's stepping-stone to a public career; now, it was to be his
son's. On May 6, 1706, Livingston announced that he wished to appoint Philip as his deputy, and the Mayor's Court accepted the young
man.[4]

Livingston then visited his eldest son, John, in New London. He
took advantage of Connecticut's comparative freedom to write a
lengthy and perceptive indictment of Cornbury which he sent to
William Lowndes of the Treasury. Recounting the governor's conflicts with the Assembly over his failure to account for funds, Liv-

2. Livingston to Lowndes, June 2, 1707, PRO, Treas. 1: 102, pp. 134-35; N. Y. Council Minutes, Oct. 14, 1706, X, 45, N. Y. State Lib.
3. Livingston to Winthrop, Dec. 28, 1706, Winthrop Papers, XIV, 160, Mass. Hist.
Soc.
4. Albany Mayor's Court Minutes, May 6, 1706, Munsell, ed., *Annals of Albany*,
V, 152.

ingston denounced Cornbury as a transvestite, a fool, and a moral bankrupt. "Tis said," he wrote, "he is wholly addicted to his pleasure ... his dressing himself in womens Cloths common[ly every] morning is so unaccountable that if hundreds of Spectators did not dayly see him, it would be incredible." Such odd behavior did not instill confidence in the governor or his government, he told Lowndes; indeed, Livingston considered himself extremely unfortunate to be involved in governmental finance because the warrants he had received seven years before (the £394 [New York] which Blathwayt had refused to approve for payment out of the customs and excise duties) were returned to him by the merchants to whom he had given them. Many wished that the governor "were not so nearly related to our gracious Souveraign," Livingston commented; "neverthelesse they hope that god in his due time will send a Deliverance."

Meanwhile, New York had "a poor dispirited people, a mixture of English, Dutch, and French ... and if they be never So much oppress'd, dare not Complain, because they are not unanimous, & doe not stick to one another, So that a governor if he be not a man of honor and Probity can oppress the People when he pleases, its but Striking in with one Party, & they assist him to destroy the other, and this is our Case." This shrewd analysis of the colony's political difficulties, read by the Lord High Treasurer, probably played a role in Cornbury's eventual replacement, although it was only one of several adverse commentaries written about the governor.[5]

Livingston's detestation of Cornbury reinforced his determination to keep his contacts with the government to a minimum and to devote his energies to trade. In the summer of 1707, he bought the "Great Island" in the Mohawk River and a twenty-four-acre tract on the adjacent riverbank. This gave him an important commercial station located on the Iroquois route to Albany. Since it was customary during the fur season for the Albany traders to go out to meet the Indians and "sell 'em goods at a dearer rate," it was possible that Livingston hoped to employ such tactics by using the "Great Island."[6]

5. Livingston to Lowndes, June 2, 1707, PRO, Treas. 1: 102, pp. 134-35; Shaw, ed., *Cal. Treasury Books*, XXIV (Part II), 571. See also Lewis Morris to Secy. of State, Feb. 9, 1707/8, O'Callaghan, ed., *N. Y. Col. Docs.*, V, 38.
6. Deeds of Jan and Bata Clute to Livingston, June 25, 26, Aug. 12, Sept. 25, 1707, Melius and Burnap, eds., *Index to Albany Records: Grantees*, VII, 4589; McIlwain, ed., *Wraxall's Abridgment*, 53, 61.

Livingston's determination to participate more actively in the Indian trade was strengthened by the receipt of £1,695 sterling worth of goods from James Douglas of London on November 17, 1707. This cargo, the largest ever shipped to Livingston, included red and blue duffels, striped blankets, hats, hat bands, Scots cloth, silks, muslins, cambrics, worsteds, buttons, 8,000 needles, and a wide assortment of other textiles and haberdashery. Arrangements for the shipment were undoubtedly made before Livingston's departure from England. He and Douglas had paid cash for only a small portion, £501 sterling, and the remainder was advanced by several merchants on four months' credit from the date of its arrival in New York City. The London merchants even agreed to bear the risk on the goods they shipped on credit, an interesting commentary on Livingston's reputation.[7]

For the next ten months, Livingston apparently concerned himself solely with private matters. His name does not appear in the public records until September 1708, when he went before the governor and Council to demand formal recognition of his royal commission. Cornbury could no longer afford to delay: it would be difficult to convince the English authorities that it took more than two years to compare two brief documents. Thus, probably much to his own surprise, Livingston heard the governor order that the document "be entered at large in the minutes of this Board." Livingston promptly demanded payment of his salary as secretary for Indian affairs, but Cornbury had anticipated him. Five days later, the Council minutes noted that "it is the opinion of his Excellency and all the Councill (Except Colonel Peter Schuyler who gave no opinion therein) that the Petition be disallowed & that it be humbly represented to her Majestie that the Petitioners office is not of any use but Burthensome to the Revenue."[8]

Livingston must have been furious, but there was nothing that he could do. He took some comfort from the knowledge that Cornbury's days were numbered; as early as March 1708, the Crown had determined upon Lord John Lovelace, Baron of Hurley, as his successor. When Lovelace stepped ashore in New York City on the

7. Invoice, Feb. 28, 1706/7, Livingston-Redmond Mss.
8. N. Y. Council Minutes, Sept. 7, 1708, N.-Y. Hist. Soc., *Collections*, 2 (1876), 453; Livingston's petition to Cornbury, Sept. 10, 1708, N. Y. Col. Mss., LII, 165, and N. Y. Council Minutes, Sept. 7, 10, 15, 1708, X, 198-200, 203, 222, both in N. Y. State Lib.

morning of December 18, 1708, he brought to an end an entirely
indefensible administration. But Cornbury did not return to England
at once; his creditors saw to that. Now that he was without authority,
they turned with delight and called him to account for his past ex-
travagance.[9]

The Baron of Hurley was clearly sent to the colony as something
more than a reform governor; his most important mission was to
expedite two imperial schemes then being readied. One, which did not
come to fruition under his guidance, was the settlement of several
thousand Palatine refugees in New York to produce naval stores.
The other, the "Glorious Enterprise," was an expedition to reduce
Canada. In both undertakings, it was expected that Lovelace would be
capable and honest and would carry out the royal directives with
dispatch.[10]

Just as the Crown expected prompt compliance from its new governor, so, too, did Livingston expect prompt redress of his grievances.
On January 20, 1708/9, he petitioned Lovelace for his salary arrears
as secretary for Indian affairs, declaring that he had continued to
discharge his duties despite Cornbury's refusal to pay his salary. A
complete stranger to the colony and its inhabitants, Lovelace wisely
insisted that he could take no action until he first learned the Queen's
pleasure on Cornbury's claim that the secretaryship was useless and
financially burdensome. Livingston apparently accepted this without
offense and, to clarify matters, asked him three weeks later to order
all the councilors except Schuyler to state in writing their reasons for
concluding that the office was useless. Livingston's petition was put
aside while the governor, following custom, concerned himself with
the new Assembly elections which he had ordered. When the new

9. Sunderland to Bd. of Trade, Mar. 28, 1708, O'Callaghan, ed., *N. Y. Col. Docs.*,
V, 39; John Livingston to Wait Winthrop, Nov. 23, 1708, Winthrop Papers, XIV,
150, Mass. Hist. Soc.; Lovelace to Bd. of Trade, Dec. 18, 1708, *Cal. State Papers, Col.*,
XXIV, no. 252. Cornbury bitterly reported: "One De Lancey a french Merchant here
had arrested me, he has since declared to severall people here that he never would
have done it if Doctor Johnston, and Mr. Blathwaits kinsman Mr. Clarke the Secretary of this Province had not pressed him to do it, and they have been with all my
Creditors to perswade them to the like, some have done it, some have not." Cornbury
to Lord (?), Mar. 9, 1708/9, Additional Mss., vol. 15895, pp. 339-40, British Museum
(Lib. Cong. transcripts). Cornbury remained in New York until he succeeded his
father as Earl of Clarendon.

10. Bd. of Trade to Lovelace, Mar. 28, 1709, Sunderland to Lovelace, Apr. 28, 1709,
O'Callaghan, ed., *N. Y. Col. Docs.*, V, 72-73.

legislature gathered on April 5, 1709, Robert Livingston was one of the members for Albany. He was soon appointed chairman of the committee on elections and a member of several other committees.[11]

Politics always held a fascination for Livingston, but his real reason for seeking an Assembly seat was personal. On June 26, 1708, the Queen-in-Council had disallowed the statute, passed by Cornbury's first Assembly, to repeal all the laws enacted during Nanfan's administration. This revived the act confiscating Livingston's estate and clouded the title to all his property. Thus, on April 29, 1709, he prayed leave of the Assembly to introduce a bill to repeal the confiscation law. Permission was granted; the bill was read for the first time, and eight days later it was referred to a special committee. Before further action could be taken, Lovelace died on May 6. Almost simultaneously, the plans for the "Glorious Enterprise" matured. This campaign against Canada, originally suggested by Samuel Vetch and now being led by him and Francis Nicholson, crowded aside all lesser matters. Livingston's bill was held in abeyance while the government prepared for war.[12]

Vetch had written to Lovelace from Boston, asking that Peter Schuyler and Robert Livingston—his uncle and father-in-law respectively—be sent "to find out two Sober trusty and sensible Indians" for use as spies at Montreal and Quebec. Schuyler and Livingston were also to investigate Wood Creek, near Lake Champlain, as a possible depot and embarkation point for the expedition. Lovelace's death altered these plans, for Lieutenant Governor Richard Ingoldesby was absent, and Peter Schuyler, as the eldest councilor in length of service, assumed the presidency. In his place, Kiliaen Van Rensselaer of the Council went with Livingston to select the Indian spies. The two agents departed on May 6, quickly accomplished their purpose, and were back in New York City on the twenty-first to make a full report to the Assembly of their negotiations.[13]

Soon thereafter, Ingoldesby returned to the colony and assumed

11. Livingston to Lovelace, Jan. 20, 1708/9, O'Callaghan ed., *Doc. Hist. N. Y.*, III, 630-32; N. Y. Council Minutes, Jan. 20, Feb. 11, 1708/9, X, 277, 287, N. Y. State Lib.; *Assembly Journal*, I, 239-42.

12. Bd. of Trade to Lovelace, June 28, 1708, O'Callaghan, ed., *N. Y. Col. Docs.*, V, 48; *Assembly Journal*, I, 242-44, 246; Samuel Vetch's "Canada Survey'd," July 27, 1708, *Cal. State Papers, Col.*, XXIV, no. 60.

13. Vetch to Lovelace, Apr. 30, 1709, Vetch Letterbook, Museum of City of N. Y.; Leder, ed., *Livingston Indian Records*, 202-5.

control of the government. Although his commission had already been revoked by the Queen, no one had notified officials in New York. This was an unfortunate oversight at a critical juncture, for Ingoldesby was not really qualified to take command of the government and direct its contribution to the Canada expedition. A lesser official noted that he was "so influenced by My Lord Cornbury and his party, that whatever his Lordship desires is put in Execution." More important, Ingoldesby was unable to cope with the "interest that... Tyrannises at New York," the *handlaers* of Albany, who feared the disruptive effects of the war on their illicit Albany-Montreal trade. They bitterly opposed the campaign, although the farmers, mindful of the possible benefits for themselves, were supporting it.[14]

There is no evidence that Livingston was involved financially in the "Glorious Enterprise." Beyond his negotiations with the Indian spies, he seemed to restrict himself to forwarding mail between Vetch in Boston and Nicholson on the Albany frontier. Perhaps he was afraid of a project whose prospects were uncertain. If so, he was most wise, for the expedition came to an inglorious end. A naval flotilla had been expected from England to lead the attack up the St. Lawrence River, but the sailing plans were canceled by the vicissitudes of the European phase of the war. Without naval support, the land army, which was only to be a diversionary force, could not march, and the scheme collapsed.[15]

The citizens of Albany quickly realized that this fiasco placed them in a dangerous position: the French would not sit by and wait for the English to gather together their forces. The leaders of the expedition met in Albany on August 12 to draft a memorial about "the Deplorable & dangerous Condition these fronteers will be in this winter." As it became more and more obvious that the English fleet would not appear, the fears of the populace increased and the Assembly in September appointed a committee, of which Livingston was

14. "Cal. of Council Minutes," N. Y. State Lib., *Bulletin 58*, 229; Bd. of Trade to Queen Anne, Sept. 2, 1709, Byerly to Bd. of Trade, June 30, 1709, Cockerill to Popple, July 2, 1709, O'Callaghan, ed., *N. Y. Col. Docs.*, V, 89, 80, 81.

15. Vetch to Nicholson, Aug. 12, Sept. 22, 1709, Vetch Letterbook, Museum of City of N. Y. For a survey of the expedition, see Bruce T. McCully, "Catastrophe in the Wilderness: New Light on the Canada Expedition of 1709," *Wm. and Mary Qtly.*, 3rd ser., 11 (1954), 441-56; George M. Waller, "New York's Role in Queen Anne's War, 1702-1713," *N. Y. Hist.*, 30 (1952), 40-53, and Waller, *Vetch*, 121-41, *et passim*.

a member, to memorialize the Queen.[16] Beset by fears of a French invasion, the colony could do little more; the next move had to come from the Crown.

In the meantime, the collapse of the "Glorious Enterprise" opened the way for consideration of less important matters which had been shunted aside during the hectic summer of 1709. Once again, Livingston plunged into legislative affairs, but his main interest remained the repeal of the act confiscating his estate. The Assembly committee, to which it had been referred, finally reported on October 21 that the allegations in Livingston's bill were true. After several minor amendments were added by the Assembly, the bill was given its third reading and sent to the Council. On November 1 the Council concurred, and on the twelfth Lieutenant Governor Ingoldesby affixed his signature.[17] Vindicated at last, Livingston, like the government as a whole, patiently awaited the arrival of the new royal governor, Robert Hunter, whose administration was to mark the dawn of a new age in New York's politics. /

16. Leder, ed., *Livingston Indian Records*, 213-14; *Assembly Journal*, I, 258-59.
17. *Assembly Journal*, I, 262-65, 270; *Legis. Council Jour.*, I, 291-92, 295. The text may be found in *Col. Laws of N. Y.*, I, 687-88.

PART THREE

Political Maturity
1710-1728

CHAPTER XIII

Governor Hunter and the Palatines

WHEN ROBERT HUNTER assumed New York's governorship on June 14, 1710, Livingston was more thoroughly dissociated from public affairs than at any time during the previous two decades. There was every indication that he had relinquished all thoughts of politics and was instead broadening the scope of his commercial activities. For some sixteen years, he had owned property in New York City, but it was not until December 1709 that he applied for and received the right to engage in business within the metropolis.[1]

Despite these intentions, however, Livingston returned to public service because of the problems and opportunities presented by the arrival of over 2,000 Palatine refugees with Governor Hunter. Having flocked to London in 1709 to escape the War of the Spanish Succession, they could not be denied sanctuary by the Crown, even though their eventual disposition posed a problem. One solution, of course, was to send them to the colonies where land was cheap and labor scarce; several halting attempts had been made to do this, but the embarkation for New York was the first real effort to solve the problem.

This mass migration was intended to answer several economic and strategic purposes. To pay for its British imports, New York needed

1. Livingston's "List of Debtors," Jan. 20, 1709/10, Mayor Willson's certificate, Dec. 13, 1709, Livingston-Redmond Mss.

a staple commodity other than furs. Strategic naval stores seemed the logical commodity; the colony had the requisite raw materials and England wanted to replace Baltic sources for the royal navy's turpentine, pitch, tar, and masts. Strengthening the Albany frontier was another purpose of the Palatine settlement. New York, as the defensive keystone of British North America, was under-populated, creating a danger that the French might overwhelm the colony, drive a wedge between New England and the South, and thereby pave the way for the ultimate conquest of all the British colonies.[2]

When the refugees landed with Hunter, they found that no official preparations had been made for them in New York, except for a Council order placing an embargo on all grain exports for three months. Designed to prevent a rapid rise in the price of grains and other foodstuffs as a result of the sudden influx, the measure did not blunt the grain dealers' eager anticipation of increased trade.[3]

As a merchant, Livingston certainly expected to profit from the settlement, and he may have had even loftier expectations because of the friendship between his son-in-law Samuel Vetch and the governor, as well as the Scottish background which he shared with Hunter. However, rather than entangle his finances again with those of the government, he sought to capture a share of the Hudson River carrying trade, which would increase greatly with the settlement. In June 1710, he contracted for the construction of a sloop, the *Caledonia*, at his manor, specifying that she was to be 34 feet long, 5½ feet deep, and 14 feet wide.[4]

While the *Caledonia* was still on the ways, the governor arrived in New York. His first concern was the establishment of his government, but after he had read his commission and sworn in his councilors, he attended a series of entertainments planned by prominent officials and merchants. On July 12, he was feted by Livingston. The relationship was cordial from the outset, and it was to become even

---

2. Walter Allen Knittle, *The Early Eighteenth Century Palatine Emigration: A British Government Redemptioner Project to Manufacture Naval Stores* (Phila., 1936), 1, 65-8, 71, 111-16, 132-34, 147.

3. Alida to Robert Livingston, Apr. 16, 1710 (Dutch), Livingston-Redmond Mss.

4. Livingston's son-in-law referred to "my worthy friend Coll: Hunter." Vetch to Lord Stair, Nov. 18, 1709, Vetch Letterbook, Museum of City of N. Y.; Indenture between Evert Pells and Livingston, June 8, 1710, "Inventory of the ... Calidonia," July 10, 1710, Livingston-Redmond Mss.

more so once the governor realized the difficulties involved in settling the Palatines on the lands designated for them—the Mohawk Patent. Not only did the Indian proprietors object, but the land was also unsuitable for naval stores production because it lacked sizable stands of pine.[5]

Selection of an alternate site was left wholly to the governor, who began negotiations with "some who have land on Hudson's river fitt for that purpose." By the end of July, he had narrowed his choice and intended to inspect several tracts with Surveyor General John Bridger. The former Evans grant of 6,300 acres on the west shore of the Hudson suited his needs, but it was too small for nearly 2,500 settlers. At Bridger's suggestion, he negotiated with Livingston for the purchase of an additional 6,000 acres from Livingston Manor, just across the river from the Evans tract. The discussions were probably conducted while Livingston and Hunter participated in a two-week conference with the Iroquois at Albany. About five weeks after the conference ended, the deed was signed transferring 6,000 acres of Livingston Manor to the Crown and authorizing the use of stands of pine on Livingston's land within certain limitations. On October 5, Hunter took possession of the property and paid £400 (£266 sterling).[6]

As far as Hunter was concerned, this was a most advantageous purchase; the soil was good, the land was near the timber supply, and it was accessible to water transportation. For Livingston, it was one of his shrewdest bargains, because it enabled him to turn his manor into a profitable investment. The coming of the Palatines would convert his relatively unsettled manor into a profitable trading area, and his manufacturing enterprises could be expanded. Still other attractive features for him were his appointment as inspector of Palatines, effective August 24, 1710, at an annual salary of £100 and his receipt of the victualing contract for the Palatines.

5. John Sharpe, "Journal of my Life–Exteriour," *Penn. Mag. of Hist. and Biog.*, 40 (1916), 292; Knittle, *Palatine Emigration*, 138; Leder, ed., *Livingston Indian Records*, 215-16.

6. Hunter to Bd. of Trade, July 24, 1710, O'Callaghan, ed., *N. Y. Col. Docs.*, V, 167; Knittle, *Palatine Emigration*, 140, 153-56; Hunter's Iroquois conference, Aug. 7-20, 1710, O'Callaghan, ed., *N. Y. Col. Docs.*, V, 217-23; Robert and Alida Livingston's deed to Hunter, Sept. 29, 1710, O'Callaghan, ed., *Doc. Hist. N. Y.*, III, 644-51.

According to the contract, signed on November 13, Livingston was to supply each settler with a daily allowance of one-third of a loaf of bread and a quart of ship-beer. His payment would be one-half in silver and the balance in merchandise, of which five-sixths was to be European (i.e., textiles, ironware, and similar manufactures) and the remainder West Indian (i.e., molasses, rum, and sugar). He was then given an advance of twenty-five tuns, or casks, of flour, and £400 in silver.[7]

Before the contract was formalized, Livingston began purchasing supplies and winning the friendship of those with whom he would be associated in the Palatine venture. He bought £72 of textiles from George Clarke, secretary of the colony and Hunter's agent for the refugees, even though he did not need the goods, simply as a means of keeping "on good terms with him, who controls much, if not everything." Both Hunter and Livingston were anxious to maintain cordial relations with one another. The governor sent the Board of Trade a copy of the law passed in Ingoldesby's administration to repeal the 1702 act which confiscated Livingston's estate, adding this note: "When your Lordships have read the Act I am perswaded you'll think it reasonable to offer it to Her Majesty for her approbation." Livingston, in turn, busied himself on the administration's behalf in the Assembly where he was one of the four members "most distinguished for their activity in the house."[8]

Livingston was undoubtedly encouraged to re-enter the political arena by the favorable reception he received from the governor, and he began to seek out new areas in which to apply his talents. He hit upon the idea of victualing the British garrison at Annapolis Royal, Nova Scotia, and suggested it to General Francis Nicholson, an intimate of many royal officials. The general sent it on to Colonel Samuel Vetch, Livingston's son-in-law and commanding officer of

7. Hunter to Bd. of Trade, Oct. 3, 1710, Contract between Livingston and Hunter, Nov. 13, 1710, Acct. of Livingston's salary, Aug. 24, 1710-Mar. 25, 1713, O'Callaghan, ed., *Doc. Hist. N. Y.*, III, 560, 653-55, 686. For an explanation of Livingston's profits see Lawrence H. Leder and Vincent P. Carosso, "Robert Livingston (1654-1728): Businessman of Colonial New York," *Business Hist. Rev.*, 30 (1956), 40-42.

8. Robert to Alida Livingston, Oct. 18, 21, 1710 (Dutch), Livingston-Redmond Mss.; Hunter to Bd. of Trade, Nov. 14, 1710, O'Callaghan, ed., *N. Y. Col. Docs.*, V, 181; *Assembly Journal*, I, 271. The three other members were Speaker William Nicholls, Stephen De Lancey, and Lewis Morris. Smith, *History of New York*, I, 179.

the garrison, who hoped for Livingston's sake that "the Generall will be wiser than to show it to any body." [9]

Livingston dropped the idea of victualing the Annapolis Royal garrison because of supply problems in New York. First of all, he discovered that the beef gathered for the settlers was spoiling. Rather than accept a loss on the meat or force the government to do so, he ordered the immediate distribution of a two months' supply; if the beef went bad, it was better that it do so in the Palatines' hands. Secretary George Clarke, the governor's agent in the Palatine arrangements, gave his unqualified blessings to this move. Livingston also encountered difficulties in securing supplies from Stephen De Lancey, Hunter's commercial agent in New York City. De Lancey, along with most of the other merchants, was infected with a speculative fever in February 1710/1 and could not furnish Livingston with wheat and barley. He explained that "all moneyd men run upon the price [of] cocoa which maketh all other commodityes of no Value, ...you must not depend upon me...for I have Layd out above Three thousand pounds in cocoa which hath dryed me up." Secretary Clarke promised to make good De Lancey's deficiency by sending a cargo of beef and flour in mid-March. But Governor Hunter was finding it difficult to supply Livingston with money. Silver, Clarke explained, "is scarcer to be met with if possible than truth and honesty; If I were in Cash I would readily do you any favour of this kind without Reminding you of your having had of Mr. De Lancey in money and goods, and of me in money above thirteen hundred and fifty pounds." [10]

Because no one could send him cash, Livingston utilized his own credit as best he could. On March 5, 1710/1, the *Caledonia* returned to the Manor with 1,376 schepels of wheat purchased on four months' credit. Livingston had no idea that there would be any difficulty in securing reimbursement, especially since the governor took such a deep personal interest in the project. However, governmental support was inadequate. From March to June, 1711, Livingston expended over £3,800 for the settlers, but George Clarke had promised more

9. Vetch was then victualing that garrison and probably a bit annoyed at his father-in-law's effort to supplant him. Vetch to Livingston, Jan. 17, 1710/1, Livingston-Redmond Mss.

10. Clarke to Livingston, Jan. 26, Mar. 5, 1710/1, De Lancey to Livingston, Feb. 14, 1710/1, *ibid*.

than he could produce. Although he desired to send money "as soon as possible," he lamented on one occasion that "if you know [what] the difficulty here is to get [money] ... you would not be impatient." [11]

In addition, the Palatines grew restless as they envisaged perpetual bondage. Living in the midst of virgin forests, they were denied land of their own and forced to labor for the Crown. When the benefits of their situation were pointed out to them, they admitted that they were better off in New York than in the Palatinate, but the "desire to possess a good deal of land upset and demolished, in a moment afterwards, all these advantages." Concerned over this unrest, Livingston reported to the governor, who decided to visit the Manor to survey the situation for himself. In the meantime, Clarke suggested that Livingston assure the Palatines that "they had better set their thoughts on the spot they are now planted upon." When Hunter arrived, he tried to reconcile the settlers to their role, but they threatened a mutiny. The governor then obtained reinforcements, disarmed the Palatines, and ordered them treated as the "Queens hired servants," appointing a court to manage them.[12]

Having suppressed an incipient rebellion, the governor turned to Livingston's victualing account for the Palatines. For the six months beginning November 13, 1710, the government still owed Livingston £279 and he demanded cash to pay off debts in London. He had not settled his accounts for the £1,695 sterling consignment of goods received in 1707, and James Douglas and the other creditors were becoming impatient. To secure his money, Douglas finally employed John Sharpe as his agent.[13] Livingston's repayment of his London creditors depended upon prompt repayment by the government of the victualing account.

However, De Lancey pointedly told Livingston not to expect any more merchandise or money from him—"you must apply for the

---

11. "Account of wheat," Mar. 5, 1710/1, Livingston to Wessel Ten Broeck, Mar. 11, 1710/1 (Dutch), Livingston to Dirk Wessels, Mar. 11, 1710/1, Clarke to Livingston, Mar. 27, 1711, *ibid.*

12. Cast to Hunter, Mar. 27, 1711, O'Callaghan, ed., *N. Y. Col. Docs.,* V, 214; Clarke to Livingston, Apr. 24, 1711, Livingston-Redmond Mss.; Hunter to Bd. of Trade, May 7, 1711, *Cal. State Papers, Col.,* XXV, no. 832; Knittle, *Palatine Emigration,* 163-64.

13. Livingston's accts., May 13, 1711, N. Y. Col. Mss., LV, 18, 19a, 19b, N. Y. State Lib.; Sharpe to Livingston, May 4, 1711, Livingston-Redmond Mss.

future to Mr. Clarke for mony when you want it (... the Country traders ... will pay me no mony and hardly any flower) I am forced to give here 4s 6d a bushel for wheat So that you must not depend upon me for any." This difficulty was compounded by Hunter's decision, before he received Parliamentary approval, to extend the subsidy of the naval stores program for another year. He had no alternative, because the settlement had been begun too late to accomplish anything during its first year, and unless it were extended another twelve months, the money already spent would be wasted.[14] No one knew whether Parliament would agree to this and vote the necessary funds. Thus there were few merchants willing to gamble on the outcome by advancing money, tempers were soon on edge, and Livingston antagonized Hunter by his old habit of demanding immediate repayment of the money due him.

As a result, Secretary Clarke carefully scrutinized Livingston's accounts, and he disagreed with him on several points. On the flour originally advanced to him, Livingston allowed only fifteen shillings a bushel, including transportation; this, Clarke charged, defrauded the government. If the higher price could be proven, Livingston countered, he would pay the difference. To Clarke's objection that the contract was violated when Livingston failed to follow a change in the assize of bread in New York City, the victualer pleaded ignorance of the change; if there had been an alteration, he was ready to adjust his accounts accordingly. Finally, Clarke did not believe that the balance of the account should be paid in cash. Nevertheless, Livingston insisted upon specie: he could not purchase wheat for goods, and his cash and credit were exhausted. "This is the only Time for purchasing wheat," he warned, "for in harvest time none is to be had." Moreover, he added, "an Expedition to Canada ... would raise the Prise of wheat Considerably." [15]

Livingston had good cause to fear the effects of war preparations on the Palatine situation. A new expedition against Canada meant that all official efforts would be directed toward the troops rather than the naval stores program. Indeed, many Palatines enlisted in

14. De Lancey to Livingston, May 18, 1711, Livingston-Redmond Mss.; *Journal Bd. Trade*, II, 232.

15. "Livingston's answer to Some objections made by george Clarke," June 13, 1711, N. Y. Col. Mss., LV, 27, N. Y. State Lib.

the army, taking able-bodied men away from the production of naval stores. At the same time Clarke ordered Livingston to secure 2,000 bushels of peas and all the bread possible for the troops' use, thus depriving the settlers. Livingston objected strongly to Hunter and Clarke.[16]

But the governor and the secretary augmented Livingston's fears instead of easing them: "There is no money here for us for all which we have advanced for the Palatines." He immediately ordered his wife "to stop the baking," and pointedly warned Hunter and Clarke that he had only a few days' supply of wheat. But warn, protest, and implore though he might, Livingston obtained no relief. The governor's bills of exchange were not being honored in London, goods were not being sent to him, and no immediate solution could be found because "All hands are occupied with this expedition."

Livingston was greatly agitated. "I do not want to run up any more debts," he wrote his wife, "I already have too many." With the Palatine settlement pushed aside by the Canada expedition, he could not even get his accounts audited, let alone paid. On the morning of July 23, he had a serious talk with Clarke, who "said positively there is no money." "What will happen to us," Livingston exclaimed, "Heaven knows." His decision was simple and characteristic: "I cannot ruin myself for someone else." He sent his wife strict orders: "Do not deliver any more bread come what may . . . I have already delivered bread two months too long and it will have to stop at once." [17]

Surveyor General John Bridger, then in Boston, heard of the difficulties hampering the naval stores program, and he immediately placed the entire blame on Livingston, whom he castigated for failing to advance his own funds. He had learned, he announced, "that the victualling of the Palatines and Not the Raiseing of Naval Stores Induced a Gentleman to undertake an Affaire he was wholy Ignorant of." Bridger's criticism was most unfair. There was no prospect of repayment for Livingston, and in any case, the responsibility for the entire situation probably belonged to the officials in London. A ministerial upheaval in the English government had displaced Hunter's

16. Clarke to Livingston, July 5, 1711, *ibid.*, 99; Intercolonial conference proceedings, June 21, 1711, O'Callaghan, ed., *N. Y. Col. Docs.*, V, 259; Robert to Alida Livingston, July 8, 12, 21, 1711 (Dutch), Livingston-Redmond Mss.

17. Robert to Alida Livingston, July 21 (2nd letter), 23, 1711 (Dutch), Livingston-Redmond Mss.

Whig friends and substituted Tory officials who had no love for dissenters, either English or Palatinate; they urged the abandonment of the settlement and the naval stores program.[18]

This turn of events placed both Livingston and Hunter in awkward positions. The governor could not allow the naval stores program to fail, but he did not have the means to maintain it. Neither could he afford to alienate Livingston and his friends. Although De Lancey took pity on the harrassed executive and extended him some credit, it did not solve the problem. Hunter finally decided to "just let things take care of themselves and let everybody go on his own way . . . to save themselves." Livingston could still sympathize with the governor who, he admitted, was "at his wits' end and does not know what to do with the Palatines." "If, before he gets further orders from England, he lets them go free, then he will not be able to get them back together again, and he is not in a position to furnish them with food and drink." However, Livingston stoutly refused to furnish any more bread and ship-beer unless he first had some assurance of repayment. He told his wife to send down all the flour on the Manor—"it is safer to have no bread or flour in the closet." [19]

Unable to get any assistance from the governor, Livingston turned to his old acquaintance, General Francis Nicholson, for help with the royal officials. The general was daily expected in New York City to take command of the Canada expedition and, when Livingston learned that Hunter was going to accompany him to Albany, he insisted on joining the party. "I will not let go," he promised Alida, "until the account has been made up, it is too much to let it stand like this." When Nicholson arrived in New York City on August 6, Livingston asked him to use his influence with George Clarke to secure some money for victualing. Nicholson's presence and seeming friendship was most reassuring, if not financially rewarding, and Livingston suggested that Alida resume baking bread for the Palatines with whatever flour she had on hand.[20]

18. Bridger to William Popple, July 23, 1711, PRO, CO 5: 865, no. 68; Knittle, *Palatine Emigration*, 181-84. The Earl of Clarendon, formerly Lord Cornbury, sought to attack Livingston on this score in revenge for Livingston's treatment of him. Clarendon to Dartmouth, Mar. 8, 1710/1, O'Callaghan, ed., *Doc. Hist. N. Y.*, III, 656-57.
19. Robert to Alida Livingston, July 31, Aug. 1, 5, 1711 (Dutch), Livingston-Redmond Mss.
20. Robert to Alida Livingston, Aug. 5, 6, 1711 (Dutch), *ibid.*

By mid-August, Nicholson, Hunter, and Livingston headed for
Albany to woo the Iroquois for the Canada campaign. During their
voyage north, the governor had agreed to sign bills of exchange for
£700 sterling if Livingston would give him a receipt for £1,050
(New York). This immediately began a new dispute: Livingston
could see no reason to pay a 50 percent discount when the current
rate was 30 percent. The governor next offered to pay half in cash
and half in merchandise, but Livingston rejected this since he could
not pay the farmers with goods. At this point, Livingston "com-
municated everything to the General who is my friend." Nicholson's
innocuous advice was "not to go too far with the Palatines without
moving very warily." [21]

Although the deadlock between Livingston and Hunter continued, the arrival of a packet boat bearing letters from England for
the governor gave Livingston cause for cautious optimism. "As far
as I can learn," Livingston told his wife, "the matter of the Palatines
is not forgotten." Because the Canada expedition so dominated men's
thoughts and actions, however, he decided to wait until the Iroquois
conferences were concluded before pressing matters further.[22]

When the conferences ended, the three men returned to New York
City and Livingston resumed his laments. There was still no money
to be had—"cannot even get enough from Mr. Clarke," he wrote, "to
pay a cartman." If his wife would agree, Livingston was now willing
to accept £500 or £600 worth of goods as part payment of the debt.
Then, with whatever bills of exchange he could get from Hunter,
he would "pay all of . . . the debt in England, for I will not have any
peace until that is done." [23]

Livingston's importunities finally had their desired effect: the governor approved his accounts on September 13, thereby clearing the
way for their payment. De Lancey then supplied him with some
merchandise, which he forwarded to his wife, instructing her that it

21. Iroquois Conference, Aug. 17-18, 1711, O'Callaghan, ed., N. Y. Col. Docs., V,
265-74; Robert to Alida Livingston, Aug. 18, 1711 (Dutch), Livingston-Redmond Mss.
When Livingston returned to New York City, his attention was diverted by the
serious illness of his daughter-in-law Mary Winthrop Livingston. She underwent
surgery on September 7, and died 16 months later. Robert to Alida Livingston, Sept. 7,
8, 1711, ibid.; "Diary of Joshua Hempstead, 1711-1758," New London County Hist.
Soc., Collections, 1 (1901), 19.

22. Robert to Alida Livingston, Aug. 22, 1711 (Dutch), Livingston-Redmond Mss.
23. Robert to Alida Livingston, Sept. 8, 1711 (Dutch), ibid.

was "good stuff and a good buy and you can sell it cheaply to attract customers and let Claverack and Kinderhook and the Flats know that you have all kinds of goods and you will give a better buy than in Albany." Livingston also received £1,050 (New York currency) in bills of exchange, but at a 50 percent discount, which he sent to his London creditors so that he could "put an end to this debt in England, for the interest eats a man up." [24]

Even more important, however, was word that the governor and secretary intended "to go on with the Palatine matter." No sooner had this decision been made than the news arrived that the British fleet in the St. Lawrence River had been destroyed—another Canada expedition had failed. Now, Clarke and De Lancey again refused to send Livingston money because of its scarcity, and Livingston ordered his wife to sell all the goods on hand for whatever cash she could get; otherwise they could never repay their obligations to local farmers.

Although Livingston insisted on specie payments while Hunter and Clarke offered him merchandise, both the victualer and the governor realized that their eventual reimbursement depended upon the success of the naval stores program, and each placed that project above personal considerations, thereby avoiding a dangerous rift. Livingston accepted Hunter's offer of a shipload of biscuits left over from the Canada expedition, Clarke's £150 of "best goods," and the promise of £500 of Dutch goods expected by Hunter.

Perhaps, as sometimes happens, their common difficulties brought Livingston and Hunter closer together. The governor intended to "keep his residence at Albany at our place all winter," reported Livingston. Moreover, Hunter agreed to continue the victualing contract and to make payments in accordance with the original terms, and Secretary Clarke offered to deliver £200 in cash within two weeks to David Jamison, Livingston's newly appointed agent in New York City.

Having reached an understanding with Hunter, Livingston set out for Albany to dispose of the goods he had received. In his absence, however, his earlier discussions with Nicholson bore some unexpected fruit. The general, who was overly impressed with his own importance, was dissatisfied with the management of the Palatine

24. Robert to Alida Livingston, Sept. 15, 1711 (2 letters), (Dutch), *ibid.*; Certificates issued to Livingston, Sept. 13, 1711, N. Y. Col. Mss., LVI, 84, 85, 86a, N. Y. State Lib.

program, and Livingston had allegedly attempted to utilize his disap-
probation to his own advantage by carrying tales against Hunter.
Word of this reached the governor who immediately wrote to
Nicholson, telling him that Livingston's action, if true, was "a most
base and villanous practice." Although he knew that the victualer was
"the most selfish man alive," Hunter could not believe "that a man
who lay under so many obligations to me as he does would take it into
his head to make any Representations to my Prejudice without ac-
quainting me at Least.... If any man has any Advantage by the
Palatines here it is he." He angrily wrote to Livingston and warned
him of the possible consequences of his treachery. "If your mistaken
Interest has led you into a Secret Contrivance with my Enemys to
my prejudice it is high time that I have attention to my real ones.
When I hear from you," Hunter ominously concluded, "I shall
send you the Continuations of your [victualing] Contract or otherwise as I think her Majesties Service may Require." [25]

Unaware of this dramatic turn of events, Livingston disposed of his
merchandise and returned to New York City to present his victualing
accounts for the period ending November 13, 1711. He intended to
insist upon cash; "if I do not get any money, I give up," he told his
wife, "for I do not want to make a trip to England again, I am too
old, it would better suit me to have some rest in my old age instead
of running around so much, I am very much discouraged." [26]

Before Livingston presented his accounts, the governor confronted
him and asked whether he had received the letter demanding an explanation of his conduct. Livingston replied in the negative, and
Hunter began to recite the charges from memory in French as they
had been written by Jean Cast. Livingston interrupted, reminded the
governor that he did not understand French, and asked for a written
translation. Two days later, Secretary Clarke supplied him with the
charges in English. Once Livingston had a chance to read them and
to understand their seriousness, he went straight to Hunter and denied
everything: "It was wrong and Cast had misunderstood us." On the

25. Robert to Alida Livingston, Sept. 18, 19, 21, 22, 26 (2 letters), Oct. 15, 1711
(Dutch), Livingston-Redmond Mss.; Hunter to Nicholson, Oct. 22, 1711, O'Callaghan,
ed., Doc. Hist. N. Y., III, 675-76; Hunter to Livingston, Oct. 22, 1711, "Historical
Documents and Autograph Letters," in Myers Mss., N. Y. Pub. Lib.

26. Robert to Alida Livingston, Oct. 24 (2 letters), Nov. 5, 1711 (Dutch), Livingston-Redmond Mss.

following day, Nicholson's testimony substantiated his denial. The governor and the victualer then met and agreed that "Cast was mistaken and was all wrong." Hunter "was very well satisfied in the matter," according to Livingston, "and hoped I would not mention it anymore, and asked me to eat with him."

Livingston benefited most from this bizarre episode; he had been the injured party and could now press Hunter even more strongly for a satisfactory settlement. He claimed £791 for victualing and insisted upon £610 in cash, but Hunter offered £200 in cash and the balance in merchandise. Taking a firm stand, Livingston replied: "I do not want to be involved anymore, for I just do not want to go to England again." To Clarke, who also rejected his demand for money, he announced: "What shall I do to continue, for without credit we cannot get anything?" [27]

Both Hunter and Clarke refused to budge from their positions. Livingston received £100 in cash and £249 worth of goods. The cash was earmarked for the local farmers from whom he had bought wheat on credit, but somehow he managed to secure 6,000 pounds of bread and some salted fish for the Palatines. He continued to victual, but he made an important qualification: "I did not commit myself unless the farmers bring wheat." [28]

Livingston's problems, as was often the case, did not come singly. He had great difficulty in securing wheat from the Ulster County farmers; his sloop was suddenly without a captain and a new one had to be found; the Palatines raided his storehouse in January; and, in February, the ice carried away the gutter of his gristmill and blocked the Roeloff Jansen Kill so that the water level rose sixteen feet. Unable to use his gristmill or sawmill, Livingston was forced to send his grain to Andries Coeyman's mill, twenty-eight miles away. Six carpenters were put to work to repair the mills by the end of April. [29]

When Livingston visited the governor in May of 1712, there was

27. Robert to Alida Livingston, Nov. 12, 1711 (Dutch), *ibid*.

28. Livingston's receipts to Clarke, Nov. 12, 15, 1711, N. Y. Col. Mss., LVI, 163a, 163b, N. Y. State Lib.; Robert to Alida Livingston, Dec. 3, 1711 (Dutch), Livingston-Redmond Mss.

29. Gilbert to Robert Livingston, Jan. 11, 1711/2, Quackenboss to Livingston, Feb. 17, 1711/2 (Dutch), Bagge to Livingston, Jan. 7, 1711/2, Livingston-Redmond Mss.; Livingston to Smith, Apr. 2, 1712, O'Callaghan, ed., *Doc. Hist. N. Y.*, III, 679-80.

no hint of their previous disagreement. After submitting his accounts to Clarke, Livingston was promised Hunter's bills of exchange for £880, as well as £300 or £400 worth of goods. "If we get this £880," he told his wife with relief, "we will then be out of the misery," for they could use the money to pay their local debts.

Six days later, a packet boat arrived from England bearing good news for some, but not for Livingston. There had been widespread uncertainty as to whether the Crown would assume the obligations of the Canada expedition, and it was now learned that the British Treasury would pay those bills "⅔ cash and ⅓ as soon as the accounts had been audited." Livingston, however, had not participated in the campaign's financing, although he had made some small speculations in its bills once it had failed.[30]

Livingston was much more concerned about the Palatine venture than in the success of his minor speculations. When two London merchants, Robert Hackshaw and John Norton, informed him that the Lord High Treasurer had refused the governor's bills for the Palatines, he immediately took their letters to Hunter, who attempted to calm Livingston by remarking that Parliament had not yet considered the basic question of whether or not to continue the naval stores program subsidy for a second year. He felt confident that a favorable decision would be forthcoming and that the treasurer would then accept the bills. To demonstrate his own confidence in eventual repayment, Hunter gave Livingston his personal bills of exchange on his own London agent, Micajah Perry. The victualer promptly took them to the Jewish merchant, Jacob Franks, who discounted them and gave him cash.

While waiting to receive another £450 in similar bills, Livingston received word that the governor's earlier bill for £100 had been protested by the Lord High Treasurer. Livingston's anxiety was now mounting daily. "If I do not get any money," he insisted, "then the Palatines cannot have any bread or beer." At this moment, the chaos was compounded when Secretary Clarke's marriage put a halt to all high level government decisions. Realizing that he could make no further headway with the governor or the secretary, Livingston re-

30. Robert to Alida Livingston, May 2, 8, 1712 (Dutch), Livingston-Redmond Mss.; Acct. Bk. of Van Brugh and Hansen, Commissioners for Canada Expedition of 1711-12, *passim*, N.-Y. Hist. Soc.

turned to his manor by June 13. He sent his sons out to buy wheat, but Philip was only able to buy 300 schepels at seven guilders each in Schenectady, and Gilbert could only get wheat in Ulster County at five shillings two pence a schepel, two pence more than the current price. Because his credit was nearly exhausted, Livingston had to accept that price and, by mid-July, had gotten 1,663 schepels of wheat, enough to carry the Palatines through September.[31]

Supplies for the winter were another matter, however, especially since Livingston's fears were now being shared by Hunter and Clarke. Despairing of any further financial aid from the Crown, they ordered Livingston to reduce the amount of ship-beer given to the settlers. Only those who were actually working were to receive it, "not . . . their familys." The governor asked him to continue baking and brewing for another two or three weeks, assuring him that "he would not lose." Hunter's last hope was James Du Pré who had gone to London as his personal emissary. There were reports that he had not met with friendly treatment at Court, but until he returned everything was held in abeyance.[32]

By August 1712, even the governor's façade of confidence crumbled, and he decided to let "the Palatines go free this winter to go and work where they will on condition that they will return in the spring and . . . they will not have to be provided for in the meantime." On September 6, the governor gathered the settlers together and brought the naval stores program to an ignominious close by advising them of his decision. Five weeks later, Du Pré's long overdue vessel arrived, but he had "indiscreetly gone ashore at Rhode Island," taking with him all the papers pertaining to the Palatines. As Hunter confided to Livingston, he was "kept still in the Dark."[33]

31. Robert to Alida Livingston, May 8, 15, 1712 (Dutch), Philip to Robert Livingston, June 13, 1712, Gilbert Livingston's acct. of wheat, July 16, 1712, Gilbert to Robert Livingston, July 17, 1712, Livingston-Redmond Mss. See also Livingston to [Clarke], July 11, 1712, Misc. Mss. no. 1458, N. Y. State Lib. The bill is in N. Y. Col. Mss., LVII, 57, ibid.

32. Clarke to Livingston, July 30, 1712, Robert to Alida Livingston, Aug. 20, 22, 1712 (Dutch), Livingston-Redmond Mss.; Hunter to Livingston, July 30, 1712, N. Y. Col. Mss., LVII, 191, N. Y. State Lib.

33. Robert to Alida Livingston, Aug. 27, 1712 (Dutch), Hunter to Livingston, Oct. 17, 1712, Livingston-Redmond Mss.; Hunter to Cast, Sept. 6, 1712, O'Callaghan, ed., Doc. Hist. N. Y., III, 683. Many Palatines scattered into Pennsylvania and throughout N. Y., but some remained on the Manor though the number is uncertain. Knittle, Palatine Emigration, 189-95.

The situation sorely depressed the governor, and he succinctly described his feelings to his friend, Jonathan Swift: "My unhappy circumstances have so soured me, that whatever I write must be vinegar and gall to a man of your mirth . . . I am used like a dog after having done all that is in the power of man to deserve a better treatment, so that I am now quite jaded." His melancholy was increased considerably by the letters which Du Pré finally delivered. Livingston rushed down to New York City to learn what decision had been made in London, and the governor gave him the bad news on November 5. The Board of Trade had twice represented to the Queen and the Lord High Treasurer without success that the naval stores program should be continued and had suggested an appropriation of £30,000 sterling for a two-year subsidy. Now that the government had failed to act, the last remaining hope was to get together a syndicate of merchants willing to take over the contract and subscribe £100,000 for the work. One-third of the sum was to be in cash to repay the program's debts, and the balance was to be ready whenever needed. Hunter and Livingston talked over such a proposal which Du Pré was to carry to England. Livingston pitied the governor at this time—he was "so tight for money that I have not yet proposed anything to him"—and finally abandoned all efforts to clear his accounts for the Palatine settlement.[34]

But fate had firmly bound the futures of Robert Livingston and Robert Hunter in a common economic tangle out of which would grow a political union strong enough to withstand many shocks and disturbances over the next eight years.

34. Hunter to Swift, Nov. 1, 1712, F. Elrington Ball, ed., *The Correspondence of Jonathan Swift, D. D.* (6 vols., London, 1910-14), II, 10; Robert to Alida Livingston, Nov. 8, 1712 (Dutch), Livingston-Redmond Mss.

CHAPTER XIV

Hunter's Search
for Political Stability

ALTHOUGH THE NAVAL stores program which dominated Hunter's first two years in New York ended in failure, the balance of his administration was much more successful as he worked out a *modus vivendi* with the strong-willed and suspicious members of the Assembly. Ending the hostility between legislature and executive put his political acumen to the test; most of his predecessors had been unable to work with their Assemblies, and few of his successors would be able to do so. Indeed, one later governor, once he realized the enormity of the task, chose suicide instead.[1]

The crux of the conflict between the two branches of government was, as always, control of the colony's finances. Because Livingston remained on the side lines during most of this dispute, he was only indirectly involved and could devote himself to his commercial and mercantile enterprises. By December 1712, after the naval stores program collapsed, he decided to seek repayment of his advances in London. This did not mean another Atlantic crossing, for Livingston relied upon James Douglas, his chief English creditor, to collect his

1. Wayne Andrews, ed., "In Flocks, Like Ill-Boding Ravens: Being an Account of the Tragic End of Sir Danvers Osborne, Bart.," N.-Y. Hist. Soc., *Quarterly*, 35 (1951), 405-7.

money and apply it to his English debts. To his son Robert, he delegated the task of securing from Hunter and Clarke certified copies of the Palatine accounts. The young man made little progress, however, and reported that "the Governor told me he has orderd the affaires of the Palatins to be negotiated by Mr. Douglas, but can't yet Perceive that there is any good news from England in relation to that." "If the money be not paid to your Creditors in England," he reminded Hunter, "they would send Powers of Attorney to recover it here," but he concluded that "there seems to be a Stagnation of affaires." [2]

This "stagnation" resulted from the anticipated arrival of General Francis Nicholson, the royal commissioner of enquiry, whom the Queen had authorized to conduct investigations in every colony from Nova Scotia to Carolina and to examine every phase of colonial life. Pending his arrival in New York, action on the claims of all the Crown's creditors was delayed.[3] But Livingston soon found other problems that required his attention. On February 23, 1712/3, he was notified that his eldest son's wife, Mary Winthrop, had died on January 8. This sad news was confirmed by the bereaved husband who eulogized, "As She did in her Life time So Likewise at her death behavd with wonderful patience and other Vertues." [4]

Livingston did not allow himself to be distracted from his work of expanding the commercial and manufacturing facilities on his manor. He had established a gristmill, a sawmill, a brewery, and a bakehouse to serve the needs of the Palatines, and he now intended to add an iron forge. From the Boston merchant, John Borland, he ordered the anvil, bellows, vise, and "Beake Iron." At the same time, he took inventory of his storehouse and found that he had £735 worth of textiles and ironware on hand for sale to the local populace.

Because the details of managing an extensive agricultural, commercial, and manufacturing establishment occupied so much of his

2. Robert to Alida Livingston, Aug. 22, 1712 (Dutch), Robert Livingston, Jr., to Robert Livingston, Dec. 13, 1712, Feb. 11, 1712/3, Livingston-Redmond Mss.; Osgood, *Colonies in Eighteenth Century*, II, 99-104, 111-12, 117.

3. Nicholson's commission, Oct. 14, 1712, *Cal. State Papers, Col.*, XXVII, no. 97. John Borland of Boston had advanced £19,000; John Livingston had expended £1,200; and Vetch claimed to have spent £7,000. John to Robert Livingston, Aug. 7, 1712, July 1, 1713, Livingston-Redmond Mss.

4. Joanna to Robert Livingston, Jan. 18, 1712/3, John to Robert Livingston, Jan. 19, 1712/3, Livingston-Redmond Mss.

time, Livingston left the conduct of his affairs with the government to his son Robert, Jr., who rapidly became discouraged about dealing with officialdom. "I very seldom wait on the Governor," he wrote, "for I dont see any advantage to be reapd by being over courteous, & he has never so much as invited me to take a meal with him, for all the civil Entertainment he has met with from you." [5]

Hunter's seeming discourtesy to Livingston's son stemmed, not from malice, but from his absorption with the Assembly. To his old friend, Dean Swift, the governor lamented: "In a word, and to be serious at last, I have spent three years of Life in such torment and vexation, that nothing in Life can ever make amends for it." In an effort to win control of the Assembly, he dissolved that body and ordered new elections. He turned for assistance to Livingston, suggesting that he serve in the Assembly "if it should be [offered to you] gratis." Livingston, however, notified Hunter that he had no desire to stand for the Assembly from Dutchess County because Leendert Lewis was too strong a candidate and because he could not spare the time away from his "own affairs at home." [6]

One such affair was the family storm created when Livingston's eldest son, John, broached the subject of his remarriage to a "young Ladey of good forttun, an only Child, that I have a Valleuw for beyond aney thing I can Express here (Daughter to Mrs. Sarah Knight)." Both of John's sisters were disturbed by his choice. Joanna declared that Elizabeth Knight had "a very Staind Carrecter" and complained that he "disperrigs our family to make it Equall with Mrs. Kniet's." Margaret Vetch charged that John had become involved with Elizabeth "whilst his late Concort was yet alive," and that people "talke very odd of unlawfull familiarityes." When she informed him of her feelings, he stalked out of her house and "tooke no more notice of mee," she wrote, "than of a Stranger ever after." [7]

Livingston remembered his son's earlier infatuations, first for Jacob Rutsen's daughter, and then for Mary Winthrop. When Sarah Knight

5. Borland to Livingston, Feb. 23, 1712/3, Inventory, Mar. 4, 1712/3, Robert Livingston, Jr., to Robert Livingston, Mar. 28, 1713, *ibid*.

6. Hunter to Swift, Mar. 14, 1712/3, Ball, ed., *Correspondence of Swift*, II, 43; Hunter to Livingston, Mar. 30, [1713], Robert to Alida Livingston, Apr. 4, 9, 1713 (Dutch), Livingston-Redmond Mss.

7. John to Robert Livingston, May 20, June 1, 15, 1713, Joanna to Robert Livingston, June 22, 29, 1713, Margaret Vetch to Livingston, June 29, 1713, Livingston-Redmond Mss.

wrote to Robert and Alida Livingston on Elizabeth's behalf, they apparently made no response. When Livingston finally broke his silence of nearly two months, he informed his son that he had an "Eille oppinion of the Ladey." John realized that Margaret's gossip was the basis of his father's attitude, and he urged him to write to Increase and Cotton Mather, ministers of the North Church in Boston, for an unbiased report on Elizabeth's reputation. He reminded his father that he was "past the years of an unthinking boy." Since the marriage took place on October 1, 1713, the Livingstons apparently succumbed to their eldest son's pleas; since it was performed by the "aged and Venerable Dr. Increase Mather," perhaps Elizabeth was the virtuous woman that John claimed her to be. Nevertheless, the Livingstons did not welcome their new daughter-in-law with any enthusiasm.[8]

Livingston soon found himself involved in another controversy—this time, with the Van Rensselaers over the northern border of Livingston Manor. In 1704, Kiliaen Van Rensselaer, the Patroon, had given his brother Henry the southern section of Rensselaerswyck, known as Claverack, which bordered on Livingston Manor. The exact boundary lines were vaguely defined, and Henry Van Rensselaer now claimed the northern section of Livingston Manor.[9] Although Livingston and Van Rensselaer agreed to arbitration in November 1713, Livingston was unwilling to rely solely on that method, and several years elapsed before a settlement was reached. Three days after he signed the arbitration agreement, he petitioned the governor and Council for a new patent for his manor. His request was tabled, however, perhaps because Hunter realized that his intervention would merely stir up new animosities and jeopardize his efforts to stabilize the colony's politics. And there was a political motive behind Livingston's request for a new patent, in addition to confirming his land title. He wanted the freeholders of his manor, a small handful of farmers, to have the right to elect their own representative to the Assembly. If granted, Livingston would then have a "pocket borough"

8. Sarah Knight to Robert Livingston, June 22, 1713, John to Robert Livingston, July 1, 9, 16, 1713, Elizabeth Knight Livingston to Robert Livingston, Oct. 6, 1720, July 6, 1721, *ibid.*; Anson Titus, "Madam Sarah Knight, Her Diary and Her Times, 1666-1726," The Bostonian Society, *Publications*, 9 (1912), 106.

9. Kiliaen Van Rensselaer's deed to Henry Van Rensselaer, June 1, 1704, Yates Papers, Box IV, N. Y. Pub. Lib.; John to Robert Livingston, May 20, 1713, Livingston-Redmond Mss.

which would guarantee him a seat in the Assembly when that body finally considered payment of the government's debts.[10]

His interest had been whetted by the Assembly's passage of an act assigning the excise duties for twenty years to payment of the public debts. The claims had not yet been compiled or audited, but Livingston's was among the largest of the government's obligations. It was not inconceivable, therefore, that he wished to answer personally when the legislature asked how much money was due him. Since his request for a new patent had been tabled, however, his scheme for an Assembly seat failed and he had to rely upon Hunter's favor. At this moment, the two men were drawn together by startling news of the investigative activities of General Nicholson in Boston.[11]

At the end of December 1713, Vetch warned his father-in-law that it was impossible to come to terms with Nicholson. "His temper is extreamly altered to the worse," and "he is so violent a party man [i.e., a Tory] that every man must fly very high that expects any favour or recommendation from him." He is "a Violent Enimy of Governor Hunter," continued Vetch, "and will Endeavour to separate you from his Intrest and sift his affairs but be upon your guard for he loves you both alike, but this to your selfe and Governour Hunter only!" There was little hope, Vetch warned, that the general would approve the Palatine accounts.[12]

John Livingston supported this estimate of Nicholson, and he warned his father, "pray do not Lay your Selfe open to him nor Damnify Governor Hunter." Vetch repeated that injunction: "Your bargain," he told Livingston, "is only with Governor Hunter, so if you either Expose your accounts or Contract to any person without his advice or consent you will prejudice your own affairs mightily." Livingston was warned to "waite upon your Governor as soon as the season will allow to Concert with him all your affairs before G: N: arrives."

Livingston rushed down to New York City to confer with the

10. Indenture between Van Rensselaer and Livingston, Nov. 16, 1713, Misc. Mss. Henry Van Rensselaer, N.-Y. Hist. Soc.; Computation of Rensselaerswyck's extent, Nov. 1713, Livingston-Redmond Mss.; Livingston's petition, Nov. 1713, and N. Y. Council Minutes, Nov. 19, 1713, O'Callaghan, ed., *Doc. Hist. N. Y.*, III, 685-86.

11. John to Robert Livingston, Jan. 1, 1713/4, Vetch to Livingston, Jan. 25, 1713/4, Borland to Livingston, Apr. 19, 1714, Livingston-Redmond Mss.

12. Vetch to Livingston, Dec. 28, 1713, *ibid.*

governor after receiving these letters on April 12. Nicholson was a serious threat, and both men realized that they must act together. Livingston apparently promised to avoid all contact with "the old madman," and Hunter, in return, promised that, when the Assembly debated the public debt bill, he would use his influence to win approval of Livingston's claim for over £1,000 sterling salary arrears as secretary for Indian affairs.[13] Unfortunately, Hunter had not yet established a firm, working relationship with the Assembly; thus his promise carried with it no guarantee of success. Livingston, however, had no alternative except to spurn Nicholson's advances; he had accepted membership in Hunter's political organization and had decided his political future. In the long run, his decision was wise, but there were still troubled times ahead.

Some of the difficulties which Hunter and Livingston faced in the Assembly were illustrated by the consideration of the debt bill in April and May 1714. "Mr. Rensselaer," Livingston told his wife, "has always been on our side and has been very zealous that justice be done to us, but the party [i.e., the opposition] is too strong." However, the governor refused to approve any debt bill "until right has been done to everyone." To strengthen Hunter's hand, Livingston asked his wife for some old financial records because "some gentlemen who are very displeased by the conduct of the Assembly would like to draw some light from them."[14]

The debt bill remained a strictly partisan measure, both in conception and evolution. Cadwallader Colden claimed that it had been proposed by the majority as an "opportunity of doing themselves justice," and Livingston echoed him when he remarked that "everything goes by favoritism."[15] Although it was unfortunate for Livingston that he was not among the Assembly's favorites, this bill marked the first real application of the theory of public office previously espoused

13. John to Robert Livingston, Jan. 1, 1713/4, Vetch to Livingston, Mar. 8, 1713/4, Robert to Alida Livingston, Apr. 13, 1714 (Dutch), *ibid.* Some months after Nicholson's visit, Hunter described the general as "old *Nick-Nack*, who has Paganiz'd himself with that Name [Androboros], which interpreted, signifies a *Man-Eater*." See Hunter's *Androboros: A Biographical Farce in Three Acts, Vizt. The Senate, The Consistory, and the Apotheosis* (New York, 1714).

14. Robert to Alida Livingston, Apr. 17, 21, 1714 (Dutch), Livingston-Redmond Mss.

15. *Ibid.;* "Colden's Letters on Smith's History," N.-Y. Hist. Soc., *Collections,* 1 (1868), 202.

by David Jamison. Government was now being used, not to destroy those out of power, but to reward those holding office.

Livingston's failure to secure a favorable consideration of his claims, according to John Collins, his brother-in-law, stemmed from personality conflicts within the Livingston-Schuyler family group. "I am of Opinion," Collins declared, "that Major Schuyler, Mr. Verbrughen, & Mr. H. Rennslars will never forward your account in the assembly lett them say what they will unless you Engage to give Coz Phill [Schuyler] Something for his part of that Service." But Livingston refused to bribe anyone—at least for something which was rightfully his. He appeared before the Assembly and presented a memorandum of his claims, which was laid aside while the governor's accounts were being considered. When Livingston learned that £4,122 had been approved for payment to Hunter, he rejoiced. It meant, he advised his wife, that the governor "will not have any more excuses now that he does not have any money." To make certain of his claim on any funds received by Hunter, Livingston asked Vetch, then in London, to prepare a caveat against the governor in case he failed to pay the Palatine accounts.[16]

Livingston then visited various assemblymen and secured from eight or ten of them pledges to support his salary claim. They apparently kept their word, because his memorandum was read and referred to the committee of the whole on May 11. He was elated by promises of favorable considerations from several of the assemblymen, but not everyone shared his confidence. Philip Livingston remained a skeptic: "I perceive the proverb to be true that kissing goes by favour . . . and I hear that they have none for you, Especially such as are of your Relations, So that I think they do not design at Last that any but some particular persons shall be paid." The complications feared by Philip soon arose. Livingston was called before the Assembly on May 14 to answer several questions about his salary as secretary for Indian affairs, particularly whether he had received payment for two warrants dated September 1700. He swore under oath that he had not, and the matter was again referred to the committee of the whole.[17]

16. Collins to Livingston, Apr. 28, 1714, Robert to Alida Livingston, May 10, 1714 (Dutch), Livingston-Redmond Mss.

17. *Assembly Journal,* I, 351; Robert to Alida Livingston, May 11, 1714 (Dutch), Philip to Robert Livingston, May 12, 1714, Livingston-Redmond Mss.

Livingston reported that he had lined up eleven votes and he believed that the only question now remaining was whether he would receive one-half or two-thirds of the money he claimed. Just before the vote was taken, however, someone noted that the Council under both Fletcher and Cornbury had denounced the secretaryship as useless and a burden to the treasury. This delayed the decision and enabled his enemies to undo his missionary work among the assemblymen. "I have heard," he wrote, "that Myndert Neeft [of Dutchess County] takes as much trouble against me as I take to push the thing through. He has gotten 3 of the votes against me, so what I construct by day, he if he can destroys at night." [18]

This delay cost Livingston his victory. On May 25, Lewis Morris reported from the committee of the whole that the governor should get £4,297, Peter Schuyler £1,581, Gertrude Van Cortlandt £1,400, Jacob Leisler, Jr., £2,025; but Livingston was to receive only £384. Although certain minor adjustments were made along the way, the pattern of the bill remained unchanged. When it received the approval of the governor, Council, and Assembly, Livingston was given £564 in full settlement of all his claims, the total of which, exclusive of £1,430 salary arrears, was £2,003.[19]

This token payment, and the terms of the law which precluded any future payments, disheartened Livingston, but there was one saving factor—the allowance of more than £4,000 to Hunter. No longer was there any reason why he could not settle the Palatine accounts, and on May 26 he debited the governor for £1,967. But he was premature if he expected prompt payment; Hunter, like all other claimants, had to await royal approval of the bill before any money was forthcoming.[20]

Livingston's distress was increased by a letter from his son-in-law in London. "Mr. Douglass and Severall others," Vetch wrote, "make very hearty complaints against you, I endeavour to Excuse you as much as possible upon account of the non-payment of your Palatine Bills which I fear will be long unpaid here as Indeed all publick

18. Robert to Alida Livingston, May 19, 22, 1714 (Dutch), Livingston-Redmond Mss.; *Assembly Journal*, I, 353.
19. *Assembly Journal*, I, 353-55; William Bradford, ed., *The Laws of His Majesties Colony of New-York* (N.Y., 1719), 247, 251-52, 257, 266.
20. Acct. between Livingston and Hunter, May 26, 1714, N. Y. Col. Mss., LIX, 36, N. Y. State Lib.

money of all sorts." Hunter undoubtedly sympathized with Livingston, but there was little that he could do for him. Having suddenly found a basis of agreement with the Assembly—its allowance of more than £4,000 was evidence of that—the governor had no intention of jeopardizing it. He implored William Popple to bend every effort to win royal approbation of the debt bill, and he addressed similar pleas directly to the Board of Trade.[21]

Opposition came from an unexpected source. Lord Cornbury, now the Earl of Clarendon, protested that the bill was "so unjust in its nature, as to direct the Payment of considerable sums of money where none is really due, and allow to other just debts, to some one half, to others a third, to others a fourth part, and to others nothing." He had been omitted entirely and he vigorously attacked the provision invalidating all debts antedating 1714 which were not recognized and paid in this bill.[22]

The Board of Trade was willing to give serious consideration to Clarendon's complaints, but in his usual erratic way he failed to appear and explain his case. The Board therefore decided to proceed with the bill, and a favorable recommendation was prepared on May 4, 1715, and sent to the King-in-Council. When Hunter learned that Clarendon had delayed approval of the debt bill, he seized the chance to consolidate his position with the Assembly by denouncing the former governor. "I shall only say," he remarked to the legislators, "that in My Opinion, he, of all Men, ought to have been silent in this Case." Hunter alluded, of course, to the fact that much of the colony's indebtedness could be traced to Clarendon's misapplication of funds. The Assembly, in a rare show of unanimity, joined the governor in denying all of Clarendon's allegations.[23]

Hunter was most anxious to improve his relationship with the Assembly. A general naturalization act was then pending whose terms,

21. Vetch to Livingston, June 7, 1714, Livingston-Redmond Mss.; Hunter to Popple, Nov. 8, 1714, Hunter to Bd. of Trade, Nov. 25, 1714, *Cal. State Papers, Col.,* XXVIII, nos. 82, 95; Hunter to Bd. of Trade, Sept. 6, 1714, O'Callaghan, ed., *N. Y. Col. Docs.,* V, 379.

22. Clarendon's caveat, Jan. 25, 1714/5, *Cal. State Papers, Col.,* XXVIII, no. 181; Clarendon to Bd. of Trade, Feb. 8, 1714/5, O'Callaghan, ed., *N. Y. Col. Docs.,* V, 398; *Journal Bd. Trade,* II, 598-99.

23. *Journal Bd. Trade,* III, 13, 14, 24, 25; Popple to Clarendon, Mar. 15, 1714/5. *Cal. State Papers, Col.,* XXVIII, no. 285; *Assembly Journal,* I, 368; Council and Assembly of N. Y. to Bd. of Trade, May 30, 1715, O'Callaghan, ed., *N. Y. Col. Docs.,* V, 405.

insisted upon by the Assembly, conflicted with the Crown's instructions. If the governor could promise the Assembly support of their naturalization bill and in return secure passage of a five years' revenue for support of the government, he would get something that had not been given any executive for a decade—independence from the legislature. In a neat bit of bargaining, the Assembly and governor each got what they wanted. "If I have done amiss," Hunter apologized to the Board of Trade. "I am sorry for't, but what was there left for me to do, I have been struggling hard for bread itself for five years to no effect, and for four of them unpitty'd, I hope I have now laid a foundation for a lasting settlement on this hitherto unsettled and ungovernable Province." [24]

Although Hunter had scored an important political victory, Livingston was not pleased. Not only had he been badly treated in the debt bill, but the revenue act also omitted the secretary for Indian affairs from the list of offices for which salaries were provided. But Livingston soon found compensation in other ways. Having won his major points with the Assembly, Hunter could now afford to be more considerate of his fellow Scotsman's desires. Financial relief was impossible, but Hunter gave the lord of Livingston Manor something else that he desired. Two years after the tabling of the petition for a confirmatory patent for the Manor, it was unearthed, and the attorney general was directed to draw up the desired document. The new patent, prepared and signed on the day it was ordered, included the usual features, together with two items specifically requested by Livingston: the freeholders of the Manor were given the right to elect their own assemblyman, and the "naturall marks and boundaryes" of the 1686 patent were replaced by "courses and distances" according to Deputy Surveyor John Beatty's running of the bounds in 1714. [25]

Livingston also wanted his manor to be politically and administratively independent of both Albany and Dutchess counties. Located within both counties, its tax assessments and collections, administration of justice, and conduct of elections were obviously complicated.

24. Hunter to Bd. of Trade, May 21, July 25, 1715, Instructions to Hunter, Dec. 27, 1709, O'Callaghan, ed., *N. Y. Col. Docs.*, V, 403-4, 416, 126-27.
25. *Assembly Journal*, I, 375; Hunter to Jamison, Oct. 1, 1715, Surveyor's map, 1714, Hunter's patent to Livingston, Oct. 1, 1715, O'Callaghan, ed., *Doc. Hist. N. Y.*, III, 689-90, 691, 697.

By the terms of the 1686 patent, for example, the freeholders were authorized to elect their own assessors and collectors, but that right had not been exercised until recent years and had then been violently opposed by the Albany authorities. Even though the right was confirmed in the 1715 patent, wrangling continued for a year or more.[26]

Politics on the Manor were predictable and Livingston was elected to the Assembly in 1716. He attended the Assembly in New York and his name was entered on the rolls on June 5. But his wife's sudden and serious illness interrupted his attendance before the House organized itself. Robert, Jr., reported: "Mother is taken with an extream fitt of Sickness Since twelve of the clock, the Symptoms seems to be worse than any she has had hitherto, She is seizd with an extream pain all over her body as if her blood was Stopd in its circulation ... I am very much afraid we shall loose our Mother & am afraid we'll be most Sensible of it when she is gone." Livingston apparently rushed home to her bedside and remained there throughout her illness, for his name disappeared from the Assembly's rolls for the next eleven months.[27]

While Livingston remained at Roeloff Jansen Kill, his friend, Attorney General Jamison, kept him informed of the latest political developments. "Our Governour's intrest," he wrote, "Stands immoveable at Court where he has all his heart can desire." He referred to the Board of Trade's success in winning royal approbation of the debt bill, as well as its handling of the controversial naturalization act. A decision on the latter would not be made for some time, so that the Assembly could revise the measure to meet any objections before it was submitted to the Privy Council.[28]

Meanwhile, the Assembly had remedied the major defect of the debt bill—its disallowance of all claims antedating 1714 which were not approved in that law. The legislature ordered that all unpaid claims, despite the 1714 statute, could be brought in for consideration

26. Deposition of Van Slyck, Feb. 29, 1715/6, deposition of Salisbury, Mar. 22, 1715/6, Livingston-Redmond Mss.
27. Robert Livingston, Jr., to Philip Livingston, May 30, 1716, *ibid.; Assembly Journal*, I, 381, 381-94.
28. Jamison to Livingston, Dec. 25, 1716, Livingston-Redmond Mss.; Order of King-in-Council, June 17, 1715, Bd. of Trade to Hunter, Mar. 15, 1715/6, O'Callaghan, ed., *N. Y. Col. Docs.*, V, 412, 470-71.

and inclusion in a supplementary act. Gilbert Livingston urged his father "to state your account Concerning the Demands on the province, ... [and] Deliver it to Colonel provoost and alderman Kip who are appointed to Receive them, belive you may have a good Chance to have them allowd."[29]

Livingston must have been cheered by this news, but he did not intend to rely solely upon the governor's influence to win approval of his claims. As the prospective assemblyman from Livingston Manor, he intended to supervise personally the handling of his claims during the legislative debates. Fortunately, his wife improved steadily, and her recovery made possible Livingston's return to politics. His friends were eager to have him enter the newly elected Assembly, and John Collins, his brother-in-law, wrote: "Your health is Continued at the Loyall Club and your Number Sacredly Observed by which means we keep our action open and are resolved to wait upon you." By the end of March 1717, Livingston acceded to their requests, and probably to his own inclinations as well. Dirk Wessels was jubilant; to him, this meant that their enemies would not gain "any mastery over us in which they would delight very much."[30]

Before leaving home, Livingston arranged with his son Philip and with Wessels to supervise the election of the assemblyman from the Manor. Livingston was the only candidate and the real question was whether the Assembly would accept him. Creation of new Assembly seats was a jealously guarded legislative prerogative, and this would add another member to the governor's party in the House. "Some of our enemies," Livingston admitted, "would love to prevent it." On April 26, Livingston learned of his election. "Just now," Wessels reported, "we have had the election ... and it has fallen on you without the slightest opposition by anybody." The Assembly was already in session, and Livingston was anxious to join its debates because "Our people on the [Hudson] river cannot get enough strength. ... Everybody feels that it will help me a great deal if I come in the House now."[31]

But unhappily no one had sent the indenture and writ of election

29. Gilbert to Robert Livingston, Jan. 7, 1716/7, Livingston-Redmond Mss.

30. Philip to Robert Livingston, Jan. 16, 1716/7, Collins to Livingston, Jan. 26, 1716/7, Wessels to Livingston, Mar. 23, 1716/7 (Dutch), *ibid.*

31. Robert to Alida Livingston, Apr. 17, 25, 1717 (Dutch), Wessels to Livingston, Apr. 22, 1717 (Dutch), Philip to Robert Livingston, Apr. 22, 1717, *ibid.*

necessary for Livingston to claim his seat. By May 1, however, he received the necessary papers, as well as a warning from his son Philip of opposition from Jacob Rutsen and the Albany members. He had anticipated this and had discussed with the governor the possibility of his rejection by the Assembly. Hunter promised to "speak about it to the members from the river so that they do not oppose it in the House." [32]

The leader of the opposition was apparently Leendert Lewis of Poughkeepsie, member for Dutchess County, who had boasted that Livingston would not be allowed in the Assembly even though he "ran with the Governor." Supporting Lewis were the Albany representatives who were especially hostile to Livingston's claims. Their attitude, Philip suggested, resulted from their having "pickd & fitched up as many accounts as ever they could gett, most part sold to them on condition to give goods if allowd and [I] therefore am of opinion theyl oppose what they can wherein theyve no Interest for fear the Sum [of all the debts] will become great and then theirs not allowd." [33]

To gain admission to the Assembly, Livingston had to overcome the self-interest of the Albany members and their allies. This he failed to do; when he presented his credentials, the House refused to seat him. Later that same day, however, the vote was reversed, and Livingston took the qualifying oaths before the governor. The Assembly's sudden reversal was the result of a simple political bargain. On the original vote, there had been ten in favor of admitting Livingston and ten opposed, and Speaker Nicolls had suggested a postponement of the decision. "In the afternoon," Livingston reported, "many of the Assemblymen said that the only reason why Leendert Lewis was against me was because of fear that I would be against the bill he had introduced...to locate the [Dutchess] County Courthouse and prison in Poughkeepsie." Livingston then made it clear that he "would not be opposed to that if he [i.e., Lewis] and the gentlemen would pass a bill that my manor is to be allowed to be in Albany County, or else that it be a county of its own. Whereupon it was thus decided, and he and the rest will assist me to have it placed in

32. Robert to Alida Livingston, Apr. 27, 1717 (Dutch), Philip to Robert Livingston, Apr. 25, 1717, *ibid*.

33. Salisbury to Livingston, May 8, 1717 (Dutch), Philip to Robert Livingston, May 9, 1717, *ibid*.

the County of Albany." On the second vote, it was twelve to eight in Livingston's favor.[34]

This bargain was typical of the small adjustments constantly being made to develop a working balance of power in the Assembly. Livingston not only took his seat, but he entered upon an entirely new phase of his political career. First as an assemblyman, and then as speaker of the Assembly, he was to get nearly everything he wanted. In the process, he became one of the chief lieutenants of Robert Hunter and of his successor, William Burnet.

34. *Assembly Journal*, I, 395; Robert to Alida Livingston, May 13, 1717 (Dutch), Livingston-Redmond Mss.

CHAPTER XV

Governors Hunter and Burnet: "A Perfect Harmony Reigning"

BY THE SPRING OF 1717, Governor Hunter was on the verge of an amicable settlement with the Assembly. Many factors were responsible, but the most important was the governor's skill in winning over men of "power and ability" by paying the price for their support. His party leaders in the Assembly, Lewis Morris and Robert Livingston, were two such men, and they headed a group of legislators "amenable to discipline." Through this combination, the governor established for the first time in two decades a period of comparative political calm.

The 1717 bill to pay the public debts created the new political alliance. Its architect was Morris; its superintendent, as well as chief beneficiary, was Livingston. Many claims had been submitted, and the decision as to which should be honored consumed much time and energy, but the fruit of their joint endeavors, "a compromise of a most complex nature," was the establishment of a workable political organization. As an ally, Livingston offered the governor forty years of political experience and considerable influence among the members of the "River Party," the assemblymen from the Hudson Valley counties.[1] Anxious for Livingston's support, the governor

1. McAnear, Politics in Provincial New York, 257, 265, 273; Charles W. Spencer, "The Land System of Colonial New York," N. Y. State Hist. Assn., *Proceedings*, 16

came to his rescue when it seemed that the merchant would lose his seat because of the Albany assemblymen's influence. The governor sent Livingston to tell the members "in his name that if they opposed the King's writ, it would be high time for him to dissolve them."

With the staunch backing of Hunter, Livingston was not reticent about pressing his demands after he entered the Assembly. "The accounts will now be received again," he told his wife; "that is my most important goal, and all the River members assist each other faithfully. With the aid of Provoost and Morris, we can always have a majority, so I hope that I will redeem some of the debt." Livingston's influence made itself evident within a short time. First, he was appointed chairman of the committee to consider Leendert Lewis' bill to erect the Dutchess County courthouse and jail in Poughkeepsie. Next, he introduced his own measure to place his manor wholly within Albany County. And finally, he and eleven others were appointed "to consider further of the Accounts laid before this House, alleged as Debts of this Colony." [2]

In desiring the annexation of his manor to Albany County, Livingston had but one purpose—enhancement of his own personal power. His chief lieutenant on the Manor, Dirk Wessels, supported that goal, although he questioned the effects of the strategy to be employed. Albany County, he thought, "will in time become very strong," and the Manor might become a mere appendage. But Dutchess County was weak, and the Manor, if attached to that county, would not gain anything. The only solution, in his opinion, was to erect the Manor into a county of its own. But Philip Livingston was sure that the Assembly would reject this proposition and he agreed completely with his father's purpose and strategy. "Without doubt it will be much Easier & less Chargeable then to be in two Countys, the one poor and the other oppressive," he remarked. "Of these two one must be Chosen in order to be freed from both in time which I perceive you aim at." [3]

The Assembly quickly approved a bill annexing the Manor to

(1917), 159; "Colden Letters on Smith's History," N.-Y. Hist. Soc., *Collections*, 1 (1868), 204.

2. Robert to Alida Livingston, May 13, 1717 (Dutch), Livingston-Redmond Mss.; *Assembly Journal*, I, 396.

3. Wessels to Livingston, May 18, 1717 (Dutch), Philip to Robert Livingston, May 20, 1717, Livingston-Redmond Mss.

Albany County, and shortly thereafter enacted the Dutchess County courthouse bill. With the passage of these two laws, it was expected that the Assembly would adjourn and Livingston promised his wife that he would bring the governor home with him. Perhaps, during this visit to the Manor, Hunter's aid could be won in the dispute with Henry Van Rensselaer, a problem which continued to bother Livingston.[4] Indeed, Livingston was so highly regarded by Hunter that there was little likelihood of anything being done to injure him or his interests.

Well aware of this, young Robert urged his father to use his influence to get him a government post, and the strategy he suggested was most revealing—Livingston should "give him a gratuity out of that debt he owes you for it, because he does not much incline to pay you." Hunter was, of course, in no position to repay the advances for the Palatines, and Livingston had used this obligation to win certain favors.[5] However, he did not oblige his son in this instance, for there were more important things that he wanted. One was settlement of the boundary dispute with Van Rensselaer. Hunter's attitude was suggested by Attorney General Jamison who promised Livingston that "nothing shall pass to prejudice you." When a motion was presented in Chancery to cancel the arbitration bond unless the Van Rensselaers showed cause why it should be continued, the attorney general told Livingston that he had mentioned this matter to Hunter again, and that the boundary line would not be changed "till the lines are run next fall." [6]

During the summer of 1717, while this affair was being managed in New York City by Robert, Jr., Livingston remained on his manor, turning his attention to domestic problems. When he discovered that his youngest daughter, Joanna, was being courted by Henry

4. *Assembly Journal*, I, 396-98; *Legis. Council Jour.*, I, 408-9, 411; *Col. Laws of N. Y.*, I, 915; Robert to Alida Livingston, May 25, 1717 (2nd letter, Dutch), Philip to Robert Livingston, June 4, 1717, Livingston-Redmond Mss.

5. Robert Livingston, Jr., to Robert Livingston, June 25, 1717, Livingston-Redmond Mss. Hunter could not repay Livingston because he was deeply in debt to others. He had spent £32,071 on the Palatines, but had gotten only £10,000 from the British Treasury and £800 from the sale of surplus goods. The remainder of £21,271 had come in part from the governor's pocket, but largely from loans such as Livingston's. Acct. of moneys paid by Hunter, Dec. 1717, *Cal. State Papers, Col.*, XXX, no. 235.

6. Robert Livingston, Jr., to Robert Livingston, July 3, 30, 1717, Jamison to Livingston, Aug. 16, 1717, Livingston-Redmond Mss.

Beekman II, he was displeased and promptly told the young man of his feelings. At least one of Livingston's sons was delighted to learn that Beekman had been rebuffed: "I should be very Sorry if she should not light of a better match," wrote Philip, "or a good young man without any such publick blott and as much estate as this has." [7] But Livingston's problems were not solely domestic.

At the same time that he delivered this unpleasant news to Beekman, Livingston received disturbing information himself. His London creditors were again pressing him for their money; James Douglas, who had employed Attorney General Jamison as his agent, sent his account. Vetch had also been approached on this matter and, after examining the account, he concluded that Douglas was being more than fair. He urged his father-in-law to settle the debt, because Douglas and the others with whom he had had dealings in London "give you the worst of names and say if you were not a rich miser they Could forgive the debts but every body from your parts represents you as such to them." Livingston was in no position to clear the London debts, and he was still too concerned about affairs at home to be greatly worried about his reputation in London's mercantile circles. [8]

When the Assembly met again in September, Livingston returned to New York City. The governor informed the House that he received a copy of a memorial delivered to the House of Commons by an expelled assemblyman, Samuel Mulford, who had harassed every governor since Dongan's time and who now attacked Hunter for his "Oppressions" of the people. But Mulford's attacks had no influence with the Board of Trade. That agency made it a point to notify Hunter that "the reports of your removal are malicious and groundless. This you may make known in such manner as you shall think the most likely to silence such reports." Nothing could have served more effectively to strengthen the governor's hand with the Assembly. [9]

Livingston was undoubtedly pleased by this evidence of the gov-

7. Philip to Robert Livingston, June 23, 1717, Henry Beekman to Robert Livingston, July 3, 1717, Robert Livingston, Jr., to Robert Livingston, July 18, 1717, *ibid.*

8. Jamison to Livingston, July 5, 1717, Vetch to Livingston, Aug. 25, 1716 (recd. July 16, 1717), *ibid.*

9. *Assembly Journal*, I, 400. For a sketch of Mulford's career, see O'Callaghan, ed., *Journal of the Voyage of the Sloop Mary*, 38n-44n; Bd. of Trade to Hunter, Sept. 4, 1717, *Cal. State Papers, Col.*, XXX, no. 69.

ernor's influence at Court, because the bill to pay the public debts was about to be considered by the Assembly. Philip had high hopes for his father's claims, but Livingston took no chances; he personally supervised the settlement of his debt. On October 17, he and three other assemblymen were directed to prepare and bring in a bill to pay the public debts. The big problem was to find a method of financing the payments. One proposal suggested that £32,000 in paper money should be printed, with £12,000 being issued to the government's creditors and the remainder loaned out at 5 percent interest. The interest, £1,000 annually, would permit the redemption of the bills given to the colony's creditors at the end of twelve years, while the other bills would be canceled as the loans were repaid. Livingston did not approve of this scheme, and offered two alternatives: an extension of the excise for twelve years, or a series of import and poll taxes, primarily on slaves, which would net the government about £1,500 a year.[10]

But Livingston was more interested in how much money he could get under this law. He now demanded £1,696 as reimbursement for his expenses in going twice to London. This claim, never before presented, was based on the assumption that the trips would have been unnecessary if the government had met its obligations when they fell due. Despite the unusual nature of the request, the Assembly committee agreed to pay him £1,484 of this sum. Philip Livingston undoubtedly reflected his father's attitude when he reported that he was "Exceedingly Rejoyced."

When the bill was referred to another committee after its second reading, Livingston sought appointment to that group so that he could prevent any obstruction of his claim. Philip Livingston suggested that "those whose accounts are rejected" were fomenting opposition, and he singled out Peter Schuyler as the person most determined "to overthrow what he can if he cant gett nothing allowed" for himself. Even Hunter took notice of this—"the angry men have threatened," he informed the Board of Trade, "that they'll have it damn'd before 'tis pass'd."[11]

10. Philip to Robert Livingston, Oct. 2, 1717, "Proposeal of ways & means to raise 12000 £," Livingston-Redmond Mss.; *Assembly Journal*, I, 405.
11. *Assembly Journal*, I, 408; Philip to Robert Livingston, Oct. 25, Nov. 6, 1717, "R. Livingston's account with the colony," 1717, Livingston-Redmond Mss.; Hunter to Popple, Nov. 9, 1717, *Cal. State Papers, Col.*, XXX, no. 194.

Despite the opposition, the governor's friends saw the measure safely through the Assembly; it received Council approval on December 18, and the governor gave his assent three days later. "A perfect harmony reigning among all parties" was Hunter's description of the political scene. Livingston was certainly in harmony; he had received the largest sum voted in the bill—3,710 ounces of plate, or £1,484, in settlement of his claim for £1,696.[12]

After this law was referred to the English authorities, Livingston gave his attention to other matters. On October 30, 1717, he and Henry Van Rensselaer settled their long-standing dispute by agreeing to the Catskill Creek as the boundary between Livingston Manor and Claverack. As chairman of the Assembly committee to farm the excise collections, Livingston also used his influence to gain this government contract for his youngest son, Gilbert, who had formed a partnership with Francis Harrison. They offered £1,500 annually to the treasury for this privilege, and the Assembly accepted it on October 24, 1717, and gave them a five-year contract.[13]

After concluding these matters, Livingston returned home to his manor. No longer a wilderness tract, his estate was now an important center of population. According to the census taken in 1718, there were 126 Palatine households, consisting of 499 people (exclusive of widows and orphans), living on the east bank of the Hudson. Although most settled on lands purchased from Livingston by the Crown, they remained within his economic orbit. The extent of their dependence on Livingston for goods was made clear by the lists of debtors which he periodically compiled. On March 1, 1717/8, the Palatines owed him £379, and ten months later their indebtedness amounted to £385. This was, of course, only a portion of the credit extended by Livingston to his customers. Settlers on his manor and at Claverack, Catskill, and Kinderhook owed him another £1,225 in March 1717/8, and those in more distant areas of the colony were indebted for over £1,200.[14]

12. *Assembly Journal*, I, 412-13; Hunter to Popple, Nov. 22, 1717, O'Callaghan, ed., *N. Y. Col. Docs.*, V, 493; *Col. Laws of N. Y.*, I, 957, 985.
13. Indenture between Livingston and Van Rensselaer, Oct. 30, 1717, Livingston-Redmond Mss.; "Memo relating to...Claverack & the manor," 1725, Misc. Mss. Henry Van Rensselaer, N.-Y. Hist. Soc.; *Assembly Journal*, I, 404, 406. For Harrison's nefarious career, see Vincent Buranelli, "Governor Cosby's Hatchet-Man," *N. Y. Hist.*, 37 (1956), 26-39.
14. Acct. of German families, 1718, O'Callaghan, ed., *Doc. Hist. N. Y.*, I, 692;

These sums suggested that Livingston had not neglected his mercantile affairs while serving in the Assembly. His wife was undoubtedly responsible for her husband's success; it was she who ran their storehouse and determined whether or not credit was to be extended. Her effectiveness as a businesswoman is to be found in the increasing sales figures in Livingston's account books.[15]

Livingston's residence on his manor during the winter of 1717-18 was cut short by the governor's summons to attend the Assembly in New York City. Before a quorum was obtained, Speaker William Nicolls resigned his post because of ill health. He had long opposed Hunter, and it has been assumed that his resignation was brought about by his inability to cope with the governor's influence. After a quorum was obtained, the first order of business therefore became the election of a new speaker. On May 27, the house "by Plurality of Voices made Choice of *Robert Livingston*, Esq., to be their Speaker, and conducted him to the Chair accordingly." [16]

At a time when Livingston's thoughts were probably turning to retirement, he was thrust even more deeply into the political fray. The blessings of retirement were not to be his for a number of years; there was still much work for him to do. Now, more than ever before, he was in a position to repay the many favors previously received from Hunter and to demand new ones from him. Among the most important tasks given to Livingston was that of helping the governor win the support of the Board of Trade for the debt bill of 1717. This legislation met with strong opposition from a group of London merchants who were being prodded by their New York correspondents, and the point most severely criticized was the method used to redeem the bills issued to the colony's creditors. Livingston and Hunter worked together to get a measure passed which modified that objectionable feature.[17]

Lists of Palatine debtors, Mar. 1, 1717/8, Mar. 5, 1717/8, Dec. 26, 1718, Livingston-Redmond Mss.

15. In the ten months following March 1717, £475 worth of goods were sold; in the following year sales jumped to £600. "The Posts in the Journall ... Sum'd up," Apr. 1, 1717-June 1, 1721, Livingston-Redmond Mss.

16. *Assembly Journal*, I, 413; Osgood, *Colonies in Eighteenth Century*, II, 114; Smith, *History of New York*, I, 200.

17. *Journal Bd. Trade*, III, 367, 374-75; Hunter to Popple, July 7, 1718, O'Callaghan, ed., *N. Y. Col. Docs.*, V, 572; Hunter to Popple, Oct. 13, 1718, *Cal. State Papers, Col.*, XXX, nos. 718, 718 i.

At the same time, the Board of Trade was considering both the 1709 statute to repeal the Leislerian act to confiscate Livingston's estate and the 1717 law to annex Livingston Manor to Albany County. In order to get the governor to use his influence at Court in behalf of these measures, Livingston signed a release in September 1718 for all debts due as a result of the Palatine settlement. Although the document solemnly declared that it was "for and in Consideration of a Competent Sum of money" paid by Hunter, no amount was mentioned and there is no evidence that any cash changed hands. Livingston's repayment came in the form of favors and political preferment, not money, and it must have looked like a good bargain to the Scot. An almost immediate favor was the action taken by Ambrose Phillips, the New York agent, to obtain the Board of Trade's approval of the 1709 law. Another was the governor's unceasing efforts to win approval of the 1717 debt bill, which would benefit Livingston greatly. It was not until June 1719 that the Board of Trade agreed upon a favorable recommendation, but gaining its support was simple in comparison to securing a favorable vote from the Privy Council.[18]

By this time, Hunter was becoming weary of his post and anxious to return to London, both to assist in winning approval of the debt bill and to settle his own private affairs. He confided his desires to Popple in May 1719, adding that "the Assembly here is now mett, & probably will Continue the Revenue, but I am afray'd only for a short time, for they begin to smoake my design in spite of all my disguise." Speaker Livingston was among those who had smoked out Hunter's plan. On June 19, he advised his wife of the rumor that the governor was returning to England, and it was confirmed five days later when Hunter addressed the Assembly. "As the very Name of Party or Faction seems to be forgot," he cautioned the legislators, "may it forever be buried in Oblivion, and no Strife ever happen among you . . . you Gentlemen have given a happy Example, which, I hope, will be followed by future Assemblies."[19]

Livingston and Morris were designated by the House to draft a

18. *Journal Bd. Trade*, III, 436, IV, 63, 68-71; Phillips to Bd. of Trade, Feb. 6, 1718/9, *Cal. State Papers, Col.*, XXXI, no. 50; Popple to West, Feb. 20, 1718/9, *ibid.*, no. 70; Livingston's release to Hunter, Sept. 6, 1718, Misc. Mss. Robert Hunter, N.-Y. Hist. Soc.

19. Hunter to Popple, May 18, 1719, O'Callaghan, ed., *N. Y. Col. Docs.*, V, 521; Robert to Alida Livingston, June 19, 1719 (Dutch), Livingston-Redmond Mss.

reply to these laudatory remarks. These two closest political associates of Hunter reciprocated with a fulsome address which the Assembly approved and delivered to the departing governor:

You have governed well and wisely, like a prudent Magistrate, like an affectionate Parent, and wherever you go, and to whatever Station the divine Providence shall please to assign you, our Sincere Desires and Prayers for the Happiness of you and yours shall always attend you.

We have seen many Governors, and may see more, and as none of those, who had the Honour to serve in your Station, were ever so justly fixt in the affections of the Governed, so those to come will acquire no mean Reputation when it can be truly said of them, their Conduct has been like yours.[20]

Thus spoke the New York Assembly. Few colonial governors were ever so honored on the conclusion of a lengthy administration. The eulogy, almost unique in the annals of the American colonies, served as a fitting climax to Robert Hunter's governorship. And the tribute was well-earned, for this Scotsman had learned and applied a cardinal principle of successful government: assemblies "must be wrought upon by degrees, he that thinks he can do every thing at once knows little of popular Assemblys." [21]

Robert Hunter departed for England in the fall of 1719 and left Peter Schuyler in charge of a caretaker government as president of the Council. The governor had not been long out of the country when Schuyler took steps which were viewed as a prelude to the dismantling of the political machine so laboriously created by the governor. He replaced Robert Livingston, Jr., "the nephew," as mayor of Albany with his own cousin, Myndert Schuyler, a move which Governor Hunter in London denounced as an effort to bring about "a dissolution of this present Assembly, the most dutifull . . . and the most attentive to the true interests of the Colony that the Province could ever boast of." [22]

Hunter immediately warned the Board of Trade of the implica-

20. *Assembly Journal*, I, 437-39.
21. Smith, *History of New York*, I, 201; Hunter to Bd. of Trade, May 3, 1718, O'Callaghan, ed., *N. Y. Col. Docs.*, V, 504.
22. Schuyler to Bd. of Trade, Oct. 31, 1719, Hunter to Bd. of Trade, Dec. 22, 1719, *Cal. State Papers, Col.*, XXXII, nos. 48 i, 488.

tions of Schuyler's actions, urging that "no alterations be made but what shall appear by the advice of the Council there to be of absolute necessity, and that he by no means dissolve ... this present Assembly." The Board readily heeded this advice and submitted a representation to the secretary of state, who sent a letter to Schuyler within three days. The speed with which Hunter's advice was acted upon testified to the extent of his influence with the English authorities. That, plus the sharpness of the royal command, evidently convinced Schuyler of the futility of trying to undermine or weaken the Hunter party in the governor's absence. He meekly replied to the Board of Trade: "Those orders were punctually comply'd with." [23]

On May 19, 1720, Hunter was equally successful in securing King George I's assent to the 1717 debt bill. Because this was the keystone of the governor's political structure, it was approved even though the Crown opposed the principle involved. Future laws for the emission of bills of credit were not to be enacted in any colony unless they included a suspensive clause which made them inoperative pending royal sanction. [24]

Hunter followed up his victories by searching for a suitable replacement as governor of New York. Although no one in the colony knew it when he left for London, Hunter did not intend to return to New York. He therefore arranged privately with William Burnet, the comptroller of customs and a son of famed Bishop Gilbert Burnet, to exchange offices. Since both men were in complete agreement on policy matters, Burnet appeared to be an ideal choice. Governor William Keith of Pennsylvania described him as one whose "good Manners sobriety and extrodinary Mild Temper, will in my opinion make any people happy under his Government." [25]

By the middle of 1720 there was no news in New York "but our Dayly Expectation of Mr. Burnet." However, several months were to elapse before he took over the government; in the interim, the

23. Cragg to Schuyler, Dec. 26, 1719, *ibid.*, XXXI, no. 496; Schuyler to Bd. of Trade, Apr. 27, 1720, O'Callaghan, ed., *N. Y. Col. Docs.*, V, 587; *Journal Bd. Trade*, IV, 132-33.
24. Order of King-in-Council, May 19, 1720, O'Callaghan, ed., *N. Y. Col. Docs.*, V, 539-40.
25. Bobin to Clarke, June 24, 1720, [Edmund B. O'Callaghan, ed.], *Letters of Isaac Bobin, Esq., Private Secretary of Hon. George Clarke, Secretary of the Province of New York, 1718-1730* (Albany, 1872), 26; Keith to Colden, July 14, 1720, N.-Y. Hist. Soc., *Collections*, 50 (1918), 103-4.

groundwork was being laid for a bold, new fur trade policy that was to become the key issue in his administration. An effective fur trade policy was long overdue in the continuing Anglo-French rivalry for North American dominance. Livingston had earlier voiced concern about the dangers the Canadian trade posed to New York, but no one heeded him. Hunter had been too busy with the establishment of his political machine to become involved with an issue which would have aroused the hostility of the Albany wholesalers. Between one-half and two-thirds of all the furs gathered in Canada found their way to Albany in exchange for the less expensive and more desirable English textiles. The wholesalers had never bothered to penetrate beyond Lake Ontario because "they sold large Quantities of Goods without any trouble, the French taking them from their doors." However, a direct trade with the western tribes would be equally profitable and more politically advantageous for the English colonies.[26]

The leader and chief beneficiary of the Albany-Montreal trade was allegedly Stephen De Lancey, whom Cadwallader Colden later labeled the "Gentleman at New-York, who almost entirely engrossed the Indian Trade of this Province, and thereby acquired a very great Estate and Influence." After serving as Hunter's commercial agent during the Palatine experiment, he formed an alliance with Adolph Philipse and Peter Schuyler, thus forming the political triumvirate which opposed all efforts to end the Montreal trade.[27]

Livingston, on the other hand, was one of the foremost opponents of the Canadian trade, and he announced his position before Burnet even arrived in New York. In August 1720, he prepared a memorial for President Schuyler in which he listed three basic dangers to the English colonies: the intermittent raiding by the Iroquois against the southern colonies, the French fort and trading house at the falls of Niagara, which diverted western furs to Canada, and the Albany-

26. Bobin to Clarke, July 30, 1720, O'Callaghan, ed., *Bobin's Letters*, 35; *Assembly Journal*, I, 409; Cadwallader Colden, *The History of the Five Indian Nations of Canada which are dependent on the Province of New York, and are a barrier between the English and the French in that part of the World* (2 vols., N.Y., 1922), II, 53-54; Jean Lunn, "The Illegal Fur Trade out of New France, 1713-1760," Canadian Hist. Assn., *Report of the Annual Meeting Held at Montreal* (Toronto, 1939), 65-66.

27. J. A[lexander] to Mr. P. C. of London, 1740, Colden, *History of the Five Nations*, II, 58; McIlwain, ed., *Wraxall's Abridgment*, lxv-lxvi.

Montreal trade. The most serious of the dangers, in Livingston's view, was the trade with Canada. It enabled the French to engross the beaver supply of the Great Lakes region and thus capture the allegiance of the western tribes. Only a strenuous effort to stamp out the contacts with Montreal, accompanied by an equally vigorous encouragement of the direct trade with the western tribes, could overcome the economic and strategic threat to the English domains.[28]

Two days after Livingston wrote this memorial, Schuyler and the Iroquois conferred at Albany. The Seneca had already turned their backs on the English because they feared that Schuyler "had a hatchet in his bosom," and the other tribes, although they attended, distrusted him. He urged them to destroy the French settlement at Niagara, but they said the greater danger lay in the Montreal trade which, they insisted, "we desire you to stop." This Schuyler refused to do.[29]

In mid-September Governor Burnet finally arrived in New York and Schuyler's presidency came to an end. The new governor quickly aroused the anger of the Schuyler-Philipse-De Lancey faction when he failed to abide by an accepted custom, the dissolution of the old Assembly and the calling of new elections. By continuing the old Assembly, Burnet upset the opposition's plans to contest the seats of many Hunter supporters. But Burnet was wise to retain the legislators who had been elected in 1716, for the majority were, as he phrased it, "tractable," and there was no reason to run the risk of going to the polls. Moreover, the existing Assembly was ready to grant him a satisfactory revenue for several years, something no governor would ever willingly jeopardize.[30]

When the governor and the speaker met for the first time on October 11, 1720, they immediately found themselves in agreement on all basic issues. "I arrived yesterday," Livingston wrote his wife, "to the great joy of the Governor who received me with great civility and I was with him nearly all day yesterday and talked of all things concerning the public. I hope that we will be very happy with him. He agrees in all our feelings and he approves of my memorandum and representation [on the fur trade].... I cannot express enough the

28. Livingston's memorial to Schuyler, Aug. 23, 1720, O'Callaghan, ed., *N. Y. Col. Docs.*, V, 559-60.
29. Iroquois Conference, Aug. 25-Sept. 4, 1720, *ibid.*, 562-69.
30. Burnet to Bd. of Trade, Sept. 24, 1720, *ibid.*, 573.

great friendship the new Governor shows me, he is very familiar." [31]

The canny Livingston intended to utilize Burnet's "great friendship" for the benefit of his sons Robert and Gilbert, and there was little question that he would have his way. Burnet's opening speech to the Assembly indicated the extent of Livingston's influence. Dwelling at great length upon the Anglo-French rivalry, the governor took the stand that Livingston had earlier adopted, warning the legislature to prevent "any Trade on this side, that may be destructive to the Publick"—the Montreal trade.[32]

Livingston's task was made much easier by Burnet's position, and this was fortunate because the speaker was now suffering from a painful ailment that was to be with him for the remainder of his life. Despite his physical pain, Livingston continued to serve Burnet as confidential adviser and as speaker of the Assembly. Never before had he enjoyed such cordial relations with a chief executive, nor such intimate ones. "The civility and respect the Governor shows me in particular and also shows to all the children is inexpressible," he jubilantly told his wife; "he will make Robert Clerk of the Chancery and Gilbert Escheator General, the place Colonel Graham had. He came and visited me Sunday night and said that I should just speak up for anything that it is in his power to give me. He knows from whom I have sprung. . . . those who have exclaimed so against the old Governor have little reason to boast about it." [33]

And Burnet kept his promises: two days later, Philip Livingston was appointed deputy secretary for Indian affairs. At the same time, he replaced some of the old commissioners for Indian affairs who had opposed the elder Livingston's views on the fur trade. They had been removed, Burnet told Philip, because "they had misrepresented the true Cause of the French success with the Indians, tho your Father had prepared Clauses for that purpose in a Memorial delivered to

31. Robert to Alida Livingston, Oct. 12, 1720 (Dutch), Livingston-Redmond Mss. The memo has not survived, but it is referred to in N. Y. Council Minutes, XIII, 11, N. Y. State Lib.

32. *Assembly Journal*, I, 439.

33. Livingston's ailment may have been a kidney, liver, or gall bladder complaint. It was first mentioned on Jan. 14, 1719/20 by Philip Livingston; he hoped his father "by voiding much sand will . . . [be relieved] from that painfull and dangerous distemper"; Livingston-Redmond Mss. On Oct. 18, Livingston was "so ill . . . with a pain in my back that I could not help myself, and yesterday I could not walk to the Assembly House but had to be carried in Cousin Bayard's Chair." Robert to Alida Livingston, Oct. 12, 18, 1720 (Dutch), *ibid.*

them, these I find they have changed so as to Shelter the Profit some of them had ... from their Pernicious Trade with the French." These moves were preliminaries to a frontal assault on the Albany-Montreal trade which Livingston, Morris, and Burnet were preparing. A "perfect example of responsible party government," the plan originated with Livingston, was supported by Burnet in his opening speech, and was introduced into the Assembly by Lewis Morris, administration spokesman. Within two weeks the Assembly had adopted the trade law and the revenue act. The prohibitory act made it illegal to trade or sell any Indian goods (i.e., cloth, guns, gunpowder, kettles, lead, or liquor) to the French, and subjected violators to forfeiture of the goods involved and a £100 fine, half of which was to go to the informer. Enforcement was entrusted to the sheriff of Albany County.[34]

At the same time that he guided the Assembly's deliberations on these administration measures, Livingston resumed his talks with the governor about matters which concerned him personally, requesting the renewal of his commission as secretary for Indian affairs with a salary from the quitrents. Burnet was agreeable, although he feared that the quitrents would be inadequate. However, Livingston was not worried; "when I have such a commission it will be a debt on the Crown and must be paid some time or other." He then presented a formal petition to the governor, but asked that the commission be given to his son Philip, an Albany wholesaler, and that it include all of his appointive offices.[35] Always generous to his sons, Livingston also recognized the debilitating effects of old age.

To facilitate approval of the petition, Livingston entered into a correspondence with George Bampfield, cousin of William Popple of the Board of Trade and a personal friend of Hunter. Bampfield wanted to become London agent for the New York Assembly, and Speaker Livingston offered to assist him if he could prove his mettle by first securing the royal commission for Philip. Then, Livingston

34. Burnet to Philip Livingston, Oct. 20, 1720, McIlwain, ed., *Wraxall's Abridgment*, 132; Robert to Alida Livingston, Nov. 4, 9, 1720 (Dutch), Livingston-Redmond Mss.; *Assembly Journal*, I, 445, 447-48; *Col. Laws of N. Y.*, II, 8-10; McAnear, Politics in Provincial New York, 334.

35. Robert to Alida Livingston, Nov. 9, 1720 (Dutch), Livingston-Redmond Mss.; Livingston's petition to Burnet, Nov. 17, 1720, PRO, CO 5: 1052, fol. 137 (Lib. Cong. transcripts).

promised, "I shall Endeavour to get you appointed agent." [36] The governor also urged that a royal commission be issued to Philip Livingston. "This I am the more earnest in," he wrote the Board of Trade, "because Robert Livingstone the speaker of the Assembly has always been serviceable to Brigadeer Hunter & has now been of the greatest use to me both in the Assembly, and in laying open the true state of affairs with the Indians ... so that this act prohibiting it [i.e., the Albany-Montreal trade] is chiefly owing to the Speaker."

Well pleased with both Livingston and the Assembly as a whole, Burnet gave much of the credit to Hunter for having made a "good impression" on the legislators. By "adhering firmly to every one of Brigadeer Hunters friends," the new governor had won passage of two important measures. Indeed, the only discordant notes came from two councilors, Philipse and Schuyler, who had never been wholly reconciled to Hunter's policies. Burnet suggested that they be replaced by James Alexander and Cadwallader Colden.[37]

Livingston had attained the pinnacle of influence and power, but there were those who were not at all pleased, particularly the commissioners for Indian affairs whom Burnet had dismissed. They claimed that the elder Livingston was senile, Philip reported, but they "ought now to acknowledge that you have been more understanding than they, for one that is grown Childish could not have them turned out of being Commissioners. ... it seems said here that you are the monarch of the whole Province." A political veteran, Livingston ignored the attacks of his enemies, which merely raised him in the esteem of Burnet who was determined to stamp out the Albany-Montreal trade, punish those who obstructed him, and reward those who aided him. "He will make it a rule," Livingston thought, "to distinguish those who are for the Interest of the Province from those who promote the french trade for their own gains." [38]

Although the ousted commissioners may have blamed the elder Livingston for their plight, they directed their animus against Philip, whose political fortunes rose in direct proportion to his father's grow-

36. Livingston to Bampfield, Nov. 18, 1720 (draft), Livingston-Redmond Mss.
37. Burnet to Bd. of Trade, Nov. 26, 1720, O'Callaghan, ed., *N. Y. Col. Docs.*, V, 576-80.
38. Philip to Robert Livingston, Dec. 4, 1720, Collins to Livingston, Jan. 19, 1720/1, Williams to Livingston, Jan. 28, 1720/1, Philip to Robert Livingston, Feb. 1, 1720/1, Livingston-Redmond Mss.

ing friendship with Burnet. As an official enjoying the governor's friendship and patronage, young Livingston had to avoid any activity which might reflect discredit on the administration. He found this difficult to do because of the inequities in the prohibitory law. He had to relinquish his trade with Schenectady residents since that town was north of the line beyond which Indian goods were not to be sold. He also objected to the elimination of all trade with the Caughnawaga Indians, agents of the Montreal merchants. "It will be hard to banish them at once," he wrote. He, John Collins, and Major Holland recommended that "there can hardly a Law be made to bridle the people of these parts in matter of trade unless every person is obligd to purge himselfe on oath," for the sheriff could not be in more than one place at a time nor could he legally deputize anyone else to perform this duty. Only by an oath could the "Angry Stroud Company" be prevented from sending "what Strouds they please" to Canada.³⁹

Although the law was not perfect by any means, it disrupted the Canadian trade and made the Albany wholesalers smart under its restrictions. Burnet was very pleased by this, for it was "a beginning to a better state of affairs." He realized that the French would not accept these changes without a struggle, and he was probably not surprised when Philip Livingston reported that Jean Coeur had been sent as a French emissary to the Seneca.⁴⁰

While considering such portentous matters, Livingston learned that his eldest son, John, had died in London. For a number of years, John suffered from a "tedious fitt of the goute," but he had decided nevertheless to go to England in October 1718 to settle his accounts with the Crown for victualing the garrison at Annapolis Royal. Before leaving New London, he sold his estate there for £4,500 with the intention, upon his return, of settling in New York.⁴¹

After Livingston learned of his son's death, he drew up a new will. John left no children by either marriage, and Philip now became the primary heir to the elder Livingston's estate. He was to get the Manor and the brick house in Albany which was then his home. To his

39. Collins to Livingston, Feb. 17, 1720/1, Philip to Robert Livingston, Feb. 20, 1720/1, *ibid.*
40. Philip to Robert Livingston, Mar. 20, 1720/1, *ibid.*; Burnet to Bd. of Trade, Mar. 9, 1720/1, O'Callaghan, ed., *N. Y. Col. Docs.*, V, 584.
41. John to Robert Livingston, Sept. 9, Oct. 9, 1717, Livingston-Redmond Mss.; John Livingston to Stoddard, Oct. 28, 1718, Edes Papers, Mass. Hist. Soc.

third son, Robert, Jr., Livingston willed the lower section of the Manor, Clermont, and the lands at Kinderhook, while Gilbert, the youngest son, was to receive the Saratoga property and the small house in Albany. The two daughters, Margaret and Joanna, were each to receive a house in New York City and small sums in cash. Alida Livingston, "during her pure widowhood," was to have all the estate's rents and profits; if she remarried, she was to receive one-third of that income until her death.[42]

Livingston was undoubtedly affected deeply by his son's death, but his mind was soon occupied by public affairs, just as it had been following the other personal tragedies of his life. He responded to Governor Burnet's summons to participate in another Assembly session; it would be a full and active meeting for the governor pledged to "set the Indian affairs aright, To which I will turn all my thoughts with all possible zeal." Burnet's firmness was backed by support he received from London. Under the guidance of Hunter, Vetch, and Bampfield, the Board of Trade had accepted the governor's recommendation that Philipse and Schuyler be replaced on the Council by two of Hunter's close friends and supporters, Colden and Alexander, and the Privy Council gave its approval on the same day. Thus was eliminated the last source of opposition within the governor's official family.[43]

By such measures as these, the Burnet party rewarded its friends. The distinguishing political characteristic in New York was no longer doctrinaire adherence to an ideal as it had been twenty years earlier, but unquestioned support of a leader. Party politics had returned to its pre-1689 character, and the governor could only be certain of a majority by combining a sufficient number of sectional interests. By uniting the Hudson River counties with certain elements in New York City and Albany, Burnet was now attempting to follow the pattern initiated by Hunter. But his task was not an easy one, and he relied heavily on his knowledgeable speaker of the house. Increasingly irritable because of his deteriorating health, Livingston complained of the arduous duties of the speakership: "I wish to be

42. Robert Livingston's will, Mar. 25, 1721, Livingston-Redmond Mss.
43. Burnet to Livingston, Apr. 20, 1721, *ibid.*; Bd. of Trade to George I, Order of King-in-Council, Feb. 10, 1720/1, *Cal. State Papers, Col.* XXXII, nos. 378, 379.

discharged from this sad work in the Assembly," he wrote on one occasion, "for it goes against the grain." [44]

Livingston had too much at stake to give serious consideration to retirement. He was most interested in the issuance of a royal commission to Philip, a subject which Hunter, Vetch, and Bampfield had not neglected in London. In mid-June, the former governor wrote Livingston, summarizing the proceedings to that date. There were delays in the secretary of state's office, Hunter explained, but he promised to "move in it swiftly." Two months later, Bampfield reported that he, Hunter, and Vetch "had two severall attendances at the Board of Trade.... there is noe Room to Doubt but the same will be Complyed with ... in favour of your Son." [45]

Although the decision was delayed by the administrative confusion of the "South Sea Bubble," the Board of Trade finally prepared a favorable recommendation and sent it to Lord Carteret for royal consideration. By the end of June 1721, the Privy Council issued a royal warrant for the preparation of the desired commission, but the salary was to be paid out of the colony's revenues, not the quitrents. It was not until September 30, 1721, however, that Philip Livingston's commission was finally completed. [46]

While these negotiations were proceeding in London, Livingston found himself enmeshed in other events at home which concerned Gilbert. The young man's partnership with Francis Harrison in farming the excise had led to bankruptcy. Harrison had withdrawn from the enterprise after the first year, but Gilbert had continued and found himself in debt to the colony's treasury and falling further behind each year. His financial recklessness bewildered his artful father, who could only comment, "Do not know what to make of it.... He worries about it less than I, so it seems." [47]

When Gilbert finally realized the hopelessness of his situation, he

44. Burnet to Livingston, May 23, 1721, Robert to Alida Livingston, June [1,] 1721 (Dutch), Livingston-Redmond Mss.

45. Hunter to Livingston, Mar. 17, 1720/1, Bampfield to Livingston, May 3, 1721, ibid.

46. Journal Bd. Trade, IV, 284-85; Bd of Trade to Carteret, June 13, 1721, O'Callaghan, ed., N. Y. Col. Docs., V, 584; Royal warrant, June 30, 1721, Cal. State Papers, Col., XXXII, no. 556.

47. Gilbert Livingston's petition to Assembly, Nov. 12, 1717, Franklin D. Roosevelt Collection of Livingston Mss., Roosevelt Lib., Hyde Park; Robert to Alida Livingston, Oct. 18, 1720 (Dutch), Livingston-Redmond Mss.

appealed to the Assembly for relief. For the privilege of collecting an excise of about £900 a year, the partners had agreed to pay the treasury £1,500 a year, a most foolish bargain. To salvage his credit and protect his reputation, Gilbert proposed to sell New York City lands which his wife had inherited, but in order to do so he had to receive governmental approval, because the colony had a prior claim on all his assets. Through his father's influence, a bill permitting the sale was introduced and passed.[48]

Gilbert's creditors were not wholly satisfied, however, and he turned for aid to his father. False pride had caused him to fear that an appeal to his father would meet "with a forbidding manner of asses," but Livingston accepted his son's penitent plea for aid and offered several proposals. None of them satisfied the ambitious young man who, in a counterproposal, suggested that he be given the farm near Albany tenanted by Jan Clute, a house, barn, cattle, two Negro slaves, the house in Albany occupied by Philip, and the office of secretary for Indian affairs. "Then (with the help of God)," he concluded, "I might maintain my family (with what assistance I might then Reasonably expect from my mother in Law) in a Reputable manner."[49]

Fortunately for Gilbert's sake, his father took a charitable view of these outrageous demands and offered a farm at Canastagione, some livestock, 600 boards, £100 towards building costs, a Negro slave, plow, harrow, and wagon. To pay the balance of Gilbert's obligations, Livingston also assigned him the proceeds from the sale of his one-seventh share of the Saratoga Patent. Gilbert had no choice but to accept his father's final offer, and the 20,000 acres at Saratoga were transferred to Philip as trustee for his brother on October 9. A year later, Livingston cut his son out of his will.[50]

Robert Livingston had now reached an age when he wished to rely more heavily upon his sons. But John was dead, young Robert had not yet proved his mettle, and Gilbert, who had been a sad

48. *Assembly Journal*, I, 455, 457-59, 463.

49. Gilbert to Robert Livingston, n.d. (recd. Sept. 14, 1721), Livingston-Redmond Mss.

50. "My Resolution on Son Gilbert's proposals," Sept. 15, 1721, *ibid.;* Deed of Robert and Alida Livingston to Philip Livingston, Oct. 9, 1721, Melius, ed., *Records of Albany County: Grantors*, VIII, 4686; Livingston's codicil, Sept. 22, 1722, Livingston-Redmond Mss.

disappointment, could not be trusted in business affairs. Philip remained, not only his father's primary heir, but the son best qualified to succeed to his father's political mantle. For each of his sons, however, Livingston had incurred certain political obligations which still had to be repaid.

CHAPTER XVI

Payment in Kind for Favors Received

R OBERT LIVINGSTON, perhaps more than anyone else in the colony, had received a full measure of favors through Governor Burnet's endeavors and the influence of Hunter and Bampfield in London. Now, payment in kind had to be made—there were many opportunities for doing so.

The debt to Bampfield came first. Hunter and Burnet had originally suggested that he apply for appointment as the New York Assembly's London agent, and Livingston promised to lend his support as speaker in return for Philip's commission as secretary for Indian affairs. Bampfield possessed valuable influence at Court; "I think the best returne I Cann make for soo Singular a favour," he candidly wrote to the speaker, "is by my Dilligence and application for the Interest and advantage of your Province . . . And my Couzen Popple (as he promised his Excellency the Governor [Burnet] before he left England) will give me all the assistance he Cann Not only in his owne office [secretary to Board of Trade] But alsoe his Interest in all other offices." [1]

Although Bampfield performed his part of the bargain, his appointment as agent was delayed because of the Assembly's suspicion of strangers, no matter how highly recommended. In a clever political maneuver, Livingston drafted a letter to Comptroller of the Customs Robert Hunter which was submitted to the Assembly and approved

1. Bampfield to Livingston, May 3, 1721, Livingston-Redmond Mss.

on June 27, 1721. The former governor was asked to assume the
agency as "the fittest person for that trust," and he was authorized
"either to accept thereof yourself, or to nominate another to be our
Agent." Immediately upon receiving it, Hunter offered the post to
Bampfield, who quickly accepted. The agent-designate assured Livingston that he would be wholly guided by the counsel of Hunter
and Popple, and later, in a personal letter, he thanked the speaker
for devising the strategem, the "most Effectuall means to promote my
Interest for that Employment." [2]

It was not until June 1, 1722, however, that a motion to appoint
Bampfield was made in the Assembly, and no action was then taken
on it. After the summer recess, he submitted his report on activities
before various imperial agencies in the colony's behalf and the House
placed it "on the Table for the Members to peruse." Four days later,
the legislators approved Bampfield as "Agent for this Colony, for
the Space of two Years, to be computed from the Time Brigadier
Hunter appointed him as such." At the next session, the Assembly
pledged to pay his salary and expenses. [3]

With one political obligation discharged, Livingston turned to
another which required even greater skill. A bitter controversy had
long been brewing between the Assembly and Horatio Walpole,
auditor general of the plantation revenues, and Governor Burnet
found it expedient to side with Walpole, even though he could ill
afford to alienate his legislature. Caught in a dilemma, Burnet asked
Speaker Livingston to work out a *modus vivendi*.

Livingston's task was difficult because the dispute was complex and
involved important officials. The Assembly, traditionally and justifiably fearful of an unscrupulous governor, had dogmatically refused
to create a permanent revenue and had authorized taxes for a limited
number of years, the length depending on the degree of trust that
the Assembly had in the executive. Moreover, the legislature had consistently refused to adhere to the Crown policy that all governmental
revenue should be at the sole disposal of the governor and Council;

2. N. Y. Assembly to Hunter, June 23, 1721 (Livingston's draft), Bampfield to
Livingston, Sept. 15, 1721, Feb. 5, 1721/2, *ibid.*; *Assembly Journal*, I, 458.
3. Bampfield to Livingston, Apr. 30, 1722, Livingston-Redmond Mss. Bampfield
thanked the speaker "for proquoring my Sallary for two years and doubt not of
your Goodness to get it Carryed along with the Revenue." Bampfield to Livingston,
Mar. 4, 1722/3, *ibid.* See also *Assembly Journal*, I, 470, 487-88.

in 1714, it had forced Robert Hunter to accede to an increase in the power of the treasurer, appointed by the Assembly, and disbursement of public money in accordance with the House's stated wishes. Thus, the government's accounts were audited by the Assembly's treasurer, not the Crown's auditor general, who was then William Blathwayt, or his deputy and cousin, George Clarke. They were only permitted to supervise customs duties and the minor, semi-feudal revenues such as quitrents, fines, forfeitures, and escheats.[4]

Although the Assembly had its way for several years, the death of Blathwayt on August 26, 1717, and the appointment of Horatio Walpole as his successor in October set the stage for a conflict which was made almost inevitable four years later by the secretary of state's instructions to Governor Burnet: "It is His Majesty's pleasure, that the money raised for support of the Civil Government...shall pass thro' the hands of His Majesty's Officers.... And you are hereby required to oppose and remove all innovations that have already been made, or shall be attempted to be made upon this head, in relation to the management of His Majesty's Revenue."[5]

Even under ordinary circumstances, this directive would have led to a political uproar; Walpole's status made the situation extraordinarily explosive. His brother was Prime Minister Sir Robert Walpole, and it behooved all who wanted favor or justice from Whitehall to support the auditor general's claims. The long-expected explosion occurred on June 15, 1721, when a letter from the Lords of the Treasury to the colony's treasurer, Abraham De Peyster, was submitted to the Assembly. It specifically demanded that De Peyster account with either Walpole or his deputy, Clarke. The Assembly responded with a memorial, prepared by Lewis Morris, which recited the many "extravagancies of those times," particularly the "allowing a fee or salary to the Auditor General of 5 per cent upon the whole amount of His Majesty's Revenue in this Province."

The objection to the fee was merely a pretext; the Assembly was determined to retain full control, through its treasurer, of the government's receipts and disbursements, but it could not openly an-

4. Jacobsen, *Blathwayt*, 377-80; Leonard Woods Labaree, *Royal Government in America: A Study of the British Colonial System Before 1783* (New Haven, 1930), 283-85.
5. Royal instructions to Hunter, Nov. 22, 1717, N. Y. Col. Mss., LX, 183, N. Y. State Lib.; Carteret to Burnet, May 16, 1721, *Cal. State Papers, Col.*, XXXII, no. 492.

nounce that it distrusted those whom the king placed in authority. Therefore, the Assembly emphasized the unfairness of the auditor general's fee which, it claimed, the Crown had never authorized, and announced its willingness to allow De Peyster to account with Walpole or Clarke provided "such accounting will not load His Majesty's Revenue here, with a debt of 5 per cent or £150 per annum." Should the auditor general's monetary claim be allowed, the House warned, "it will be impossible to pay the Officers of the Government their salaries." [6]

Walpole was furious when he learned of the New York memorial, and he declared it was "a meer pretence to prevent my Deputies auditing & Inspecting their accounts and by that means to have the Collecting and Disposing of the Revenues of that Province entirely in their own Power." The 5 percent fee was not the crux of the matter: "The Question is of much greater Importance," he warned the Treasury Lords, "than my fees" which, however, he refused to relinquish. The Treasury Lords, well aware of political realities, supported Walpole and warned Burnet that De Peyster's refusal to account was "a very arbitrary and unwarrantable proceeding, and a contempt of His Majesty's authority, and that this excuse relating to the Auditor's fee has no manner of colour or foundation in it." [7] Fortunately, the Assembly was in adjournment when this message was received and there was time to work out a compromise.

In the fall of 1722, Livingston was given the unwelcome task of convincing the assemblymen of the propriety of acceding to Walpole's demands. It was to their advantage to retain the "frindship and Intrest" of the Walpoles, the speaker suggested, and the auditor general's fee would amount to no more than that being paid to the colony's treasurer, whose services would then be unnecessary. "It will be farr more for our honor advantage and Intrest to do it willingly than by Compulsion." Livingston advised the Assembly to submit to the Crown's will and give a kind word and a pension to De Peyster." [8]

6. *Assembly Journal*, I, 455-57; N. Y. Assembly to Burnet, June 30, 1721, *Cal. State Papers, Col.*, XXXIII, no. 554.
7. Walpole to Treasury Lords, Apr. 26, 1722, PRO, CO 5: 1085, no. 40 (Lib. Cong. transcripts); Treasury Lords to Burnet, Apr. 28, 1722, *Cal. State Papers, Col.*, XXXIII, no. 119.
8. "What I [Livingston] am of opinion Relating the auditor general and agent," Oct. 29, 1722, Livingston-Redmond Mss. A pension was also advisable for De Peyster

This was not easy counsel for the Assembly to accept, because it went contrary to the history of the House in financial matters. On first consideration, the Assembly rejected the speaker's proposal and drafted its own instructions to Bampfield. Roundly condemning Walpole for his greed, the legislators announced that the king might create the position of auditor general, but the colony had no responsibility to pay his salary. "The Country seems Rather Disposed to pay their own Treasurer," they concluded, "than Run the hazard of falling into an Other Laborynth of Publick Debts." [9]

These were strong and dangerous words, and it was only with diplomacy and tact that Livingston and Burnet finally convinced the Assembly of the recklessness of its position. The letter to Bampfield was tabled, but Livingston sent him a copy for his information. The agent replied: "I am very glad that the Letter . . . was quashed for that Gentleman [i.e., Sir Robert Walpole] at present being at the head of the Ministry it would have been a very difficult task to obtain what I am therein ordered to do." [10]

The Assembly had seen the wisdom of not attacking Horatio Walpole, but getting it to pay his salary and arrears was another matter. Before that could even be considered, some means had to be found to raise additional funds. The colony's revenues were greatly diminished because of a decline in trade. By May 1722, the tax receipts were £1,700 in arrears and the governor and other officials had not been paid for six months. Livingston had a strong personal interest in this problem because his son's commission as secretary for Indian affairs authorized a salary of £100 sterling out of the colony's revenues. Burnet had suggested that the commission be withheld from the Council's official notice until the colony's debts were paid. Otherwise, Philip Livingston might meet the same difficulties that his father had earlier experienced. [11]

Livingston and Burnet agreed that the problem existed, but they disagreed on the means to solve it. The governor suggested a land

because he was "quite distracted and is closely confined by his family." Burnet to Bd. of Trade, June 17, 1722, O'Callaghan, ed., *N. Y. Col. Docs.*, V, 649.

9. "Letter designed for the agent but on further consideration not approved of by the Assembly," Nov. 1, 1722, Livingston-Redmond Mss.

10. Bampfield to Livingston, Mar. 4, 1722/3, *ibid.*

11. Robert to Alida Livingston, May 16, 19, 1722 (Dutch), *ibid.*; Bobin to Clarke, Sept. 12, 1721, O'Callaghan, ed., *Bobin's Letters*, 90.

tax, with the greatest burden falling on untenanted property. Livingston objected strenuously; as a large landowner, he would be one of those most adversely affected. However, Burnet was not one to brook opposition to his plans, even from his closest friends, and when Livingston called on him on May 29, he was refused admittance. "It is presumed," the speaker remarked, "that he is busy preparing an act to destroy the great [land] patents or to tax them so much that they will open up the lands... they may try what they want. I do not think they can put their intentions into effect."

When the governor delivered his opening address to the Assembly the following day, Livingston reported that it was "very sharp and consisted of many articles which mentioned the shortage and lack of all money." On June 8, Burnet announced his plan for a six pence tax on every hundred acres of untenanted land in private hands. This was not confiscatory, but it would force speculators to open their holdings for settlement. Livingston estimated that it would cost Rensselaerswyck about £200 a year and be "very inconvenient" to him. He promised to oppose it with all his strength.

The governor's scheme was doomed to failure, primarily because it was aimed at the very group which gave him his Assembly majority, the "River party" of Hudson Valley landowners. Their opposition, plus the fact that "the expenses of measuring would amount to more than the tax," insured its defeat; but Burnet blamed Livingston for this setback. When confronted with this accusation, the speaker freely admitted his responsibility and warned the governor that "those who suggest such things to him are not his friends; it is putting the country upside down, and if he thinks twice he will thank me."

Although a new tax was passed by the end of June, it bore no resemblance to Burnet's proposal. It was a levy on "the real and personal estate, excluding the vacant land," designed to raise £1,200 by July 1723. Still angry, the governor attempted to embarrass the speaker by sending to the Assembly Philip Livingston's earlier request for payment of his salary as secretary for Indian affairs. Any new monetary demand would not be looked upon favorably, Burnet thought, but he underestimated the speaker's influence, for the Assembly simply ignored the request. Before long, the whole affair was forgotten: "It is all finished," Livingston told his wife, "and I have been invited to eat with him tomorrow in the fort." [12]

Disagreements such as this between the governor and the speaker were the exception rather than the rule. They usually worked together in close harmony, as was demonstrated by the revision of the prohibitory trade act, which had hindered but had not halted commerce between Albany and Montreal. Adept at finding loopholes, the *handlaers,* or wholesalers, evaded its provisions by sending "off their Goods to the Mohacks Country . . . and then it is out of the Power of Any Officer to Discover them." Burnet had tried unsuccessfully to deal with the subterfuge of using the Indians as intermediaries in the prohibited trade, but neither a private lecture to ten sachems on comparative British and French constitutional history nor a detachment of militia in the Seneca country served to cut off the French trade and initiate a trade with the Far Nations. Philip Livingston complained of the frequency with which the law was being violated and suggested that it should be amended and made more effective, or abandoned. [13]

As spokesman for the governor's party, Lewis Morris finally introduced a bill to amend the original statute on June 21, and it was enacted into law on July 8. Under its terms, anyone suspected of illegal trading was to be tendered an oath which denied not only personal participation in the trade after August 16, 1722, but also knowledge of any violations by others. Refusal to take the oath would mean that the person was guilty of "having Traded with the Subjects of the French King." More effective enforcement procedures were also authorized; the oath could be administered by the mayor, an alderman, or a justice of the peace of Albany, by the commander of the garrison at either Albany, Schenectady, or Fort Hunter, or by anyone employed to discover the trade. No longer would enforcement be hampered by the sheriff's inability to be in more than one place at a time. [14]

12. Robert to Alida Livingston, May 26, June 1, 8, 12, 30, 1722 (Dutch), Livingston-Redmond Mss.
13. Henry Holland to [Livingston (?)], June 16, 1721, Burnet's "Discourse with 10 Sachims," Sept. 4, 1721, Leder, ed., *Livingston Indian Records,* 229, 229-30; Burnet to Peter Schuyler, Jr., Sept. 8, 1721, O'Callaghan, ed., *N. Y. Col. Docs.,* V, 641-42; Philip to Robert Livingston, Feb. 15, 1721/2, Livingston-Redmond Mss.; McIlwain, ed., *Wraxall's Abridgment,* 140.
14. *Assembly Journal,* I, 475, 481-82; *Col. Laws of N. Y.,* II, 98-101.

In August and September 1722, the importance of the Iroquois to all the English colonies was emphasized by a conference at Albany attended by Governors Alexander Spotswood of Virginia, Sir William Keith of Pennsylvania, and William Burnet of New York, each with an impressive retinue. Many citizens of Albany must have vied for the privilege of accommodating them, but the Livingstons carried off the honors. Spotswood stayed with Robert Livingston, Jr., "the nephew"; Sir William resided with Philip Livingston's father-in-law, Peter Van Brugh; and Burnet, along with several councilors from each colony, lodged at Robert Livingston's.

Livingston and his son Philip played important roles in the behind-the-scenes discussions at Albany. "All the 3 Governors . . . have consulted me concerning their proposals," wrote the speaker; "there has been a general meeting of all the Governors . . . and Councilors, at which I and our son were the only ones present of those who live here." [15] His prominent role at the conference gave Livingston renewed hope that he might yet obtain a more secure salary out of the quitrents for the post of secretary for Indian affairs. But he was to find it increasingly difficult to deal with the Crown and royal officials in London.

During the eighteenth century a subtle but significant differentiation occurred between the British and their colonial cousins. While the British were growing more rigid in their approach to political and administrative problems, the Americans were beginning to realize the limitations inherent in the old ways and were seeking newer, more effective solutions to their problems. This change would eventually have a profound influence on the relations between the two segments of the empire.

Although the divergence sprang from a variety of causes, perhaps the most basic was the need of the British to protect the Glorious Revolution and its results from all possible assaults. To do so, they erected about it an impregnable fortress of tradition and custom. In America, on the other hand, the situation was far more dynamic: new problems constantly clashed with custom and demanded new solutions. Coupled with this growing difference in outlook was a change

15. Robert to Alida Livingston, Aug. 25, 1722 (Dutch), Livingston-Redmond Mss.

in British administrative procedures. Preoccupied with international war and diplomacy, as well as its own pleasures, the upper echelon of government allowed colonial problems to pass by default into the hands of a burgeoning bureaucracy of undersecretaries and clerks. Petitioners to the Crown for favors or rights were forced increasingly to apply to lower-level officials whose authority was carefully circumscribed by the traditions and customs which had grown up about them.

Robert Livingston's dealings with British officials illustrate graphically the effect of these changes on the relations between the mother country and the colonies. During his first visit to London in 1695-96, he presented a complex set of claims for offices and large sums of money without adequate proof, but he secured a settlement within a year. On his second trip in 1703, his claims were substantially similar and more thoroughly documented, but it took him three years to accomplish his purpose. Now, in the 1720's, when his requests were much simpler and his influence much greater, it was even more difficult to obtain satisfaction.

He desired two things in the 1720's which needed the approval of the increasingly inflexible and rigid imperial bureaucracy at Whitehall. Both were relatively simple and neither called for an appropriation from the Crown. A more satisfactory salary for Philip as secretary for Indian affairs, and royal approval of the method devised to enable Gilbert to settle his debts to the government required no major departure from tradition; but the royal officials were exceptionally dilatory in both matters.

Gilbert Livingston's debt to private merchants, incurred during his partnership with Francis Harrison in farming the excise, could not be paid until he had discharged his obligations to the government. The impatient merchants turned to Gilbert's father for satisfaction. "I was not yet on land," the speaker wrote on his arrival in New York City in May 1722, "when Moses Levy spoke to me because our Gilbert owed him £70 and the payment date had passed, and he said, if he did not come from Esopus to pay him, he would have him arrested." But a Mr. Morin had anticipated Levy; Gilbert had already been arrested on a complaint for £50 and been released on his own recognizance, and a Mr. Reed, who claimed £200, refrained from arresting him only because of his high regard for the speaker. "There is," sighed Livingston, "no end to it." [16]

In 1721 the Assembly passed a law permitting Gilbert to sell the New York City lands which his wife had inherited so that he might repay his debt to the government, but a defect in the act dissuaded potential purchasers. Since there was no guarantee that Gilbert would transfer the proceeds of the sales to the government, the colony's claim to the lands might not be extinguished and the buyers could only sue Gilbert.[17] Only a new law would attract purchasers, and the speaker interceded with the governor. In November 1722, the Assembly passed a statute to appoint trustees to manage and sell Gilbert's properties and to hold the proceeds for the government, thus ensuring valid titles because there could then be no diversion of funds. Burnet lost no time transmitting the measure to the Board of Trade with this comment: "It is the only way the Debt to the Revenue can be paid by this Gilbert Livingston. . . . I hope your Lordships will favour me with an effectual & speedy recommendation of this Act to His Majesty." [18]

The Board of Trade promptly referred the act to its counselor Richard West for an "opinion in point of law." He reported "as much in our favour as we could desire," Bampfield informed Livingston, but the Board, in the late summer of 1723, referred the question back to West for a further report. "Some Scruples" had been raised because the law authorized Gilbert to pay £800 to the government in settlement of his obligation of £1,100. "Whether compositions of that kind are usually or proper to be made," the counselor suggested, "your Lordships will judge." [19] Before any action was taken, however, the king went abroad and all public affairs were suspended. At the end of February 1723/4, Bampfield still hoped to get royal approval of the law, but he had no idea when. After the law was referred to West for a third time, he finally stated that he had no objection to the matter of the composition, and the Treasury Lords, with the aid of Peter Le Heup, a clerk in their office, added their

16. Robert to Alida Livingston, May 19, 1722 (Dutch), *ibid.*
17. Robert to Alida Livingston, June 8, 12, 19, 30, 1722 (Dutch), *ibid.*
18. *Assembly Journal,* I, 481, 483, 486, 488-89; Burnet to Bd. of Trade, Nov. 21, 1722, O'Callaghan, ed., *N. Y. Col. Docs.,* V, 656-57.
19. *Journal Bd. Trade,* V, 2; Popple to West, Jan. 10, 1722/3, West to Bd. of Trade, Aug. 16, 1723, *Cal. State Papers, Col.,* XXXIII, nos. 410, 684; Bampfield to Livingston, Mar. 4, 1722/3, May 15, Aug. 6, 1723, Livingston-Redmond Mss.

endorsement. On April 30, 1724, the Privy Council at last approved
this statute as well as the one passed for Gilbert's benefit in 1721.[20]

Although the measures relating to Gilbert received royal approbation, the Livingstons were most unhappy about the delays in London.
Not only had they been kept waiting a long time for the Crown's decision on the laws relating to Gilbert, but the negotiations for payment of Philip's salary as secretary for Indian affairs were still continuing. Livingston had requested a salary out of the quitrents for the
secretaryship as early as 1696, when he received his first commission,
but he accepted the less satisfactory provision of a salary drawn out
of the colony's general revenues. When his commission was renewed
by Queen Anne, the same thing occurred. Now, at the very peak of
his political influence, he was determined to get a more certain reward for his son Philip.

Livingston expected aid from a number of influential men, including Hunter and Burnet. The former governor was still indebted
to the speaker for financial assistance rendered during the Palatine
settlement, and Philip suggested that Hunter "would be very unjust
if he did not Show you some favours for that Considerable Sum of
money you Lost by him." He also believed that Burnet would support them because of his dependence upon the speaker in effecting
his legislative program.[21]

To a man of Livingston's position, £100 sterling a year was not of
the utmost importance, but the salary issue had become a matter of
principle to the family, and stubbornness was a family trait. The salary
had been granted by the Crown and, even though the Assembly and
Council of New York had consistently refused to pay it, Livingston
would not give up. By 1722, the salary arrears due the secretary for
Indian affairs amounted to about £1,700 sterling. Had he attempted
to present such a claim to the Assembly, he would have caused con-
sternation and lost all his friends in the House. Instead, he took the
firm position that the money should come from the quitrents, a fund
wholly at the Crown's disposal and not subject to the control of the
governor, Council, or Assembly. In May 1722, he wrote to Hunter,

20. Bampfield to Livingston, Sept. 13, 1723, Feb. 25, 1723/4, May 23, 1724, Livingston-Redmond Mss.; *Journal Bd. Trade*, V, 73, 81, 82; West to Bd. of Trade, Mar. 14,
1723/4, John Scrope to Popple, Apr. 9, 1724, Order of King-in-Council, Apr. 30,
1724, *Cal. State Papers, Col.*, XXXIV, nos. 89, 122, 144.
21. Philip to Robert Livingston, Feb. 15, 1721/2, Livingston-Redmond Mss.

Bampfield, Vetch, and his London correspondent Samuel Baker, telling them "that there must be an order from the king to get the salary out of the quitrents rather than the revenue" and, a month later, he restated his demand in even stronger terms.[22]

Bampfield consulted with Hunter and Vetch, and they agreed to submit a memorial to the Lords of the Treasury representing "the Difficulty & Hardships your Son lies under on Account of his Receiving his Salary out of the Publick Revenue and praying that the same may be paid out of the quit Rents." He was not overly optimistic, for he noted that the commissions previously issued for the office had always stipulated a salary paid out of the revenue, and royal officials were noticeably reluctant to break with tradition.[23]

For nearly a year the memorial was enmeshed in the web of colonial administration, but in May 1723 Vetch notified his father-in-law that he and Bampfield had waited on Sir Robert Walpole who informed them that "there will be no chance of getting a salary out of the quitrents except by a new commission." However, Horatio Walpole was willing to lend his assistance in gratitude for the aid which the speaker had given him during his dispute with the Assembly. During the summer of 1723, Bampfield began to lay the groundwork for the issuance of a new commission to Philip Livingston. He did not "apprehend that any Obstruction will be made," but he expected delays because Secretary of State Lord Carteret was in Hanover with the king and Horatio Walpole was resting at his country estate. In their absence, "the Under Secretaryes here make a Difficulty to alter their usuall Forms as they are entered in their Books." However, Bampfield assured Livingston that Walpole would "use his utmost Interest to return the favour you have done him." [24]

Philip Livingston, unacquainted with British administrative procedures, was exasperated by what appeared to be unfulfilled promises and irrational delays. He suspected Bampfield of deluding his father and suggested that there was no point in spending any "more money about it without a prospect of obtaining your aim"; it was time to repay the agent "in his own Coin and to get another in his Room." Presumably, the governor agreed. A few months later, he dismissed

22. Robert to Alida Livingston, May 16, 26, June 19, 1722 (Dutch), *ibid.*
23. Bampfield to Livingston, Aug. 13, 1722, *ibid.*
24. Bampfield to Livingston, Mar. 4, 1722/3, Aug. 6, Sept. 13, 1723, Robert to Alida Livingston, May 11, 23, 1723 (Dutch), *ibid.*

Bampfield as of July 1723. The astonished agent swore that he had performed his duty "to the uttermost" of his ability and denied all responsibility for the delays that had been encountered. The blame, he announced, belonged to those officials who remained "so long abroad" or "at their Country Seats." [25]

Burnet's action was both precipitous and dangerous. By dismissing a capable agent, he ran the risk of alienating William Popple, Bampfield's cousin and secretary to the Board of Trade. Hunter immediately realized the possible consequences and tried to undo the mischief. Burnet had ordered Bampfield to turn over all papers to his successor, Peter Le Heup, a clerk in the office of the Treasury Lords, but Hunter worked out a compromise agreement at a meeting in February 1723/4 with Bampfield, Le Heup, Popple, and Vetch. [26] "In order to avoid all Controversyes that might happen," Bampfield reported, "they thought and agreed on this Expedient which is that Mr. Le Heup and I should be joynt Agents for the Province and divide the Sallary and in pursuance of such Agreement we have mutually entered into an Instrument in Writing for that purpose." Speaker Livingston was asked to arrange for the agreement's ratification by the Assembly. [27]

But the next Assembly session was still a few months away and Livingston, tormented by the devils of old age, spent the time at his "country seat." He was still bothered with an embarrassing kidney ailment which caused him to complain: "I always walk here with a wet sail"; his wife suffered from a painful swelling of her legs, possibly the result of a circulatory ailment. Nevertheless, he continued to give close attention to the development of his manor. Although its actual management was left in his wife's capable hands, he constantly sent her advice on current prices in New York City and the West Indies for wheat, flour, butter, and other commodities produced on the Manor. He also suggested new techniques which could be applied: "The Dutch as well as the English on Long Island," he once wrote,

25. Philip to Robert Livingston, Jan. 4, 1722/3, Bampfield to Livingston, Feb. 25, 1723/4, *ibid*.

26. Livingston's son-in-law Samuel Vetch played a role in effecting this compromise. For several years, he had been in London pursuing the elusive prize of royal favor without success. See Philip to Robert Livingston, Feb. 15, 1721/2, Jan. 4, 1723/4, Robert to Alida Livingston, May 13, 26, and June 19, 1722, May 23, 1723, May 16, 1724 (Dutch), Edmund Knight to Livingston, Feb. 26, 1722/3, *ibid*.

27. Bampfield to Livingston, Feb. 25, 1723/4, *ibid*.

"do not reap anymore with the sickle but with the scythe and cradle.
. . . I believe that . . . there are several of the High Dutch [i.e., Pala-
tines] who can reap with the scythe and cradle." [28]

Flour milling was one of the oldest activities on Livingston Manor.[29]
In addition, several new manufacturing processes were introduced by
Livingston. One was a cider press, built in accordance with suggestions given him by the Virginia delegates to the Albany conference
with the Iroquois in August 1722. A more ambitious project was the
development of a copper mine on the Manor which had been discovered by Philip Livingston in the winter of 1721-22.[30] For about
a year, Philip's discovery lay dormant, but in the spring of 1723,
Livingston inquired about hiring a miner. Several were available, but
they were too expensive, and he consoled his wife with words which
reflected his childhood as the son of a Calvinist minister: "If one
cannot find treasures in the earth by digging and spading, let us be
contented, for they would only be treasures that the rust and moths
could spoil, but in God's word are eternal treasures." Although he
eventually hired a man for £3 per month, Livingston made no further
mention of the apparently unsuccessful mine.[31]

Among Livingston's more successful new ventures was the construction of a new vessel to replace his sloop *Caledonia,* now fourteen
years old. When it was completed in June 1724, Livingston proudly
told his wife that "everyone praises it as such a beautiful sloop." He
used the maiden voyage of the new vessel as a device to entice his
wife to leave the Manor and visit New York City. "Do not let anything prevent you from coming down at the first opportunity. When
we are dead," he reminded her, "who will look after the work? Do
not let us become bound." [32] But Livingston failed to realize that both
he and his wife had become "bound"; she, to their estate on the banks
of the Hudson, and he, to the Assembly chamber in New York City.
Forged by a lifetime of habit, such chains were not easily broken.

28. Robert to Alida Livingston, June 27, July 1, 1724 (Dutch), *ibid.*
29. See Robert to Alida Livingston, June 20, 24, 1724 (Dutch), *ibid.,* for a discussion of a milling agreement with a Mr. Webb for 1,000 bushels of grain in
October and 1,400 or 1,500 bushels the next spring.
30. Robert to Alida Livingston, Aug. 25, 30, 31, 1722 (Dutch), Philip to Robert
Livingston, Feb. 15, 1721/2, *ibid.*
31. He hired a miner from the copper mine being worked by Arent Schuyler, his
brother-in-law, near the Passaic River in New Jersey. Robert to Alida Livingston,
May 23, 25, June 6, 1723 (Dutch), *ibid.*
32. Robert to Alida Livingston, May 11, 29, June 3, 8, 18, 1724 (Dutch), Cornelius
Van Horne to Livingston, July 18, 1723, Jan. 27, 1723/4, Mar. 25, 1724, *ibid.*

CHAPTER XVII

"And This, Too, Shall Pass Away"

THE CLIMAX OF Burnet's administration, in reality, came well before its close, for the middle years of the 1720's saw him at the apex of his power. His friendship with Livingston, Morris, and Colden in New York and his close association with Robert Hunter and Horatio Walpole in London assured him of sufficient strength to put his legislative program into effect with a minimum of difficulty. And he needed the close cooperation of his friends when the Assembly met in the spring of 1723. The government's revenue was due to expire in the following September, and the colony was already in debt for more than £3,600, including £2,400 claimed by Horatio Walpole as salary arrears for the office of auditor general of the plantation revenues. Where the money was to come from, Speaker Livingston complained, "we do not yet know."

On May 21-22, the Assembly received formal notice of Walpole's claim and then adjourned for the Pentecostal holiday. The interruption was most opportune, for it gave the members time to consider the knotty financial problem. The speaker feared that they would "hardly allow Mr. Walpole's money," and there was a good chance that the question might start a revolt in the House. Not only could this embarrass the governor politically, but warrants had already been

issued for Walpole's salary arrears, and some of them had been redeemed by the Treasurer.[1]

Exceptional tact had to be used to get the Assembly to accept this
fait accompli and vote the necessary funds. At a dinner which he
gave for all the assemblymen, the governor "talked heartily about
Mr. Walpole's money," and his charm, logic, and oratory combined
to sway the legislators. On June 21, they voted £1,600 for the auditor
general, as well as £500 for the support of the militia, and provided a
three-year tax on real and personal property for payment. Somewhat
jubilantly, Livingston reported that Burnet was "quite pleased that
we have gotten this far. It was not without a great deal of trouble,
but it was necessary." [2]

Although the relations between the governor and the Assembly
were as harmonious as they had been during Hunter's last year, there
were storm clouds on the horizon. A "great rebellion" had occurred
in Albany, Livingston noted, because of "the enforcement of the law
about the Canadian trade." In the ensuing months, hostility to that
law, one of the governor's most important programs, became one of
the rocks on which his political organization eventually foundered.
Despite all of Burnet's measures, the situation on the Albany frontier
was deteriorating. Peace between England and France had not in-
hibited New York's northern neighbor from making strenuous efforts
to undermine English influence among the Iroquois. As secretary for
Indian affairs, Philip Livingston reported that the Iroquois had allowed
Jean Coeur to build a fort at Niagara; he added that the French agent
intended to build a trading house there as soon as the weather permitted. "When done," Philip dolefully predicted, "adieu a trade with
the far Indians." [3]

Philip denounced the operation of the fur trade law as detrimental
to English interests, but he despaired of any truly effective statute.
"Our Legislators," he believed, "have always wrong notions & Inven-
tions which never Suceed. They aim and attempt a Trade with
Remote Nations and in the mean time Suffer the french in the Bowells

1. Robert to Alida Livingston, May 25, June 6, 14, 15, 1723 (Dutch), Livingston-
Redmond Mss.; *Assembly Journal*, I, 491, 493.

2. Robert to Alida Livingston, June 18, 21, 1723 (Dutch), Livingston-Redmond
Mss.; *Assembly Journal*, I, 496.

3. Robert to Alida Livingston, July 1, 1723 (Dutch), Philip to Robert Livingston,
Jan. 8, 1723/4, Livingston-Redmond Mss.

of their country to debauch the Indians. All their Schemes will faile unless forts be built & Garrisons kept among the Indians but I know its in vain to propose any such thing." As if to confirm his fears, several Albany traders returned from Canada two months later and announced that the French were well supplied with goods from Bristol or Boston and planned to send fifty men to Lake Ontario in the following spring to intercept the western Indians and divert them from Albany. "If so," Philip cautioned, "we may expect a melancholy Summer." [4]

The discontent of the secretary for Indian affairs probably reflected the feeling of his fellow merchants in Albany. Without a channel of expression, however, they could do little more than hope for a change. But the death of Hendrick Hansen, assemblyman from Albany County, gave them a means of demonstrating their opposition to the governor's policies by supporting Myndert Schuyler, who, Philip warned, would "take Revenge on the Governor." [5] In the ensuing election, all of the avowed candidates were hostile to the governor's party; no one seemed willing to run under its banner. Philip Livingston even thought of running himself, but he rejected that idea for a reason his father must have understood: "While the Assembly sits its commonly the best trade here which must be attended as well as a farmer his plow." It seemed likely that the winner by default would be Myndert Schuyler who, Philip noted, "has Long since made Interest with the Canada traders and feeds them with hopes he'll open that trade." That promise even appealed to the secretary for Indian affairs, for "it would be much better to have it open & free for the french to bring & send their beaver to buy what they want then to be wholy without trade."

Philip Livingston was especially bitter because he was singled out by his fellow merchants for discriminatory treatment as a close associate of the governor. He complained that "the whole Currant of our trade goes to the young men who have Refuzd to take the oath prohibiting a trade with Canada.... I cant sell anything to them. My Relations of my own & wifes side Envy me to that degree that if it

4. Philip to Robert Livingston, Jan. 8, Feb. 24, 1723/4, *ibid.*
5. Schuyler had two grievances: Burnet had expelled his recently deceased brother, Peter, from the Council, and he had fined his son for a violation of the fur trade law. Philip to Robert Livingston, Feb. 24, 1723/4, Apr. 21, 1724, *ibid.; Assembly Journal*, I, 500.

was not for Strangers I . . . could not sell what goods I have now in an age." Young Livingston sent these warnings and complaints to his father, who approached the governor with them, but was rebuffed. Burnet was apparently unwilling to take the matter seriously. "If the great man will not be Advized & take other measures," Philip replied, "the french will settle Thierondequat & then he'll Repent he has not taken your Advice." [6]

Meanwhile, the electoral picture in Albany seemed to brighten a bit for the Burnet group. Robert Livingston, Jr., "the nephew," accepted a nomination for the Assembly seat, and he was less objectionable to the governor's supporters than the other candidates. However, Burnet felt that he owed a favor to Francis Harrison and therefore supported his candidate, David Van Dyck. By dividing his own supporters, he almost certainly gave the Albany election to his opponents. Not only was Philip Livingston bitter over the acquisition of power by his enemies, but he viewed the governor's refusal to support Robert Livingston, Jr., as a personal affront. The secretary for Indian affairs had become the victim of the administration's enemies for his espousal of the fur trade law; now, the governor publicly denied him his support. [7]

While Philip Livingston nursed this grudge against Burnet and fought an election campaign that had already been lost, his father joined the assemblymen gathering in New York City in May 1724. The speaker's health was rapidly deteriorating. On May 25, his spirits were unusually low and he failed for the first time to close a letter to his wife with the usual terms of endearment. "I have not felt well for three days," he wrote, "it seems as if the pain increases a bit now. Have been unable to sleep at night, had to get up every half hour." Because he had "to water so badly at night," he desperately needed additional nightshirts, and he told his wife to send them from the Manor or he would have to buy them in New York City. "They come or they do not come," he angrily concluded, "and thus adieu." His spells of illness became so frequent and severe that the governor

6. Philip to Robert Livingston, Mar. 16, 1723/4, Mar. 25, Apr. 10, 1724, Livingston-Redmond Mss.

7. Philip suggested that he be compensated by having his friend, Harme Vedder, appointed commander of the detachment in the Seneca country. Philip to Robert Livingston, May 7, 25, 1724, *ibid*.

had to adjourn the Assembly for a day on June 1 because of the speaker's inability to attend.[8]

Livingston's discomfort must have been increased by the news sent nim from Albany by Philip: Myndert Schuyler had been "Elected a Representative . . . by a majority of 40 od." Since Philip had been unable to support the governor's candidate, Van Dyck, he remained away from the polls "for fear to disoblidge the grande man." Schuyler's victory was a bitter blow, particularly because Burnet, by failing to heed the advice of those committed to serve his interests, had assisted in elevating this enemy to power. Perhaps the governor himself explained the reason for this blunder when he wrote at a later date: "I am lazy enough in . . . matters where I have less expectations of doing any good, and therefore leave them to be managed by others." In politics, as he was learning, this could be dangerous unless he were careful in his choice of managers.[9]

However, the Schuyler misadventure shocked the governor into a realization of the value of his alliance with the Livingston family, and he promptly began to mend his political fences. When Livingston again broached the subject of a salary out of the quitrents for his son as secretary for Indian affairs, he hinted that he would enter into direct negotiations for this with the authorities in London. Burnet disliked this prospect and tried to woo the Livingstons by nominating Philip to his Council. "It pleases me to see," commented Philip, "that his Excellency's apprehensive that you will make Interest to gett an order from home to have it done . . . and to gett you in his Interest in what will be transacted at this Sessions [of the Assembly] may be the Chief Reason that he write to the Lords to have me one of the Councill."

Philip's elevation to the Council would smooth the way for that group's acceptance of a royal order for payment of his salary as secretary for Indian affairs. The Council would presumably look with more favor upon such an order if it benefited one of its own members. In return for the governor's recommendation of his son, Livingston supported Burnet's program in the Assembly, doing his best to deflect the blows aimed at the trade law. He also guided the Assembly's de-

8. Robert to Alida Livingston, May 11, 17, 25, 29, June 3, 1724 (Dutch), *ibid.;* *Assembly Journal,* I, 500, 502.

9. Philip to Robert Livingston, May 30, 1724, Burnet to [Philip Livingston], May 31, 1725, Livingston-Redmond Mss.

liberations on the problem of the colony's debts. Lewis Morris was directed to draft a measure taxing real and personal property, exclusive of unimproved lands, but when he finally brought in the act on July 1, it was incredibly long—fifty-six pages—and, reported Livingston, detested by everyone. Morris had "put so many impossible things in it that everybody is astonished at it. . . . it will be the last bill he will ever draw up for the House," promised the speaker.[10]

Livingston was also disgusted by a last minute flurry of measures dumped into the legislative hopper. He was in so much pain that he wanted to return home as quickly as possible; "I am so tired of it here," he announced two weeks later, "that I do not think I shall ever intend to return to New York in this job, it is too difficult for me and I cannot take it anymore." When the Assembly finally adjourned on July 24, 1724, Speaker Livingston wearily returned home.[11]

Finally free from legislative duties, Governor Burnet hurried to Albany for a conference with the Iroquois. There, he received firsthand proof of the hostility of the *handlaers*. He wanted a fort erected at Oswego to protect the Indian trade, but the Iroquois insisted that it be located at Lake Oneida. He had named Harme Vedder, Philip Livingston's nominee, to command the detachment in the Seneca Country, but the Iroquois urged his replacement by Abraham Schuyler. In his usual direct, blunt fashion, the governor announced his decisions and told the Indians: "I do not like this answer which the *Handlaers* have put into your mouths for they neither love you nor me but mind their own profit." [12]

Vedder's appointment was clearly designed to mollify Philip Livingston. The governor also sought to strengthen his ties with the Livingstons by writing to the Board of Trade and the Duke of Newcastle to urge Philip's appointment to his Council. Such conciliatory acts were made all the more necessary by unwelcome news from London that the governor's Indian trade policy had come under a scathing attack. A group of London merchants charged that the law, although well intended, "would have quite a contrary effect"; the

10. Philip to Robert Livingston, June 10, 1724, Robert to Alida Livingston, June 18, 20, 27, July 1, 1724 (Dutch), *ibid.; Assembly Journal*, I, 506, 508.

11. Robert to Alida Livingston, July 9, 21, 1724 (Dutch), Livingston-Redmond Mss.; *Assembly Journal*, I, 509, 513.

12. Burnet's Iroquois Conference, Nov. 17, 19, 1724, O'Callaghan, ed., *N. Y. Col. Docs.*, V, 718-19.

French could readily procure goods in Europe if they were denied them in Albany. Furthermore, the Iroquois were 200 or 300 leagues from Albany and had to travel through French territory to get there. Finally, the trade law had precipitated a serious decline in commerce between New York and England.[13]

This attack was based upon inaccuracies which were not immediately recognized in London. The Iroquois did not depend on French permission to trade at Albany; rather, it was the French who needed Iroquois consent, but the Board of Trade's geographical knowledge was as limited as the London merchants'. Equally mistaken was the assertion that the French could obtain Indian trade goods as easily from Europe as from Albany, because only England or its colonies could supply the duffels, stroudwaters, and West Indian rum so highly desired by the natives. Only one of the merchants' statements may have been correct: there may have been a decline in trade between New York and England, and this was a most important point to the merchants and the Board. However, trade statistics for this period confuse the picture more than they clarify it, and it is questionable whether the trade law was wholly responsible for any decline.[14] Nevertheless, the arguments were referred to Governor Burnet for a rebuttal, and he delegated that task to Cadwallader Colden, the Scottish physician who was surveyor general and a member of the governor's Council. Colden carefully corrected the merchants' errors in his memorial on the fur trade which was sent to London.[15]

Robert Livingston took no active part in the defense of the fur trade policy because he was growing very weary of the burdens of public life. Having been troubled over his land boundaries by some

13. Burnet to Bd. of Trade, Nov. 7, 1724, Burnet to Newcastle, Nov. 21, 1704 [i.e., 1724], *ibid.*, 713-14, 734; *Journal Bd. Trade,* V, 94-5, 98, 102, 104.

14. McIlwain, ed., *Wraxall's Abridgment,* lxxiii, lxxiiin. The figures of one author suggest that there was no decline. Murray G. Lawson, *Fur: A Study in English Mercantilism 1700-1775* (Toronto, 1943), Univ. of Toronto, *Studies, History and Economics Series,* IX, 108, 135, 138. However, Mr. Wm. I. Roberts, III, of Penn. State Univ., presently working on the fur trade, has questioned the validity of these statistics.

15. *Journal Bd. Trade,* V, 108, 112-13; Colden's memorial, Nov. 10, 1724, O'Callaghan, ed., *N. Y. Col. Docs.,* V, 728-33. Three years later Colden completed his task by writing the first part of his famous *History of the Five Nations.* In preparing both the memorial and the *History,* he undoubtedly had the advice of the Livingstons, who possessed the records of the commissioners of Indian affairs as well as a tremendous fund of information.

argumentative Palatines, he wrote a lengthy complaint to Burnet and expressed his feelings: "If I had Employed my time & industry in Trade (to which I was bred) Since I came to this Country I might in all Probability (with the blessing of God) have been in better Circumstances than now I am tho I Praise God for his goodness I have more than I deserve, and am well Satisfyed with my Lott and Condition." [16]

Reaching the eventide of their lives, both Robert Livingston and his wife were suffering greatly from illness. Philip was so concerned about his parents' health that he sent his wife, Catherine, to visit them at the Manor in June 1723. She was immediately alarmed by her father-in-law's condition. "Found father very bad and getting still worse," she hastily wrote her husband; "I wish you would come . . . for your father is really in a bad state." Alida Livingston was just as seriously ill as her husband. Their New York City physician depreciatingly described her condition: "As for the swelling of Madam Livingstons feet, it is very usuall for persons of her age to be so troubled." Unable to offer any medical advice for either of his patients, the doctor told Livingston, "The good Lord grant You patience and strength to bear it, and Send you reliefe from it, for vain is the help of man." [17]

Despite his physical pain and his wife's suffering, Robert Livingston did not shirk his duties. He had been summoned to attend the Assembly in New York City on August 21, 1725, and he was determined to make the trip. When he was unable to do so, the governor adjourned the Assembly from day to day for nearly a week. Finally, on August 31, the members asked Burnet for advice. He told them that "they might immediately proceed to the Choice of a new Speaker," which they did, electing Adolph Philipse. Five days later, Livingston finally arrived. En route, he had learned of Philipse's election, which he considered "good news." He commended the assemblymen for their action: "They had good reason to do so. For one, I had requested it." An unwelcome burden had been lifted from Livingston's aged shoulders.

16. Livingston to [Burnet], Nov. 17, 1724, N.-Y. Hist. Soc., *Collections*, 67 (1937), 175-77.

17. Catherine to Philip Livingston, June 15, 1725 (Dutch), Dr. John Nicolls to Livingston, July 7, Aug. 12, 1725, Livingston-Redmond Mss.

Livingston's retirement as speaker created new difficulties for the governor; Philipse was not his friend. In addition, there were vacant Assembly seats for New York City, Queens County, and Staten Island, and there was a distinct possibility that these might fall to the opposition party. Notwithstanding the chance that he might lose control of the Assembly, Burnet remained loyal to his old friends, and he told Livingston that he was "not displeased" at him for having forced the election of a new speaker.[18]

Livingston's gratification was enhanced by word from Peter Le Heup that a royal warrant had been issued for payment of Philip Livingston's salary out of the quitrents. Since the Livingstons had all but abandoned any hope of collecting the arrears, they were not disturbed that the effective date of the payments was to be December 25, 1724. Indeed, if there was any disappointment on that score, it was more than compensated for by Le Heup's advice that the king had approved Philip Livingston's appointment to the governor's Council.[19]

An aura of good feeling prevailed as Robert Livingston retired from active politics. His eldest son had received two important signs of royal favor, the governor was still "very friendly and kind," and the Assembly was most generous. When the former speaker appeared before the House to apologize for his tardiness, he was asked to assist the members whenever his health permitted, and he was "ordered always to sit on the right hand of the Speaker in the House." Although the governor would soon dissipate the good feelings which prevailed in New York politics, nothing could destroy Livingston's status as an honored elder statesman.[20]

Throughout the first half of the eighteenth century, New York politics remained in a state of flux. "Neither side held a fixed set of political tenets," one historian has written; "party feeling was

18. Bobin to Livingston, June 26, 1725, Robert Livingston, Jr., to Robert Livingston, Aug. 25, 1725, Robert to Alida Livingston, Sept. 6, 11, 1725 (Dutch), *ibid.*; *Assembly Journal*, I, 513, 514.

19. After this warrant was signed, Walpole ordered that no further salaries were to be paid out of the quitrents. Peter Le Heup to Livingston, July 13, 1725, Robert to Alida Livingston, Sept. 11, 1725 (Dutch), Livingston-Redmond Mss.

20. Robert to Alida Livingston, Sept. 13, 15, 1725 (Dutch), *ibid.*; *Assembly Journal*, I, 514.

moulded by circumstances." [21] Many events and conditions helped to mold factional spirit, and one of the most important was the character and the personality of the governor who, as the Crown's direct representative, had a strong influence for good or evil in the body politic.

Both Hunter and Burnet provided cases in point. The former, by uniting a diverse group of supporters in the Hudson Valley counties and elsewhere, made possible a working Assembly majority which held together for more than a decade. Burnet, who inherited this group intact, was neither as skillful nor as sagacious as his predecessor, and the unity created by a consummate politician was gradually dissipated by an obstinate administrator. Too often abrupt in his demands and unwilling to yield or compromise, Burnet soon found himself opposing those who once had supported him.

In many respects, Burnet created his own difficulties. Early in his administration, instead of courting the powerful Philipse and Schuyler families, he alienated them by dismissing Adolph Philipse and Peter Schuyler from his Council. Later, by insisting upon a rigorous enforcement of the punitive fur trade law without making any real effort to replace the lost trade, he embittered the Albany *handlaers* who had influential mercantile and political contacts in London.

The decline of the Burnet coalition, however, was gradual. He placed his initial reliance upon skilled and experienced politicians such as Livingston, and they were able to relieve some of the friction that normally developed in politics. Livingston's retirement as speaker cost the governor an important pillar of strength, because a retired speaker, no matter how highly honored by his fellow assemblymen, was an elder statesman, not a politician wielding power. Since Livingston's ability to influence or control votes was markedly diminished, Burnet was no longer as willing as he once had been to heed his advice. He turned instead to the impetuous and radical Lewis Morris, ignoring the more conservative leaders of the Hudson Valley counties.

On September 13, 1725, the very day on which Livingston congratulated the House on the election of Philipse as speaker, Burnet committed a serious blunder. In the by-elections to fill vacancies, Stephen De Lancey, an opponent of Burnet, won the New York City

21. Alexander C. Flick, *Loyalism in New York During the American Revolution* (N.Y., 1901), Columbia Univ., *Studies in History, Economics, and Public Law*, XIV, 17.

seat formerly held by David Provoost, one of the governor's party. When the assemblyman-elect appeared to claim his seat, the House followed the customary procedures, and escorted him to the governor's chamber to take his oaths. Knowing that De Lancey had been born in France, Burnet asked him how he became "a Subject of the Crown," and De Lancey replied that he had been "denized" in England many years before. "Doubtful whether this was a sufficient Qualification to sit as a Member," the governor decided to give the matter further consideration, thus barring his opponent from the House.[22]

Burnet's action seemed to usurp the Assembly's prized right to determine the qualifications of its own membership, and it threw the House into turmoil. Although De Lancey was an avowed opponent of the governor's policies, even Burnet's supporters disliked the maneuver. There were many in the colony whose citizenship was no less questionable than De Lancey's, and if his were successfully challenged, what would then happen to them? While Chief Justice Morris was examining De Lancey's case for the governor, Cadwallader Colden returned to New York City on the evening of September 13. Unaware of what had happened until Livingston visited him the next morning, Colden immediately arranged to see Burnet, but before he did so, he met with Colonel Hicks, a man "much in the governors interest and a leading member of the house," who privately told him that "the house was in a ferment," and that "the Governors friends would oppose him" on this issue.

Colden then related both conversations to the governor in detail. Burnet "was staggered" and penned an apologetic message to the Assembly in which "he yielded by halves and under apparent reluctancy." When Colden warned him that this was not enough, that he "must either yield or break with the Assembly," the governor wrote a statement explaining that his sole motive had been to bring the objections against De Lancey to the House's attention. In no way, he continued, did he intend to infringe on the Assembly's prerogative of judging the fitness of its own members.[23]

But the damage had already been done. Livingston predicted that

22. *Assembly Journal*, I, 514-15.
23. "Colden's Letters on Smith's History," N.-Y. Hist. Soc., *Collections*, 1 (1868), 210-11.

these developments would "produce an eternal hatred and consterna-
tion among the people"; no matter what Burnet might say or do, the
House would vote to accept De Lancey as a fully qualified member,
if only to spite the governor. The town, Livingston reported a few
days later, was "full of uneasiness and grumbling," because it was
rumored that Chief Justice Morris would support the governor's
original objections to De Lancey. But Morris' report, though noting
all the weaknesses in De Lancey's claim to citizenship, conceded that
he might have been included in the proclamation issued by the governor and Council in 1687 for the naturalization of aliens. However,
the chief justice refused to commit himself on the legality of the
proclamation and firmly avoided every opportunity to evaluate the
evidence presented. He summed up his report by giving the governor
a face-saving suggestion: since De Lancey had been considered a
subject of the Crown for so many years, he might as well "receive the
Benefit of it, so far as you [Burnet] may legally allow it."

The chief justice had effectively side-stepped the responsibility of
deciding De Lancey's qualifications, but he had given Burnet an opportunity to recant his original error. The governor refused to demean
himself, simply referring Morris' report to the Assembly without
comment. The members thereupon unanimously resolved that De
Lancey was fully qualified and, on the afternoon of September 21,
he was given the necessary oaths by Burnet.[24]

The governor's effort to purge a leader of the opposition created
more enmity and unrest than would have existed had De Lancey
been permitted to take his seat quietly. By failing to consult with
Livingston, Colden, or some other cautious politician, Burnet had
committed a serious blunder which alienated a number of his followers.[25] Although Livingston deserted the governor on this issue,
they were in complete accord on one major problem—the fur trade
law. Both favored revision, and the former speaker hoped to "put it
in a different form than the previous law." Philip Livingston warned

24. Robert to Alida Livingston, Sept. 15, 17, 1725 (Dutch), Livingston-Redmond
Mss.; Assembly Journal, I, 518-19, 520.
25. "The Refusing the oath to Mr. DLancey is a great Surprize to Maney here
as well as at N: York. . . . it will Certainly Create much trouble. Coll. Renselaer tells
me that DLancey is Resolvd to go for England if the Chief Justice gives his opinion
that he is an alien. It is a great blow to dispute the [land] titles of all that are not
naturalized. There can be no good Expected from it." Philip to Robert Livingston,
Sept. 23, 1725, Livingston-Redmond Mss.

his father, however, that "if the oath be Slackd or left out its better than broake." Indeed, he suggested that the only way to make it really effective was to banish or imprison violators for life. Neither idea was practical, and both had probably been suggested facetiously.

A new approach was needed; Livingston recognized that five years of punitive measures had not answered the purpose. On September 24, he was appointed to the committee to revise the law, along with Morris, Philipse, Rutsen, Kipp, Cuyler, and Beekman. Livingston's task was complicated by the governor's insistence that a five-year revenue law should be passed before the trade measure was considered. Only Livingston and three other members voted for the governor's proposal; the overwhelming majority of the House refused to consider anything more than a two-year extension of the revenue law. "The Governor," Livingston reported, "is very angry," but he had only himself to blame: he had antagonized the Assembly, and this was his reward.[26]

Livingston wisely refrained from opposing the majority on this issue, and he accepted appointment to the committee to draft the tax law in accordance with the majority's stated wishes. The committee recommended the retention of import duties on wine, rum, cocoa, and Negro slaves, but suggested the replacement of excises on salt and molasses, as well as the tonnage duty on vessels, with a three shilling poll tax on Negro slaves. By joining the majority on this question, even though its tax proposals were not in his own interests, Livingston hoped to court support for the revision of the fur trade law. His strategy apparently worked, for the Assembly took up that regulation on November 2, but the shortness of time and the complexity of the problem forced the House to postpone further action and to extend the existing law until the end of the next Assembly session.[27]

After the governor prorogued the Assembly, he notified the British authorities of recent developments, suggesting two reasons for his difficulties: his support of Auditor General Walpole's demand for a 5 percent fee on all revenues collected in the colony, and the hostility of the merchants who had been unable to destroy the fur trade law.

26. Robert to Alida Livingston, Sept. 23, Oct. 1, 6, 1725 (Dutch), Philip to Robert Livingston, Sept. 23, 1725, *ibid.; Assembly Journal,* I, 521.

27. *Assembly Journal,* I, 524-25, 527-28; Robert to Alida Livingston, Oct. 16, 1725 (Dutch), Livingston-Redmond Mss.

Perhaps, he added, the assemblymen would be "disposed to do things in a handsomer manner" in the spring when he would again apply for a revenue measure of more than two years' duration.[28]

An astute report by George Clarke, secretary of New York, penetrated more deeply than the governor's explanation. Livingston's replacement as speaker by Philipse, observed Clarke, and the election of several new assemblymen, including De Lancey, had "given a great turn to the Councils of that house." The majority's insistence upon a modification of the tax structure reflected the shift in the balance of power from the Hudson Valley to New York City and Long Island. New York City's commercial interests, not the Valley's landowners, would benefit most from the changes: ending the tonnage duty would encourage shipping; abandoning the salt and molasses taxes, which fell "heaviest on the poorer people," would win the support of Long Island's small farmers and New York City's artisans; a poll tax on Negroes, "which the rich will chiefly pay," would transfer an added share of the burden to the wealthy landowners.

As an example of the political ineptness of Burnet, Clarke pointed to the governor's failure to realize the implications of this economic discontent and to understand the political change taking place. Not only had he gone too far in the De Lancey affair and set an unhappy tone for the entire session, but he had also exhibited an arrogant attitude towards the members. When he learned that several of his former supporters were going to vote to limit the revenue extension to two years, he called them in and "reproached them with ingratitude." This, Clarke believed, "had an effect contrary to his expectations ... all in general resenting the threatment [sic] they had received."

As his plans continued to go awry, the governor became increasingly irritable with those whose support he should have sought. He complained to Clarke that Philip Livingston's salary for the secretaryship was a "thing unreasonable ... which old Livingston himself actually promised and engaged to the Assembly never to ask or insist on for the future, in consideration of the money they gave him in the last long Bill [to pay the public debts] in 1717." When Clarke repeated this to Walpole, he commented: "This I mention to You Sir

28. Burnet to Newcastle, Nov. 17, 1725, Burnet to Bd. of Trade, Nov. 24, 1725, O'Callaghan, ed., *N. Y. Col. Docs.*, V, 765-66.

as he bid me, without enquiring into the reasons of it." Clarke strongly
suspected, however, that the governor was annoyed over Livingston's
unceasing efforts to find governmental places of profit for his sons,
especially since he believed that Livingston "has no manner of interest
in the house and therefore probably may never come to the Assembly
again." [29]

Burnet was mistaken, for even though Livingston's influence in the
Assembly was diminished, he was still highly regarded by the other
members. Despite the limitations of advanced age and ill health, he
was also surprisingly vigorous. When the governor reconvened the
Assembly in April 1726, Livingston returned to New York City, was
appointed to the all-important committee on grievances, and played
a prominent role in resolving the financial dispute which had disrupted the previous Assembly session. The governor and the legislature smoothed over their differences, reaching a compromise on
the tax schedule and extending the revenue law for three years. Duties
on wine were increased and those on rum, cocoa, and Negro slaves
were continued unchanged, but the taxes on salt, molasses, and tonnage were dropped.[30]

Time had soothed impassioned feelings, and Livingston reported
that Burnet was "very kind, has sent me two dozen bottles of white
wine and French wine." Livingston now found himself the object of
solicitation by both political groups. When he suffered a recurrence
of his illness which left him temporarily unable to move, his sickbed
was visited by Philipse, De Lancey, and other members of the opposition, each of whom offered their kindest respects and fullest assistance.
One reason for their friendship, as well as Burnet's, became apparent
a few days later when he heard a rumor that the governor intended
to press for a discriminatory tax on large landed estates.

On May 10, Livingston left his sickbed in response to a personal
plea from Speaker Philipse and was immediately appointed to the
committee to consider the governor's land tax proposal. The opposition gathered sufficient strength to defeat Burnet's proposal and to
substitute a levy on real and personal property scheduled to yield
£1,200 a year for three years. At the same time, the Assembly

29. Clarke to Walpole, Nov. 24, 1725, *ibid.*, 768, 770-71.
30. Robert to Alida Livingston, Apr. 27, 30, 1726 (Dutch), Livingston-Redmond
Mss.; *Assembly Journal*, I, 535.

showed its contempt for the governor and his chief adviser, Lewis Morris, by voting to reduce the salary of the chief justice from £300 to £250 a year, and by authorizing similar reductions in the remuneration of lesser officials. Because there was "hate and malice in this," sentiments which he did not share, Livingston refused to support the vindictive legislation.[31]

With the financial controversy out of the way, the Assembly turned to more constructive matters—in particular, revision of the fur trade law. They quickly agreed on a new approach to this perennial problem. By the end of May, the committee of the whole had decided that "the stroudwaters going to Canada have to pay 30 shillings, kettles 4 pence the pound, baize and plets [i.e., cotton goods] 4 pence the yard, and that which goes to the West half as much." [32]

Five years of outright prohibition of the Canadian trade had failed; now, the trade was to be recognized and regulated by taxation, but the undesirable Canadian phase was to be discouraged with a higher tax than the desirable western phase. Although Burnet claimed full credit for devising this approach, Livingston, too, deserved some of the praise as chairman of the committee which drew up the law.

On June 17, the fur trade law and nineteen other measures received gubernatorial assent, and the Assembly adjourned until late September, much to Livingston's relief. He notified his wife that he was returning home and added: "I am very glad to be released from such a difficult burden and duty." This "release" was to be final for Livingston. When the Assembly reconvened that fall, his son Robert, Jr., represented the Manor.[33]

After an active career of nearly half a century, Robert Livingston finally retired in the summer of 1726. But his long-anticipated happiness lasted only a year. Sometime between August and December 1727, Alida died and the lord of the Manor was left alone. "One can indeed believe with certainty," wrote a friend and business associate in The Netherlands, "the great sadness you found yourself to be in

31. Robert to Alida Livingston, Apr. 30, May 4, 7, 12, 1726 (Dutch), Livingston-Redmond Mss.; *Assembly Journal*, I, 535-36.
32. Robert to Alida Livingston, May 17, 26, 1726 (Dutch), Livingston-Redmond Mss.; *Assembly Journal*, I, 538-39.
33. Burnet to Bd. of Trade, Oct. 14, 1726, O'Callaghan, ed., *N. Y. Col. Docs.*, V, 781; *Assembly Journal*, I, 540, 543, 544, 545; Robert to Alida Livingston, June 4, 11, 16, 18, 1726 (Dutch), Livingston-Redmond Mss.; *Col. Laws of N. Y.*, II, 281-87.

upon the death and loss of such a spouse with whom you had lived for 48 years in great love and unity." [34] Although he survived another year, Livingston led a secluded life.

On August 2, 1728, Livingston prepared his last will and testament. To his eldest surviving son, Philip, he left the Manor of Livingston exclusive of the portion known as Clermont, which he gave to Robert, Jr. To Gilbert who had caused so much anguish over finances, he left nothing other than what he had already given. He also made minor bequests to each of his two daughters and provided for the support of the manor church.[35]

Sometime within the next ten weeks, Robert Livingston joined his wife in death. His passing evoked no eulogy in the colony's fledgling newspaper, and his family papers contain no letters of condolence from friends or relatives. Even the letters of contemporaries, as far as can be determined, made no mention of his demise. Yet, Robert Livingston did not need black-bordered newspaper notices or letters as memorials to his life; he left behind more substantial monuments.[36]

Robert Livingston's death was more than the natural release sought by a weary old man who had led a full and active life—it was the passing of an age. By his role in bridging the transformation of New York from a ducal proprietary into a royal province, he helped formulate the fundamental patterns and practices which succeeding generations of politicians would utilize. And he was eminently qualified for this task by his background as the son and grandson of outstanding Scottish Presbyterian divines, and by his training in the cosmopolitan community of Rotterdam. Inculcated in him were the basic precepts of Presbyterianism, but the excessive zeal which so frequently characterized it was sharply modified by his years in The Netherlands. He could thus adhere with dogged persistence to a policy, whether for personal gain or public service, without falling into the snare of demagoguery which trapped so many of his contemporaries.

34. Bernardus Holthuysen to Robert Livingston, Apr. 12, 1728 (Dutch), Livingston-Redmond Mss. According to Holthuysen, Livingston had notified him of Alida's death either on Aug. 10 or Dec. 5.
35. Robert Livingston's will, Aug. 2, 1728, N.-Y. Hist. Soc., *Collections*, 26 (1894), 341-48.
36. The will was probated on Oct. 15, *ibid.* For the absence of comment, see *New-York Gazette*, Aug.-Dec. 1728, *passim.*

Within Livingston's personality were elements which could easily have made him repugnant had they not been balanced by qualities which, though they did not endear him to his enemies, made him at least palatable to his friends. He was eager for success, ambitious and often grasping; he was stubborn, deceitful, and self-seeking, but he was able to blend the concepts of private gain and public service more effectively than most of his fellow New Yorkers. As much as he bewailed his inability to follow mercantile pursuits exclusively, Livingston was a master politician who stood ready to capitalize upon any situation that presented itself and, if need be, to create the situation. And, whether through fate or ability, he frequently found that his interests and those of his colony and the Crown were compatible, if not identical. Thus, by keeping his eye to the main chance, Robert Livingston served himself, the province, and the empire equally well.

BIBLIOGRAPHICAL NOTE

THE most fruitful sources for this study have been several collections of unpublished manuscripts. Foremost among these are the Livingston-Redmond papers, now on deposit with the Franklin D. Roosevelt Library, Hyde Park, New York. Without the information contained in these documents, a detailed examination of Robert Livingston's career would have been impossible. Nearly half the collection pertains to Robert and Alida and their children. Remarkably complete, it is a family archive unique for New York history in this period.

That the Livingston-Redmond collection has been given scant attention by scholars is in no way a reflection upon the papers' value; instead, it is a commentary upon the difficulties of working with seventeenth-century Dutch, for many of these documents have remained untranslated since the day they were written. Indeed, some of the most important materials, Robert's letters to his wife, were unavailable for research use until the present author had them translated by Mrs. Alida J. Kolk O'Loughlin of Cambridge, Massachusetts. Such translations have been identified by the term "Dutch" affixed to the appropriate citations.

Supplementing this basic collection are several others located in various depositories. The most significant are the Winthrop Papers at the Massachusetts Historical Society, the Blathwayt Papers at Colonial Williamsburg, and the De Peyster Papers at The New-York Historical Society. Twelve volumes of the Winthrop Papers have been neither published nor catalogued; they contain numerous letters from and documents relating to Robert Livingston and his eldest son, John. The Blathwayt Papers supply an unusually rich source of comments, written largely by participants, on events occurring in New York. The De Peyster Papers, a less comprehensive familial collection, shed light on politics during the Bellomont administration.

Several collections of public documents were indispensable. The two most important are the New York Colonial Manuscripts at the New York State Library, Albany, New York, and the British Public Record Office materials, some of which have been transcribed for the Library of Congress. Despite the damage wrought by the New York State Capitol fire of 1911, the New York Colonial Manuscripts remain a prime source of information about colonial life. The Public Record Office papers, mainly petitions, reports, financial accounts, council minutes, and decrees, fill in many of the gaps in the New York Colonial Manuscripts and, at the same time, provide a more complete picture of the relations between the colony and the mother country.

Although these unpublished materials are a treasure trove for the scholar, he has equally rewarding published materials available. The documentary sources of New York's history in print are perhaps as rich as those for any state. In the nineteenth century, the state's authorities took seriously their responsibility for preserving and disseminating the records upon which history must be based. Among the outstanding results of their work are: Edmund B. O'Callaghan's edition of the *Documentary History of the State of New York* (4 vols., Albany, 1849-50), and his *Documents Relative to the Colonial History of the State of New York* (11 vols., Albany, 1853-61).

Those collections are primarily historical in nature, but the state has also published other official records which deal largely with political institutions. The most noteworthy among these are: *Journal of the Votes and Proceedings of the General Assembly of the Colony of New-York* (2 vols., New York, 1764-66), *Journal of the Legislative Council of the Colony of New-York* (2 vols., Albany, 1861), and the compilation by the Commissioners of Statutory Revision of *The Colonial Laws of New York from the Year 1664 to the Revolution* (5 vols., Albany, 1894).

At the same time that state authorities were accepting their responsibility, private agencies were also undertaking the publication of historical records. Indeed, the state was actually spurred on to its task by The New-York Historical Society. The numerous volumes of that organization's *Collections* and their importance attest to its diligence in this field. Their variety is merely suggested by the following list of topics in the volumes consulted for this study: Cadwallader Colden's letters and papers, records of the Supreme Court of Judicature, New York City tax lists, abstracts of wills, papers relating to the New York-Massachusetts dispute over Vermont, records of the Leisler administration, and "The Case of William Atwood, Esq."

The fruitful efforts of both the state and The New-York Historical Society have often been supplemented by publications under the auspices of other agencies or private individuals. In the field of Indian affairs, there are three basic works: Cadwallader Colden's *History of the Five Indian Nations* (2 vols., New York, 1922), Charles H. McIlwain's edition of Peter Wraxall's *An Abridgment of the Indian Affairs* (Cambridge, 1915), and the present author's *The Livingston Indian Records, 1666-1723* (Harrisburg, Pa., 1956). Privateering, an important industry of early New York, is well documented in J. Franklin Jameson's edition of *Privateering and Piracy in the Colonial Period: Illustrative Documents* (New York, 1923).

Still another form of documentary material, often of great importance, is the diary, journal, and autobiography. For Robert Livingston's background, the "spiritual" autobiography of his father is most helpful—Thomas Houston, ed., *A Brief Historical Relation of the Life of Mr. John Livingstone, Minister of the Gospel . . . Written By Himself* (Edinburgh, 1848). One of the best descriptive journals for the early period of New York life is that edited by Bartlett B. James and J. Franklin Jameson, the *Journal of Jasper Danckaerts, 1679-1680* (New York, 1913). A more recent publication is Wayne Andrews, ed., "A Glance at New York in 1697: The Travel Diary of Dr. Benjamin Bullivant," The New-York Historical Society, *Quarterly*, 40 (1956), 55-73. Bullivant also kept another important journal: "Benjamin Bullivants Journall of Proceedings from the 13 Feb. to the 19th of May [1690 in Boston]," Massachusetts Historical Society, *Proceedings*, 1st ser., 16 (1879), 101-8.

Local history, of primary importance in studying Livingston's early career, is amply documented. Joel Munsell's *The Annals of Albany* (10 vols., Albany, 1854-71), Berthold Fernow's *Documents Relating to the . . . Towns along the Hudson and Mohawk Rivers* (Albany, 1881), Arnold J. F. Van Laer's *Minutes of the Court of Albany, Rensselaerswyck and Schenectady, 1668-1685* (3 vols., Albany, 1926-32), and the same editor's *Early Records of the City and County of Albany and Colony of Rensselaerswyck* (3 vols., Albany, 1916-19) illume the story of Albany's growth and Robert Livingston's part in that development.

For unpublished colonial and local records, there are several calendars in print, some of which give more detailed summaries of documents than others. The most important are: Edmund B. O'Callaghan, ed., *Calendar of Historical Manuscripts* (2 vols., Albany, 1866); "Calendar of Council Minutes, 1668-1783," New York State Library, *Bulletin 58 (March 1902) History 6;* Wheeler B. Melius, ed., *Index to the Public Records of the County of Albany ... Grantors* (14 vols., Albany, 1902-7); and Wheeler B. Melius and Frank H. Burnap, eds., *Index to the Public Records of the County of Albany ... Grantees* (12 vols., Albany, 1908-11).

In studying the career of a man prominent in colonial administration and politics, an examination of the British records is most necessary. The English government has made an outstanding effort to present the pertinent documents to the scholar by means of well-annotated calendars. These materials from the Public Record Office were most useful in this study: W. N. Sainsbury *et al.*, eds., *Calendar of State Papers, Colonial Series, America and West Indies* (40 vols., London, 1860-1939); Joseph Redington, ed., *Calendar of Treasury Papers* (6 vols., London, 1868-89); and William A. Shaw, ed., *Calendar of Treasury Books* (25 vols., London, 1904-52). Two other works which, although not calendars, certainly deserve mention are: W. L. Grant and James Munro, eds., *Acts of the Privy Council of England, Colonial Series* (6 vols., London, 1908-12), and *Journal of the Commissioners for Trade and Plantations, 1704-83* (14 vols., London, 1920-37).

Voluminous private papers have also been published in England. This has been done mainly in the form of calendars, and the Historical Manuscript Commission deserves a large measure of credit. Its reports on the Portland Papers (no. 29), Buccleuch and Queensberry Papers (no. 45), Downshire Papers (no. 75), Finch Papers (no. 71), and House of Lords Documents (no. 17) were found most helpful for this work.

Less has been done on this side of the Atlantic in the publication of private papers, but those that have appeared have usually been edited selections rather than calendars. These were especially helpful: R. N. Toppan and A. T. S. Goodrick, eds., *Edward Randolph: Including His Letters and Official Papers* (7 vols., Boston, 1898-1909); Arnold J. F. Van Laer, ed., *Correspondence of Maria Van Rensselaer, 1669-1689* (Albany, 1935); Edmund B. O'Callaghan, ed., *Letters of Isaac Bobin* (Albany, 1872); and "The Winthrop Papers," Massachusetts Historical Society, *Collections*, 5th ser., 8 (1882), and 6th ser., 3 (1889).

In addition to the documentary materials, both published and unpublished, examined for this study, all secondary works which seemed to have any bearing on the subject were utilized. Some have been cited in footnotes, but many did not supply specific information or statements which could be so credited. Often, however, they provided interesting generalizations and clues to the location of important documents.

Secondary accounts in several instances provided a basic frame of reference for this study. For a history of The Netherlands, one of the most useful analyses is Petrus Johannes Blok, *History of the People of The Netherlands*, translated by Oscar A. Bierstadt and Ruth Putnam (5 vols., New York, 1898-1912). Perhaps the most interesting and suggestive interpretation of Livingston's native land is Wallace Notestein's *The Scot in History* (New Haven, 1947). Herbert L. Osgood's *The American Colonies in the Eighteenth Century* (4 vols., New York, 1924), and Charles M. Andrews, *The Colonial Period of American History* (4 vols., New Haven, 1934-38) provide the standard histories of politics in this period.

Certain specialized secondary studies also warrant individual notice. The first history of the colony, William Smith's *The History of the Late Province of New York* (2 vols., New York, 1829), falls somewhere between the categories of source material and secondary works; its value for a study of political history is undeniable. More modern works which have been profitably consulted include: Beverly McAnear's often perceptive and useful Politics in Provincial New York, 1689-1761 (unpublished doctoral dissertation, Stanford University, 1935); Walter Allen Knittle, *The Eighteenth Century Palatine Emigation* (Philadelphia, 1936); Samuel G. Nissenson's scholarly *The Patroon's Domain* (New York, 1937); Dixon Ryan Fox, *Caleb Heathcote, Gentleman Colonist* (New York, 1926); Harvey E. Fisk, *English Public Finance from the Revolution of 1688* (New York, 1920); Gertrude Ann Jacobsen, *William Blathwayt* (New Haven, 1932); and Stanley M. Pargellis, "The Four Independent Companies of New York," *Essays in Colonial History Presented to Charles McLean Andrews By His Students* (New Haven, 1931). Two important studies appeared as this volume went to press: G. M. Waller's *Samuel Vetch: Colonial Enterpriser* (Chapel Hill, 1960) and Michael Garibaldi Hall's *Edward Randolph and the American Colonies, 1676-1703* (Chapel Hill, 1960); both add depth to our understanding of this period.

Finally, a comment should be made about the two earlier efforts to delineate Robert Livingston's life—Edwin Brockholst Livingston's *The Livingstons of Livingston Manor* (New York, 1910), and John A. Krout's "Behind the Coat of Arms: A Phase of Prestige in Colonial New York," *New York History*, 16 (1935), 45-52. Although these works were satisfactory for their times, both authors were handicapped by the unavailability of the Livingston-Redmond Manuscripts. Each study suffers therefore from an inability to penetrate the surface of Livingston's public career as exemplified in the somewhat stylized official records.

INDEX

Adventure Galley, 110, 125

Agriculture, 57-58

Albany, economy of, 11, 12-13, 18-19, 37; RL in, 11, 15, 17; description of, 13, 83; government of, 44-45; Convention, 61-65, 66, 68, 69; discontent against Fletcher, 127-28, 132, 134; and Canada campaign, 206; defense of, 206, 212; assemblymen of oppose RL's claims, 239; merchants of attack Philip Livingston, 255-56; against fur trade law, 276

Albrough, John, 105

Alexander, James, 255, 257

Allyn, John, 67, 71-72

Amsterdam, 125-26

Andros, Sir Edmund, creates Indian commissioners, 15; relations with RL, 17, 20, 24, 25, 26, 32, 58, 85; trade restrictions of, 18-19, 37-38; excise tax created by, 40; and Dominion of New England, 50-51, 58, 59, 60

Annapolis Royal, 214-15 and *n.* 9

Anne, Queen, 194

Anti-Leislerians, 75-76, 77, 129-30, 132, 145, 173-74, 178-79

Army, 137

"A Satyr Upon The Times," 178-79

Ashton, Thomas, 42

Ashurst, Sir William, 135, 137-38, 149-50

Assembly, creation of, 40, 41, 43; role in 1680's, 58; conflict with Fletcher, 90; RL's relations with, 119, 139, 171-72, 183, 205, 207, 230-31, 239-40, 247, 271, 283; Bellomont's relations with, 132, 133, 140, 145; Leislerian control of, 140, 145, 162, 163; Hunter's relations with, 227, 235-36, 241-42, 248, 249; and debt bill of 1714, 231, 232-33, 234, 237-38; and debt bill of 1717, 245, 246; Burnet's relations with, 252, 265-66, 283, 284-86, 287, 289-90; and Bampfield, 261, 262; and Walpole dispute, 262-65, 275-76; passes law for Gilbert Livingston, 270; elects Philipse Speaker, 282

Atwood, William, 168, 170, 176, 178, 179, 180, 181

Auditor General, 262-65

Baker, Samuel, 272

Bampfield, George, 254, 257, 261, 265, 272-73

Bancker, Evert, 121, 127-28

Barbados, 37-38

Bayard, Nicholas, and Leislerians, 59, 63, 75-76 and *n.* 52, 144, 174, 177; described by Randolph, 84; plots against Bellomont, 131-32, 136

Beekman, Gerardus, 64

Beekman, Henry, 145

Beekman, Henry, II, 243-44

299